Sexual Rhetorics

"*Sexual Rhetorics* moves beyond an engagement with the gendered and sexual subject. The sexed rhetorics animated in this collection will move readers to confront and consider the pervasiveness of sex/uality in structuring social life and discourses in public/s sphere/s. In bringing together a range of sexed methods—from archival research to textual and rhetorical analyses to ethnographic-style inquiry and case studies—Alexander and Rhodes effectively argue that to fully understand rhetorical action in contemporary (counter)publics, we must also know and understand the primacy of sexual rhetorics."
—*Adela C. Licona, University of Arizona, USA*

Sexual rhetoric is the self-conscious and critical engagement with discourses of sexuality that exposes both their naturalization and their queering, their torquing to create different or counterdiscourses, giving voice and agency to multiple and complex sexual experiences. This volume explores the intersection of rhetoric and sexuality through the varieties of methods available in the fields of rhetoric and writing studies, including case studies, theoretical questioning, ethnographies, or close (and distant) readings of "texts" that help us think through the rhetorical force of sexuality and the sexual force of rhetoric.

Jonathan Alexander is Professor of English, Education, and Gender & Sexuality Studies at University of California, Irvine, USA, where he was the founding Director of the Center for Excellence in Writing and Communication.

Jacqueline Rhodes is Professor of English at California State University, San Bernardino, California, USA.

Routledge Studies in Rhetoric and Communication

1 Rhetorics, Literacies, and Narratives of Sustainability
   Edited by Peter Goggin

2 Queer Temporalities in Gay Male Representation
   Tragedy, Normativity, and Futurity
   Dustin Bradley Goltz

3 The Rhetoric of Intellectual Property
   Copyright Law and the Regulation of Digital Culture
   Jessica Reyman

4 Media Representations of Gender and Torture Post-9/11
   Marita Gronnvoll

5 Rhetoric, Remembrance, and Visual Form
   Sighting Memory
   Anne Teresa Demo and Bradford Vivian (editors)

6 Reading, Writing, and the Rhetorics of Whiteness
   Wendy Ryden and Ian Marshall

7 Radical Pedagogies of Socrates and Freire
   Ancient Rhetoric/Radical Praxis
   S.G. Brown

8 Ecology, Writing Theory, and New Media
   Writing Ecology
   Edited by Sidney I. Dobrin

9 The Rhetoric of Food
   Discourse, Materiality, and Power
   Edited by Joshua J. Frye and Michael S. Bruner

10 The Multimediated Rhetoric of the Internet
    Digital Fusion
    Carolyn Handa

11 Communicating Marginalized Masculinities
    Identity Politics in TV, Film, and New Media
    Edited by Ronald L. Jackson II and Jamie E. Moshin

12 Perspectives on Human-Animal Communication
    Internatural Communication
    Edited by Emily Plec

13 Rhetoric and Discourse in Supreme Court Oral Arguments
    Sensemaking in Judicial Decisions
    Ryan A. Malphurs

14 Rhetoric, History, and Women's Oratorical Education
    American Women Learn to Speak
    Edited by David Gold and Catherine L. Hobbs

15 Cultivating Cosmopolitanism for Intercultural Communication
Communicating as Global Citizens
Miriam Sobré-Denton and Nilanjana Bardhan

16 Environmental Rhetoric and Ecologies of Place
Edited by Peter N. Goggin

17 Rhetoric and Ethics in the Cybernetic Age
The Transhuman Condition
Jeff Pruchnic

18 Communication, Public Opinion, and Globalization in Urban China
Francis L.F. Lee, Chin-Chuan Lee, Mike Z. Yao, Tsan-Kuo Chang, Fen Jennifer Lin, and Chris Fei Shen

19 Adaptive Rhetoric
Evolution, Culture, and the Art of Persuasion
Alex C. Parrish

20 Communication, Public Discourse, and Road Safety Campaigns
Persuading People to Be Safer
Nurit Guttman

21 Mapping Christian Rhetorics
Connecting Conversations, Charting New Territories
Edited by Michael-John DePalma and Jeffrey M. Ringer

22 Identity and Power in Narratives of Displacement
Katrina M. Powell

23 Pedagogies of Public Memory
Teaching Writing and Rhetoric at Museums, Archives, and Memorials
Edited by Jane Greer and Laurie Grobman

24 Authorship Contested
Cultural Challenges to the Authentic, Autonomous Author
Edited by Amy E. Robillard and Ron Fortune

25 Software Evangelism and the Rhetoric of Morality
Coding Justice in a Digital Democracy
Jennifer Helene Maher

26 Sexual Rhetorics
Methods, Identities, Publics
Edited by Jonathan Alexander and Jacqueline Rhodes

Sexual Rhetorics
Methods, Identities, Publics

Edited by Jonathan Alexander
and Jacqueline Rhodes

LONDON AND NEW YORK

First published 2016
by Routledge

2 Park Square, Milton Park, Abingdon, Oxfordshire OX14 4RN
711 Third Avenue, New York, NY 10017

Routledge is an imprint of the Taylor & Francis Group, an informa business

First issued in paperback 2017

Copyright © 2016 Taylor & Francis

The right of the editor to be identified as the author of the editorial material, and of the authors for their individual chapters, has been asserted in accordance with sections 77 and 78 of the Copyright, Designs and Patents Act 1988.

All rights reserved. No part of this book may be reprinted or reproduced or utilised in any form or by any electronic, mechanical, or other means, now known or hereafter invented, including photocopying and recording, or in any information storage or retrieval system, without permission in writing from the publishers.

Notice:
Product or corporate names may be trademarks or registered trademarks, and are used only for identification and explanation without intent to infringe.

Library of Congress Cataloging in Publication Data

Sexual rhetorics: methods, identities, publics / Edited by Jonathan Alexander and Jacqueline Rhodes.
   pages cm. — (Routledge Studies in Rhetoric and Communication; #26)
Includes bibliographical references and index.
   1. English language—Rhetoric—Study and teaching—Social aspects.
   2. Authorship—Study and teaching—Social aspects. 3. Gender identity.
   4. Sex. I. Alexander, Jonathan, 1967- editor. II. Rhodes, Jacqueline, 1965- editor.
PE1404.S43 2015
809'.933538—dc23   2015022068

ISBN: 978-1-138-90687-7 (hbk)
ISBN: 978-0-8153-9634-5 (pbk)

Typeset in Sabon
by codeMantra

Contents

Acknowledgments   ix

Introduction: What's Sexual about Rhetoric, What's Rhetorical about Sex?   1
JONATHAN ALEXANDER AND JACQUELINE RHODES

PART I
Sexed Methods

1 Promiscuous Approaches to Reorienting Rhetorical Research   17
HEATHER LEE BRANSTETTER

2 "Intersecting Realities": Queer Assemblage as Rhetorical Methodology   31
JASON PALMERI AND JONATHAN RYLANDER

3 Consciousness, Experience, Sexual Expression, and Judgment   45
JACQUELINE M. MARTINEZ

4 Hard-Core Rhetoric: Gender, Genre, and the Image in Neuroscience   58
JORDYNN JACK

5 Historicizing Sexual Rhetorics: Theorizing the Power to Read, the Power to Interpret, and the Power to Produce   72
META G. CARSTARPHEN

6 Milk Memory's Queer Rhetorical Futurity   79
CHARLES E. MORRIS III

PART II
Troubling Identity

7 The Trope of the Closet   95
DAVID L. WALLACE

8 Sex and the Crip Latina 108
ELLEN M. GIL-GÓMEZ

9 Affect, Female Masculinity, and the Embodied Space Between: Two-Spirit Traces in Thirza Cuthand's Experimental Film 121
LISA TATONETTI

10 The Unbearable Weight of Pedagogical Neutrality: Religion and LGBTQ Issues in the English Studies Classroom 134
G PATTERSON

11 The Story of Fox Girl: Writing Queer about/in Imaginary Spaces 147
MARTHA MARINARA

12 "As Proud of Our Gayness, as We Are of Our Blackness": Race-ing Sexual Rhetorics in the National Coalition of Black Lesbians and Gays 159
ERIC DARNELL PRITCHARD

PART III
(Counter)Publics

13 "Gay Boys Kill Themselves": The Queer Figuration of the Suicidal Gay Teen 175
ERIN J. RAND

14 Consorting with the Enemy?: Women's Liberation Rhetoric about Sexuality 188
CLARK A. POMERLEAU

15 Sex Trafficking Rhetorics/Queer Refusal 203
IAN BARNARD

16 Sexual Counterpublics, Disciplinary Rhetorics, and Truvada 217
J. BLAKE SCOTT

17 Presidential Masculinity: George W. Bush's Rhetorical Conquest 231
LUKE WINSLOW

18 Liberal Humanist "Rights" Discourse and Sexual Citizenship 244
HARRIET MALINOWITZ

List of Contributors 259
Index 265

Acknowledgments

We thank our contributors for their wonderful work in forwarding the understanding of sexual rhetorics. Special thanks to Elizabeth Catchings for early assistance in hunting down sources and authors.

We are also grateful to the editors of *Enculturation*, which published an earlier version of our introductory comments in "Queer Rhetoric and the Pleasures of the Archive" (January 26, 2012).

Harvey Milk's "You've Got to Have Hope" speech used with permission from the Harvey Milk Archives, The James C. Hormel Gay & Lesbian Center of the San Francisco Public Library, San Francisco, CA. A special thanks to Susan Goldstein, San Francisco City Archivist at the San Francisco Public Library, for her help with the Harvey Milk collection.

Introduction
What's Sexual about Rhetoric, What's Rhetorical about Sex?

*Jonathan Alexander and
Jacqueline Rhodes*

Sexual rhetoric is self-conscious and critical engagement with discourses of sexuality that exposes both their naturalization and their queering, their torquing to create different or counterdiscourses, and gives voice and agency to multiple and complex sexual experiences. Such engagement, often comprising rich ecologies of meaning making and exchange, takes myriad forms, and it benefits from a history of liberatory, feminist, and queer rhetorical practices designed to critique patriarchal and capitalist hegemonies. Often, sexual rhetorics, as in the case of queer rhetorical practice, focus in particular on sexual normalization and the regimes of discursive control through which bodies are disciplined and subjectivities reified as "straight," others "bent," and yet others illegible in different public spheres.

Sexual rhetoric thus relies on (1) a recognition of the dense and complicated ways in which sexuality, *pace* Foucault, constitutes a nexus of power, a conduit through which identities are created, categorized, and rendered as subjects constituted by and subject to power; and (2) a careful tracing of attempts to disrupt and reroute the flows of power, particularly but not exclusively discursive power, as mediated through sex and sexuality. We see "sexuality" as robustly rhetorical—a set of textual, audiovisual, affective, and embodied tools through which bodies and psyches are shaped and cast in particular identity formations and through which such bodies and psyches might potentially be recast and reformed. We assert that the discourses, identities, affects, and embodied practices clustered under the rubric "sexuality" are all themselves inherently rhetorical in the sense that they carry and vector the weight of ideological pressures on bodies and minds.

Sexuality is both terministic and dramatistic in the Burkean sense; it is simultaneously one of the dominant filters for and zones of conflict through which we understand, negotiate, and argue through our individuality and our collectivity. What are the current shapes and contours of such understanding and negotiation? And how might we use rhetoric the better both to understand "sexuality" and the "sexual" in contemporary private and public spheres? Moreover, how might we understand the rhetorical as always already sexualized, as imbued with the persuasive forces of bodies, intimacies, affects, erotics, and varied partnerings?

We believe that a robust sexual rhetoric focuses theoretical and methodological attention on those strategies that seek to broaden, even to the breaking point, what counts or passes as "normal." To that end, this collection seeks to offer a challenging but productive way to expand our awareness of the rhetorics of sex/uality, looking at how those rhetorics move multiply and intersectionally to articulate the complexities of desire and discourse. Such movement seeks to remedy the impoverishment of our imaginations, of our sexual and gender imaginary, and to reintroduce into public discourse the imagination of bodies that exceed the normalizations of the juridical, political, medical culture that "fixes" things.

Lessons from the Archives

In our 2012 "Queer Rhetoric and the Pleasures of the Archive," we explore the affordances of online queer archives, noting that work with archives of sexuality often shows us the conflicting and alternative modalities of rhetorical practice accruing around and generated by the discussion of sex/uality. At a time when "information" and "data" about sex and sexuality are readily accessible, we wonder about the challenges of making such information and data meaningful. Certainly, rhetoric offers us a number of strategies for such meaning-making, showing us the various ways in which information about sex/uality can be constructed. One powerful modality of research in this area is Foucault's revisioning of history, a revision produced through a genealogical approach to the past. A genealogy, as Foucault writes (1977), is "an examination of descent [which] permits the discovery, under the unique aspect of a trait or concept, of the myriad events through which—thanks to which, against which—they were formed" (146). A genealogy shows multiple, contradictory pasts that reveal the interplay of power and knowledge evident in given constructed concepts such as madness or sexuality. As we look for such interplay in concepts of sexual liberation and political protest, we look at the discursive constructions of those concepts as they emerge from the rhetorical and material needs of specific peoples working at particular times.

For instance, for many scholars of LGBTQ history, archives of sexuality have become important sources not only of information but also of theorizing about queer experience and possibility. As Charles Morris writes, queer archives show us how "queer lives, past and present, are constituted by voices that swell with the complex measures of our joys and our struggles against annihilating silence" ("Archival" 146). Archives established primarily to document the lived experiences of queer people, such as the Lesbian Herstory Archives in Brooklyn and The ONE National Gay and Lesbian Archives in Los Angeles, provide historians, scholars, and laypeople a sense of what it was like to be queer at particular moments. They also suggest how a narrative of emerging—and changing—queer experience might be constructed over time. As recovery projects, providing us resources to narrativize past and often painful experiences of individual and cultural homophobia and trauma, archives of LGBTQ experience may provide us powerful opportunities to think critically about systems of oppression and the interlocking mechanisms of the "personal" and the "political."

Such archives serve not only historians, however, seeking to recover a buried LGBTQ past. They also point to the contestations about that past, particularly as many queers seek to locate their experiences (of oppression, but also of community building and the formation of productive counterpublics) in particular sociohistorical circumstances. The work, for instance, around carefully documenting the New York City's Stonewall Inn Riots in 1969 is an exercise both in recovery of specific historical moments and in interpreting those moments to narrate a sense of the queerly historical. Judith Halberstam, writing about transgender archives in *In a Queer Time and Place*, notes that

> [t]he archive is not simply a repository; it is also a theory of cultural relevance, a construction of collective memory, and a complex record of queer activity. In order for the archive to function, it requires users, interpreters, and cultural historians to wade through the material and piece together the jigsaw puzzle of queer history in the making. (169–70)

The particular difficulties of this work—this piecing together that Halberstam notes—present both challenges and opportunities not just for historical work but also for understanding the rhetorical dimensions of queer archiving.

Similarly, as Morris writes, "archives are indeed rhetorical sites and resources, part of a diverse domain of the usable past that ... functions ideologically and politically" ("Archival" 146). Working extensively with a variety of lesbian archives, Ann Cvetkovich in *An Archive of Feelings: Trauma, Sexuality, and Lesbian Public Cultures* argues that queer archives "address particular versions of the determination to 'never forget' that gives archives of traumatic history their urgency" (9). However, archiving that traumatic history is often difficult, particularly given the fact that so many queer or homoerotically inclined individuals led secret or double lives deep in the closets of systemic homophobia. Cvetkovich explains:

> That gay and lesbian history even exists has been a contested fact, and the struggle to record and preserve it is exacerbated by the invisibility that often surrounds intimate life, especially sexuality. Even the relatively short history (roughly "one hundred years") of homosexuality as an identity category has created the historiographical challenge of not only documenting the wide varieties of homosexual experience but examining documents of homophobia along with earlier histories of homoeroticism and same-sex relations. (242)

Given this difficulty, historians and archivists often rely on "ephemera, the term used by archivists and librarians to describe occasional publications and paper documents, material objects, and items that fall into the miscellaneous category when being catalogued" (Cvetkovich 243). Underground newsletters, photographs, and letters, as well as court documents—all become part of a potential queer archive that not only collects but connects incidents in narratives reconstructing particular queer experiences.

In general, because so much of the public sphere is increasingly mediated in online venues, and because the web in particular facilitates the creation of counterpublic spaces, we see a potential diversification of rhetorical practices, some of which may question or even seek to subvert some of the dominant practices of the public sphere. This potential seems particularly rich in queer archives. As Cvetkovich argues, it is imperative that we understand "gay and lesbian archives as archives of emotion and [potentially of] trauma" (242). Such trauma may not be fully representable. However, the articulation of complex emotions—from anger to resentment to pain and an acute sense of loss, as well as delight in desire and the pleasures of naming desire and claiming community—becomes central to queer rhetorical work. As such, ethos and pathos often assume dominance, while logos, traditionally vaunted as the superior form of argumentation and persuasion, is less queerly compelling. The concomitant significance of ethos and pathos to the rhetorical performance of queer rhetorical practices may have much to do with the fact that such practices often present us with actual individuals or groups, not just with minds articulating a sense of the queer but also with bodies performing sexually and queerly. As such, the online queer archive offers us a nearly unprecedented opportunity to think the body in rhetorical practice—and in this case, the queer body in queer rhetorical practice.

Entering—and Expanding—the Conversation

What our work on online queer archives taught us was that more work needed to be done. Certainly, others have attempted similar projects, primarily from the vantage point of queer perspectives—from the 1992 *Pre/Text* special issue on queer rhetorics to Alexander and Gibson's cluster on queer theory in a 2004 *JAC* to a 2009 *College Composition and Communication* article by Wallace and Alexander on the "queer turn" in composition studies. However, with these exceptions, as we argue in "Queer: An Impossible Subject for Composition," scholarship on the potent intersections of queer theory and rhetoric/writing "remains relatively sparse and under-read" (178). More explicitly:

> Queer compositionists have contributed important essays that prod us to think critically about the importance of LGBT content in our writing curricula, to be attentive to the particular literacy and instructional concerns of LGBT students, and even to consider the potential implications of queer theory for the teaching of writing. However, while comparable work in feminist thinking, critical pedagogies, and postmodernity in general have created significant movements within

the field of rhetoric and composition studies, queerness and queer theory have not, despite their significant contributions "across the hall," that is, to literary study. (178)

With this critique in mind, we broaden our current scope of inquiry to ask about the possibilities of not just queer theory but of thinking sexuality in general for rhetorical studies.

Previous relevant studies have turned attention to *particular* spaces and media through which sex/uality has been figured, often focusing on either identity issues or on sex/uality as a problem. For instance, Meta G. Carstarphen and Susan Zavoina's *Sexual Rhetoric: Media Perspectives on Sexuality, Gender, and Identity* (1999) offers one of the earlier attempts to think through the social constructions of gender and sexuality through different mass media, ranging from newspapers and magazines to film, television, and the early public Internet. Indeed, many subsequent studies focus on the rhetorical power of media representations of gender and sex/uality and their influence on how we understand and conceptualize intimacies, bodies, desires, and pleasures. There's even a study of *Sexual Rhetoric in the Works of Joss Whedon* (2010).

In addition to studying sexuality in contemporary mass media, some scholars take a much-needed historical view, filling in gaps in our long-term understanding of how rhetorics about sex have shaped both public discourses and public policies. *Dirty Words: The Rhetoric of Public Sex Education, 1870–1924* (2010) by Robin E. Jensen usefully documents the development of sex education efforts at the turn of the century, particularly as such were aimed at the working classes and African Americans, often in an attempt to contain or control these populations. Miriam G. Reumann's *American Sexual Character: Sex, Gender, and National Identity in the Kinsey Reports* (2005) is noteworthy for historicizing the development of rhetorics of sexuality in relation to national identity in the United States, especially after the Kinsey Reports "outed" the diversity of US sexual practices and helped provide a rudimentary discourse for discussing sex and sexuality in public spaces.

At times, studies examining the intersections among publics, rhetorical practices, and sex/ualities focus on particular instances in which the sexual emerges as a problematic. For instance, Julie Thompson's *Mommy Dearest: Contemporary Rhetorics of Lesbian Maternal Identity* (2002) looks specifically at how lesbian mothers have been rhetorically figured in many different public spheres as untenable or illegible subjects. In a different set of public realms but still focused importantly on women, Linda K. Fuller's *Sexual Sports Rhetoric: Historical and Media Contexts of Violence* (2009) analyzes discourses surrounding public discussions of topics such as spousal abuse and gender orientation in contemporary media about sports. The intersections, or sometimes collisions, among sexual and religious rhetorics have drawn particular attention. Michael Cobb's *God Hates Fags: The*

Rhetorics of Religious Violence (2006) focuses on Fred Phelps and his church's notorious antigay rhetorics as well as how various queers have attempted to cultivate alternative rhetorics of spirituality to counter the violence directed at them. Christine J. Gardner's *Making Chastity Sexy: The Rhetoric of Evangelical Abstinence Campaigns* (2011) looks specifically at recent "chastity movements" among Christian communities attempting to convince young people to wait until marriage to have sexual relations.

Queer subjects—as instructors, students, and topics—have drawn attention in several studies, with a few in composition and rhetoric being particularly noteworthy. Harriet Malinowitz's *Textual Orientations: Lesbian and Gay Students and the Making of Discourse Communities* (1995) was the first book-length study to look specifically at writing-intensive courses focused on queer students. Malinowitz lays out how engagement with sexual identity can form an important part of a writing and rhetoric instructor's critical pedagogy, especially as such marks and values queer outsider knowledge. Zan Meyer Gonçalves's *Sexuality and the Politics of Ethos in the Writing Classroom* (2006) was, after Malinowitz's study, the next book-length analysis of gay and lesbian students' identity performances, particularly in composition courses. Gonçalves discusses the complexities of identity in negotiating shared spaces, arguing that lesbian and gay students' experiences offer us unique opportunities to see the construction of personal ethos as such students attempt to articulate their concerns in sometimes indifferent or even hostile environments. Gonçalves argues that writing teachers can assist such students in becoming rhetorical agents, as well as use their experiences to illuminate the power of ethos in rhetorical contexts.

Arguing more broadly about sexuality beyond lesbian and gay identity in *Literacy, Sexuality, and Pedagogy: Theory and Practice for the Composition Classroom*, Jonathan Alexander seeks to "bring critical work in sexuality studies ... to bear on our understanding of literacy" (36), taking as his starting point an "understanding of the ways in which sexuality is constructed in language and the ways in which our language and meaning-making systems are always already sexualized" (18). Alexander's purpose is to investigate possibilities for thinking sexuality critically in the composition and rhetoric classroom, as a topic of inquiry and even an approach when investigating with students a range of literacy practices.

What happens if we push this work outside the classroom, understanding public spheres as always already sexualized, as ecologies imbued with the formation, contestation, regulation, and queering of sex/ualities?

We take our understanding of the public sphere from Michael Warner, who, writing with Habermas in mind, attempts to theorize a rhetorically active public sphere, one that considers issues and debates them vigorously—if not always as "rationally" as Habermas intends. Indeed, Warner argues:

> Public discourse ... is poetic. By this I mean not just that it is self-organizing, a kind of entity created by its own discourse, or even that

this space of circulation is taken to be a social entity, but that in order for this to happen all discourse or performance addressed to a public must characterize the world in which it attempts to circulate and it must attempt to realize that world through address. (113–14)

Warner's public is embedded in and constructed out of discourse, and he argues that participation in public discourse must be rhetorically acute; that is, any rhetorical action must recognize how it either constitutes or exists in relation to a set of world views already in circulation in discourse. Put simply, a "public is poetic world making" (Warner 114), and any discursive activity within the public must recognize and situate itself rhetorically vis-à-vis the preexisting projects of "world making." Of course, most public lifeworlds are densely heterosexual, heteronormal—a situation we know all too well.

Warner's distinction between publics/counterpublics notes how agency in the public sphere relies on being able to articulate and maintain the dominant lifeworld—lifeworlds that are often interimbued with sexualized subject positions, identifications, and normative trajectories of desire. This move toward maintenance explains the high level of activity around gay marriage issues; for instance: opponents of gay marriage attempt to preserve a particular view of what marriage is and how it should be defined, whereas proponents argue that gay relationships are often just like straight ones, so they should be labeled and understood as such—not just rhetorically but in material reality. Indeed, the marriage debate offers a rich example of Warner's assertion that "all discourse or performance addressed to a public must characterize the world in which it attempts to circulate." If queers are to have agency within the dominant public sphere, they must address how that sphere characterizes itself to itself. In this case, queer lives become intelligible—one wants to say "legible"—only when they articulate themselves in the rhetoric of the dominant. That is, queers who claim marriage rights narrate their lives through the structures of the dominant public, the dominant lifeworld.

With such an understanding of the interimbrication of sexualities and public spheres, what would a serious engagement with multiple theories of sexuality do to rhetorical studies? Answers to this question in previous scholarship—from the *Pre/Text* issue on queer rhetorics to Charles Morris's recent anthology, *Queering Public Address: Sexualities in American Historical Discourse*—have focused on deep readings of authors and orators whose sexuality has often been elided in discussion of their work. Although such recovery work is useful, it often eschews the thorny question of what, precisely, might be a sexual rhetoric. How does it function rhetorically, not just in the life of the individual seeking a voice, declaring an identity, but also publicly, beginning to circulate in and impact public spheres, spaces of public discourse? Further, how do we think sex rhetorically, and think rhetoric sexually, to make room for alternative voices, alternative modalities of being, and divergent approaches to pressing debates and social issues? An individual, a subject, can be disciplined, silenced. But rhetorical acts, developed through interventions such as disidentification, emerge collectively over time to show us how the public sphere argues, considers issues, and/or debates the polis often through the sexual. Thus, our purpose here is to trace the emergence, not of the sexual subject, but of sexual rhetorical practices and their simultaneous creation and intervention into the public sphere.

The present volume brings together leading voices in the fields of rhetorical studies, composition, communication, and writing studies to explore the deep interimbrication of sexualities and rhetorical practices. Our contributors explore the intersection of rhetoric and sexuality through a variety of methods available in our fields, including case studies, theoretical questioning, ethnographies, and close (and distant) readings of "texts" that help us think through the rhetorical force of sexuality and the sexual force of rhetoric. We have divided this collection into three sections: Sexed Methods; Troubling Identity; and (Counter)Publics—each reflecting a major area of contribution to the field of rhetorical studies when we think rhetoric and sexuality together.

The first section, *Sexed Methods*, brings together scholars who grapple with how different methods, such as archival research, challenge what we think we know about the relationship between sexuality and rhetoric. Moreover, they also attempt at times to show how thinking sexuality rhetorically, as well as rhetoric sexually, might require new methods and approaches. Part of any methodology approaching sexuality and rhetoric must interrogate sexed and sexist assumptions about our objects of study. And as we noted earlier, a key method in revealing and troubling assumptions and predispositions is careful archival work. In "Promiscuous Approaches to Reorienting Rhetorical Research," Heather Lee Branstetter describes a queer and promiscuous orientation for scholars whose work intersects with sexuality studies and rhetorical historiography. To invite an intense revisiting of the past and affirm intimate engagement with multiple perspectives and facilitate possibilities for scholarly invention, Branstetter advocates a reexamination of professional norms in terms of methodology, style, and expression. Other generative methods involve assembling materials to read them queerly, as Jason Palmeri and Jonathan Rylander argue in "'Intersecting Realities': Queer Assemblage as Rhetorical Methodology." For these authors, a "queer turn" in thinking about sexuality and rhetoric resists binary models of sexuality, explores interrelation with other axes of embodied difference, and rearticulates rhetorical subjectivities as complex assemblages of bodies, technologies, and discourses that transform over time. As a model for their work, they draw on Jasbir Puar's articulation of queer assemblage to develop a rhetorical methodology that might engage resistance against the complex networks of "homonationalism" that have worked to ally LGBT rights rhetorics with imperialist and nationalist agendas. Jacqueline M. Martinez understands some of the difficulties of defining objects and subjects of study in sexual rhetorics when considering trans subjects' sexual experience. In her chapter, "Consciousness, Experience, Sexual Expression, and Judgment," she uses a semiotic and phenomenological lens to examine the political ambiguity of sexual desire and perceptions of self as exemplars that reveal the socially and culturally specific predispositions that come to constitute biases in commonly taken judgments regarding the relative health or value of specific sexual expressions. Her approach aims to investigate the relationship between our ideas about sexuality and a "corporeal intending," which often functions as a misalignment and makes judgments regarding the relative value of sexual expression difficult.

The next chapters in this section turn to the consideration of methods for approaching sexual rhetorics in broader contexts of knowledge production and even political activity. In "Hard-Core Rhetoric: Gender, Genre, and the Image in Neuroscience," Jordynn Jack examines how heterosexist and heteronormative assumptions function in scientific rhetorics about sex, desire, and the brain. She argues that even a feminist perspective alone is not sufficient to dislodge a heterosexual perspective in studies of the sexed/gendered brain. In "Historicizing Sexual Rhetorics: Theorizing the Power to Read, the Power to Interpret, and the Power to Produce," Meta G. Carstarphen traces the themes of "sex" and "gender" through the body of work invoking sexual rhetorics in different ways, and then she aligns these conceptualizations against rhetorical frameworks. This chapter, then, offers a reading of this body of scholarship, mindful of Judith Butler's performativity of gendered rhetoric, as evidence of a broader, global and historically resonant evolution of sexual rhetorics. Such work often draws energy from history as its seeks future transformations, and Charles E. Morris III writes in "Milk Memory's Queer Rhetorical Futurity" that any hope for an as-yet-unrealized queer futurity be understood and pursued in some significant measure in relation to the rhetorical wellsprings of the past. Using the Harvey Milk archive, Morris explores key modes of sexuality's rhetorics: destabilization, candor, recruitment, coalition, and memory, noting how they amply embody rhetoric's queer deployment, its constraint and possibility, in projects dedicated to LGBTQ worldmaking.

The chapters in this opening section often suggest that any sexing of method in rhetorical studies positions identity as a key category through which sexuality works rhetorically, as well as through which rhetoric uses the sexual in acts of persuasion. Identity (and the workings of power through it) is multifaceted, and authors in the second section, *Troubling Identity*, consider a range of intersections among identity, sexuality, and rhetorical action. David L. Wallace starts us off with "The Trope of the Closet," noting how, as the concept of coming out of the closet has gained currency in both popular culture and scholarly discourse, it has been increasingly appropriated to describe acts of self-disclosure and self-identification that do not involve sexual identity or gender expression. Wallace unpacks the use of tropes in popular culture generally, in academic discourse, in queer theory, and in his own personal experience—all to complicate our understanding of the trope of the closet by identifying how the concept shapes discourses related to the revelation of identity issues that are either not immediately apparent or that may be apparent but remain unvoiced. How do such tropes of identity play out in different social groupings?

Considering sexuality, race, and ability together in "Sex and the Crip Latina," Ellen M. Gil-Gómez autoethnographically explores how her experiences of her own body, sexuality, and academic identity have shifted dramatically as she has joined the ranks of the disabled and chronically ill. Her chapter considers the rhetorical disjunctions of an attractive woman in a wheelchair—how can someone who's "attractive" be ill or disabled?—as this juxtaposition is not consistent with cultural norms of how a body appears attractive. In "Affect, Female Masculinity, and the Embodied Space Between: Two-Spirit Traces in Thirza Cuthand's Experimental Film," Lisa Tatonetti picks up on the rhetorical problematization of gender introduced in the first section of the book in her analysis of queer Cree filmmaker Thirza Cuthand's articulation of female masculinity, which she discusses through the lens of affect and embodiment as part of a sexual rhetoric.

Reminding us that religious affiliation is a powerful marker and constructor of identity, G Patterson considers "The Unbearable Weight of Pedagogical Neutrality: Religion and LGBTQ Issues in the English Studies Classroom." Patterson notes how conservative Christian rhetors have at times deployed "religious freedom" as a prophylactic against charges of bigotry. Drawing from queer, feminist, and critical race theorists' critiques of neoliberalism, she reads such "neutrality" against the grain and locates key tropes among these neutrality narratives—an analysis that might make for an astute approach to teaching rhetorical awareness. Continuing a focus on the classroom, Martha Marinara writes both analytically and autobiographically in her chapter, "The Story of Fox Girl: Writing Queer about/in Imaginary Spaces," about how work in queer composition and rhetorical studies has become domesticated, queered positions often reduced to more comfortable identities. Marinara, wanting teachers and students to rethink the tensions between language and social behaviors, invites reconsideration of the pedagogical possibilities of thinking rhetoric sexually.

And finally, turning to a broader public pedagogic in "'As Proud of Our Gayness, as We Are of Our Blackness': Race-ing Sexual Rhetorics in the National Coalition of Black Lesbians and Gays," Eric Darnell Pritchard focuses critical attention on the sexual rhetorics of the national activist group to examine how the organization and its members forged new paradigms for social action that synthesized race and sexuality in their efforts to document and build upon the contributions of black LGBT people to the Black freedom and gay and lesbian civil rights movements.

As essays in this section remind us, identities are inevitably never simply personal, and the turn to classroom considerations in the final essays of the previous section remind us that identities always take shape in publics, often numerous publics. Similarly, the sexual rhetorics that individuals and groups deploy, as personal as they might feel, are often mobilized to do work in multiple public spheres. The chapters in our last section, *(Counter)Publics*, consider the rhetorical work of the sexual, and the sexual work of the rhetorical, as a persuasive force, problematic, and possibility in several socialities.

Because rights are often predicated on or mobilized through identities, consideration of their relationship seems pressing, particularly at a time of increased expansion in some public spheres of rights based on sexual identity. The operation of identities and rights in sexual rhetorics achieves sharp focus in the examination of particular contemporary cases. Erin J. Rand's chapter, "'Gay Boys Kill Themselves': The Queer Figuration of the Suicidal Gay Teen," picks up the pressing problem of homophobic bullying to trace the circulation of a "collectively imagined symbol," the suicidal gay teen. This figure performs not just the work of raising awareness of homophobic bullying, but also may in itself constitute "an enactment of insidious and injurious rhetorical violence." In the process, heteronormativity remains unquestioned.

The contradictions inherent in rights-based work sometimes come to the fore in activist projects. In "Consorting with the Enemy?: Women's Liberation Rhetoric about Sexuality," Clark A. Pomerleau historicizes the complexities of basing liberation movements and activism on identity, noting how the "realization that sexuality changes and gains its meaning from our social situations collides with the seemingly comforting commonplace that sexuality is stable." Paying particular attention to feminist engagements with sexualities, including heterosexuality, lesbianism, and bisexuality, reveals the ongoing struggle to negotiate between the need for a legible and inclusive activist politics and the desire to honor different lived experiences. Similarly, in "Sex Trafficking Rhetorics/Queer Refusal," Ian Barnard shows how anti-sex trafficking rhetorics, like other sex panics, are imbricated in heteronormative attachment and defensiveness, though in the case of sex trafficking panic the routes of attachment are often more elliptical and dispersed. For instance, Barnard argues that, ironically, queer panic and queer reactive impetuses inform and even impel much anti-sex trafficking rhetoric and activism. And in "Sexual Counterpublics, Disciplinary Rhetorics, and Truvada," J. Blake Scott offers a rhetorical-cultural analysis of the ongoing controversy surrounding Truvada, the first HIV antiretroviral drug approved (in 2012) for pre-exposure prophylaxis. Blake analyzes how discourses surrounding Truvada often function as a "disciplinary rhetoric," or body of persuasion, that works to "shape the normalization, identification, and embodied experiences of sexualized subjects."

Finally, our last two contributors consider how sexual rhetorics function in overtly political discourses in the public sphere. Luke Winslow's "Presidential Masculinity: George W. Bush's Rhetorical Conquest" considers how voters rely heavily on affective shortcuts to navigate what might otherwise be an unmanageably complex political process. Specifically, he explores the role sexuality plays in facilitating those shortcuts, taking as his case study different representations of masculinity in the presidential political discourse of

George W. Bush. And in "Liberal Humanist 'Rights' Discourse and Sexual Citizenship," Harriet Malinowitz examines how notions of "rights" and "fairness" have been historically—and still presently are—used in the LGBT movement, as well as in many academic contexts, to persuade people that "gay is OK." The rightness of "rights" achieves widespread recognition and sympathy through various (and often sentimentalized) vehicles of symbolization that could well bear closer inspection.

Taken together, these chapters speak not only to the diversity of methods and objects of study available in the study of sexual rhetorics, but also to the saturation of public discourses with sexual appeals. In so many ways, the rhetorical is the sexual, and any understanding of rhetorical action is necessarily hampered, if not indeed damaged, without robust attention to the sexual. We hope this collection goes some length in demonstrating the necessity of considering sexual rhetorics as a fundamental part of understanding rhetorical action in contemporary public spheres.

Works Cited

Alexander, Jonathan. *Literacy, Sexuality, and Pedagogy: Theory and Practice for the Composition Classroom*. Logan: Utah State UP, 2008. Print.

Alexander, Jonathan, and Michelle Gibson, eds. "Special Cluster: Queer Theory." *JAC: A Journal of Composition Theory* 24.1 (2004). Print.

Alexander, Jonathan, and Jacqueline Rhodes. "Queer Rhetoric and the Pleasures of the Archives." *Enculturation*. Jan. 2012. Web. 3 May 2015.

Alexander, Jonathan, and Jacqueline Rhodes. "Queer: An Impossible Subject for Composition." *JAC: A Journal of Composition Theory* 31.1 (2010). 177–206. Print.

Alexander, Jonathan, and David Wallace. "The Queer Turn in Composition Studies: Reviewing and Assessing an Emerging Scholarship." *College Composition and Communication* 61 (2009): 300–20. Print.

Carstarphen, Meta G., and Susan Zavoina, eds. *Sexual Rhetoric: Media Perspectives on Sexuality, Gender, and Identity*. Westport, CT: Greenwood, 1999. Print.

Cobb, Michael. *God Hates Fags: The Rhetorics of Religious Violence*. New York: New York UP, 2006. Print.

Cvetkovich, Ann. *An Archive of Feelings: Trauma, Sexuality, and Lesbian Public Cultures*. Durham, NC: Duke UP, 2003. Print.

Foucault, Michel. "Nietzsche, Genealogy, History." *Language, Counter-Memory, Practice: Selected Essays and Interviews*. Ed. Donald F. Bouchard. Ithaca, NY: Cornell UP, 1977. 139–64. Print.

Fuller, Linda K. *Sexual Sports Rhetoric: Historical and Media Contexts of Violence*. New York: Peter Lang, 2009. Print.

Gardner, Christine J. *Making Chastity Sexy: The Rhetoric of Evangelical Abstinence Campaigns*. Berkeley: U of California P, 2011.

Gonçalves, Zan Meyer. *Sexuality and the Politics of Ethos in the Writing Classroom*. Carbondale: Southern Illinois UP, 2006.

Halberstam, Judith. *In a Queer Time and Place: Transgender Bodies, Subcultural Lives*. New York: New York UP, 2005. Print.

Jensen, Robin E. *Dirty Words: The Rhetoric of Public Sex Education, 1870–1924.* Urbana: U of Illinois P, 2010. Print.

Malinowitz, Harriet. *Textual Orientations: Lesbian and Gay Students and the Making of Discourse Communities.* Portsmouth, NH: Heinemann, 1995.

Morris, Charles E. "Archival Queer." *Rhetoric and Public Affairs* 9.1 (Spring 2006): 145–51. Print.

Morris, Charles E., ed. *Queering Public Address: Sexualities in American Historical Discourse.* Columbia: U of South Carolina P, 2007. Print.

Morrison, Margaret, ed. *Queer Rhetoric.* Special issue of *Pre/Text* 13.3–4 (1992). Print.

Reumann, Miriam G. *American Sexual Character: Sex, Gender, and National Identity in the Kinsey Reports.* Berkeley: U of California P, 2005.

Thompson, Julie M. *Mommy Dearest: Contemporary Rhetorics of Lesbian Maternal Identity.* Amherst: U of Massachusetts P, 2002. Print.

Waggoner, Erin B., ed. *Sexual Rhetoric in the Works of Joss Whedon.* Jefferson, NC: McFarland, 2010. Print.

Warner, Michael. *Publics and Counterpublics.* New York: Zone, 2002. Print.

Part I
Sexed Methods

1 Promiscuous Approaches to Reorienting Rhetorical Research

Heather Lee Branstetter

> *"Isn't this what good scholarship already does?"*
> *"This sounds sexy and all, but it also sounds unethical."*
> *"Aren't you just reifying harmful stereotypes?"*
> *"What about the negative aspects of promiscuity, like disease?"*

It was a packed room, the biggest audience I'd ever had for a presentation, despite the fact that all three of us—Risa Applegarth and Jean Bessette along with me—were relatively new scholars. The intersection of methods and memory studies was having a moment, it seemed, at this 2009 Feminisms and Rhetorics conference. I have now come to believe that methodology was having a moment in the field of rhetoric more broadly. I had spoken about the need for a more "queer and promiscuous" approach to feminist scholarship, and I advocated its usefulness for scholars whose work intersects with memory studies and women's rhetorical historiography. I had been inspired by the RSA Institute workshop with Charles Morris, Karma Chávez, and Isaac West a few months prior. The barrage of excited yet critical questions that hit me afterward showed me that I had touched a sensitive spot. Some members of the audience saw the approach I was outlining as not being an example of "legitimate" scholarship, whereas others didn't see what was new about it at all, and still others perceived it as inappropriate or even immoral. Was I doing something wrong, I wondered?

My presentation was meant to guide, to inspire others to mix up our scholarship, moving and shaking the traditional ways of doing things, but ever since I've tried to talk about it in academic spheres, it's been met with demands that it make itself more communicable without "infecting" traditional scholarship with its vector potential. I know some questions come from an empathetic place, a true desire to understand, to connect. But some questions also come from a defensive impulse to sequester or suppress perspectives or approaches ("let them have their 'special issues' and 'alternative rhetorics'"). And of course some others want to control (aka "professionalize") what might potentially be dangerous—on the *loose*, running around stirring up shit. What is the value of diversity—why on earth do we even bother to admit students from a variety of backgrounds, affirm equal opportunity hiring practices, or talk about the need for different perspectives and epistemic processes—if our goal is merely to program everyone to work in monologous tongues that reify a tower of ivory babble?

In their introduction to this collection, Jonathan Alexander and Jacqueline Rhodes assert that sexuality is robustly rhetorical. To this statement, I add that rhetoric is also robustly promiscuous. And promiscuity is also inherently queer insofar as it challenges mainstream sexual values and ideas about what sexuality should be: the terms overlap where they challenge "normal" paradigms of morality and what constitutes deviance. In this case, queer does not simply point us toward a gay or lesbian identity, nor to a homo versus hetero perspective, since the term *queer* can have the effect of covering over difference and mischaracterizing a diversity of voices when it is used synecdochically (or metonymically ... maybe both at the same time).[1] And, as I will explain throughout the remainder of this piece, the term *promiscuity* does not indicate the inability to control one's sexual impulses or desires. Nor does it point us toward inherently indiscriminate sexual behavior. Rather, I wish to describe and inspire more diverse orientations to research, a way of doing scholarship by embracing the historical linkage of promiscuity (and its inherent queerness) with deviance and pathology. I hope to unsettle and confound our notions of scholarly decorum, propriety, and tradition. The approach I describe is often performative, playful, and mischievous. It embraces peculiarity, suspends expectations, and follows hunches in order to go deeper without being "properly introduced." This orientation is usually subversive insofar as promiscuity has traditionally been used as an accusation against someone whose behavior is perceived as indiscreet, suspicious, and generally disreputable. A promiscuous approach does not seek to redefine norms—rather, it seeks to *disrupt normalcy altogether*, to intimately engage with and vicariously inhabit multiple perspectives, to live through the desires of strangers, to simultaneously invite and affirm the variety of human experience.

An explicit focus on sexual rhetorics and research methodology offers the unique opportunity to examine intersections of sexual-rhetorical approaches with the productive conceptual potential of promiscuity, "a constellation of discursive practices that emerge at different times for different groups in order to articulate resistance to regimes of sexualized normalization," as Alexander and Rhodes put it in 2012 ("Queer Rhetoric and the Pleasures of the Archive"). Our field would benefit from a more sustained engagement with the perspectives, people, and acts often seen as sexually deviant but not necessarily LGBTIA. To be more specific, I'm thinking of slutty women, sex workers, interracial sex, or fetish, kink, and polyamorous orientations. For the purpose of this piece, the regimes of sexualized normalization include our own research and academic institutional contexts. By inhabiting and exploring the value of sexual-rhetorical perspectives that have traditionally been denigrated or dismissed, we enhance possibilities for scholarly invention and persuasive action.

Our research topics and methods should reflect the variety of our rhetorical activity as humans. I focus here on describing the productive potential

I see for more promiscuous approaches to rhetorical scholarship, connecting my examples to rhetorical historiography and community or cultural rhetorics. I address the liabilities I've encountered while experimenting with a promiscuous approach and suggest ways to justify the value of this sexual-rhetorical perspectival lens during those times when it becomes strategically necessary to make ourselves tactically communicable to those who might otherwise find us illegible, interpret our work as immoral, or dismiss our contribution as "personal," dilettantish, or niche. I close with brief applications and extensions. In this chapter, I orient toward some potential lines of flight I see for reapproaching (don't I really mean "reproaching" my smart-ass spell check wants to know? maybe, I think) rhetorical research by embracing its promiscuous nature as a methodological hermeneutic.

Academic Freedom
Means Polyamorous Ideas
Creative Movement
Promiscuous Approaches

"What is an Approach? Define Your Terms. Fit Your Ideas in with Others Who Have Come Before."

No. (Not yet—that's the next section.) But okay, fine, I will try to explain what I mean by "approach": I mean an orientation, inspiration, feeling, philosophical investments, theoretical contexts, and methodological implications.

In "The Idea of Rhetoric in the Rhetoric of Science," Dilip P. Gaonkar observes that a "striking and commonly noted feature" inherent in rhetoric's interdisciplinary resurgence "is the sheer promiscuity with which the term *rhetoric* is deployed" (37). He critiques what he calls several times "the promiscuous use of the term rhetoric" as "almost talismanic," a surface-level substitute for making an analysis rhetorical (71) that *"severely undermines rhetoric's self-representation as a situated practical art"* (76). I love this piece and appreciate the observations about how rhetoric's supplementarity—the rhetoric of X, rhetorical X, X and rhetorics, or, as in the case of this book, simply X rhetorics—functions as a hermeneutic. Gaonkar notes the interpretive roles of rhetoric in pedagogy, critique, and theory, but what has arisen more recently as rhetoric has become more thoroughly disciplined, is increasing interest in methodology. The way *rhetoric* is paired with the word *promiscuous* in the essay reveals the following undercurrent: if rhetoric is being so slutty, sleeping around with all the other disciplines, it may no longer be unique or valuable to have sex with rhetoric. In the case of methodology, however, I would argue that rhetoric's promiscuity has made it *more* valuable as an interpretive lens. And that's what I mean by an "approach."

I stumbled upon a promiscuous approach when I jumped down the rabbit hole of social movement rhetoric and collective invention for my dissertation and discovered that the critique of institutional structures I'd been studying applied to the very scholarship I was expected to engage in order to demonstrate field competence and earn my degree. I began to wonder: Which of our practices were suspect, and how and why? I began to feel like we needed a "Students' Right to Their Own Language" adapted to scholarly rhetoric and research. Which of our professionalization, incentive systems, and citation practices continued to exist primarily because they reaffirmed the dominance of the preexisting system, and which of our practices were truly oriented toward forwarding significant, ambitious, and legitimately creative new ideas?

A promiscuous approach to rhetorical research acknowledges and experiments with multiple ways of being, wants research to be self-determined and free, wants to "have sex" with lots of different kinds of projects in lots of different ways and understand those projects on their own terms in order to bring something unique out of the result, without feeling economically coerced to publish in traditional venues or conform–contort one's spectrum of ideas and skills into a "coherent research agenda." And again, if we are to affirm the variety of our human rhetorical activity, there should be room for promiscuous approaches, topics, perspectives, and styles in our rhetorical scholarship and professional spheres.

Rhetorical promiscuity is a reorientation of our traditional academic ways of doing style, expression, and genre. Promiscuous rhetorics question where we put our acknowledgments, who we cite, and how we write. A promiscuous approach transcends traditional ways of judging propriety—it is a radical orientation toward openness, trying on different ways of looking at the world and spreading that knowledge around. Promiscuous approaches attempt to be transparent and truthful, even as they are inherently complex, role playing, embracing the iterative yet unpredictable and at times parallel process energy of simultaneity, interactivity, multiplicity, excess, rhythm, collective invention, social movement, connection, exchange, give and take, service, performance, a dialogic interplay of power and strategy or moving in intuitive empathic approaching telepathic ways. Yes, I'm talking about sex. And I'm also talking about rhetoric. Promiscuous approaches to rhetoric challenge our complacent acceptance of what "proper" scholarship *feels* like, looks like, acts like. It engages memorable, flexible, improvisational ideas at event horizons in communal ways. It's rhetoric outside the confines of marriage to the academy, not limited to higher education echo chambers for the purposes of reproduction.

For those of us whose writing and teaching intersect with sexuality and sexual topics, our research often arises organically out of the content and context, and our approaches have been inherently risky. It is therefore even more important for us to be relentlessly thorough when translating our process and relevance to others. Our profession continues to need more representative understandings of rhetoric in the lives of real people, people whose relationship to sex and sexual desire range across a spectrum. Because our field has looked to the classical Greek and Roman canon to legitimate our research, we have missed out on valuable perspectives as we play a rigged game: the weight of our academic heritage requires those of us working in more promiscuous ways to jump higher procedural hurdles in terms of developing new theories, discovering relevant methodologies, and justifying broader applications for the ones we already have.

A Slutwalk of Hir Own
(Or, Promiscuity Shacks up with Traditional Ways of Doing Scholarship and Methodology. And yes, even Deleuze. At the same time.)

In which our protagonist attempts to sexually orient hirself within incongruous perspectival lenses, simultaneously throating self-destruction and fisting self-preservation in search of freedom ...

This section is about the liabilities and challenges of promiscuous approaches. It is also about trying to make promiscuous methods tactically communicable and theoretically alive.

Whore. Contaminated. "Inappropriate." "Unprofessional."

How many times have these words been used to regulate and control? Promiscuity's free-spirited approach threatens the stability of a well-controlled, regulated, "professional" situation.

The word *appropriate*—as in square, but also as in cultural appropriation, as in, *to appropriate* someone else's culture—has colonial problems. Similarly, the word *professional* [and professor] is caught up in the "middle class" values language games of:

                        confusing self with [academic] corporation.
          caught up enforcing rules you didn't write, don't endorse
      (trying not to get kicked down) =
   moving up the economic ladder
profession =

It's the working professional classes or those trying to move from the so-called working class over to the working professional classes who are colonized by the overly complex and self-contradictory hierarchy of mainstream values. Even socially progressive academics reify traditional values by default and—often in small-talk situations or grad school/job market/tenure and promotion/research committee/grant foundation behind-closed-doors and off-the-official-record evaluation situations—make erroneous assumptions or question those who have taken the time to consider which mainstream values and practices are worth continuing to reinforce. The academic world remains monogamous and/or square in practice, especially in terms of research subjects and methods.[2] So often it's the already less visible research subjects, people, and projects that suffer. Our profession's socialized demand that we appeal to the traditionally dominant norms of scholarship that have actively worked to exclude a diversity of voices is a social justice problem for me: the expectation that we *appeal rhetorically to those very norms to adequately defend our divergence from them* turns into an ethical imperative to do otherwise, to get with others who are similarly oriented and resolve not only to do scholarship differently but also to inhabit our scholarly personas in different ways, acting in accordance with our conscience regarding the social responsibility we have to those beyond the traditional boundaries of the academy, even when that work is not already recognized by existing academic incentive mechanisms. Because otherwise nothing will change. A promiscuous approach to rhetoric chooses topics based on ambition and significance, idealistically (yet not naïvely) oriented toward making the world a place where difference is embraced.

Resources are allocated and assumptions are made in part according to what others read when they scan your CV. And square scholarly professional imperatives can feel alienating to promiscuous approaches, which draw inspiration from varied realms. But a promiscuous approach also strives to be *communicable* at times (and perhaps at times contagious) in its search for connection with others who might be working in more traditional ways but who also feel restricted by scholarly norms and who thus might be recruited (if not converted) in the quest for a greater diversity of approaches. A promiscuous approach challenges norms, but is also varied and diverse, and at times engages with traditional and perhaps necessary professional tasks. It does not dismiss the work of others that is truly relevant, even when that work has at times excluded truly relevant and valuable perspectives from its own intellectual harems. So for the next three paragraphs, I'll engage with the traditional approach to legitimating promiscuous, intimate, or sexual methods according to disciplinary expectations.

Previous published work that explicitly addresses methods in rhetorical historiography has emphasized the importance of democratizing our understanding of the past in order to work toward more socially progressive futures. In my own research, I have found *Working in the Archives* and *Beyond the Archives* valuable collections that bring together much of the rhetorical historiography methods already visible within the field. We can extend the methodological and practical lessons more broadly as we emphasize connections. For example, the introduction to *Working in the Archives* points us toward primary sources found not only in traditional university libraries but also unpublished writing in unexpected places, such as those found in records kept by local historians in small towns, with Charlotte Hogg's work on rural women emerging as a useful example. Scholars in feminist historiography have forged significant paths to extend our discussion of rhetorical methodology beyond traditional topics and approaches (for more on feminist recovery and methods, see also Royster and Kirsch or Enoch and Jack). Yet, as Kate Davy points out: "If women in general are absent from the historical record, lesbians are aggressively missing; for reasons of survival, their history unfolds in acts of hiding from a hostile culture" (134). Davy's discussion highlights the heightened sense of stakes for those of us working on topics that intersect with sex and sexuality, those of us who have had to be particularly creative when searching for, inventing, and justifying our research. When our research material is actively camouflaged or when it doesn't come preassembled in a narrative form, we need to invent a wider range of interpretive and methodological tools.

Connections with more typically sexed and/or intimate methods—dealing with emotions, desire, and ethics regarding the use of past—also find justification in the above collections already deemed legitimate by Southern Illinois University Press (SIUP) disciplinary standards. Even scholars discussing more typically square topics in purely pragmatic ways admit the voyeuristic "guilty pleasures" of reading private letters and diaries, emotional investment in discovering the lives of those we research in intimate ways, and complex reality of balancing these feelings as we share our personal encounters within a critical academic context (Bergmann). Wendy Sharer explains how she moved from ensuring she had "responsibly revealed" her biases as she was "debating the validity" of her ideas before finally realizing that her "most significant (to date) research project originated within the emotion-laden family and life experiences that preceded that research" (54). Our passions and lived contexts inspire and improve our scholarship as we make educated guesses and feel the movements of our research, as we "try not to cling too tightly to a hypothesis" nor wander around the archives without one (Mastrangelo and L'Eplattenier 164). The intimate dynamics, creative unpredictability, intuition, and general messiness inherent in any rhetorical methodology that deals with subjects not already given to a researcher in a coherent narrative has already been seen as a strength, as Nan Johnson has discussed, comparing her own archival experience to "making art" (292). Maybe it's just me, but the way she describes it also sounds like sex.

Scholars doing the already-visible research have lately expressed their desire that we relate to the past in ways that move beyond what Royster and Kirsch have described as "the three Rs" of "rescue, recovery, and (re) inscription" (75), despite the fact that many perspectives continue to remain "aggressively missing" from our rhetorical historiographies. Royster and Kirsch advocate engaging with the past using the "dialectical and dialogical analytical tool" they call "critical imagination," so that we work "in symbiotic partnership" across time by "re-creating and honoring a more fully textured view of involvement, participation, rhetorical prowess, and indeed leadership" (ibid.). Part of the critique here is that by focusing on "recovering" personally interesting topics rather than "a more fully textured view," we repeat the very conditions that excluded those we have sought to "rescue" from historical obscurity and in the process become hero protagonists in our own colonizing Western master narratives.

Charles Morris and K. J. Rawson outline a different critique of the potential integrity problem inherent in contemporary historiographic scholarship as they discuss our discipline's [sacred] "lineage of revisionist rhetorical historiography, with its critical shift from historical subjects to historical production itself," which is "materially and ideologically constitutive and thus consequential" (74). In their piece, promiscuously embedded in an SIUP-legitimate edited collection that gathers a range of theoretical perspectives on histories of rhetoric, Morris and Rawson "chart and mobilize queer archives and archival queers," calling our attention in a non-resentful, matter-of-fact sort of way to "ongoing disciplinary heteronormative neglect and omission" that continues "despite a decade of visible scholarship in this field and twenty-five years' worth of influential scholarship in the academy writ large" (ibid.). Sexuality and gender studies scholarship, they point out, offers rich rhetorical resources for a more fully textured view of relating to the past and has long had a complex relationship with timespace, history, imagination, critical agendas, impossible desire, and archives. See, for example, Ann Cvetkovich's 2003 *An Archive of Feelings*, Eve Kosofsky Sedgwick's 2003 *Touching Feeling*, Judith Halberstam's 2005 *In a Queer Time and Place*, Heather Love's 2007 *Feeling Backward*, and José Esteban Muñoz's 1999 *Disidentifications* and 2009 *Cruising Utopia*, or Lauren Berlant's 2011 *Cruel Optimism*. This sort of work should provide sufficient resources for scholarly legitimation and methodological tools for sexual-rhetorical topics. Yet perhaps it has been excluded from the already-visible rhetorical historiography—which, Rawson argues ("Queering Feminist Rhetorical Canonization"), has now taken on the force of a canon that our discipline expects us to cite (*disciplines* us into citing!)—in part because work having to do with sexuality is often reduced to that scholarly death phrase: special interest.

Even though there is value to promiscuously engaging with dominant perspectives by choice, in order to make ourselves communicable, promiscuous approaches to rhetoric also intentionally seek inspiration from other disciplines or art, music, public culture, and community spheres specifically in search of perspectives not limited by the terministic screens, trained incapacities, and occupational psychoses (Burke, *Permanance and Change* and *Attitudes Toward History*) of our discipline or specialty. There is value in ignoring the coercive expectation to be legible (and thus surveillable or servile and reduce-able or reproducible) to traditional scholarship. A promiscuous approach can sidestep this control by publishing in different ways, rewarding nontraditional publication venues with our attention. There's *Harlot*, also drawing inspiration from rhetoric's disreputable ethos as harlot of the arts. The journal *Enculturation* recently extended into a new venue called *Intermezzo*, seeking to publish scholarship that is smart and provocative, yet coming (multiple ways) "from a variety of disciplinary approaches or a mixture of approaches" engaging "rhetorical gestures not normally appreciated in traditional, academic publishing" (par 3). Promiscuous approaches can look to journals like *Rhizomes*, which has taken Deleuze's approach as a launching point, as the manifesto explains:

"New thinking need not follow established patterns. ... we encourage migrations into new conceptual territories resulting from unpredictable juxtapositions."

Engaging the past promiscuously may require that at times we strap on our sex prosthesis of memory (to adapt Derrida's famous phrase) and say, "fuck it." ("Wait, so let me understand this: I can do you while you're doing her? Cool.") Or, if you prefer, make love. If you are (the ostensibly straight) Deleuze, you approach the past from behind in a not-entirely-consensual yet nevertheless affectionate reorientation of "the straightforward linear relation between space and time that associates the behind with the completed past" (Stockton 6). When I first became enamored of Deleuze, I didn't know that his work has been seen as incompatible with social movement rhetoric and especially feminism (despite Elizabeth Grosz's work), which is supposedly more "appropriately" read in connection with Marxist thought, even though lesbian feminists in the United States developed their *own* rich theoretical tradition and have historically enriched their perspectives through a promiscuous variety of theoretical means, not by declaring monogamous allegiance to any particular rhetorical lineage or theoretical heritage.

But even though Deleuze is not widely seen as playing well with some others, I consider that kindred, promiscuous approaches at times accept pleasure and influence from strange bedfellows. I also enjoy the D. Perhaps I am attracted to him because he is kindred: recently, Flaxman called Deleuze "[a]n incorrigibly promiscuous thinker" insofar as he has "entertained relationships with countless philosophers, 'friends' and 'enemies' alike" (22). Promiscuity, as embodied in Deleuze's approaches, impels us not only to do our scholarship differently, but also to express our work in multifaceted, disorderly ways that elide abstract categorization, inventing intercourse as we go, relating to other fresh concepts that attract us, producing concepts "created in amorous relations with other domains," following "a profligate line, forming new associations, experimenting here and there, and always returning—fondly, but without promises—to those associations that have produced the most conceptual joy" (Flaxman 181). But at the same time a promiscuous approach need not "*just fuck anyone*"; instead, "promiscuity demands that we cultivate tastes and develop a sensibility (where, when, how, how many?) that the ascetic anchorite will never know" (Flaxman 181–182, emphasis in original).[3] To be promiscuous does not necessarily mean you are "easy," does not mean that you spread yourself thin or lower your standards. Approaching scholarship in a Deleuzian-promiscuous way means "formulating alliances with other means of expression, with the sensations and intensities that affect us, disorient us, move us" (Flaxman 182). A fresh, bold, more creative way of doing rhetorical scholarship requests that our words and concepts invite further exploration and use an "otherwise" kind of language and expression, spinning within and among chaotic landscapes.

What Now?

> "'Let me give you some counsel, bastard,' [Tyrion] Lannister said. 'Never forget what you are, for surely the world will not. Make it your strength. Then it can never be your weakness. Armor yourself in it and it will never be used to hurt you.'"
> —George R.R. Martin, *A Game of Thrones* (57)

Venturing outside traditionally sanctioned spheres and media requires researchers to adopt experimentally unique approaches to rhetorical research. It also requires a willingness to develop better vocabularies and share a wider range of narratives about how rhetoricians actually go about conducting research. K. J. Rawson, Jean Bessette, and John Howard have demonstrated some of the ways in which we can expand our understanding of historiographic work as we engage the past in temporally, materially, and technologically complex ways to reimagine power and reapproach our relationships with the past. We might call this "critical imagination," or "strategic contemplation" oriented toward honoring our past, as Royster and Kirsch do, or we might think of it as fantasy, fetish, "opening up," or becoming-ethical-timespace-sluts. For example, scholars who work on subjects that document the lives of people seen as liminal or people who challenge mainstream expectations and values often need to seek out or help create homegrown or community-built archives. Like Morris and Rawson, we need more people who are proactive in the actual process of rhetorical historiography, stepping outside the bounds of the academy to see anew those whose lives we've dismissed, and value a wider variety of perspectives as we redefine what "counts" as an item of value.

We also need more scholars helping to bring greater visibility (and improved preservation practices) to preexisting informal community collections, both locally and transnationally. Because, as Ekaterina Haskins has pointed out, "museums and archives have traditionally valued objects and texts, selected for their enduring cultural value, over ephemeral manifestations of cultural heritage," we too often limit ourselves to the ideologies and spaces of "intellectual and artistic elites" when we rely on traditionally sanctioned institutions of memory (402). It enriches our rhetorical scholarship to learn about archivists' approaches to organizing, preserving, and describing materials, as Sammie L. Morris and Shirley K. Rose have explained. We can take more initiative—and recruit our students—to engage nonacademics as we build more inclusive histories and identify basement, attic, and closet archives that should be better preserved and more accessible to others. Forging connections with local leaders, working with community and oral historians, local museum directors, and public librarians, and helping other keepers of the past to build different kinds of memory institutions is in itself *rhetorical work*—it's the promiscuous application, theory, and practice of rhetoric. As humanistic studies continue to explain our worth to increasingly vocationally oriented institutions, we should seriously consider arguing along these lines in our local contexts: time spent doing what has traditionally been classified by hiring and tenure-promotion committees as "community service" might be more adequately recognized as applied rhetorical scholarly engagement.

After sorting through my rabbit hole of a dissertation, I began a second major project to see if I could apply the community-oriented-immersion-participant-researcher methodology I had begun innovating and experimenting with along the way. After working in coalition with museums in my hometown to identify and preserve historical records, build a digital repository, and construct interactive virtual exhibits from materials contributed by local historians and community recordkeepers, I have become convinced of promiscuity's value as an approach to rhetorical research and I hope to inspire others by sharing my own experience. In my case, I was exploring the rhetorical contributions of women engaged in brothel-based sex work, and it has helped extend my understanding of the possibilities inherent in attending to the creation, interpretation, and influence of public memory and collective invention beyond institutional boundaries and within new media contexts.

As I have been helping augment my hometown's preexisting archives by enhancing our community memory and connecting it with the lived experiences of historic madams and working girls, I've learned so much about how they contributed rhetorically to our town's sense of history and culture. Engaging with others outside academic spaces through scholarly service has worked in a reciprocal way. By working with research participants to document and preserve oral histories, comparing them to previously unpublished historic and archival materials, and creating digital repositories connected to virtual exhibits, I have discovered how stories travel across time and space as the most persuasive lines of argument appeal to the collective local values and gather into fractal patterns, pulling the past into present and vice versa.

It may be that the approach I am describing here is indeed what good scholarship already does, but shouldn't we continue to seek new ways to describe it, finding inspiration in a more diverse body of thought so that our practices better reflect our rhetoric? Only by revising our methodologies to include a range of perspectives not limited to our traditional approaches can we make room for the greater range of voices we profess to want to include in what is becoming a promiscuously-mixed-no-longer-merely-ivory tower. I cannot generalize out to all sexual rhetorics or to all rhetorical research (despite what my chapter title might imply) because that value will be as varied as the individuals who might seek to engage it, but I do believe organically arising methodological approaches that draw inspiration from sexual rhetorics, such as the promiscuous orientation I have here described, have the potential to enrich rhetorical research more generally, especially when aligned with other emergent areas such as global human rights rhetoric, or nonlinear virtual and interactive narrative modes of communication.

I want to close with a question that adapts Deleuze's retrospective on his own approach in the letter that opens up *Negotiations*: How about instead of "all that crap where everyone's supposed to be everyone else's guilty conscience and judge," instead of "being this or that sort of human," we orient toward "becoming inhuman," imagine the loosening of our "human organization, exploring this or that zone of bodily intensity, with everyone discovering their own particular zones, and the groups, populations, species that inhabit them" (11)?

Acknowledgments

I would like to thank my writing group, Risa Applegarth, Erin Branch, Sarah Hallenbeck, Chelsea Redeker, and Lindsay Rose Russell, for reading and responding to my writing. My VMI women's writing group provided feedback as well—thank you Deidre Garriott, Julie Brown, Meagan Herald, Valentina Dimitrova-Grajzl, Jessica Libertini, Kristen Rost, Sara Whipple, and Jennifer Gerow. I would also like to express my continuing gratitude for the contributions of my dissertation co-directors, Jane Danielewicz and Jordynn Jack, as well as extend my thanks for the material support, funding, and mentorship provided by the Sallie Bingham Center for Women's History and Culture and the Wallace District Mining Musuem, especially Executive Director Jim McReynolds. My major research projects have been generously encouraged by grants from the University of North Carolina and the Virginia Military Institute.

Notes

1. Despite its inclusive potential and varied application opportunities, when we use queer as an identity category, bi- or pansexual, polyamorous, transgender, socioeconomic class concerns, and critical race perspectives are often subsumed to monogamous, middle-class or elite sexual values, whites-only contexts, or homonormative concerns.
2. See, for example, David Wallace's 2002 article for more on how this can play out in terms of heteronormativity.
3. For caveats about "discriminating" tastes, see Michael J. Faris and M. L. Sugie in "Fucking with Fucking Online: Advocating for Indiscriminate Promiscuity."

Works Cited

Alexander, Jonathan. "Beyond Identity: Queer Values and Community." *Journal of Gay, Lesbian, and Bisexual Identity* 4.4 (1999): 293–314. Print.

Alexander, Jonathan, and Jacqueline Rhodes. "Installation, Instantiation, and Performance." *College Composition and Communication Online* 1.1 (January 2012) Web. 14 Aug. 2014.

———. "Queer Rhetoric and the Pleasures of the Archive." *Enculturation: A Journal of Rhetoric, Writing, and Culture.* 16 Jan. 2012. Web. 26 Apr. 2015.

Anderson, Dan. "Performing Rhetoric: Embodying Rhetoric Through Screens and Space." *Computers and Writing.* Frostburg, MD, June 2013. Conference presentation.

Applegarth, Risa. "Inhabiting a Field: Memory Texts and Discipline Formation." *7th Biennial Feminisms and Rhetorics Conference.* East Lansing, Michigan, Oct. 2009. Conference presentation. Print.

Bergmann, Linda. "The Guilty Pleasures of Working with Archives." In Alexis E. Ramsey, Wendy B. Sharer, Barbara L'Eplattenier, and Lisa S. Mastrangelo, eds., *Working in the Archives: Practical Research Methods for Rhetoric and Composition.* 220–31. Carbondale: Southern Illinois UP, 2010.

Berlant, Lauren. *Cruel Optimism.* Durham, NC: Duke UP, 2011. Print.

Bessette, Jean. "An Archive of Anecdotes: Raising Lesbian Consciousness after the Daughters of Bilitis." *Rhetoric Society Quarterly* 43.1 (2013): 22–45. Print.

———. "Feminist Historiography, Methodology, and Memory: Interpretations of Margaret Fuller's *Feminisms.*" *7th Biennial Feminisms & Rhetorics Conference.* East Lansing, Michigan, Oct. 2009. Conference presentation.

Branstetter, Heather Lee. *An ALFA-Omega Approach to Rhetorical Invention: Queer Revolutionary Pragmatism and Political Education.* The University of North Carolina at Chapel Hill, 2012. Ann Arbor, MI: *ProQuest.* Web. 13 Dec. 2014.

———. "Queering Feminist Historiography." *7th Biennial Feminisms & Rhetorics Conference.* East Lansing, Michigan, Oct. 2009. Conference presentation.

Burke, Kenneth. *Attitudes Toward History.* 3rd ed. Berkeley: U of California P, 1984. Print.

———. *Permanence and Change: An Anatomy of Purpose.* 3rd ed. Berkeley: U of California P, 1984. Print.

Cvetkovich, Ann. *An Archive of Feelings: Trauma, Sexuality, and Lesbian Public Cultures.* Durham, NC: Duke UP, 2003. Print.

Davy, Kate. "Cultural Memory and the Lesbian Archive." *Beyond the Archives: Research as a Lived Process.* Ed. Gesa E. Kirsch and Liz Rohan. Carbondale: Southern Illinois UP, 2008. 128–35. Print.

Deleuze, Gilles. "Letter to a Harsh [Severe] Critic." *Negotiations: 1972–1990.* Trans. Martin Joughin. New York: Columbia UP, 1997. 3–12. Print.

Derrida, Jacques. "Archive Fever: A Freudian Impression." *Diacritics* 25.2 (Summer 1995): 9–63.

Enoch, Jessica, and Jordynn Jack. "Remembering Sappho: New Perspectives on Teaching (and Writing) Women's Rhetorical History." *College English* 73.5 (2011): 518–37. Print.

Faris, Michael J., and ML Sugie. "Fucking with Fucking Online: Advocating for Indiscriminate Promiscuity." *Why Are Faggots So Afraid of Faggots?* Ed. Mattilda Bernstein Sycamore. Oakland: AK, 2012. 45–52. Print.

Flaxman, Gregory. *Gilles Deleuze and the Fabulation of Philosophy.* Powers of the False, Volume 1. Minneapolis: U of Minnesota P, 2011. Print.

Gaonkar, Dilip Parameshwar. "The Idea of Rhetoric in the Rhetoric of Science." *Rhetorical Hermeneutics: Invention and Interpretation in the Age of Science.* Ed. Alan G. Gross and William M. Keith. State U of New York P, 1997. 25–85. Print.

Glenn, Cheryl, and Jessica Enoch. "Invigorating Historiographic Practices." Ramsey et al. 11–27.

Grosz, Elizabeth. *Volatile Bodies: Toward a Corporeal Feminism.* Bloomington: Indiana UP, 1994. Print.

Halberstam, Judith. *In a Queer Time and Place: Transgender Bodies, Subcultural Lives.* New York: New York UP, 2005. Print.

Haskins, Ekaterina. "Between Archive and Participation: Public Memory in a Digital Age." *Rhetoric Society Quarterly* 37.4 (2007): 401–22. *CrossRef.* Web. 13 Dec. 2014.

Hogg, Charlotte. *From the Garden Club: Rural Women Writing Community*. Lincoln: U of Nebraska P, 2006. Print.

Howard, John. *Men Like That: A Southern Queer History*. Chicago: U of Chicago P, 1999. Print.

"Intermezzo Announcement." *Enculturation: A Journal of Rhetoric, Writing, and Culture*. Intermezzo Series ed. Jeff Rice. Web. 26 Apr. 2015.

Johnson, Nan. "Autobiography of an Archivist." Ramsey et al. 290–300.

Love, Heather. *Feeling Backward: Loss and the Politics of Queer History*. Cambridge, MA: Harvard UP, 2007. Print.

Martin, George R.R. *A Game of Thrones*. New York: Bantam, 1996. Print.

Mastrangelo, Lisa, and Barbara L'Eplattenier. "Stumbling in the Archives: A Tale of Two Novices." *Beyond the Archives: Research as a Lived Process*. Ed. Gesa E. Kirsch and Liz Rohan. Carbondale: Southern Illinois UP, 2008. 161–69. Print.

Morris, Charles E., III. "Introduction: The Archival Turn in Rhetorical Studies, Or, The Archive's Rhetorical (Re)Turn." *Rhetoric and Public Affairs* (Spring 2006): 113–15. Print.

Morris, Charles E., III, and K. J. Rawson. "Queer Archives and Archival Queers." *Theorizing Histories of Rhetoric*. Ed. Michelle Ballif. Carbondale: Southern Illinois UP, 2013. 74–89. Print.

Morris, Sammie L., and Shirley K. Rose. "Invisible Hands: Recognizing Archivists' Work to Make Records Accessible." Ramsey et al. 51–78. Print.

Muñoz, José Esteban. *Cruising Utopia: The Then and There of Queer Futurity*. New York: New York UP, 2009. Print.

———. *Disidentifications: Queers of Color and the Performance of Politics*. Minneapolis: U of Minnesota P, 1999. Print.

Ramsey, Alexis E., Wendy B. Sharer, Barbara L'Eplattenier, and Lisa S. Mastrangelo, eds. *Working in the Archives: Practical Research Methods for Rhetoric and Composition*. Carbondale: Southern Illinois UP, 2010. Print.

Rawson, K. J. *Archiving Transgender: Affects, Logic, and the Power of Queer History*. Syracuse University, 2010. Ann Arbor: *ProQuest*. Web. 13 Dec. 2014.

———. "Queering Feminist Rhetorical Canonization." *Rhetorica in Motion: Feminist Rhetorical Methods and Methodologies*. Ed. Eileen E Schell and K. J. Rawson. Pittsburgh: U of Pittsburgh P, 2010. 39–52. Print.

"Rhizomes Manifesto." *Rhizomes: Cultural Studies in Emerging Knowledge*. Ed. Ellen Berry and Carol Siegel. Web. 13 Dec. 2014.

Royster, Jacqueline Jones, and Gesa E. Kirsch. *Feminist Rhetorical Practices: New Horizons for Rhetoric, Composition, and Literacy Studies*. Carbondale: Southern Illinois UP, 2012. Print.

Sedgwick, Eve Kosofsky. *Touching Feeling: Affect, Pedagogy, Performativity*. Durham, NC: Duke UP, 2003. Print.

Sharer, Wendy. "Traces of the Familiar: Family Archives as Primary Sources Material." *Beyond the Archives: Research as a Lived Process*. Ed. Gesa E. Kirsch and Liz Rohan. Carbondale: Southern Illinois UP, 2008. 47–55. Print.

Stockton, Will. "Reading Like a Sodomite: Deleuze, Donne, Eliot, Presentism, and the Modern Renaissance." *Rhizomes: Cultural Studies in Emerging Knowledge* 17 (Winter 2008). Web. 13 Dec. 2014.

"Students' Right to Their Own Language." *College Composition and Communication* 25.3 (1974): 1–18. Print.

Wallace, David L. "Out in the Academy: Heterosexism, Invisibility, and Double Consciousness." *College English* 65.1 (2002): 53–66. Print.

2 "Intersecting Realities"
Queer Assemblage as Rhetorical Methodology

Jason Palmeri and Jonathan Rylander

Within rhetorical studies, scholarship on sexuality has evolved from an initial focus on the inclusion of seemingly stable gay and lesbian identities in pedagogy to a broader "queer turn" (Alexander and Wallace) that calls us to resist binary models of sexuality and to recognize how sexuality is interrelated with other axes of embodied difference (Alexander and Rhodes; Fox; Gibson, Marinara, and Meem; McRuer; Pritchard). Similarly resisting stable or simplistic notions of identity, proponents of ecological and networked approaches to rhetoric have been rearticulating rhetorical subjectivities as complex, shifting assemblages of bodies, technologies, material spaces, and discourses that emerge and transform over time (Dingo; Hawk; Reid; Rice; Rivers and Weber; Sheridan, Ridolfo, and Michel). Although this turn to viewing rhetorical subjectivity in terms of networks has been productive, feminist rhetorical scholars have critiqued, importantly, how many of these emerging theories of rhetorical assemblage have too often elided material power dynamics of gender, race, sexuality, and nation (Dingo; Jung; Micciche).

Seeking to outline a networked sexual rhetoric approach attuned to complex power relations, this chapter draws on Jasbir Puar's articulation of queer assemblage to develop a rhetorical methodology for understanding "sexuality not as identity, but as assemblages of sensations, affects, and forces" (Puar, "Homonationalism" 24). Employing Puar's work to engage the sexualized rhetorics of US immigration discourses, we demonstrate how a queer assemblages approach can help us critique and ultimately develop tactics of resistance to the complex networks of "homonationalism" (Puar) that have worked to ally LGBTQ rights rhetorics with imperialist and nationalist agendas. To demonstrate how queer assemblages can work as a methodology for analyzing queer activist rhetorics, we perform a close rhetorical analysis of the "UndocuQueer" activist movement—focusing especially on the collaborative political work of visual artist, Julio Salgado.

Sexuality as Process: Moving Toward A Queer Assemblages Methodology

Resisting both the definition of "queer" as a stable identity category and the uncritical celebration of queerness as inherently transgressive, we turn to Puar's formulation of *queerness as an assemblage* uncontained within a single body as well as one that can be coopted by state and otherwise oppressive regimes. Placing Deleuze and Guattari's theory of *agencement* in dialogue with queer of color critique, Puar reconceptualizes sexuality as assemblage of complex "affective processes, ones that foreground normativizing and resistant bodily practices beyond sex, gender, and sexual object choice" (Puar, *Terrorist Assemblages* 221). Pushing beyond a singular focus on sexual identities and desires, a queer assemblages methodology seeks to elucidate unfolding networks or fields of "psychic and material identification" with forces that one may not immediately associate with sex, sexuality or queerness—forces such as patriotism and American imperialism (221). As a form of sexual rhetoric operating through seemingly disconnected forces, queer assemblages constantly unfold and expand, resisting epistemological closure. Their full dynamics cannot be known in advance because they are made up of a complex, ever-shifting array of forces that escape the control of any single individual. Following this understanding of queer assemblage, we are concerned with ways in which queer politics, even seemingly radical queer interventions and queer theorizing, can be coopted through neoliberal and otherwise normative discourses, especially those discourses that mark and exclude racialized others.

In highlighting this methodological approach, we are building upon and extending (not seeking to replace) intersectionality as a viable theoretical framework for complicating rhetorics of identity and identity politics (Anzaldúa; Crenshaw; Lorde; Pough; Royster; Wallace). Resisting the common theoretical move of replacing one theory for another, we follow Puar's more recent articulation of intersectionality and queer assemblage as related analytical frameworks that might work together in "frictional ways" to better understand relations of power (Puar, "I Would Rather Be a Cyborg"). Within a queer assemblages framework, identities (even intersectional ones) are not stable and are not analogous, especially when axes of embodied difference—race, class, gender, sexuality, nation, disability, age, religion—are conceived not as "separable analytics" but as "interwoven forces that dissipate time, space, and body against linearity, coherency, and permanency" (Puar, *Terrorist Assemblages* 212). Further, categories such as race, gender, and sexuality operate "not as simple entities and attributes of subjects" but as events transformed through the interplay of human and non-human actors influencing subjects and systems of oppression at varying levels of scale and power (Puar, "I Would Rather Be a Cyborg"). For Puar and for us, then, the recognition of nonhuman agency is not a disavowal of feminist, queer of color critique, but rather a way to better understand the wide array of forces (including the nonhuman) that influence shifting constructions of race, gender, and sexuality.

In seeking to understand queerness as a messy assemblage of both dominant and transgressive forces, we have been influenced in particular by Puar's articulation of "homonationalism" as an assemblage that reveals how the claiming of "queerness" can be coopted to support or elide neoliberal and imperialist regimes. Building on Lisa Duggan's understanding of homonormativity as a privatized and "depoliticized gay culture anchored in domesticity and consumption" (50), Puar defines *homonationalist assemblage* as follows:

> the concomitant rise in the legal, consumer and representative recognition of LGBTQ subjects and the curtailing of welfare provisions, immigrant rights and the expansion of state power to engage in surveillance, detention, and deportation.
> (Puar, "Homonationalism as Assemblage," 25)

In articulating the concept of homonationalism, Puar powerfully calls scholars and activists to pay more attention to unfolding relations among what may initially appear as disparate and disconnected forces.

In the context of our work analyzing the UndocuQueer art, we employ Puar's theory of homonationalist assemblage as a methodology for analyzing the complex intersections among mainstream LBGTQ rights activism and repressive immigration regimes in the contemporary United States (Chavez; Nair). Specifically, Puar's theory of homonationalism can help explicate the contradictions of our current moment when many mainstream LGBTQ groups are celebrating Obama's support for gay marriage and gays in the military while remaining largely silent about how the Obama administration has been deporting more people annually than previous administrations (Lopez and Gonzalez Barrera). Although homonationalist LGBTQ activists often ignore questions of migrant justice, a queer assemblages methodology encourages us to remember that oppressive discourses of sexuality and migration have long been intertwined in the United States: indeed, gays and lesbians were explicitly banned from immigrating to the United States until 1990, and still today immigration law privileges heteronormative conceptions of family in reviewing applications for citizenship (Cantú; Reddy).

As we seek to untangle the complex array of forces that shape and contain dominant conversations about LGBTQ and migrant "rights," we also turn to Jennifer Wingard's understanding of "branding" as a neoliberal assemblage through which normative bodies are included and granted protection through national citizenship and family values appeals, while minoritized bodies are marked as threats to be contained or eliminated. In particular, Wingard details how affective neoliberal rhetorics "have made immigrant and GLBT citizen bodies into 'brands' that serve as cautionary tales of what to avoid, whom to fear, and who is outside norms of citizenship" (2). When migrant and queer bodies both function as brands against which normative American family values are defined, not just identities but histories of racism, colonialism, misogyny, homophobia, and sexism are "flattened" in order to "forward a 'simpler' vision of the American family" that elides "the deep material differences between those who are seen as part of this family and those who are not" (Wingard 29).

As a result of the dominance of the family brand in our neoliberal political times, it is not surprising that some of the most visible advocacy on behalf of LGBTQ migrants has centered on the plight of binational LGBTQ couples who could benefit from the ability to apply for citizenship on the basis of same-sex marriage (Chávez; Nair). Although this kind of advocacy has important material consequences for some undocumented migrants, it also problematically enables LGBTQ groups to keep the focus on marriage rather than on more capacious activism against the diverse forms of structural violence that queer migrants face (Chávez; Nair). By more thoroughly tracking the assemblages that render the complex experiences of queer migrants as illegible within neoliberal LBGT rights discourses, we can begin to elucidate tactics of rhetorical resistance to dominant branding regimes that flatten queer migration experiences.

Tactical Queer Assemblage: Tracing Bodies, Discourses, and Technologies in the "I Am UndocuQueer" Art Project

In addition to viewing queer assemblage as a powerful way to map affective, material networks of normativity, we also articulate queer assemblage as an activist methodology not only for reading but also for contesting dominant brand representations. To this end, we analyze Julio Salgado's collaborative "I am UndocuQueer" art project as a potentially subversive queer assemblage. In particular, we map the potentially resistant ways the project works (1) to reconceive identity formation as a collaborative and tactical assemblage of bodies; (2) to reassemble and complicate queer activist discourses; and (3) to reimagine rhetorical action as a shifting assemblage of bodies, discourses, and material technologies that evolves over time.

Working in conjunction with the Queer Undocumented Immigrant Project and the Queer Undocumented Youth Collective, Julio Salgado organized the collaborative "I am UndocuQueer" art project in January 2012 in an attempt to "give us undocumented queers more of a presence in the discussion of migrant rights" (Salgado, "I am UndocuQueer"). Offering a platform for undocumented queers to take control of their own representations, Salgado put out a call on Tumblr and other social media to invite participants to join the project by emailing him "a photograph of yourself from the waist up and a quote telling us what does it mean to be UndocuQueer for you" (Salgado, "UndocuQueer" Archive). Salgado then turned these photographs and quotes into digital images circulated both online and as printed posters. Each image in Salgado's collection includes the words "I am UndocuQueer" in the top right corner as well as a drawing of an individual person next to a quote in which they describe what being UndocuQueer means to them. In a stylized form reminiscent of both comics and advertising images, the drawings of the participants are placed on a solid color background. By developing a visually striking and easily recognizable design template for the "I am UndocuQueer" images, Salgado reveals a savvy understanding of and subversion of the visual technology of branding—creating an iconic image campaign that is highly memorable, extensible, and circulatable.

In mapping Salgado's "I am UndocuQueer" project as a queer assemblage, we have been influenced by Karma Chávez's and Hinda Seif's astute rhetorical readings of UndocuQueer rhetorics. In particular, Chávez offers an important reading of how the "I am UndocuQueer" project enacts a transformational "queer coalitional ethic" while also at times problematically reifying an individualist model of social change (101). Further deepening our understanding of the rhetorical and material implications of the project, Hinda Seif's person-based research with queer migrant activists (including Salgado) usefully elucidates the conscious rhetorical choices Salgado and other participants have made in crafting the project—focusing especially on theorizing the complex, material implications of employing "coming out" as a political strategy for migrant justice. In this chapter, we seek to extend Seif and Chávez's analytic work by demonstrating how the "I am UndocuQueer" project enacts queer assemblage as a methodology of rhetorical action.

Reassembling Bodies: Identity as Collaborative and Tactical Assemblage

One of the key tactics of Salgado's project is the collective claiming and repetition of the term *undocuqueer* itself–often but not always hyphenated. By claiming a single word *undocuqueer* to describe the experience of being both queer and undocumented, Salgado's work powerfully insists that sexuality and citizenship status must be considered together. As one participant puts it, "I am Undocu-Queer ... because I can't be one without the other" (Claudia), or as another asserts "UndocuQueer: Taking Control of my own identity. I exist" (Seleny). By claiming *undocuqueer* as a singular term, participants in Salgado's project strategically ensure that queerness and undocumentedness cannot be divided into separate words that can then be elided. In this way, usage of the term *undocuqueer* can be seen as a kind of *ontological* activism making visible material experiences that are often erased. Further demonstrating the ontological implications of the UndocuQueer project, another participant, Tony, powerfully describes the term *undocuqueer* as marking "intersecting identities *and realities*" (italics ours). In other words, undocuqueer is not a simple, easily reducible identity brand; rather, it is a process of mapping the intersecting realities that work to both constrain and enable particular kinds of action for bodies marked as queer and undocumented.

In addition to highlighting the complex experiences of queer and undocumented people, the term *UndocuQueer* also implicitly highlights other positionalities in relation to immigration status and sexuality— the "undocu-straight" and the "docu-queer"—that call viewers to more critically interrogate intersecting privileges and oppressions. For example, for us as two white male "docu-queers" with US passports, the very word *undocu*-queer demands that we account not just for the ways in which our queerness denies us particular kinds of recognition by the state but also to recognize the many material privileges we claim as documented US citizens whose racial identification causes our citizenship not to be questioned by authorities.

Although the consistent and repeated use of the term *undocuqueer* in the project makes visible the experiences of people who identify as both queer and undocumented, it, like all brand representations, risks flattening the complex embodiments of those it seeks to represent. Yet, when we look closely at the diverse quotes that accompany the "I am UndocuQueer" images, we can see that many participants explicitly position "undocu-queer" as but one of many identity markers that they might use to describe themselves. For example, numerous participants choose to compose quotes that blend English and Spanish while also claiming additional identifications such as "Latina," "Jota," or "Mujer"—framing their images in ways that "insist on the interlocking identities that constitute UndocuQueer" (Chávez 102). Indeed, some participants explicitly call out the limitations of the "UndocuQueer" brand in the quotes accompanying their images. For example, Yahaira argues that "We grow into our multi-faceted selves each and every time we embrace who we are. ... Undocumented? Yes. Queer? Yes. All of me? No." In this way, Yahaira deliberately refuses claiming UndocuQueer as a totalizing brand—positioning it instead as a provisional marker that ontologically describes just a part of her existence.

In addition to pointing to the limits of UndocuQueer or any branded identity to describe the complexity of their "intersecting realities," participants in the project also resist the tendency to position branded identities (including "UndocuQueer") as "new" and ahistorical. For example, one participant, Prerna, credits the foundational influence of Audre Lorde in her own conception of UndocuQueer identity: "To borrow shamelessly from Audre Lorde, as a queer, undocumented person I know that their [*sic*] is no such thing as single issue struggles because we don't lead single issue lives" (Prerna). Further, Salgado himself has noted how the traditions of women of color feminism have influenced his conception of the project:

> [I]n the feminist movement you had [...] white women leading movements. And you had women of color trying to say your experience is different from my experience. Knowing that history, I knew that my experience as an undocumented man in California was different than Yesenia [a member of the UndocuQueer activist movement] who grew up in St. Louis. I wanted to hear from them, what that experience was like.
>
> (Salgado, quoted in Seif 112–13)

In this way, Salgado reveals his own conscious desire to resist the sedimentation of "UndocuQueer" as a one-dimensional brand and to instead reconceive the project of identity representation as necessitating a collaborative assemblage of voices that reveals the complex differences of positionality among those who identity as UndocuQueer.

Reassembling Discourses: Normativity as "Common Enemy"

Resisting a "single-issue" model of social change, the UndocuQueer project powerfully draws connections between the affective rhetorics of queer and migrant activist struggles. In their statements accompanying their images, participants often draw on LGBTQ rhetorics of "resisting normativity" to explain their experiences as both queer and undocumented. Although some of the individual images could be read as arguing for a simple equivalence of LGBTQ and undocumented struggles, the broader assemblage of the project reveals a much more nuanced approach to highlighting the affinities and differences in the discourses of LGBTQ and migrant activism. In a savvy move, Vincent's image articulates the UndocuQueer movement as "about crossing borders of normativity which allows us to celebrate all our identities and live in a space of liberation." Instead of arguing for inclusion within current regimes of border regulation or state-sanctioned marriages, Vincent calls undocumented and queer activists to "cross borders of normativity." By connecting the refusal of border control regimes with queer activist traditions of resisting heteronormativity, Vincent suggests that queer liberation must necessarily include resistance to all normative borders—both *national and sexual.*

Further emphasizing how queer refusal of normativity must encompass a resistance to normative immigration regimes, another participant, Jonathan, is pictured holding a microphone and leading the chant: "We're here, we're queer, we're undocumented. Get used to it!" Although mainstream LGBTQ and immigration reform groups often argue for inclusion by telling stories of "model" families who adhere to normative values, Jonathan remixes a classic queer liberation chant that demands justice and recognition for queers (and, in his version, undocumented people) on their own terms. In this way, Jonathan's protest chant powerfully enacts Salgado's professed activist goal of "finding a common ground and becoming a huge fist to punch the one bully we have in common" (Salgado *Tumblr*, "Being").

While "resisting normativity" can be a useful frame for connecting queer and migrant struggles, invoking "normativity" as a common "enemy" can also risk effacing differences in the experiences of "undocumentedness" and "queerness." Although there are affinities between resisting heteronormativity and refusing border regimes, the material consequences of that resistance differ greatly depending on positionality and context. Emphasizing this point, one participant writes, "just like being queer has allowed me to say forget the norms, I want to be able to say forget the laws (immigration laws specifically) and start living" (Ireri). For Ireri, both queer and undocumented activism involve resisting normativity, but she finds it easier to "forget" heteronormativity than to "forget" normative immigration regimes when the very act of claiming undocumentedness could result in her deportation. Although US citizen queers face substantial violence and discrimination, they cannot legally be removed from the nation for refusing to fit into heteronormative structures (and white queers are unlikely to ever have their citizenship questioned). In this way, Ireri's poster powerfully highlights the important material differences in the experiences of queerness and undocumentedness—refusing to let "resisting normativity" function as a flattening brand slogan. Rather than challenging normativity through a unitary model of oppression, Ireri and other participants in the project cleverly rearticulate normativity as a complex array of shifting forces that can be strategically hacked by flexible coalitional networks of differentially positioned activists.

Reassembling Technologies: Materiality, Circulation, and the Politics of Access

Although our analysis thus far has focused on reading the project as a collaborative and tactical assemblage of discourses and bodies, we turn now to considering how material technologies and spaces have influenced the composition and circulation of the project. Notably, Salgado was first introduced to the term *UndocuQueer* via his use of Facebook (Seif 111), and he first popularized the term through composing and distributing images across diverse digital media, including the blogging platform Tumblr. Although Tumblr does allow for longer alphabetic text-based posts, its interface strongly encourages the sharing and *recirculation* of visual images by prominently positioning the uploading of photos as a distinct kind of posting (with captions denoted as optional). Thus, it's not surprising that Salgado's Tumblr project emphasized composing and circulating single images that feature only brief text—a constraint that may have limited participants' ability to tease out the nuances of their positionings in relation to "UndocuQueer" identities and politics.

Tumblr is an excellent tool for enhancing digital circulation, but we must remember that the Tumblr network (like all digital networks) is limited in its reach because of persistent inequalities of Internet access (Banks; Yergeau et al). Reflecting in part his own experience as a person who has struggled at times to compose digital art without Internet access at home (Lopez), Salgado importantly conceived the "UndocuQueer" project as flexibly circulating through multiple digital and analog technologies, including print posters to be used by activist groups. In an interview with Rogelio Alejandro Lopez, Salgado explained the importance of print circulation to his artivism:

> People like to have something to hold on to ... much like the newspaper ... I think holding a piece of artwork created by one of their

peers who is also undocumented ... empowers them in a sense. They're like, "damn, one of us did this." It's not somebody else who doesn't really understand what we're going through, but it's like somebody who is actually also undocumented. This art [is] for them, and for us too.

By highlighting the importance of distributing tactile posters for use by undocumented activists at on-the-ground protests, Salgado points to a model of queer technological activism that recognizes the necessity of constructing activist texts that can be developed and circulated through a range of digital and analog technologies—refusing a colonialist technological progress narrative (Baca; Haas) that might privilege the circulatory power of digital technologies over printed and hand-drawn media that may be more accessible to communities with limited access to online spaces.

In addition to looking at how the project was initially distributed across digital and print media, a queer assemblages approach also encourages us to look at tactical ways that the "I am UndocuQueer" project has continued to evolve and shift over time in response to particular kairotic moments, media, and material spaces. For example, in June 2013 (more than a year after most of the images were originally created), Salgado composed a billboard of five of the UndocuQueer images that was installed in the Mission neighborhood of San Francisco in collaboration with Galleria de La Raza—an art space committed to showcasing the work of Latin(a) artists who have long resided in the Mission. In a YouTube video documenting the unveiling of the billboard, Salgado explicitly positions his public artwork as a critical response to homonormative politics that focus attention on marriage and joining the military while eliding the broader struggles of queers of color in the city. Salgado argues that his billboard seeks to reveal that "it's not all about marriage and the army. Queers are more than that. You know, it's just an FYI for Gay Inc" ("Julio's First"). Couched within a comedic and playful tone in this video overall, this line in particular rhetorically articulates a direct message of activism and coalition building. Highlighting the ways in which politicians in San Francisco claim to support LGBTQ rights while also enacting gentrifying "development" policies that have been displacing many queer people of color from longstanding latino/a neighborhoods such as the mission, Salgado explicitly positions his billboard as part of a movement to "gentefy" the mission—to recenter dominant discourses about housing in the city on the needs of the people (or *gente*) who have long resided and made art in the district.

Although the project's initial manifestation on Tumblr might be read as lacking a deeper structural analysis of interlocking racialized power structures (Chávez), the assemblage of the billboard and associated online coverage of it works to draw connections between the state violence of repressive immigration regimes and the state-sanctioned violence of so-called development plans that marginalize and displace queer people of color. Although the initial deployment of the project did not explicitly focus on critiquing how homonormative

LGBTQ groups are complicit in supporting racist gentrification policies, the images take on different meanings when transformed into a billboard in the Mission in San Francisco during LGBTQ pride month and framed as an act of "*gente*-fication." If we had just read a single image of the project at a single moment in time, we would miss the complexly evolving ways in which the images take on new meanings and call forth new coalitional possibilities as they circulate through diverse media, geographic locations, artivist networks, and kairotic moments. We have only begun to trace the many ways the images were recirculated and reframed over time; to gain a clearer picture, we would need to combine queer assemblage theories with emerging rhetorical methodologies such as "iconographic tracking" (Gries) to more systematically document the ever shifting meanings of the images in different contexts—a project that is unfortunately beyond the scope of this chapter.

Conclusion: Reassembling Queer Rhetoric

In outlining queer assemblages as a rhetorical methodology, we call on sexual rhetoric scholars to move beyond situating our research in relation to stable identity categories and instead work toward analyzing and enacting resistant queer assemblages that strategically build connections among seemingly disparate (and perhaps unthinkable) social movements, discourses, spaces, technologies, and erotic intimacies. Drawing on Salgado's work which resists positioning "UndocuQueer" as a stable identity by instead offering a shifting, collaborative assemblage of embodied voices, we call for scholars of queer rhetoric to both analyze and practice collaborative forms of composing that highlight and tactically reassemble the complex, shifting, affective forces—both dominant and transgressive—through which the very idea of "queer rhetoric" is constructed and deployed.

As a model of what collaborative and tactical assemblage work might look like in the field of rhetorical scholarship, we could look to the collaborative work of Michele Gibson, Martha Marinara, and Deborah Meem's "Bi, Butch, and Bar Dyke: Pedagogical Performances of Class, Gender, and Sexuality." For these scholars, the complex and shifting dynamics of identity make it difficult to meaningfully discuss through essentializing narratives composed by solo authors. By interweaving layered narratives of the always shifting interplay of various spaces and actors—*academic and nonacademic*—in the lives of queer teachers, Gibson, Marinara, and Meem offer an inspirational vision of a queer assemblage that resists epistemological closure in favor of engaging the messy connections among bodies and materialities across seemingly disparate locations. Similarly, in "Queer: An Impossible Subject for Composition," Jonathan Alexander and Jacqueline Rhodes resist epistemological closure by composing a collaborative assemblage of collaged images, fractured narratives, and radical queer artistic texts that ultimately revels in the "impossibility" of fitting queer experiences into conventional professional structures of pedagogy or research.

Although we are profoundly inspired by Alexander and Rhodes's resistant assemblage of queer impossibility, we also recognize that it in fact is all too possible for evocations of transgressive queerness to unwittingly serve dominant ends within the academy. Our work in this chapter, then, calls attention to the ways in which queer activism and rhetorical scholarship shapes—and is shaped by—a complex assemblage of both dominant and resistant forces. The term *queer* for us does not immediately signify radical or transgressive bodies and actions; queer relations are often facilitated through—and normativized—by our associations with forces that engender homonormative and homonationalist ideals, whether we are aware of them or not. If queer rhetoric is to truly be a resistant force in the academy, we must commit to not only highlighting the importance of sexuality to rhetorical study but also to emphasizing the ways in which sexuality is always already enmeshed in broader material networks of race, gender, class, disability, nation, and neoliberal economics (Alexander and Rhodes; Fox; McRuer; Pritchard).

As we move toward a more capacious understanding of queer rhetoric as an assemblage, we also can work to challenge static, human-centered models of rhetorical situation that can limit our ability to understand both the dominant and resistant possibilities of particular queer rhetorical practices. As Rebecca Dingo has argued in her articulation of transnational feminist rhetorical methodology, a networked approach to rhetoric must necessarily "look not just at static rhetorical occasions but how rhetorics move across occasion, time, space, and geopolitical location" (146). As we work to trace how rhetorics travel and shift across time and space, we can also attend more carefully to how rhetorics are shaped by a diverse array of human and nonhuman actors (e.g., social media tools, architectural structures, military technologies).

In addition to recognizing how technologies can function as repressive tools that enable the "branding of bodies" in flattening and exclusionary ways (Wingard), we also suggest that queer rhetoricians explore how branding technologies might be subverted to generate and circulate resistant sexual rhetorics such as the "I am UndocuQueer" project. In particular, Salgado's work calls us to ask: What might queer rhetorical scholarship look like if it didn't take the form of a print manuscript or static online publication but rather emerged as a collaborative and tactical assemblage unfolding across diverse media over time? What kind of academy would we have to build for such an assemblage to be recognized, valued, and supported? What kinds of alliances can queer rhetoricians make with critical scholars in allied disciplines to challenge the neoliberal academic regimes that constrain our work and flatten our experiences?

We may not be able to ever fully step out of the neoliberal academic structures in which we are embedded, but we can fuck with them by engaging critically with queer rhetorical assemblages (such as Salgado's project) that resist homonormative and homonationalist agendas. We can fuck with them by insisting on composing our work across multiple forms of media—resisting both the digital progress narratives and traditional print conventions that limit the accessibility of our arguments. We can also fuck with the neoliberal academy by reveling in a state of ontological unknowing—by acknowledging up front that our own attempts to map and resist dominant formations are always partial, incomplete, unfolding, cut off *in media res*. In sum, a queer assemblages methodology invites us to be *audacious* in reconceiving sexual rhetoric as a shifting assemblage of bodies, discourses, and technologies, but also to be *humble* in recognizing how any assertion of a queer rhetorical methodology (including our own) may be subtly shaped by dominant forces in ways we cannot yet envision or trace.

Works Cited

Alexander, Jonathan, and Jacqueline Rhodes. "Flattening Effects: Composition's Multicultural Imperative and the Problem of Narrative Coherence." *College Composition and Communication* 65.3 (2013). 430–54. Print.

———. "Queer: An Impossible Subject for Composition." *JAC* 31.1–2 (2011): 177–206. Print.

Alexander, Jonathan, and David Wallace. "The Queer Turn in Composition Studies: Reviewing and Assessing an Emerging Scholarship." *College Composition and Communication* 61.1 (2009). Web. 26 Apr. 2015.

Anzaldúa, Gloria. *Borderlands/La Frontera*. San Francisco: Aunt Lute, 1987. Print.

Baca, Damian. *Mestiz@ Scripts, Digital Migrations and the Territories of Writing*. New York: Palgrave Macmillan, 2008. Print.

Banks, Adam. *Race, Rhetoric, and Technology: Searching for Higher Ground*. New York: Routledge, 2005. Print.

Cantú, Lionel. *The Sexuality of Migration: Border Crossing and Mexican Immigrant Men*. New York: New York UP, 2009. Print.

Chávez, Karma R. *Queer Migration Politics: Activist Rhetoric and Coalitional Possibilities*. Champaign-Urbana: U of Illinois P, 2013. Print.

Claudia. "I Am UndocuQueer" *Julio Salgado: Activist, Lecturer, Queer*. Julio Salgado. Tumblr, 13 Jan. 2012. Web. 29 Sept. 2014.

Crenshaw, K. W. "Mapping the Margins: Intersectionality, Identity Politics, and Violence against Women of Color." *Stanford Law Review* 43 (1991): 1241–299. Print.

Dingo, Rebecca. *Networking Arguments: Rhetoric, Transnational Feminism, and Public Policy Writing*. Pittsburgh: U of Pittsburgh P, 2012. Print.

Duggan, Lisa. *The Twilight of Equality?: Neoliberalism, Cultural Politics, and the Attack on Democracy*. Boston: Beacon, 2004. Print.

Fox, Catherine. "From Transaction to Transformation: (En)Countering White Heteronormativity in 'Safe Spaces.'" *College English* 69.5 (2007): 496–511.

Gibson, Michelle, Martha Marinara, and Deborah Meem. "Bi, Butch, and Bar Dyke: Pedagogical Performances of Class, Gender, and Sexuality." *College Composition and Communication* 52 (2000): 69–95. Print.

Gries, Laurie. "Iconographic Tracking: A Digital Research Method for Visual Rhetoric and Circulation Studies." *Computers and Composition* 30 (2013): 332–358. Print.

Haas, Angela. "Wampum as Hypertext: An American Indian Tradition of Multimedia Theory and Practice." *Studies in American Indian Literatures.* 19.4 (2007): 77–100. Print.

Hawk, Byron. "Reassembling Postprocess: Toward a Posthuman Study of Public Rhetoric." *Beyond Postprocess.* Ed. Sidney Dobrin. Logan: Utah State UP, 2011. 75–93. Print.

Ireri. "I am UndocuQueer." *Julio Salgado: Activist, Lecturer, Queer.* Julio Salgado. Tumblr, 18 Jan. 2012. Web. 29 Sept. 2014.

Jonathan. "I am UndocuQueer." *Julio Salgado: Activist, Lecturer, Queer.* Julio Salgado. Tumblr, 13 Jan. 2012. Web. 29 Sept. 2014.

Jung, Julie. "Systems Rhetoric: A Dynamic Coupling if Explanation and Description." *Enculturation* (2014). Web. 26 Apr. 2015.

Lopez, Mark Hugo, and Ana Gonzalez Barrera. "High Rate of Deportations Continue Under Obama Despite Latino Disapproval" *Pew Research Center.* 19 Sept. 2013. Web. 15 Sept. 2014.

Lopez, Rogelio Alejandro. "Interview Highlights: Contextualizing Media Practice with Julio Salgado." *MIT Center for Civic Media.* MIT, 2010. Web. 29 Sept. 2014.

Lorde, Audre. *Sister Outsider: Essays and Speeches.* The Crossing Press feminist series. Trumansburg, NY: Crossing, 1984. Print.

McRuer, Robert. "Composing Bodies; or, De-Composition: Queer Theory, Disability Studies, and Alternative Corporealities."*JAC* 24.1 (2004): 47–78. Print.

Micciche, Laura. "Writing Material." *College English* 76.6 (2014): 488–505. Print.

Nair, Yasmin. "How to Make Prisons Disappear: Queer Immigrants, the Shackles of Love, and Invisibility of the Prison Industrial Complex." *Captive Genders: Embodiment and the Prison Industrial Complex.* Ed. Eric A. Stanley and Nat Smith. Oakland, CA: AK, 2011. Print.

Pough, Gwendolyn D. "'Each One, Pull One': Womanist Rhetoric and Black Feminist Pedagogy in the Writing Classroom." *Teaching Rhetorica: Theory, Pedagogy, Practice.* Ed. Kate Ronald and Joy Ritchie. Portsmouth, NJ: Boynton/Cook, 2006. Print.

Prerna. "I am UndocuQueer." *Julio Salgado: Activist, Lecturer, Queer.* Julio Salgado. Tumblr, 11 Jan. 2012. Web. 29 Sept. 2014.

Pritchard, Eric Darnell. "For Colored Kids Who Committed Suicide, Our Outrage Isn't Enough: Queer Youth of Color, Bullying, and the Discursive Limits of Identity and Safety" *Harvard Educational Review* 83.2 (2013): 320–345. Print.

Puar, Jasbir K. "Homonationalism as Assemblage: Viral Travels, Affective Sexualities." *Gindal Global Law Review.* 4.2 (2013): 23–43. Print.

———. "I would rather be a cyborg than a goddess:" Intersectionality, Assemblage, and Affective Politics." *EIPCP: European Institute for Progressive Cultural Policies.* 2011. Web. 26 Apr. 2015.

———. *Terrorist Assemblages: Homonationalism in Queer Times.* Durham, NC: Duke UP, 2007. Print.

Reddy, Chandan. *Freedom with Violence: Race, Sexuality, and the US State.* Durham: Duke UP, 2011. Print.

Reid, Alexander. "Exposing Assemblages: Unlikely Communities of Digital Scholarship, Video, and Social Networks." *Enculturation.* 8 (2010). Web. 29 Sept. 2014.

Rice, Jeff. *Digital Detroit: Rhetoric and Space in the Age of the Network.* Carbondale: Southern Illinois UP, 2012. Internet resource. 29 Sept. 2014.

Rivers, Nathaniel A., and Ryan P. Weber. "Ecological, Pedagogical, Public Rhetoric." *College Composition and Communication* 63.2 (Dec. 2011): 187–218. Print.

Royster, Jacqueline Jones. *Traces of a Stream: Literacy and Social Change Among African American Women.* Pittsburgh: U of Pittsburgh P, 2000. Print.

Salgado, Julio. *Julio Salgado: Activist, Lecturer, Queer. tumblr.* Web. 28 Feb. 2014.

———. "Julio's First Billboard." Online video clip. *YouTube*, 13 June 2013. Web. 29 Sept. 2014.

Seif, Hinda. "'Coming Out of the Shadows' and 'UndocuQueer': Undocumented Immigrants Transforming Sexuality Discourse and Activism." *Journal of Language and Sexuality* 3 (2013). 87–120. Print.

Seleny. "I am UndocuQueer" *Julio Salgado: Activist, Lecturer, Queer.* Julio Salgado. *Tumblr*, 11 Jan. 2012. Web. 29 Sept. 2014.

Sheridan, David M, Jim Ridolfo, and Anthony J. Michel. *The Available Means of Persuasion: Mapping a Theory and Pedagogy of Multimodal Public Rhetoric.* Anderson, SC: Parlor, 2012. Print.

Tony. "I am UndocuQueer" *Julio Salgado: Activist, Lecturer, Queer.* Julio Salgado. *Tumblr*, 20 Jan. 2012. Web. 29 Sept. 2014.

Vincent. "I am UndocuQueer" *Julio Salgado: Activist, Lecturer, Queer.* Julio Salgado. *Tumblr*, 16 Jan. 2012. Web. 29 Sept. 2014.

Wallace, David L. "Alternative Rhetoric and Morality: Writing from the Margins." *College Composition and Communication* 61.2 (2009): 18–39. Print.

Wingard, Jennifer. *Branded Bodies, Rhetoric, and the Neoliberal Nation-State.* Lexington, MA: Lexington, 2012. Print.

Yahaira. "I am UndocuQueer" *Julio Salgado: Activist, Lecturer, Queer.* Julio Salgado. *Tumblr*, 20 Jan. 2012. Web. 29 Sept. 2014.

Yergeau, Melanie, Elizabeth Brewer, Stephanie Kerschbaum, Sushil K. Oswal, Margaret Price, et al. "Multimodality in Motion: Disability in Kairotic Spaces." *Kairos* 18.1 (n.d.). Web. 26 Apr. 2015.

3 Consciousness, Experience, Sexual Expression, and Judgment

Jacqueline M. Martinez

> "I can live more things than I can represent to myself, my being is not reduced to what of myself explicitly appears to me."
> —Maurice Merleau-Ponty[1]

Staying in and Coming Out

Whether we are talking about the many court battles surrounding the issue of "gay marriage," the mediacraze that emerges when a high-profile public figure "comes out" as lesbian or gay, or the hypocrisies that are revealed when our "moral leaders" such as clergy or politicians are exposed as living sexual lives in direct conflict with their stated "moral" commitments, nothing about sexuality seems simple or clear-cut. These social and political struggles related to sex and sexuality are complex because sex and sexuality are, more than any other aspect of personal life, at once both deeply private and profoundly social. Indeed, how we are perceived as a sexual and gendered person often has a significant impact on how we are confronted within the circumstances of our lives. And that, in turn, has an impact on even our most private and intimate experiences of ourselves, sexual and otherwise.

One does not have to personally know public figures who have "come out" to great media fanfare to know that, although they often "come out" at a specific moment in time, drawing lines between "staying-in" and "coming-out" has been a central aspect of their decision making as they have navigated their way through the whole of their careers and lives. For public figures such as professional athletes or corporate leaders, professional success often depends on their ability to look and behave as heterosexuals in public. This is also often the case in the everyday lives of gay, lesbian, and trans people in general. Surrounded by the presumptions of heterosexuality and the presumed determinacy of biological sex, those who recognize themselves as not heterosexual or non-gender-normative must negotiate between those presumptions and the fact of who they know themselves to be, sometimes as a relentless feature of everyday life. For many lesbian and gay couples, the recognition of relational commitments via marriage offers a visibility and legitimacy that carries a unique public weight that is otherwise unachievable regardless of how much their relationships resemble the healthiest of heterosexual marriages. This aspect of sex and sexuality, as involving something that is simultaneously deeply personal and publicly consequential, creates particular challenges in our effort to understand and assess the meaningfulness of our experience. It also complicates the judgments we come to make related to sex and sexuality—both our own and others' judgments.

Understanding meaningfulness is crucial because the range of possible meanings available to any person is provided in advance of our taking them up—we are born in a specific time and place that are themselves saturated through and through with complex and interrelating systems of meaning and structure. We are, in short, inescapably situated within discursive systems that always precede our existence, and therefore we are always bound, though never fully determined, by the shape and flow of those discursive forces. This coexistence of the givens of the discursive systems within which we live and the facticity of what becomes actualized in our immediate, embodied, and communicative experience, can be understood in the distinction drawn by Maurice Merleau-Ponty between speech speaking (*parole parlante*) and speech spoken (*parole parlée*) (*Phenomenology* 202). It is at this very juncture of a person engaged in a discursive world—the site at which meaning becomes actualized as experience—to which we must turn to adequately understand and assess the relative health or "goodness" of sexual expression, sexual relationships, and sexuality as a concept that comes to saturate the possibilities of meaning for human beings and the communities in which we live. And, as the chapter-opening epigraph suggests, simple self-consciousness is inadequate as a basis for accessing the relative health or value of what is lived and experienced in the immediacy of embodied engagement in the world.

The Phenomenology of Sexual Rhetorics and Rhetorical Ethics

My effort in the present work is to demonstrate how Merleau-Ponty's phenomenological distinction between speech speaking (*parole parlante*) and speech spoken (*parole parlée*) informs a study of sexual rhetorics that betters our capacity to understand and assess the relative health or goodness of sexual expression and experience. This inherently communicative understanding of sexual expression and experience leads directly to an argument in favor of a *rhetorical ethics* as distinguished from *ethical rhetoric* (Lanigan, *Phenomenology* 3). This distinction, signified by the switch in subject-predication, locates engagement prior to judgment. It eschews the idea that, when it comes to human expression and perception, judgments of healthy and unhealthy, good and bad, or right and wrong can be made outside of our communicative engagement within the discursive systems in which we live, the people with whom we are in communication, and the rhetorical practices we take up. Our *ideas* of healthy and unhealthy, good and bad, and right and wrong certainly do precede our communicative engagements within discursive systems, but no matter how much we may want them to be, ideas are never identical to experience. In fact, our ideas about things are often so powerful that we cannot see the obviousness of a wrong. Why else would a victim of even the most brutal stranger-rape blame herself for having been raped? A rhetorical ethic recognizes this difference between our *ideas about* and our *experience of*, and demands that our intellectual practices recognize this difference as well.

My interest in the immediacy of embodied engagement in the world derives from a phenomenological understanding of the relationship between consciousness and experience.[2] This phenomenological understanding allows me to examine not only the difference between *ideas about* and *experience of*, but also how the *distances between* them are concealed, stumbled upon, and sometimes articulable within the immediacy of our communicative engagements. It is this potential of articulation that requires an application of a *phenomenological reduction*, and that, in turn allows us to discover the rhetorical spaces and practices through which we might come, *a posteriori*, to stipulate as having been ethical, good, or healthy—a stipulation that always requires an ongoing reexamination.

Experience, Not Idea, as Intellectual Practice

Sorting through the difference between our *ideas about* and *experience of* is a difficult task for many reasons. It is difficult because *ideas about* emerge from complex discursive systems that situate and subject persons within networks of interrelations that structure the possibilities for meaning. Within these very discursive systems, language and speech are the only available means through which we can explicitly articulate what we judge as healthy or good about sexual expression or experience. This deeply set orientation toward the world is what Merleau-Ponty calls a "constituting consciousness," and when it monopolizes our investigations of the human world, it constitutes an "intellectualism" where language remains in the grasp of the idea, that must be rejected (*Phenomenology* 148). And this is no easy task, particularly when we are working in a milieu of scholarly work where articulate language in the form of fully thought ideas constitutes the collective body of our work.

Because neither language nor speech can be taken as self-evident, our efforts must have the capacity to interrogate the networks of interrelation through which both language and speech make possible the exact experience that becomes actualized in a moment that is always, at best, just past. Rejecting language and speech as self-evident means that we must identify a "rhetorical treatment of evidence" that does not depend on a "referential notion of evidence" (Scott 24). Thus, the question becomes one of "how to analyze language" (Scott 34) so as to see how it is at work in the networks of interrelations that constitutes our situatedness within discursive systems. By directing our "rhetorical treatment of evidence" toward the phenomenological, we can take language and speech not as a "reflection of the real," but as the means through which a deeper interrogation of the discursive conditions through which the particularities of experience emerge. Experience is not taken "as the discovery of truth" or a "prediscursive reality" (Scott 35) but rather as something that comes to exist only within the "constitutive constraint" of discourse, as "immanent to [the] power" of discourse in its subjectification of all who operate within its terms (Butler 15). In phenomenological terms, the capacity to interrogate these "constitutive" networks of interrelation through which language and speech make possible the exact experience that becomes actualized in a moment of communicative embodiment lies in the very fact that experience comes to be actualized as consciousness—thus making it possible for consciousness to be actualized as experience.

This *reversible* relationship between consciousness and experience is crucial. Let me make the point more concretely. There was a specific moment in my life when I "came-out" to myself, when I recognized with absolute certainty that I was a woman who had sexual desire toward another woman. In the moment of that recognition, I experienced a *consciousness of* my sexual desire. I recognized something about myself that had been silently present and inarticulable in the totality of my life preceding that moment. At that moment, my knowledge of my sexual desire became actual, concrete, and immediately available as a felt reality that I recognized as myself. From that moment forward, it became possible for me to reflect back upon many experiences in which I had also experienced sexual desire toward another woman (or girl), but had no consciousness of it. Now, after that moment of *experiencing consciousness* of my sexual desire, previous experiences that I had had throughout my life became a *consciousness of experience* wherein I recognized that I had, in fact, from my earliest memories, experienced sexual attraction toward members of my own sex.

Lived experience is never just a straightforward event. Rather, it is a pivot point through which the complexity of my situatedness in my lived world is both revealed and concealed in the stuff (*hyle*) of my life that often appears as happenstance or arbitrary but that is always bound to my concrete world as anchored through my body, speech, and language. Our imbrication within the discursive forces of our time and place, our boundedness to those forces through body, speech, and language, make this reversible relationship between consciousness and experience possible; it also provides a potential access to those very discursive forces, not as an "objectivist" project but as a means of accessing the very conditions of possibility of our human existence in its particularity. This potential access lies in an application of the phenomenological reduction,[3] which I am developing specifically through Merleau-Ponty's distinction between *speech speaking* and *speech spoken*. The phenomenological reduction can lead us directly to the radicalization of philosophy or intellectual projects by taking exact account of the murkiness of consciousness and experience through which one must travel to arrive at articulate language and thought—that is, discovering this murkiness that remains out of view when language and thought remain within the grasp of the idea. As Merleau-Ponty puts it,

> A philosophy becomes transcendental, that is, radical, not by taking up a position within absolute consciousness while failing to mention the steps that carried it there, but rather by considering itself as a problem, not by assuming the total making-explicit of knowledge, but rather by recognizing the presumption of reason as the fundamental philosophical problem.
> (*Phenomenology* 64)

A phenomenologically inflected rhetorical treatment of evidence developed from Merleau-Ponty's distinction between *speech speaking* and *speech spoken* allows for an examination of this reversible relationship between experience and consciousness through a focus on the facticity of lived experience that is robust and nuanced enough to locate judgment closer to *experiences of* rather than *ideas about*. As a result, we are less directed toward establishing a "position within absolute consciousness" that seeks an ethical rhetoric that presupposes judgment. Rather, we are more directed toward attending to the steps that have carried us both to and from the idea, and thus toward a rhetorical ethic that discovers judgment (or reason). This approach allows greater confidence in the *evidence* that we have generated in the attempt to access the specific networks of interrelations that make a particular moment of experience emerge within the immediacy of our communicative engagements.

Determining how to generate and evaluate evidence based in lived experience that adequately accounts for the difference between *speech speaking* and *speech spoken* is a major challenge because it is a difference that can only be generated after the fact of experience—as a matter of reflection capable of meeting the conditions for a phenomenological reduction. Much of this challenge lies in the fact that our personal reflection directed toward our own experience is itself subject to superficiality, self-deception, self-serving denial, and cultural rootedness. Reflection requires thinking, and thinking as an intellectual project directed toward one's own lived-experience easily slips into a referentiality that takes itself as the "discovery of truth" (Scott, 35). In reflecting on one's own lived experience, it is easy to perceive our language as objective to our world. Indeed, this perception of language as objective constitutes much of our taken-for-granted normalness of everyday life—to wit, given differences of opinion or perspective, we are quick to believe in the objectivity of what *we said* or what *we heard*. There is a certain confidence in our perception of an objective world that is our deeply set orientation within it. As a result, we perceive no need to account for the steps through which we have arrived at this certainty in our own speaking or hearing. Moreover, Western and Eurocentric cultures cultivate deeply set commitments to our own articulate language as objective, as well as deeply set beliefs that posit human existence as essentially autonomous, that supremely values independence in thought and action, and that conceives of knowledge as separable from the particularity of human experience (Nisbett, 2003). Taken together, these circumstances create a situation in which even our most dedicated efforts to understand our deep imbrications within the folds of our collective discursive and communicative life are continually thwarted.[4] As Merleau-Ponty puts it, "The true Cogito does not define the existence of the subject through the thought that the subject has of existing. ... Rather, it recognizes my thought as an inalienable fact and it eliminates all forms of idealism by revealing me as 'being in the world'" (*Phenomenology* lxxvii).

Sexual Freedom, Feminine Sexual Masochism, and Rhetorical Treatments of Evidence

To illustrate this conception, the phenomenological reduction, and its application as a way to arrive at a rhetorical ethic of sexual expression and perception, I turn to Sandra Lee Bartky's (1990) incisive phenomenological study of "The Story of P.," a particular case of feminine sexual masochism. Bartky defines sadomasochism as "any sexual practice that involves the eroticization of relations of dominance and submission" (46). Bartky considers the "Story of P.," a woman who is "deeply ashamed" of her masochistic sexual fantasies that "have involved painful exposure, embarrassment, humiliation, mutilation, domination by Gestapo-like characters" (cited in Bartky 46). "The Story of P." is a case of masochistic sexual fantasy that seeps deeply enough into P.'s consciousness of experience that it creates a condition of psychic distress wherein she recognizes that her own "structures of desire" are "at war with [her feminist] principles" (45). P.'s consciousness of experience emerges as deeply felt shame through which she "suffers a continuing loss of esteem in her own eyes" (47).

In her study of this case, Bartky takes up the 1980s feminist debate concerning the meaning and reality of sexual freedom and liberation for women living within a patriarchal and misogynistic culture. On each side of the debate, we have opposing arguments featuring specific offerings of evidence that favor different sets of relations between the person and the communicative world in which she lives; each position thus arrives at very different ideas about the achievement of sexual expression as exertions of human freedom and liberation. On one side of the debate are "feminists" who argue in favor of a "'politically correct' sexuality of mutual respect [that] will contend with an 'incorrect' sexuality of domination and submission" (45). On the other side of the debate is Samois, "the first lesbian S/M group in the United States" led by a small group of women including Pat Califia and Gayle Rubin ("Samois"). Samois argues that "the critics of sadomasochism conflate fantasy and reality" and that "representations of violent acts should not be regarded with the same loathing as the acts themselves" (Bartky 48). Samois argues for "moral values" inherent in sadomasochistic sexual practices that emerge from the "heightened trust that the submissive member" must have in the "dominant member," and the "unusual attentiveness and sensitivity to the partner [that] are required of the one who has permission to inflict pain" (48).

Both the feminists and Samois use articulate language—language remaining within the grasp of the idea—to argue the case for an ethic of sexual expression conceived of as an exertion of human freedom and intimacy that must be rooted in reciprocities of respect, desire, and human recognition. Each side differs, however, in its understanding of the relationship between the eroticization of dominance and submission, and what constitutes those reciprocities with human relationships. Each side offers evidence in the form of arguments about what one should strive to experience, and our judgments of the quality of this evidence naturally falls within the logic of the community toward which we are already invested.

Each side in this debate urges P. to recognize specific features of her experience in specific ways, and thus toward a particular experience of consciousness that can lead to a specific consciousness of experience that each side formulates as "good" or "healthy" sexuality expression. Each side urges P. toward very different conceptions of herself and her sexual desire based on the rhetorical treatments of evidence that remains strongly within the "presumptions of reason" (Merleau-Ponty, *Phenomenology* 64) at work for each side. Feminists urge P. to recognize the pervasiveness of the patriarchal structures of society in which the eroticization of male sexual dominance and female sexual submissiveness is "precisely the instrument by which men are able to accomplish the subordination of women" (Bartky 47). Feminists argue that as P. experiences masochistic sexual desire, her experience is made possible because she has internalized the misogynistic meanings that structure desire itself. Feminists urge P. to develop a consciousness of experience rooted in a political critique with the goal of subverting the misogynistic meanings and structures that constitute her desire. Feminist treatment of evidence in this case features a consciousness of an experience of oppression so as to usurp it.

In contrast, Samois encourages P. to "set aside [her] shame, to accept [her] fantasies fully, to welcome the sexual satisfaction such fantasies provide and even, in controlled situations, to act them out" (48). Setting aside shame as an experience of consciousness would allow P. to explore precisely the meaning and structure of desire as she experiences them for herself. Separate from any critique of the larger meaning and structures that subject all persons collectively, Samois argues that the pursuit of sexual freedom must come from the satisfaction of sexual desire that can only be located through the actual experiencing of it. Samois's treatment of evidence in this case features a consciousness of sexual desire seeking sexual satisfaction (and excluding a consciousness of shame) as the proper location from which judgments of "good" or "healthy" sexuality must come.

Speech Speaking, Speech Spoken, and the Phenomenological Reduction

At issue in the "story of P." is the question of how we arrive at the evidence upon which we make judgment, both P.'s own and ours of the society in which we live. For both feminists and Samois, this evidence lies in an argument formed through the selection of particular aspects of experience as they are in keeping with a consciousness of misogynistic oppression (feminists) or sexual desire (Samois). Phenomenologically speaking, evidence "requires a rigorous method of seeing, *noein*, in the widest sense of the word." This does not mean that we can "dispense with the discursive procedures of demonstrating and arguing in searching for truth. But all such orderings are themselves to be grounded on evidence." Evidence, in other words, "must be brought to light" (Ströker 203).[5] As Merleau-Ponty suggests, "The absolute contact of myself with myself, or the identity of being and appearing, cannot be posited, but merely lived prior to all affirmation" (*Phenomenology* 309).

Thus, strictly speaking, it is impossible for anyone other than P. to bring to light the evidence upon which she must make her own judgment of the relative health or goodness of her sexual expression. This is because, as Merleau-Ponty puts it, "if we wish to reveal the genesis of being for us, then we must ultimately consider the sector of our experience that clearly has sense and reality only for us, namely, our affective milieu." Taking up this effort directs us toward seeing "how an object or a being begins to exist for us through desire or love." Such an effort allows us to "thereby understand more clearly how objects and beings can exist in general" (*Phenomenology* 156). The affective milieu through which desire becomes available as experience is, for Merleau-Ponty, a site through which we can bring to light evidence of our embodied existence that is less beholden to the grasp of the idea that comes with articulate language. This is because, for Merleau-Ponty, "there is an erotic 'comprehension' that is not of the order of the understanding, given that the understanding comprehends by seeing an experience under and idea whereas desire comprehends blindly by linking one body to another" (*Phenomenology* 159).

Both feminists and Samois argue for an ethic located in the reciprocities of respect, desire and human recognition, but neither offers a way to bring to light the evidence from the embodied and communicative world of P. that can reach beyond each side's presumptive reasoning that encourages P. to select specific aspects of her experience *a priori* as a basis for judgment. To move beyond the presumptive reasoning that informs the judgments of each side in this debate requires more than just asking P. to reflect on her experience. This is because "our natural attitude is not to experience our own feelings or to adhere to our own pleasures, but rather to live according to the emotional categories of our milieu" (Merleau-Ponty, *Phenomenology* 399). P.'s affective milieu includes both the feminist experience of misogyny and the experience of masochistic sexual desire; the conflicting nature of each of these milieus is what constitutes P.'s psychic distress, her experience of being at war with herself. Each aspect of P.'s experience adheres to the "emotional categories" featured in each milieu, and as both she and we argue for or against an ethic through which P. should move, we often simply reinforce the reasoning at work in the formation of those affective categories to start with. What must be at issue in directing our rhetorical treatment of evidence is P.'s experience and consciousness as they become available to her as she moves through their inherent reversibility. And this can be achieved through a phenomenological reduction informed by Merleau-Ponty's distinction between speech speaking and speech spoken. This also marks out the space through which we can begin to discover what Foucault refers to as the "radical possibility of speech" (87).

Understanding the distinction between speech speaking and speech spoken means that we must not only consider what distinguishes each from the other, but that we must also understand their relationship and how our embodied existence in the world carries us through and between each. We begin with understanding language as "constituted systems of vocabulary and syntax, or the various empirically existing 'means of expression.'" These constituted systems "are the depository and the sedimentation of acts of *speech [parole]*, in which the unformulated sense not only finds the means of expressing itself on the outside, but moreover requires existence for itself, and is truly created as sense [meaning]"[6] (Merleau-Ponty, *Phenomenology*, 202). In the case of speech speaking "the meaningful intention is in a nascent state." As such, there is no "natural object" (202) to which speech refers, no "prediscursive reality" (Scott 35) we can hope to discover. Rather, in the case of speech speaking, "existence seeks to meet up with itself beyond being, and this is why it creates speech as the empirical support of its own non-being," and why "speech is the excess of our existence beyond natural being" (Merleau-Ponty, *Phenomenology* 202–3).

At the same time, however "the act of expression constitutes a linguistic and cultural world," and "it makes that which stretched beyond fall back into being. This results in spoken speech, which enjoys the use of available significations like that of an acquired fortune" (Merleau-Ponty, *Phenomenology* 203). This "fall back into being" is an "ever-recreated opening in the fullness of being [that] is what conditions ... the construction of the world and the construction of concepts. Such is the function revealed through language, which reiterates itself, depends upon itself, or that like a wave gathers itself together and steadies itself in order to once again throw itself beyond itself" (Merleau-Ponty, *Phenomenology* 203).

A phenomenological reduction grounded in the distinction between speech speaking and speech spoken must find in speaking something beyond the taken-for-grantedness of our direct or natural sense of our own being. But, because language itself provides us with an "acquired fortune" of "empirically existing 'means of expression,'" it is easy to remain within this speech spoken state carried in the natural sense of our own being. For Merleau-Ponty, the key pivot point of experience through which we can "bring to light" the aspects of human being that are not self-contained within the grasp of the idea but which is the "thrown beyond itself," lies in understanding speech as *gesture*. As Merleau-Ponty puts it, "my corporeal intending of the objects of my surrounds is implicit and presupposes no thematization or 'representation' of my body or milieu" (*Signs* 89). Lacking the presuppositions provided in the "acquired treasure" of empirically available expression that leaves language within the grasp of the idea, the corporeality of existence functions "as a mute presence which awakens my intentions without deploying itself beyond them" (Merleau-Ponty, *Signs* 89).

The moment we take up this "corporeal intending" toward the objects that constitute my world, we have a circumstance in which the acquired fortune of significations held within our shared linguistic and cultural world can no longer enclose the possibilities of consciousness or experience, and we find that "signification arouses speech as the world arouses my body" (Merleau-Ponty, *Signs* 89). To explicate these intersubjective relations through which the possibilities of consciousness and experience emerge requires bringing to light the corporeality of a speech speaking that is our interconnectedness with others and a world. To achieve this, however, is to recognize the importance of *our perception of others* because, as Merleau-Ponty puts it, "the *Cogito* has, up until our present day, devalued the perception of others" (*Phenomenology* lxxvi). Moreover, "in order for the word 'other' not to be meaningless, my existence must never reduce itself to the consciousness that I have of existing; it must in fact encompass the consciousness that *one* might have of it, and so also encompass my embodiment in a nature and at least the possibility of an historical situation" (Merleau-Ponty, *Phenomenology* lxxvi).

Returning to P., we must ask the question concerning her perception of others. Although it is clear that both feminists and Samois urge her to view her experience in light of specific kinds of evidence, neither side considers how P.'s perception of others itself is at work as she is "at war" within herself. And this, of course, is only the first of what must be many more questions to come—questions of her perception of the other from whom she seeks sexual domination and of the others before whom she feels shamed. Proceeding through a phenomenological reduction could, in fact, reveal that the perception of others most powerfully at work in P.'s consciousness and experience is neither the one from whom she seeks sexual domination nor the others before whom she feels shamed. As the possibilities of a historical situation are taken up within this phenomenological reduction, experience itself explodes beyond any sense of correspondence to an objectivist real, and reveals its genesis in its reversibility with consciousness. It also reveals why an ethical rhetoric is incapable of providing judgment concerning the relative "goodness" or "health" of P.'s experience. Rather, we must take up a rhetorical ethic buttressed with a phenomenological reduction developed from Merleau-Ponty's distinction between speech speaking and speech spoken as the milieu from which such judgments can be made. Such an effort has no endpoint but rather requires an ongoing examination because, as Merleau-Ponty puts it, "the most important lesson of the reduction is the impossibility of a complete reduction" (*Phenomenology* lxxxvii).

Conclusion

If we wish to understand sexuality as it reaches from the most public and socially shared systems of meaning to the most private and intimate moments of experience, we must understand the tightly intertwined relationships among perception, language, and experience. Working from within the immediate and embodied circumstance of persons existing within a world is crucial in the effort to adequately and accurately understand our contact with the various discursive systems within which we live. We can recognize the significance of this point only when we acknowledge that no matter how insightful any one of us might be, no matter how studied or experienced, we always remain anchored in those discursive systems *through a body* that locates us in the specificity of time and place that retains, sustains, and alters those very discursive systems in ways that can we can never make fully transparent. In fact, it might very well be the case that the greater our ability to name the terms of the discursive systems within which we live, the easier it is to presume that we are not as subjected by them as those who cannot offer such articulations. We become, in other words, capable of forgetting the fact of our existence as embodied beings located in the specificities of time and place. It is a matter of developing ways of seeing critically that opens the horizons of lived experience without making lived experience into a known artifact. To reflect on experience—the experience of coming-out as lesbian or gay, or of making one's outer gender/sex correspond to the felt sense of the inner self, or of experiencing a sexual desire of which one also feels shamed, for example—is to take up sets of rhetorical practices already available and circulating within our social world, but not in a way that mistakes those already available rhetorical practices as a totality of the possibilities of our existence.

Although it is difficult to disagree with Socrates' adage that "the life which is unexamined is not worth living," that adage doesn't get one very far in assessing what kind of contact one must have with oneself within such an examination in order for one to reach this implicit and presumed threshold of worth. A phenomenological reduction developed through Merleau-Ponty's distinction between *speech speaking* and *speech spoken* allows us to move far beyond this simple adage and toward a way of seeing that can not only reveal what is implicit and presumed, but can direct us toward intellectual practices less susceptible to the tendency to forget that we will always return to the implicit and presumed as carried in speech spoken, to language that remains in the grasp of the idea.

In Merleau-Ponty's work, phenomenology emerges as a philosophical discourse that challenges that discourse itself and its practices fundamentally. The practice of philosophy must take place within the relations of the lived world, the one in which the philosopher herself is situated.[7] We must, in other words, privilege the rhetorical and communicative over the philosophical, which is a matter not of abandoning the philosophical effort, but rather of holding it to a different standard—one that takes the immediacy of lived experience and its relationship to consciousness as paramount. It is a standard that is beholden to its own limitations and therefore also the specificities of its possibilities. Clearly, the legacy of the heterosexual–homosexual distinction and the presumptions related to the biological determinacy of a two-sex system has failed in its ability to provide any sort of criteria for judgment as to the relative health of sexual identity or expression (Martinez, *Communicative* 36–40). Thus, we are left with the challenges of examining sexual experience itself as the only place where the relative goodness or health of sexual expression may come to be judged.

Notes

1. This epigraph is taken from the 2012 translation of *Phenomenology of Perception* (310). All citations to *Phenomenology of Perception* refer to this translation. I use this translation over the 1962 version (Colin Smith, Trans. with revisions by Forrest Williams and David Guerrière) because of its wide availability.
2. Those who write under the influence of phenomenology vary widely in purpose and style, often have deeply conflicting views of what phenomenology does and does not achieve, and sometimes disagree fundamentally as to what in fact qualifies as "phenomenology." My own use of the term follows the trajectory of thought from Edmund Husserl through Martin Heidegger to Merleau-Ponty. Richard Lanigan's exposition of communicology, and its methodological cognate semiotic phenomenology, is central in this trajectory (Lanigan 2008).
3. The phenomenological reduction is, arguably, the most important feature in the development of phenomenological thought and practice (Moran 2000, 146–47). It is a topic that Husserl returned to again and again throughout his long and prolific career (Merleau-Ponty 2012, lxxiv).
4. See Martinez (2003) for a fuller discussion of this point.
5. See Martinez (2011b) and Gordon (2006) for further discussion of evidence understood phenomenologically.
6. Once characteristic of the 2012 English translation of *Phenomenology of Perception* is use of "sense" and "meaning." In most cases, where the earlier translation uses "meaning," the more recent translation uses "sense." In this particular quotation, it is necessary to recognize this difference.
7. Merleau-Ponty 1964; see also, Gordon 2006; Ahmed 2006.

Works Cited

Ahmed, Sarah. *Queer Phenomenology: Orientations, Objects, Others*. Chapel Hill, NC: Duke UP, 2006. Print.

Bartky, Sandra Lee. *Femininity and Domination: Studies in the Phenomenology of Oppression*. New York: Routledge, 1990. Print.

Butler, Judith. *Bodies That Matter: On the Discursive Limits of "Sex."* New York: Routledge.

Foucault, Michel. *The Order of Things: An Archaeology of the Human Sciences*. New York: Vintage, 1970. Print.

Gordon, Lewis R. *Disciplinary Decadence: Living Thought in Trying Times*. Boulder, CO: Paradigm, 2006. Print.

Lanigan, Richard L. "Communicology." *International Encyclopedia of Communication*." 2008. Print.

——. *The Human Science of Communicology: A Phenomenology of Discourse in Foucault and Merleau-Ponty*. Pittsburgh, PA: Duquesne UP, 1992. Print.

———. *Phenomenology of Communication: Merleau-Ponty's Thematics in Communicology and Semiology*. Pittsburgh: Duquesne UP, 1988. Print.

———. *Semiotic Phenomenology of Rhetoric: Eidetic Practice in Henry Grattan's Discourse on Tolerance*. Washington, DC: U of America P, 1984. Print.

Martinez, Jacqueline M. *Communicative Sexualities: A Communicology of Sexual Experience*. Lanham, MD: Lexington, 2011. Print.

———. *Communicative Sexualities: A Communicology of Sexual Experience*. Lanham, MD: Lexington, 2011. Print.

———. "Culture, Communication, and Latina Feminist Philosophy: Toward a Critical Phenomenology of Culture." *Hypatia* 29 (2014): 221–36. Print.

———. "Lewis Gordon's Contribution to the Study of Communication: Beyond Disciplinary Decadence." *Atlantic Journal of Communication* 19 (2011): 17–27. Print.

———. *Phenomenology of Chicana Experience and Identity: Communication and Transformation in Praxis*. Lanham, MD: Rowman and Littlefield, 2000. Print.

———. "Racisms, Heterosexisms, and Identities." *Journal of Homosexuality* 45 (2003): 109–27. Print.

———. "Semiotic Phenomenology and Intercultural Communication Scholarship: Meeting the Challenge of Racial, Ethnic, and Cultural Difference. *Western Journal of Communication* 70.4 (2006): 292–310.

Merleau-Ponty, Maurice. "On the Phenomenology of Language." *Signs*. Chicago: Northwestern UP, 1964. 84–97. Northwestern Studies in Phenomenology and Existential Philosophy. Print.

———. *Phenomenology of Perception*. Trans. Donald A. Landis. New York: Routledge, 2012. Print.

Moran, Dermot. *Introduction to Phenomenology*. New York: Routledge, 2000. Print.

Nisbett, Richard E. *The Geography of Thought: How Asians and Westerners Think Differently ... and Why*. New York: The Free Press, 2003. Print.

"Samois." Wikipedia.org. 3 Feb. 2015. http://en.wikipedia.org/wiki/Samois.

Scott, Joan. "Experience." *Feminists Theorize the Political*. Eds. Judith Butler and Joan W. Scott. New York: Routledge, 1992. 22–40. Print.

Ströker, Elisabeth. "Evidence." *Encyclopedia of Phenomenology*. 1997. Print.

4 Hard-Core Rhetoric
Gender, Genre, and the Image in Neuroscience

Jordynn Jack

With the rise of contemporary neuroscience, public audiences have become accustomed to brain-based explanations for nearly every aspect of human behavior. Sexual behavior is no different. We are now schooled to understand the brain as the most important "sex organ," a view that both popular news outlets and scientific ones espouse. Popular writer Daniel G. Amen asserts that "Even though it feels genital, the vast majority of love and sex occurs in the brain" (1), which is "the largest sex organ in the body" (1). Recognizing the significance of the brain, Amen states, can enhance your sex life. Feminist writer Naomi Wolf posits a direct brain–vagina connection in *Vagina: A New Biography* (3), whereas psychologist William M. Struthers warns that pornography can "hijack a man's brain, hypnotizing him and rendering him incapable of making good decisions" (11). These popular books draw on science to explain sexuality. In doing so, they become part of a broader cultural rhetoric that informs how we discuss sexuality itself, as well as related issues, including addiction (to drugs and food as well as porn), romantic relationships, marriage, and divorce.

In these popular discussions, authors often use neuroscience as factual evidence to support their claims. The scientific research remains uninterrogated, however, and by failing to examine it more closely, we risk an oversimplified understanding of sexuality, one that glosses over sexual differences and naturalizes culturally specific patterns as universal and biologically determined.

Isabelle Dussauge has expertly addressed the methodological assumptions underlying neuroscience studies of sexuality in her article, "The Experimental Neuro-Framing of Sexuality." Based on her review of studies of homosexuality, sexual behavior, and desire, she finds the following tendencies. First, the studies begin by choosing "ideal subjects"—typically highly responsive, young (between 18 and 40), and most often heterosexual males (126). Second, Dussauge explains, a heterosexual orientation is taken as the norm in these studies, and participants are most often selected based on their response to a Kinsey scale. Those who report same-sex desire are excluded in most studies (127). Despite this exclusion, the results of the study are taken to represent sexuality writ large, not sexuality in that particular group. Any other study group that may be chosen by researchers (women, homosexual men, lesbians, people with disabilities, etc.) is marked by their deviance from the default, and the findings do not tell us about sexuality, in general, but about sexuality in that particular group.

Dussauge also explains how these neuroscience studies assume that sexuality is defined and operationalized in ways that are meant to evoke a predictable response at a predictable level of intensity. For example, subjects might view pornographic images that have been preselected for their appeal to a test group, with the goal of ensuring that participants in the study will respond similarly to the stimulus. In this way, Dussauge argues, these studies assume "that there is a universal desire and pleasure which, once triggered, is the same for everyone" (131) and that leads to a predictable sequence of events (desire, arousal, orgasm) (132). Often, what counts as sexual response is defined in part by a set of control stimuli (often, images of bodies engaged in sports) that presumably do not evoke desire (134). Finally, Dussauge describes how neuroscience studies eliminate the body, locating an idealized desire in the brain: "pure (ageless), perfectly oriented along the homo/hetero-axis, bodiless, distilled to an essence independent of its objects and feelers" (144).

However, Dussauge does not address how scientists draw upon images as stimuli in their experiments to evoke sexual response. In this chapter, I focus on how research on genre and visual rhetoric can help us to better understand the kinds of responses images evoke. One large epistemological gap in these studies is their reliance on pornographic images to elicit sexual responses. Too often, these images are taken at face value, as natural stimuli for predictable sexualized responses. Neuroscience studies takes for granted sexualized identities as preexisting the images and the images simply producing inevitable responses, considered as genres; however, pornographic images can be understood as constituting participants based on conventionalized patterns of expectation and response, or what Kenneth Burke refers to as "the creation of an appetite in the mind of the auditor, and the adequate satisfying of that appetite" (31). A rhetorical and cultural perspective suggests that these images are not pure, natural, or devoid of culture, and neither are physical responses to them.

In this chapter, I examine two studies that typify the use of pornographic images as a stimulus. These studies were chosen in part because they are actually better than most: both seem to stem from a social perspective; one is even feminist. In other words, both studies sought to offer a somewhat richer interpretation of sexuality as culturally influenced. Yet, both studies end up naturalizing sexual responses by relying on the genre of the pornographic image without inquiring about how those images work. By using pornographic images (usually chosen because they purport to represent a "pure" or natural "core" sexual act, such as a male penetrating a female), scientists participate in the process that Judith Butler describes as the naturalization of sexual difference, which occurs as a "sedimented effect of a reiterative or ritual practice" (*Gender* 10). In the process, these kinds of studies reproduce a heteronormative understanding of sexual response that is harmful because it curtails the range of what is considered "normal"; they simultaneously produce "the more and the less 'human,' the inhuman, the humanly unthinkable" (Butler, *Gender* 8).

Genre and the Image

Neuroscientific studies that rely on visual images partake in a set of cultural practices, or a visual culture, that shapes how those images are viewed and what they are taken to represent. In *Techniques of the Observer,* Jonathan Crary explains that "[v]ision and its effects are always inseparable from the possibilities of an observing subject who is both the historical product *and* the site of certain practices, techniques, institutions, and procedures of subjectification" (5). An observer is "one who sees within a prescribed set of possibilities, one who is embedded in a system of conventions and limitations" (6). These conventions include image genres, or types of images that share similar rhetorical situations and purposes.

For example, David Park's study of Civil War image genres demonstrates how different types of images included in Civil War era newspapers in the United States required conventionalized ways of seeing. For example, images featuring battle scenes relied on realist ways of looking inculcated by landscape painting and photography (291), whereas portraits of famous figures inculcated an epideictic orientation to the subject (299). For Park, each new image genre (used in Civil War newspapers) "was based on its own set of assumptions regarding its relationship to the outside world, possessed its own rhetorical sensibility, and generated its own range of national symbols" (290). These images, in turn, influenced how actors understood the Civil War, helping to constitute viewers' identities as well as their attitudes toward the subjects.

As Cara Finnegan has explained, one practice shaping photographic images, in particular, is the naturalistic enthymeme: we tend to take images as "true" or "real" representations (135). The photograph embeds the visual convention of a "fixed, monocular eye that [bears] an apparently identical resemblance to nature" (141)—despite the fact that the photograph differs from human vision in several ways. For instance, we do not perceive the world as bounded by a rectangular frame, as in a photograph, nor do we see objects as uniformly focused across our field of vision (instead, humans only see objects sharply at the center of our field of vision). The photographic image is accepted as "real" to us, but it actually tropes and exaggerates reality: the photograph is meant to stand in for the real thing, yet it augments reality by being sharper, more colorful; it is hyperreal. As Jean Baudrillard explains, the hyperreal emerges when images no longer refer to an origin or a reality, nor do they even seek to dissimulate a reality; instead, they are used to "dissimulate the fact that there is nothing" (6). The images have no "relation to any reality whatsoever" (6). One of Baudrillard's examples is Disneyland, a "play of illusions and phantasms." Pornography operates similarly.

Hard-Core Rhetoric 61

For contemporary pornographic images, produced with the help of digital technologies such as airbrushing and computer animation, it is not simply that an image of sex stands in for the reality of sex; the image masks the fact that the sexual acts themselves are fake, an elaborate masquerade based on signs (a facial expression, an item of clothing, a prop) and often bodies that have themselves been reconfigured through plastic surgery to become signs.[1] The bodies are often equally exaggerated: skin may be waxed, tanned, and oiled; body parts may be surgically enhanced; camera angles may emphasize curves and shapes. The viewer of the pornographic image is expected to suspend disbelief, taking what is depicted as a spontaneous, real sexual act, despite knowing that the image displays models or actors in an exaggerated sexual choreography.

Yet viewers continue to view pornographic images as erotic and are conditioned to respond in certain ways because pornographic images constitute an image genre or a rhetorical form. In Burke's words, rhetorical form itself constitutes a rhetorical appeal in that it "gratifies the needs which it creates" (138); in the case of pornogrpahic images, we might find an especially apt example of this. That is, viewers of a pornographic image expect to have a specific embodied response (sexual arousal) and to respond in certain ways (perhaps not just viewing the image but acting upon their feelings of arousal).

These images also help to constitute sexed and gendered identities for those who produce, view, and are depicted in them. Anis Bawarshi argues that "[g]enres have this generative power because they carry with them social motives—socially sanctioned ways of 'appropriately' recognizing and behaving within certain situations—that we as social actors internalize as intentions and then enact rhetorically as social practices" (341). A straight man, for instance, is socially conditioned to respond sexually to pornographic images that prominently feature women (either with other women or with men) but is expected to be turned off by pornographic images featuring gay male sex. Women, in contrast, are often expected to be turned off by all pornography, although this assumption seems to be changing as pornography becomes more and more mainstream.

Experiments in neuroscience that rely on images similarly depend on image genres and their attendant ways of seeing and responding. As we will see, even studies that take a relatively sophisticated view of gender and culture still tend to naturalize images and fail to take into account the rhetorically and culturally inscribed ways of seeing that inform them. Understanding these stimuli as image genres offers a richer way of interpreting the findings as well as possibilities for richer study designs.

Hard Core

To begin, let's examine how one study deployed pornographic images in order to examine how women respond to visual sexual stimulation (VSS). In this study, published in the journal *Social, Cognitive, and Affective*

Neuroscience, Charmaine Borg, Peter J. de Jong and Janniko R. Georgiadis begin with a promising acknowledgment that sex (especially visual sexual stimulation) is "under strong social control" and at least partially influenced by cultural norms (158). This is an insight seldom acknowledged in neuroscience studies, which tend to sanitize stimuli (rhetorically and visually) in order to operationalize the concept in question.

The article continues by narrowing the focus of the investigation to sexual penetration. Because "the act of penetration lies at the very core of sexual activity" (159), the authors reason, it should "carry considerable sexual incentive value" (159) in a visual form. For this reason, in the study, researchers showed a series of pornographic images to "exclusively" or "predominantly" heterosexual women (all of whom had been in a heterosexual relationship for at least six months, were not virgins, and did not have "sexual complaints"). These images, according to the authors, featured "hardcore coital interaction" with no faces and limited context. They featured only Caucasian, heterosexual couples, and included "easily recognizable features" (159).

All of this information is presented in the space of a paragraph or two, but it packs in a staggering set of assumptions about gender, sexuality, and the image. For one, the assumption that penetration constitutes the "core" of sexual activity is based on cultural norms in contemporary Western culture. Throughout the twentieth century, the focus of sexual pleasure for women has fluctuated, and penetration has not always been considered central. Prior to the 1980s, the clitoris was featured prominently in discussions of women's sexuality. In the canonical essay, "The Myth of the Vaginal Orgasm" (1970), Anne Koedt argued that the vagina "is not a highly sensitive area and is not constructed to achieve orgasms"; the clitoris, for Koedt, was the "center of sexual selectivity," one that was largely ignored during conventional heterosexual lovemaking (198). This insight led to greater emphasis on clitoral stimulation, but also broader rhetorics of sexual freedom for women. In the 1980s, however, the focus shifted from the clitoris to the newly rediscovered (and controversial) G-spot, with a resulting increase of emphasis on penetration (in lesbian as well as heterosexual pornography for women) (Hohmann). Borg, De Jong, and Georgiadis's decision to feature penetration in sexual stimulation shown to women reflects this cultural shift. If the researchers were doing their study in the 1970s (at least if they were sympathetic to feminist insights), their choice to show women images of penetration would require explanation.

Of course, one might question the very idea that there is one "core" of sexual activity that would comprise the best type of image to show women in order to elicit sexual responses. As Marti Hohmann puts it, "There is no 'natural' or 'good' sexuality to be recovered from pornography representations" (23). That is, pornography always tropes sexuality or highlights certain cultural preferences and beliefs about sex. A focus on penetration reflects a goal-oriented model of sex in which orgasm (and especially male orgasm) is the endpoint, not a natural "core" of sexual activity. In fact, research on men's and women's responses to pornography suggests an interesting difference: "Heterosexual men show greater responses to depictions of women than to depictions of men, whereas gay men show the converse pattern. In contrast, both heterosexual and lesbian women respond substantially to both depictions of women and depictions of men" (Chivers et al. 1108). In other words, the choice to depict heterosexual, penetrative sex does not necessarily reflect women's preferences. In one study, Meredith L. Chivers, Michael C. Seto, and Ray Blanchard used a wide range of visual stimuli. For each of the image types involving sexual activity, the researchers included male–male, female–female, and male–female examples. Here, Chivers and his colleagues found that women responded to sexual activity (including the bonobos) regardless of whether the people pictured in it reflected their own sexual preferences (1116).

Although the Chivers et al. study found that sexual response (when measured vaginally) did not differ among female participants for different types of stimuli, it does not necessary follow that neural responses would not be different for different visual stimuli. The choice of penetration as the stimulus in the Borg, De Jong, and Georgiadis study therefore reflects a rhetorical choice. The authors are seeking to distill "visual sexual stimulation" into a common experimental stimulus that can then be universalized across study participants. By not dwelling on this choice, and instead presenting it as an obvious, natural one, the authors rhetorically shift the reader's attention away from other options.

The types of pornographic images available to researchers likely reflect conventions for that image genre. The authors do not describe exactly where they got their images, but there is certainly no shortage online for them to choose from. Mainstream pornographic images reflect a set of visual conventions; they are a genre. As Berkeley Kaite has argued, pornographic images contain "[c]ertain features—objects, discursive strategies, fetishized exchanges—[that] occur and recur with a vengeance and have a textual effect" (viii). As genres, these images carry with them a set of formal conventions designed to elicit an embodied response. The pornographic image might be considered the paradigmatic form in this sense. If a form "is the creation of an appetite in the mind of the auditor, and the adequate satisfying of that appetite" (Burke 31), what genre does this better than porn?

In contemporary pornographic images, according to Kaite, the female body is carefully staged, often not appearing completely naked but almost always with various accoutrements such as jewelry, shoes, or lingerie. Soft-core pornography may feature conventionalized poses, with women gradually removing clothing to reveal a nipple, a breast, the vulva, and so on, but usually alone or perhaps in the context of other women (the classic "pajama party" fantasy) (Kaite 80). Hard-core heterosexual pornography tends to feature women with a male partner, often in the act of penetration or cunnilingus. These images are posed so that women's breasts and genitals are exposed and the male's penis is clearly in view. Thus, some sexual positions (woman on top or "cowboy" style; "doggie style"; etc.) may be more conducive than others (such as missionary position) where the woman's body is not on full display. This type of pornography may also feature close-up images that work by "zoning" the body, for example by showing a single breast or a rear view of a woman's genitals, to simulate the "keyhole" viewpoint of the voyeur (Kaite 81). A series of these "zoned" images may form a narrative, usually one that depicts spontaneous sex among strangers (Kaite 80). These images feature typified facial expressions; these are of course historically and culturally dependent. In contemporary images, according to Kaite, the female partner displays pleasure (closed eyes, open mouth, head tilted back) (81), may gaze at the male's genitals, and/or may gaze naughtily at the camera (80), while males never look at the camera. By excluding faces from the images used in the study, de Borg et al. abstracted out facial expressions and gaze. Thus, the images they used participated more in the convention of what Kaite refers to as the "keyhole" perspective, positioning participants as observers and the photographic subjects as exhibitionists.

The fact that these images are carefully staged genres suggests that we should be careful not to interpret studies that draw on them to mistake the stimulus (pornographic images) for the broader category of sexual desire as it occurs in other settings. Borg, De Jon, and Georgiadis are actually quite careful in this regard, since they describe their study as one of "visual sexual stimulation" via pornographic images, in particular. But we should be careful not to interpret their results as representing some kind of natural essence. As Karen Ciclitira has noted, the types of pornographic images that are most widely available are premised on cultural topoi, or commonplaces, such as women's sexual willingness, specific types of bodies and body parts, and so on (285). Exposure to these types of images likely conditions our responses to them.

The researchers' choice of only Caucasian subjects for the stimuli is not explained in the article. The authors do not indicate the race of the study participants. We might assume, however, that only Caucasians were chosen in photos because the study participants were Caucasian. Presumably, the authors assumed that showing pictures of people of another race might represent a confounding variable, or that race might disrupt the kind of response they sought to elicit. Here, the study assumes, but does not acknowledge, a rhetoric of interpellation and identification between study participants and the people represented in the images.

Borg, De Jong, and Georgiadis were surprised by their findings: when shown images of hard-core sex (featuring penetration), participants' neural responses paralleled responses to the emotion of disgust as well as pleasure (161). For the authors, this finding "raises doubt whether all brain activity induced by such stimuli can safely be assumed to be a signature of a positive sexual incentive value, which is nonetheless the dominant sentiment in VSS neuroimaging studies" (165). The authors seem unable to reconcile the idea that pleasure and disgust could commingle in responses to pornography. Yet a social and rhetorical perspective makes it much easier to understand why (if we take these findings to be true) pleasure and disgust might both characterize women's responses to pornographic images of penetration. For one, as Karen Ciclitira explains in her study of women's attitudes and responses to pornography, feminist critiques of pornography have been influential. In interviews, Ciclitira found that some women drew on these critiques, noting that pornography was "degrading," that it involved abuse and exploitation of women, and so on. Others expressed ambivalence, noting that they found pornography arousing but felt guilty for feeling that way (293). Another possibility, of course, is that the situation of the experiment itself evoked feelings of disgust. After all, the participants in question would be in an unfamiliar environment, with their heads in an fMRI machine, knowing that researchers were recording their responses to the images they saw. Who wouldn't feel a bit creeped out? Or perhaps some might find the situation titillating. Who knows? The point is that the situation itself is also rhetorical: it produces effects and cannot be excluded from the variables.

Thus, this example demonstrates that researchers seeking to engage cultural perspectives might do better if they seek out insights from researchers in rhetorical (and other humanistic) studies. In this particular case, cultural studies of pornography and rhetorical studies of science and genre can combine with psychological and neuroscience research to provide a richer interpretation of the study findings and a more nuanced understanding of what the experiment itself sought to measure (and how).

Soft Core

One might hope that a feminist orientation might lead researchers to develop a richer perspective. Yet a feminist orientation is not, in and of itself, sufficient: a feminist *rhetorical* perspective is needed. Mina Cikara, Jennifer L. Eberhardt, and Susan T. Fiske's article, "From Agents to Objects: Sexist Attitudes and Neural Responses to Sexualized Targets," offers a case in point. The authors clearly operate from a feminist perspective. That is, they seek to answer a question about the effects of sexism, namely, how the sexualization of women affects men. Sexualized images of women, they report, "disrupt[] the typical course of social cognition" (541) by lessening the extent to which men viewing such images attribute mental states to the women pictured. More specifically, they seek to show how men fail to grant agency to women pictured in sexualized poses or dress—especially in the case of men who hold sexist attitudes.

The study also draws on a model of sexism articulated by Fiske and her colleague, Peter Glick, one that is particularly savvy in that it identifies two valences to sexist beliefs. This model, the Ambivalent Sexism Inventory (ASI), offers a bivalent understanding of sexism. Fiske and Glick suggest that sexism can fall along two intertwined tendencies: hostile sexism (HS) and benevolent sexism (BS). Hostile sexism encompasses beliefs that express aggression toward women, such as the belief that women unfairly claim discrimination, that they seek to have power over men (not equality with men), and so on. Benevolent sexism entails beliefs that express a more paternalistic attitude toward women, such as the belief that they need men's protection, that they are the more moral and sensitive of the two sexes, and so on. Both views, Fiske and Glick suggest, are harmful to women (Glick and Fiske). In the study by Cikara, Eberhardt, and Fiske, the ASI scale is used to find out whether men holding more hostile sexist beliefs are also more likely to view women as objects.

Clearly, there is much to appreciate about this study, one of the few neuroscience inquiries to take an explicitly feminist orientation. Certainly, the effects of sexist beliefs are important, and studies like this one help us to understand those deleterious effects. Yet the feminist orientation of this study unfortunately leaves sex/gender and sexuality as unexamined essences, and also fails to consider the rhetorical construction of the images used as stimuli.

A closer look at the study methodology demonstrates how this occurs. For one, the authors chose to include women in one part of the study, a test of verbal attribution of agency to images of men and women, but not in the second part, a brain imaging study using functional magnetic resonance imaging. Yet the second part of the study was the one that was taken up most in popular accounts owing to the persuasiveness of brain images and the flashiness of brain imaging research. In the functional magnetic resonance imagery (fMRI) portion of the study, 22 men were recruited. While in an fMRI scanner, they viewed images of the following image types: "sexualized female," "clothed female," "sexualized male," and "clothed male." In these images, subjects were "smiling and gazing directly at the camera." The images were cropped from "mid-thigh to top of the head," and any clothing depicted was digitally altered to "minimize detail" (543). These images, we learn, were "of the sort that are frequently observed in public spaces (e.g., advertisements, billboards)" (542).

The sexualized images used in this study also constitute an image genre. Like the pornographic images used in the previous example, these images involve a set of recurring features and audience expectations. For one, in the United States, at least, certain conventions govern what is displayed in these images and what is not shown. If the images are to be used in mainstream advertising targeting heterosexual males, for instance, they usually depict young, attractive, slender women in abbreviated clothing (bikinis, short shorts, cropped tops, etc.). In some of these images, women may be topless, but if that is the case, they are posed in a way that conceals their nipples—either with their hands, hair, or arms. If the woman is completely naked, she is similarly posed so that her breasts and vulva are not visible. Buttocks are acceptable, but only if the woman is not posing in such a way that her vulva is exposed. For men, the conventions similarly require that he does not expose his penis or testicles. Increasingly, these kinds of images remediate the techniques of pornographic images, using similar types of poses and camera angles, only with key body parts concealed.

Aside from what is concealed or revealed, these images reply on a repertoire of heterogendered body positions. For instance, images often depict women with their back arched and head thrown back, either to emphasize the size and shape of their breasts or to mimic the ecstasy of orgasm; or they may be posed sitting or leaning back with their legs in the air, toes pointed. Another common pose involves leaning over, sticking the buttocks out. All of these poses position the woman's body to thrust key parts toward the viewer, inviting the viewer's gaze, or to simulate sexual positions. It is not clear what kinds of poses were used in the images Fiske et al. selected for their study, but it is likely that they may have participated in some of these visual conventions.

Although the Borg, De Jong, and Georgiadis study cropped images to include only the genitals, Cikara, Eberhardt, and Fiske included faces in their images. Thus, participants would be participating in the visual conventions of facial expressions and gaze. These conventions echo those of the heteropornographic image. According to Kaite, in these images women typically take on one of three gazes: (1) at the camera, (2) at a male partner or the product being advertised, or (3) away from the camera, in an expression of desire, longing, or pleasure. In this study, the researchers chose the first. In these images, models tend to take on a knowing, naughty look or a flirtatious smile that invites readers to ogle them. In other words, the images help to constitute the viewer as a consumer of the woman's body: they help to constitute the sexism that Fiske seeks to measure.

In their study, Cikara, Eberhardt, and Fiske found that men who had previously tested higher in Hostile Sexism were more likely to show deactivation in several brain regions associated with mentalizing: the medial prefrontal cortex, posterior cingulate, and bilateral temporal poles (547). However, as is the case with most brain research, the areas linked here to mentalizing have also been linked to any number of other qualities or concepts. For instance, the medial prefrontal cortex (mPFC) appears regularly in neuroscience abstracts alongside concepts such as attention, control, executive function, and vision (Beam et al.). Hence, other interpretations are possible, depending on which concepts the author connects, rhetorically, to the brain region in question.

It is worth considering here how the gender and sexual identities of participants may have been invoked. Of the 22 men recruited, one was ultimately excluded from the study because he reported being homosexual (543). This fact is notable for three reasons. For one, the study design must have included some kind of measure (not described in the paper) as part of the prescreening in which participants indicated their sexuality. The particular measure used is not described, so it could have been a simple checkbox. By invoking sexuality *a priori*, the study design primed sexuality; it invoked a sexual orientation in participants. It is very possible that doing so changed the rhetorical situation of the experiment. In other words, participants may have known (consciously or unconsciously) that their sexuality was at stake in the experiment. (Of course, viewing pornographic images of women probably cued them in if they didn't already know.) Changing the way in which gendered or sexualized identities are invoked in a study can change the results. What if participants were informed, for instance, that this was not a study of sexual response but of something else? What if they displayed women bikinis, for instance, and asked participants to correctly indicate the color of the bikini—to distract them from the actual purpose? Would their results have changed?

In addition, the study design assumes that sexual orientation and gender are both static essences. Participants were defined based on their declared gender and sexual orientation, which precludes the possibility that both gender and sexuality might be something more than a single, static entity. For instance, a person might identify as female in one context or as androgyne or genderqueer in another. This broader range of options might include agender/genderless, gender fluid, transgendered, or third-gendered. L. Ayu Saraswati argues that we might better understand sexuality as a fluid, multiple process, taking on various forms in different situations and across time. She sees sexuality as both something constituted by the interpellations of others and something that we perform for an audience: sexuality "necessitates an audience (the other) in order for it to be fully articulated" (594). We might apply this concept to gender as well, understanding it not as an *a priori* identification or essence, but as something that gets invoked within a rhetorical situation that includes an audience. In these studies, gender gets invoked explicitly in prescreening forms that require participants to choose from a limited set of sex/gender and sexuality options (usually male/female and heterosexual/homosexual).

In the context of this study, participants are also interpellated into a gender role during the act of viewing pornographic images in a scanner. The latter condition, in particular, likely activates previous experiences viewing such images (such as viewing porn on the Internet). Knowing that their results will be viewed by scientists, participants are performing their sexual orientation within a particular context of surveillance and observation. They are, in essence, being asked to perform compulsory heterosexuality and masculinity for an audience.

Moreover, the design implies that gay men do not hold sexist beliefs. The ASI, as articulated by Fiske and Glick, rests upon three tenets of sexism: paternalism, gender differentiation, and heterosexuality. This last item deserves special consideration. Sexist beliefs, Fiske and Glick argue, arise out of a system of heterosexual desire, wherein men both fear women and are attracted to them. In this way, Fiske and Glick do not suggest how homosexual (or asexual or bisexual) men might come to hold sexist beliefs. As Jane Ward has argued, "queer sexism" is an understudied phenomenon. Often, she writes, gay men are "understood to exist outside of heterosexual relations of gender" (154), as natural allies of women given that both are victimized in a male/hetero dominant culture. Yet, Ward argues that gay men are not immune to sexist beliefs. For instance, Ward argues, some gay men are positioned as arbiters of female fashion and the female form, a subject position that has led some women to suffer disparaging comments and inappropriate touching from gay men. As another example, Ward suggests, gay men may perform disgust for women as a way to demonstrate their own sexuality (165). These would both be examples of what Fiske and Glick call hostile sexuality. Yet, Ward argues that we might also see examples of benevolent sexism among gay men, as in the examples she cites of drag performers who simultaneously champion femininity and describe feelings of "distance, alienation, or bitterness" toward women (162).[2]

Certainly, not all gay men hold such beliefs, nor would all share Ward's take on drag, which others interpret as a way of calling attention to the idea that gender is always "a kind of impersonation and approximation" (Butler, *Gender Trouble* 21). Yet to ignore sexism among gay men papers over the ways sexism can infiltrate homosexual men's belief systems as well as those of heterosexual men. By excluding homosexual men from their study, Cikara, Eberhardt and Fiske constrain the model of sexuality they seek to explain.

The fMRI portion of the study also excludes women, and so it also precludes the possibility that women objectify other women—but they certainly do. One situation in which women are likely to do so occurs in tabloid magazines, which often print articles body-shaming celebrities (by pointing out cellulite, poor fashion choices, and other flaws) or by celebrating the best bikini bodies. The primary audience for these magazines is women. Granted, in this situation women view images of other women in a context of judging, not simply one of attraction, but sexuality should not be excluded from these contexts (since here women are affirming their own sense of what is sexually attractive to men or to themselves). For this study, then, consideration of gender, genre, and images from a rhetorical perspective offers an enriched understanding of what the study might have been doing and how we might interpret the results.

Conclusion

Any neuroscience study of sexuality can benefit from a humanistic perspective. In particular, when pornographic images are used as a stimulus, a humanistic perspective can help to unpack what, exactly, is being operationalized. Although neuroscientists might choose pornographic images as a clear or obvious stimulus to evoke a natural sexual response, a rhetorical perspective demonstrates that this stimulus is anything but (and neither is the response). Instead, we might understand these findings with more nuance, suggesting how they reflect and reproduce social and cultural expectations about sexuality, arousal, and desire.

This is not to say that neuroscience studies cannot tell us something interesting about our sexuality, our brains, and how we respond to images. If anything, these studies suggest that images are indeed rhetorical in the deepest sense of the word: they produce embodied effects much in the way Burke suspected. They seem to create and fulfill audiences' expectations at a deep, affective level. Yet interpreting those effects outside of a broader rhetorical and cultural framework can be difficult, as we saw in the first case study, where researchers had trouble understanding why pornographic images evoked arousal as well as disgust. To take those effects as simply natural and inevitable overlooks the ways those effects are also embedded in cultural and rhetorical modes of production, in ways of seeing, in gendered, raced, and sexualized identifications.

Notes

1. Use of the term *porn* to describe other kinds of images that circulate through contemporary media, such as food, yarn (in knitting and crocheting circles), and the like, attests to the extent to which photographic and digital technologies honed in porn have spread to other settings, and along with them, certain ways of looking and certain kinds of hyperrealities.
2. Similarly, Steven P. Schacht argues that "female impersonators' strict adherence to conventional standards of female and male, combined with their masculine embodiment of the feminine, still results in a masculine hierarchy" (252).

Works Cited

Amen, Daniel G. *Sex on the Brain: 12 Lessons to Enhance Your Love Life*. New York: Harmony, 2007. Print.

Baudrillard, Jean. *Simulacra and Simulation*. Trans. Sheila Faria Glaser. Ann Arbor: U of Michigan P, 1994. Print.

Bawarshi, Anis. "The Genre Function." *College English* 62.3 (2000): 335–60. Print.

Beam, Elizabeth, L. Gregory Appelbaum, Jordynn Jack, James Moody, and Scott Huettel. "Mapping the Semantic Structure of Cognitive Neuroscience." *Journal of Cognitive Neuroscience* 26.9 (2014): 1949–965. Print.

Borg, Charmaine, Peter J. de Jong, and Janniko R. Georgiadis. "Subcortical Bold Responses during Visual Sexual Stimulation Vary as a Function of Implicit Porn Associations in Women." *Social Cognitive and Affective Neuroscience* 9.2 (2014): 158–66. Print.

Burke, Kenneth. *Counter-Statement*. 1931. Berkeley: U of California P, 1958. Print.

Butler, Judith. *Bodies that Matter: On the Discursive Limits of "Sex."* New York: Routledge, 1993. Print.

———. *Gender Trouble: Feminism and the Subversion of Identity*. New York: Routledge, 1990. Print.

Charland, Maurice. "Constitutive Rhetoric: The Case of the Peuple Quebecois." *Quarterly Journal of Speech* 73.2 (1987): 133–50. Print.

Chivers, Meredith L., Michael C. Seto, and Ray Blanchard. "Gender and Sexual Orientation Differences in Sexual Response to Sexual Activities Versus Gender of Actors in Sexual Films." *Journal of Personality and Social Psychology* 93.6 (2007): 1108–121. Print.

Ciclitira, Karen. "Pornography, Women and Feminism: Between Pleasure and Politics." *Sexualities* 7.3 (2004): 281–301. Print.
Cikara, Mina, Jennifer L. Eberhardt, and Susan T. Fiske. "From Agents to Objects: Sexist Attitudes and Neural Responses to Sexualized Targets." *Journal of Cognitive Neuroscience* 23.3 (2010): 540–51. Print.
Crary, Jonathan. *Techniques of the Observer: On Vision and Modernity in the Nineteenth Century*. Eds. Joan Copjec, Rosalind Krauss and Annette Michelson. Cambridge, MA: MIT Press, 1992. Print.
Dussauge, Isabelle. "The Experimental Neuro-Framing of Sexuality." *Graduate Journal of Social Science* 10.1 (2013): 124–51. Print.
Finnegan, Cara. "The Naturalistic Enthymeme and Visual Argument: Photographic Representation in the 'Skull Controversy.'" *Argumentation and Advocacy* 37 (2001): 133–49. Print.
Glick, Peter, and Susan T. Fiske. "The Ambivalent Sexism Inventory: Differentiating Hostile and Benevolent Sexism." *Journal of Personality and Social Psychology* 70.3 (1996): 491–512. Print.
Hohmann, Marti. "The Politics of the G-Spot: Penetrative Sex in Feminist Pornography, 1981–1991." *The Harvard Gay and Lesbian Review* 3.3 (1996): 23. Print.
Kaite, Berkeley. *Pornography and Difference*. Bloomington: Indiana UP, 1995. Print.
Koedt, Anne. "The Myth of the Vaginal Orgasm." *Radical Feminism*. Eds. Anne Koedt, Ellen Levine, and Anita Rapone. New York: Quadrangle, 1970. 198–207. Print.
Park, David. "Picturing the War: Visual Genres in Civil War News." *Communication Review* 3.4 (1999): 287. Print.
Saraswati, L. Ayu. "Wikisexuality: Rethinking Sexuality in Cyberspace." *Sexualities* 15.5/6 (2013): 587–603. Print.
Schacht, Steven P. "Gay Female Impersonators and the Masculine Construction of 'Other.'" *Gay Masculinities*. Thousand Oaks, CA: SAGE. 247–269. Print.
Struthers, William M. *Wired for Intimacy: How Pornography Hijacks the Male Brain*. Downers Grove, IL: InterVarsity, 2009. Print.
Ward, Jane. "Queer Sexism: Rethinking Gay Men and Masculinity." *Gay Masculinities*. Thousand Oaks, CA: SAGE. 152–76. Print.
Wolf, Naomi. *Vagina: A New Biography*. New York: HarperCollins, 2012. Print.

5 Historicizing Sexual Rhetorics

Theorizing the Power to Read, the Power to Interpret, and the Power to Produce

Meta G. Carstarphen

History-Making Futures: How a Sexual Rhetoric is Born

It was a relatively quiet announcement, in media terms. There was no news conference or staged announcement from corporate principles. Instead, in a simple written announcement, social media giant Facebook revealed a revolutionary decision that would affect its estimated 890 million daily active users: all would now have 59 options to describe gender—including a "write your own" selection (Guynn).

Popular media provide the worlds, even if these are virtual, in which the rhetoric of gender is most pronounced. Their economic imperatives—the dependency upon advertising and the demand for profitability—create a cultural context in which sexual roles and expectations are a given. Media also provide illusionary spaces, where what seems to be clear-cut lines are not always true. In their analysis of photos within magazine icons *Playboy* and *Cosmopolitan*, Krassas, Blauwamp, and Wesselink found that, despite their oppositional market positions, "women's sexuality is constructed in similar ways by both magazines" (168); their rhetorical positioning of women is the same. Women are presented as visual gifts for a gaze that sexualizes their identities.

It was in contexts like these that I first began, in 1999, to explore if there was indeed a "sexual rhetoric" that could be decoded and described through the lens of media texts. Then, as now, the proposition is challenging.

With a vision for where this discussion positions itself in the twenty-first century, David Gauntlett connects the points of knowledge between media and their roles in gendering identity (2008). Media may seem pervasive and feel immersive, but the theories on how media affect us revolve around the two essential ideas of agency and influence. In other words, how much control do we as individuals have over how we see ourselves, or do the media override that control with a powerful ability to project representations of who we should be?

The Power to Read

Sequoyah is a name that should be universally known, but much about this Cherokee scholar and teacher remains unknown. In 1821, he completed a task that took him 12 years to complete—he invented a syllabary that translated the spoken Cherokee language into a written alphabet. Easily taught and easily learned, the syllabary became the tool that enabled Cherokees to translate and read English. Sequoyah's innovation also propelled this Native American Nation to produce its own newspaper in 1828 (Carstarphen and Sanchez, 2010). What is fascinating about this cross-cultural true account of the innovation of an alphabet-like "reading" is how it navigated identities through a three-way negotiation: from spoken word to an Indigenous alphabet and then ultimately to English.

I often think about the privileged status of the written text and what that means to identity. An obvious implication is that, from the earliest writings, whoever served as author, as writer, had the power to shape the observed world and preserve those perceptions for the ages. Simultaneously, the markings of a printed text have the power to forge a misperception that resists erasure or to make invisible the palpable presence of the other. A haunting example of this power is the life of sixteenth-century Spanish educator and writer Catalina Hernández, a *beata*[1] from Spain sent to educate Indigenous girls in "New Spain," or Mexico. In her meticulous historiography, Susan Romano strives to re-create a snapshot of this religious woman who was known to have written two letters of concern about the treatment of her female students under the control of Franciscan friars (2007).

The letters themselves have disappeared from history, as did Catalina Hernández herself, shortly after she wrote these complaints. But as she apparently tried to communicate her concerns to Spanish Queen Isabel through the male hierarchy established in the Americas, her actual words were paraphrased and passed on through layers of interpretation, and probably, misdirection. The ability to write has historically been a hard-won privilege for those without financial or social status, for communities of color, and for women. But if we consider the power to produce as going beyond having the skill and education to do so, then we must complicate what it means to enable ideas to be recorded in a "fixed" medium—and to stay there.

When Theodor Adorno reflected on how he first coined the term *culture industry* with his colleague Max Horkheimer in 1947, it was to clarify and demystify the term once more. In his article nearly 30 years later, Adorno delineated the qualities of art from the mass-produced culture he disparaged: "All of the practice of the culture industry decidedly applies the profit motive to the autonomous products of the spirit" (9). Once the creative attributes of an artifact becomes subordinate to the economic forces that made it, then its essential nature as an artistic expression ceases to exist. Adorno's "culture industry" was quite plainly meant to spotlight the media industries, which in his words provided a range of amusements not deemed important from the "photonovels" to the "advice-to-the-lovelorn columns" (10). But he takes aim at those who dismiss the idea that such entertainments have any influence over our lives, lest we underestimate what he describes as industry's relentless pursuit of the masses.

In 1975, Laura Mulvey's "Visual Pleasure and Narrative Cinema" reached into the cinematic arts to describe the "male gaze" and has served as a powerful manifesto about the deceptive allure of what is seen. Making the position of the viewer an artifact of the visual experience, she shifted our own analyses of the content of film to the framing of these images. The female body, caught in a voyeuristic construct, could only really be known for the visual pleasure it allowed audiences. But years later, as Mulvey reflects on the changes in technology from analog to digital, she talks about a break in narrative consciousness that becomes equally available to viewers:

> People could and did watch a Hollywood film, against the grain, to quote the term used at the time, but to a certain extent to take up that position would always involve a shift away from the magic and fascination of the look, the subject position that was established by the aesthetic of the film itself, into a position which could be one of pleasure but would also suggest an alternative and self-conscious spectatorship.
> (quoted in Sassatelli 128)

Mulvey's reflection here, delivered in a small, off-handed way, is nevertheless potentially stunning for its implications about uncovering multiple identity constructions and interrelationships in texts. Consider the certainly rigid, highly structured reading of a letter, a book, a newspaper, and even a theater movie showing. We know that readers and audiences bring multiple readings to even these relatively static texts, but they have not had the tools to change these texts to suit their purposes—until the digital age. One can have "alternative" spectator roles because we have the tools to insert our own writing into texts, or self-made video or photos, or artistic embellishments. Perhaps the "alternative" spectator exists because the "alternative" author coexists with her.

The power to read, it seems to me, anticipates claiming a stake in the power to interpret. If we engage with texts by performing the acts of decoding and encoding a shared language with authors, we are led to wonder what to do with such new knowledge acquired.

The Power to Interpret

Intersectionality articulates what Susan J. Hekman describes as an obvious insight: "[I]dentities are complex, that not only gender but race, sexuality, and myriad other factors constitute identity" (145). But in the long and rich tradition of feminist theory and critiques, it wasn't until African American scholars gave voice to how identities "intersect" that this notion gained currency. To be a woman in a body that is gendered can be a different experience within the community. Feminism faced the challenge of articulating how to be one within a community, while affirming the primacy of an individual's experience.

Hekman ponders openly the question of whether scholarship has come full circle. The social construction of identity has dominated our perceptions of the sheer reality of what it means to be a male and a female. We have lived with this perception that Western civilization has been the course of our gender binaries; that the essentialism of male and female was formed in the crucible of sociopolitical circumstance.

But we must wonder if our understanding the rhetoric of gender can ever separate itself from the physical reality of being born humans and of having to learn to read the bodies in which we appear. Thus, body studies and studies of materialism bring us to a reexamination of the gender and sex as an emblem of the physical world we inhabit as understood within the sociopolitical contexts we share. In this way, we can give recognition to the lived experiences of all of us. We can empower the necessary challenge of an individual's ability to read, write, and interpret what it means to be gendered.

Media technologies over the ages have forced a rereading of the texts as well as the identity representations that are woven within the inescapable textures in the narratives. Whether our texts are linearly constructed as in ages past, or whether they exist in multidimensional planes the way that hypertext makes possible now, the power to read seems a necessary first step in our understanding of gendered and other identities.

In *Gender Trouble,* with a theory made for a highly mediated age, Judith Butler introduced the notion of performativity to gender and identity (1990). Splitting the conceptual links between sex (the material body) and gender (the social roles), Butler's work challenges us to view gender identities as performances, some voluntary and some not. When media inscribe men and women in the performativity of gender, such narratives become vivid and understood as dramatic renderings or artful narratives of fact. The power to interpret gendered identities becomes a mass event, a communal activity reaching far beyond the parameters of neighborhoods' visible communities. For example, Gauntlett argues that a reality TV show, such as *Big Brother,* and superhero movies about *The Fantastic Four* and the *X-Men* exemplify the "mostly convention" but sometimes "alternative vision" of gender representations (155).

In defining feminist philosophy, Rosalyn DiProse raises a provocative question that is a key part of any exploration of identity construction. That is, what is the role of the variable "other" in our philosophy-making? Can we know of identities besides our own, and most importantly as scholars, discuss these other realities without hierarchy? Sometimes, these understandings express themselves in restrictive binaries. For instance, to know feminism is to counter chauvinism. To describe gender difference is to react to the mores of gender normativity.

And to describe the experience of being racialized is to counter the presumptive stance of a nonraced subject. Given these certainties, DiProse sees it as an imperative to understand feminism without hierarchy and to encourage all scholars who embrace this identification to welcome, not avoid, the challenges of exploring that which is different from ourselves:

> To open ourselves to thinking through the affective field of the other and to the transformations this implies does not lessen that inspirational

sensibility, the passion for thinking, the enjoyment of ideas. But it would and has given us time to address other problems that touch our lives that may not be explicitly feminist. (128)

The Power to Produce

The promise of eternality, even immortality, through the power to produce texts is an unseen contract between writers and willing readers. The mass media amplify this notion, and the allure is attractive. What one person could see, millions could now view. What once was as transitory as a letter could be archived in multiple ways through the database precisions of technologically advanced media.

The power to produce becomes more salient to us in light of challenging political and social contexts, even as orality serves as the catalyst for vital self-expressions of identity. In her analysis of the speeches and writings of African American "club" and "church" women, Shirley Wilson Logan maps the path of public discourse for these women through the resources closest to them at the time (1999). One can imagine how the fevered and ritualized expressions of worship created bridges for these women to amplify their social concerns to more public audiences. In a strategic sense, the space of the spoken became intertwined with the written, transferring a deeper sense of permanence

We also know, for example, how women—largely European American women—organized antislavery societies through which they became vocal, and sometimes prominent critics of slavery and other dehumanizing practices toward African Americans and Native Americans. For instance, in her analysis of almost 1500 female-authored petitions, Alisse Portnoy examines these writings and speeches, uncovering a dance of identity that would redefine feminine abilities and roles (2005).

What then, does it mean to consider the power to produce? Certainly, it involves the agency to represent one's own identity and to make it known to others. In this way, self-awareness must be coupled with "other" awareness. Our perceptions of who we are can be internalized and can even be acted out. But what meaning can we draw from that enactment without the reflection or recognition in others' eyes? We may experience some version of this in everyday living, where we speak about some personal experience, only to hear someone else describe it in a very different way. That difference of a shared experience can be viewed through power constructs, positionality, and even eloquence. Understanding such an identity position can also, must also, incorporate the many-splintered lived reality of being.

In one of the most eloquent dissections of "intersectionality" as a lived experience, Jacqueline Jones Royster lays out a repositioning of voice as an essential element in what she describes as "cross-boundary discourse" (29). She privileges subjectivity, often decried as a valid tool of understanding experience or a visible factor in understanding phenomena, as central to understanding the role of voice. There are three elements to her expansive thinking about this: the personal account; the limitations of thinking about voice solely within the dual streams of spoken or written discourse; and the need for a transformation in our theories and practices of discourse.

Voice, in its grammatical sense, allows us to recognize where speakers situate themselves in an exchange. Voice, as Royster expands upon it, is central to understanding the ability to produce, to be authors of our experiences through which we can participate in constructing our own identity. Royster focused her examination on what it means to be "raced" and positioned as the "Other," but we can easily hear the applications of these ideas to gendered identities. In fact, we must. We remain in the throes of finding ways to express what a full identity, including gender, means.

Without the privilege of voice and of a subjectivity that acknowledges voice we are left mute, invisible and siloed. We may still be the originators of the self-production of our identities, but they cannot resonate with the full body of authenticity unless they can vibrate among the chorus of others who are both like us, and completely different from us.

Finally, as Royster challenges us, we can expand our conceptual thinking to imagine what identity means beyond the constraints of written texts or spoken oralities. Our hypermediated worlds have brought this need into sharp focus. Our network of communication tools grows more diverse, complex, and interconnected. We live with as well as teach new generations of media consumers ,whose whole experience is defined by the simultaneous interplay of sound, text, image, touch, and emotion.

Coda: Future-Making Histories

I began this chapter with a moment from social media that illustrates just how tangible this need is. Our tomorrow is now, and our past exists alongside the contemporaneous unfolding of the present. History now awaits comparative milliseconds instead of millennia in an infinite quest to replace what was old with what is new.

We are called upon, now more than ever, to know ourselves and to know others with an authenticity that previous epochs have denied us. We were made for such a time as this, and we are ready.

Note

1. According to Romano, there is no exact contemporary English translation for this Spanish term, but she translates *beatas* as "spiritual women who belong to some form of spiritual community" (p. 456).

Works Cited

Adorno, T.W., and Rafael Cook. "The Culture Industry." *Cineaste* 5.1 (1971): 8–11. Print.
Butler, Judith. *Gender Trouble: Feminism and the Subversion of Identity*. New York: Routledge, 1990. Print.

Carstarphen, Meta G., and John P. Sanchez. "The Binary of Meaning: Native/American Indian Media in the 21st Century." *Howard Journal of Communication* 21.4 (2010): 319–27. Print.

Carstarphen, Meta G., and Susan C. Zavoina, eds. *Sexual Rhetoric: Media Perspectives on Sexuality, Gender and Identity, Contributions to the Study of Mass Media and Communications*: Westport, CT: Greenwood, 1999. Print.

DiProse, Rosalyn. "What Is (Feminist) Philosophy?" *Hypatia* 15.2 (2000): 115–32. Print.

Gauntlett, David. *Media, Gender and Identity: An Introduction*. 2nd ed. New York: Routledge, 2008.

Guynn, Jessica. "Facebook's New Gender Option: Fill in the Blank." *USA Today* 26 Feb. 2015. Web. 28 Feb. 2015.

Hekman, Susan J. *The Feminine Subject*. Malden, MA: Polity, 2014. Print.

Krassas, Nicole R., Joan M. Blauwamp, and Peggy Wesselink. "Boxing Helena and Corseting Eunice: Sexual Rhetoric in Cosmopolitan and Playboy Magazines." *Sex Roles* 44.11/12 (2001): 751–71. Print.

Logan, Shirley Wilson. *"We Are Coming": The Persuasive Discourse of Nineteenth-Century Black Women*. Carbondale: Southern Illinois UP, 1999.

Mulvey, Laura. "Visual Pleasure and Narrative Cinema." *Screen* 16.3 (1975): 6–18. Print.

Portnoy, Alisse. *Their Right to Speak: Women's Activism in the Indian and Slave Debates*. Cambridge, MA: Harvard UP, 2005. Print.

Romano, Susan. "The Historical Catalina Hernández: Inhabiting the Topoi of Feminist Historiography." *Rhetoric Society Quarterly* 37.4 (2007): 453–80.

Royster, Jacqueline Jones. "When the First Voice You Hear Is Not Your Own." *College Composition and Communication* 47.1 (1996): 29–40.

Sassatelli, Roberta. 2011. "Interview with Laura Mulvey: Gender, Gaze and Technology in Film Culture." *Theory, Culture and Society* 28.5 (2011): 123–43.

6 Milk Memory's Queer Rhetorical Futurity

Charles E. Morris III

Harvey Milk has been hyper-present in my world lately. On the occasion of Milk Day in California (Milk's birthday) in late May 2013, my colleague Jason Edward Black and I were in San Francisco promoting our new University of California Press volume *An Archive of Hope: Harvey Milk's Speeches and Writings*. We were invited to talk about Milk's life and legacy at the esteemed Hormel Gay and Lesbian Center at the San Francisco Public Library, and—even more queerly festive—at Book's Inc. in the Castro, where our panel commenced with a rousing rendition of Happy Birthday by the SF Gay Men's Chorus. That we were joined by Dan Nicoletta and Frank Robinson for these discussions (Frank now gone) made these occasions queer living history events, themselves a powerful form of epideictic politics, all the more poignant. These memory engagements mattered in part because they were intergenerational and diverse, generating a discourse about the past and its promises collaboratively created by those who knew and worked with Harvey Milk as well as those born two decades after his death. In the same space, evening, a nonagenarian and a twenty-something wept over Harvey's life and loss, this history, and an HIV+ ACT UP veteran productively chastised us during Q & A for complicity in representational politics that erased many other San Francisco activists, especially queers of color, who had contributed invaluably to LGBTQ worldmaking past and present. For all these reasons, in that moment and beyond (that experience convinced us to continue the project), Milk's discourse and memory brings to mind José Esteban Muñoz's *Cruising Utopia*, his final utopic striving—critical, concrete, collective, emotional, anticipatory—a vision of queerness as potentiality, futurity.

All of what I have just described underscores for me that "Milk memory," all memory, is centrally an inventional resource, both limitless and limited, which is one more way of saying that sexuality is inherently and consequentially rhetorical. It is of course the case that sexuality is rhetorical in myriad complex ways that imbricate body, discourse, desire, difference, sensorium, space, time, relations, generation, identity, ideology, politics, pleasure, precarity, and so much more. Our archival engagement with Harvey Milk centers on public and private modalities performed in the personal and collective interest of sexual justice and worldmaking both in the 1970s and in our own times. Like sexuality and rhetoric themselves, such an effort is radically contingent and left wanting, anticipation and striving some of the best byproducts persuasion produces. It is also the case of course that rhetoric is sexual—embodied and effervescent, suasory and seductive, consummatory and constitutive, ephemeral and enduring. Both sexuality and rhetoric *matter*.

And both are related to the matter of memory. In the preface to *An Archive of Hope*, Black and I identified two ongoing challenges to any queer project that includes LGBTQ memory, which we called the difficulties in the *where* and the *please* of GLBTQ memory and history (xi). The where challenge concerns discovery, preservation, and circulation of GLBTQ pasts. Even as we strive successfully for greater accumulation, preservation, and exhibition of GLBTQ pasts, we also face the challenge of the *please* of GLBTQ memory and history, the rhetorical challenge of packaging and performing and circulating these pasts in ways that will appeal, seem relevant, prove applicable in these times and those to come. There remains still too much indifference to GLBTQ pasts, for reasons that are easily explicable, if unforgiveable, and difficult to overcome.

With these prefatory notes in mind, in this brief meditation let me cull Milk memory—specifically the topoi of hope, candor, and recruitment—in the interest of proffering from my perspective some, but certainly not all, key elements in sexuality in/as/through/by/with/against rhetoric.

Hope

In March 2013, a Midwestern blogger named Amelia told a story in the Gay Voices section of the *Huffington Post* titled "When My 8-year-old Gay Son Taught His Class about Harvey Milk." The boy's second-grade class, as part of a unit on civil rights, was given the exciting assignment of writing a report about a heroic figure selected from a list of provided options, and then presenting the report to the class. Because this teacher "knew that she had a gay student in her class (my kid)," Amelia remembered, she "added Milk to the list of potential essay subjects" (par. 3). Amelia's response:

> I have to admit that I was thrilled—thrilled that his teacher is so awesome that she thought to put Milk on the list, thrilled that my kid picked Milk all on his own, and even more thrilled when I learned that the kids were going to be allowed to dress up as their subjects as part of their report (oh, the cuteness!). (par. 4)

But the tough-loving work of teaching Milk memory ensued, handled with aplomb—gay pride and worldmaking understood in relation to the trauma of homophobia, in relation to the closet, in relation to Dan White's violence that took Harvey Milk's and George Moscone's lives. But, oh, the difference LGBTQ pasts can make for some non-normative schoolchildren[1] and perhaps their normative classmates. Dressed in a tan suit with a gold-and-yellow-striped 1970s tie, Amelia's son shared his report for the children who had never heard of Harvey Milk—they listened, they engaged, they expressed disbelief, they asked questions. Most of all, Amelia concluded, "There was no silence in a second-grade classroom where an 8-year-old boy, a gay boy who has never seen the need for a closet, told Harvey Milk's story" (par. 15).

No doubt, similar experiences could be shared throughout the United States, and thanks to the peculiar memory politics of Stuart Milk and his Harvey Milk Foundation, elsewhere around the globe. Amelia's story exemplifies Harvey Milk's vision of hope; evidences the significance of Milk's tireless and ultimately triumphant fight against the venomous Briggs Amendment; and manifests the dream of the California FAIR Education Act. Milk's legacy may inspire a generation of latter-day Medora Paynes—descendants of that precocious 11-year-old who arrived of her own will at Castro Camera to help Milk get elected in 1976—that we all hope will transform the meaning of LGBTQ freedom and futurity (Shilts 135, 280).

Milk understood the power of such symbolism. After all, upon finally winning in November 1977, he likened himself to Jackie Robinson, observing that, "In the same way, I am a symbol of hope to gays and all minorities" ("Homosexual on Board" 24). However, what I take as the core lesson of Milk's legacy and Amelia's story is that hope's empty optimism alone is not enough; poster-child panaceas will not suffice. His best-remembered phrase from his best-loved speech, "You've Got to Have Hope," importantly was first delivered in the Gay Community Center in San Francisco on June 24, 1977, on the occasion of his declaration of candidacy for Board of Supervisors and would become his stump speech that summer and fall. This was Milk's fourth campaign in five years, and he'd lost each of the first three times. As this rousing speech built to its climax, Milk said, "And now it's time to tell you why I've run so persistently for public office":

> I'll never forget what it was like coming out. I'll never forget the looks on the faces of those who have lost *hope,* whether it be young gays, or seniors, or blacks looking for that almost-impossible-to-find job, or Latin[o]s trying to explain their problems and aspirations in a tongue that's foreign to them. I'll never forget that people are more important than buildings, and neighborhoods are more important than freeways. I've deliberately scheduled this announcement for Gay Pride Week. I've watched a million people close their closet doors behind them and I know they cannot go back. ... These were strong people ... people whose faces I knew from the shops, the streets, the meetings, and people whom I never saw before, but who I knew. They were strong and even they needed hope ... and those young gays in Des Moines who are "coming out" and hear the Anita Bryant story [of taking away our rights and protections]—to them the only thing that they have to look forward to is hope. And *YOU* have to give them hope. Hope for a

better world. Hope for a better tomorrow. Hope for a place to go to if the pressures at home are too great. Hope that all will be alright. Without *hope* not only the gays but the blacks, the seniors, the poor, the handicapped, the US's give up ... if you help me get elected, that election. No, it is not my election, it is yours—will mean that a green light is lit. A green light that says to all who feel lost and disenfranchised that you now can go forward—it means *hope* and we—no you and you and you and, yes, *you* got to give them hope. ("You've Got ...")

Even at the distance of decades, this purple peroration is a moving personal reflection on hope's entailments of vision, struggle, community, and coalition, and a rousing rally cry for queer communication, for embodied action.

It is crucial to understand, again, that Milk was not merely offering a politician's platitude, the sweet nothings of an office-seeker. Milk embodied hope's *labor*—material, situated, performative—as prerequisite of any constitutive claim to hope's futurity. Hope is not passive optimism; it is comprised and performative of modesty, reflexivity, a work ethic, a critical perspective, a recurrent sounding of one's voice, coalition in the interest of what queerness might yet become but not determined in advance. As C. Riley Snorton asserts, hope is

> an orientation toward politics (cultural, electoral, and otherwise), which demonstrates a willingness to engage, even if it seems hopelessly naïve to do so ... forcing us to contend with the political and personal investments we have in belonging, recognition, and legibility. ("New Hope" 88–89)

Hope so conceived enacts what Ramón Rivera-Servera, in his study of late 1990s protest by defenders of San Antonio's Esperanza Peace and Justice Center, calls the "praxis of hope" (102). These hopeful activists embodied and mobilized trauma, memory, sociality, anger, courage, and love (Rivera-Servera ch. 3). As Rivera-Servera observes, such praxis comports with Muñoz's theory of an educated, critical, affective, humble hope.

For Milk, being an activist, an advocate, and a leader instilled hope because it was a coalitional mission, embodied action. Building bridges from community to community, as he described it, and building bridges within communities, across sexuality, gender, race, ethnicity, and income, was prerequisite and vital to transformation and success. Karma Chávez calls this "differential belonging," or a coalitional subjectivity that

> engenders a refusal to make a perceived audience comfortable by privileging mostly white and middle class citizens. Instead differential belonging involves a commitment to political alliances based on human and labor rights/violations, and connections built on overtly challenging racism, xenophobia, and homophobia. (*Queer* 144)

As Milk said in 1976, "When we have common battles, we have to fight together. I think that's what Harvey Milk stands for."

Such labor, bridging, belonging also entails critical reflexivity-in-futurity, such as is found in this blogger's suggested grounds of optimism within the fraught 2014 racial context of Ferguson:

> The issue at hand is that we have a situation in our society where the behavior of black people, and black young males particularly, is more likely to be regarded as criminal and dangerous than the same behavior in non-black people. And where those black people are more likely to suffer death or unnecessary levels of violence for that behavior. It is still unclear to me why with all the evidence around us we refuse to admit that this is true. There is so much hope in the admission. We have the power to do something about it. (Mitchell par. 20)

It is also important to contextually remember that Milk's most quoted comment on hope—"The important thing is not that we cannot live on hope alone, but that life is not worth living without it"—was uttered in his first major address as City Supervisor, an incisive systemic analysis and critique, and call to coalition and action, entitled "A City of Neighborhoods" (172).

Milk's hope, then, is critical reflection and deliberation; Milk's hope is taking a stand; Milk's hope is humility and empathy and collaboration, across difference. Milk understood his influence in office and on the streets by example and through restlessness about the always ongoing work yet to be done: an apt definition of social movement, an apt definition of hope.

Candor

Hope's enactment and fulfillment begins with, is sustained by, and can only provisionally culminate through candor. In a Western rhetorical tradition that has prized and inculcated prudence and civility, candor may be the queerest of rhetorical commitments and practices. Milk's philosophy and performance of candor most significantly emerged through his passionate espousal of coming out. Milk believed that this act of declaration and disclosure, intimacy and identity, vital visibility, was crucial to political progress, to eroding the stranglehold of homophobia, to creating bonds across multiple and diverse communal boundaries. As Milk urged in a speech he delivered in Dallas in June 1978, amid escalating death threats because of his own candid sexuality and activism:

> [I]t's important that you come out to everybody that you know—to your relatives, to your friends, to your next door neighbor, to the person you work with, to the people in the restaurants you eat in, and to the people in the store where you shop. So that they know it's not the rights of some gay people, but it's your personal rights that they're discussing. ("Keynote" 210)

Coming out, as Milk understood and lived it, is about openness, self, community, productive exposure, and transformative discomfort (Gross; Seidman). Candor from this perspective served as a chief antidote to bigotry, and the grounds upon which to thwart discrimination and violence against LGBTQ peoples.

The meanings, doings, and valuing of coming out has changed in the nearly four decades since Milk made it a mantra and mandate. Queer interventions have usefully challenged many of the premises on which coming out as a personal and political act rests. Yet, I would argue that coming out remains a worldmaking act in the twenty-first century in the United States. To offer one anecdote (without any claim to its representativeness), in the fall of 2009 my 31-year-old sister Mary Kate anxiously called me on a Sunday afternoon from the parking lot of M&T Bank Stadium in my hometown Baltimore, where she and her girlfriend had been escorted out of the Ravens football game by Charm City's finest for having kissed in public, having refused to stop kissing when they were told by security to "stop making a scene." (Heterosexual couples, Mary Kate and Nic insisted while being escorted out, were similarly expressing affection without such harassment). Adding insult to injury, the pretext for their ejection was that they had stolen empty plastic cups at the concession stand. LGBTQ people have a long history of being labeled an affront to public decency and of being legally and illegally disciplined as criminals; despite many political advances, such silencing and containment, all too frequently violent, still happen, more often than you'd think, and still make for harrowing and humiliating experiences that most often render LGBTQ victims mute.

The statistics are harrowing, or should be. I should also tell you that my sister, at the time, was partially yet substantially in the closet. But that moment transformed her. Mary Kate asked me to contact the local gay press, which I did, and when her story gained unexpected media attention, she came out in order to speak out against homophobia—as it happened, in the gay press such as *Baltimore Out Loud* and the *Washington Blade*, on ABC as well as on FOX News, in the *Baltimore Sun* and *Huffington Post*, and in other outlets. There was some trembling, of course, on my part as well as hers (a local news reporter outed her to our parents through an unanticipated phone call), but Mary Kate had found her voice in the courageous act of coming out and speaking out. A brother's love: I'm not sure I've ever been prouder to be queer.

Acts of coming out and being out in one's performance(s) of gender and sexuality are still queer courageous performative and strategic enactments of self, love, justice, community, protest, pleasure, and memory through expression, touch, dialogue, debate, movement, recognition, performance by going public in domains large and small, not necessarily as an essentialized identity but in whatever complex, messy, flawed, fascinating, vexing, sexy, humbling, inspiring being that one is, does, aspires to be. Earlier, lasting theories and articulations of the closet and coming out have been powerfully undone and reconfigured in relation to sexuality, race, trans/gender, class, trans/nationality, health, and ability. Cultural and political contexts of precarity, survival, and thriving that shape visibility, discretion, surveillance, discipline have been historicized and foregrounded, especially those not central to the experience of white, middle-class gay men (Chávez, *Queer Migration Politics* ch. 3; McCune; Snorton, *Nobody is Supposed to Know*; Decena). Critiques of a presumptively dated, privileged closet paradigm, however, does not disqualify *public candor*—its rhetorical complexity and affective force, arresting, enraging, catalytic, transformative; it is typically characterized as ill-advised and inferior to diplomacy, back-channeling, the-better-left-unspoken; from my perspective, it is indispensable—as a key resource of queer political potentiality. This is what I had in mind, for instance, when in a 2008 speech at a protest rally against Prop 8 and worker exploitation in San Diego, I invoked Milk memory:

> One of [Harvey Milk's] key principles was that in order to fight one must come out. And I think he meant a couple of things by that. The first thing that he meant, of course, is that you can't fight against discrimination and exploitation if you're in the closet. But he also meant ... that you have to be out about your politics. (qtd. in Gunn and Lucaites 404)

My protest performance on that occasion in San Diego was only possible because of a longer political emergence through radically particular but culturally situated processes, engagements, utterances, and embodiments of "coming out," from the late 1980s forward. And in particular, the espousal of public candor in 2008 was precipitated and enabled by my quite unexpected enactment of it while on the faculty of Boston College in 2007. Six weeks after receiving tenure (because I promised my partner I would not jeopardize our material security), I spoke out on campus in a public address against the administration's amply manifested homophobia. Here is what I said in part that evening, specifically what was deemed the offending passage—without the names this time, for I'd rather not have to seek legal counsel, again:

> We must not only be out but *call out*, call out the homophobia that degrades and pinions us, coerces us into less of a life intellectually, emotionally, and spiritually than is granted to straight members of this community. This requires vigilant and vocal attention and response to any act, in word or deed, which does violence to us. ... And, whether or not we like it, that means *naming names*, naming our community's chief homophobes, those responsible for making BC an unsafe place for GLBT students, faculty, and staff. ... Shame on them for their bigotry, packaged disingenuously in the rhetoric of Catholic doctrine and faith. Shame on us for not pressing them on these issues with the same vigor with which we claim to love one another.

In response to my speech, beginning the very next morning and lasting nearly three months, the administration twice came after me with the threat of a lawsuit for defamation of character, twice the insinuation of a university grievance, a demand for an explicit apology I would not give, and the experience of being officially censured for what was called my "uncivil discourse."

My story, of course, must be understood contextually in relation to multiple privileges, affordances, and experiences, but the centrality to it of candor, the ongoing relevance of "closetness" and its complex history, offers much to any consideration of queer rhetorics and gives broader meaning, if in the same spirit, to Milk's victory speech in November 1977, when winning for him was just the beginning of candor's promise: "This is only the first step. The next step, the more important step, is for all those ... who did not come out, for whatever reasons, to do so now. ... the coming out of a nation will smash the myths once and for all" (qtd. in Shilts 250).

Recruitment

Among the queer rewards of hope and candor, and a queer rhetorical modality in its own right, is *recruitment*. Milk would often begin a speech with the declaration, "My name is Harvey Milk and I'm here to recruit you," followed by his giggling and audience laughter, if it were a LGBTQ audience. This was nervous laughter because Milk and his LGBTQ brothers and sisters knew too well the vicious and insidious scapegoating that smeared the queers as those who brainwashed and molested the young. For at least eight decades, a pernicious associative logic, conflation conspicuous for its "studied imprecision," has linked homosexuality, pedophilic predation and despoilment, and social contagion (Harris 151). Queer religion scholar Mark Jordan observes that "[t]he most effective American rhetoric for condemning civil or religious toleration of homosexuality has repeatedly warned of dangers to the young" (Jordan xiii). As this old canard goes, homosexual degeneracy inherently embodies desire for the vulnerable young, compulsion sated by their allurement and molestation. In turn, traumatic infection and indoctrination during this particularly formative life phase thus convert the victim into a debauched existence, including a future of corrupting queer evangelism. Such predation, construed collectively as a cause and culturally as a threatening effect, was labeled in 1949 "the vicious circle of proselytism"; in our own time, it is known as "the gay agenda" (Herman 78–80; Jenkins 63; Sears and Osten). According to cultural anthropologist Roger Lancaster, the logic of recruitment is so "loosely construed" that "it need not involve any physical contact. The mere presence of homosexuals in the vicinity of children ... would confuse children and divert them from the path of normal heterosexuality" (42–43). Queer theorist W. C. Harris argues that with homosexual recruitment, "visibility itself constitutes proselytizing" (153).

As his LGBTQ audiences knew, Milk's recruitment "joke" was deadly serious in its political message: "We must let them know that we are not child molesters. ... we must dispel the myths. ... we must talk about that, we must talk about those issues on a one-to-one basis" ("Keynote" 210). But here, too, is what Milk also meant by "recruitment": a handshake, a laugh together, a serious face-to-face conversation, perhaps especially with someone who didn't already identify as LGBTQ or know LGBTQ people, especially someone who believed the lies that circulated, tarnished, and endangered LGBTQ people. And, I want to emphasize, recruitment was a local, intimate rhetorical project with rippling implications. If I have one lament about reviews of *An Archive of Hope*, which have been mostly laudatory, it's that some engage in a fundamental misunderstanding of Milk's recruitment politics. Daniel Cohen wrote in his otherwise favorable review in the *Times Literary Supplement* that "Despite his growing profile at the time of his death, [Milk] was fundamentally a local politician, and the documents that concentrate on city politics are of limited interest today" (27). Cohen is missing the good stuff; the "local" of the past matters more than Cohen suggests, and it is a matter of memory work that that purchase be amply conveyed. Milk remarked in 1978:

> History is made by events ... sometimes by large events with the world watching, but mostly by small events which plant the seeds of change. A reading of the Declaration of Independence on the steps of a building is widely covered. The events that started the American Revolution were the meetings in homes, pubs, on street corners. ("Milk Stool")

Harvey Milk's words teach us that successful activists *speak* locally, that the art of queer activist eloquence should be measured by the singularity of each ordinary persuasive opportunity, quotidian audience, fleeting performance. Milk's purple passages and stump clichés teach us that hope's discourse, at close hearing by real people, is by turns and toil both sublime and hackneyed in situ. And with each of those hit-or-miss moments of rhetorical invention and embodiment, with each handshake, with each overbearing exchange, shameless self-promotion, flirtation, corny joke, and lump-in-the-throat moment when he was on a roll, Milk brought the LGBTQ folk of San Francisco that much closer to sexual justice and freedom, to gay rights. Milk campaign staffer Jim Rivaldo remembered, "I accompanied Harvey around the city and saw how readily people from all walks of life responded to an openly gay man with good ideas and an extraordinary gift for communicating them" (Rivaldo 40).

Let me offer one example. It is often not part of the standard narrative of the Coors Boycott, often dated to the nationwide boycott begun by the AFL-CIO in 1977, that its roots are traceable to Teamster and California Coors Boycott Director Allan Baird's seeking out of Harvey Milk and an unsung gay hero named Howard Wallace in 1974–1975 to gain gay support, along with Arab and Chinese grocers, of beer drivers' strike against six distributors (Milk, "Milk Forum"; Shilts 83–84, 93–94). Milk asked for union jobs for gays, not Baird's endorsement for his supervisor campaign in return. And with the exception of holdout Coors, they succeeded, leading to an expanded boycott of Coors. As gay chronicler Randy Shilts observed, Baird was impressed by Milk's no-bullshit approach, organizing acumen, and broader vision that included, for instance, equal outrage concerning Coors's discrimination against the Latino community. Milk, in turn, relished "the symbolism of tying gays to the conservative Teamsters union" (Shilts 83). It is also noteworthy, as reported in a number of accounts, that Baird endured homophobic slurs on the job and in the neighborhood for his work with Milk and the gay community. It is well known that Milk's vision for gay economic and political power centrally depended on bridge building among diverse communities throughout the city. As he wrote in his Milk Forum column "Reactionary Beer" in the gay weekly *Bay Area Reporter* in March 1976:

> Here is a way that the gay community could show its economic power. It is not too hard to switch brands of beer. (After the second one, not too many people can really tell the difference …). The point: if the gay community continues, even leads, the boycott, then the Spanish and labor groups fighting Coors will understand who their friends are and what it means to join together in fighting for a common goal, ending discrimination. The point: we will also be building bridges with others who in turn will aid us in our fight for equal rights.

Such local acts of recruitment and resistance led to national consequences for the national Coors Boycott, lessons still vital today, from BDS to #BlackLivesMatter. Milk and others performed, on the streets and at union meetings and in gay bars, the necessary local work within the larger injustice frame, within the overarching logic of antidiscrimination as a ground for coalition politics, to undermine homophobic, racist, sexist, and classist obstacles to such a common vision. In other words, anecdotal accounts of Milk's stump efforts to undermine homophobic stereotypes at union meetings, or similar accounts of Baird's jamming of homophobic exchange with his colleagues and neighbors, must figure in combination with eloquent espousals of bridge-building against discrimination in any account of these boycotts.

Milk Continued

Having now conjured Milk memory for the purposes of LGBTQ worldmaking presence and futurity, I want to close by returning to the *where* and *please* problems of LGBTQ memory and history. In addition to sounding the familiar droning regarding mnemonic moth-erosion of complacency and indifference, I want to warn, too, of the acids of mnemonicide (Morris 93–120), and not the typical homophobic threat that first comes to mind. Milk's legacy in this regard is no different from that of so many other, perhaps most, cases of consequential collective memory: shared interest becomes selfish self-interest; propulsion becomes proprietary interference; insistence and obstinacy regarding a particular variation on the past, rotten with perfection, spoils it. I would offer, as a close observer of Milk memory politics since 2007, and now in my own experience as one of those surprisingly few memory agents directly involved in the circulation of the Milk archive, that Milk's inheritance is becoming increasingly treated as capital, with the lamentable misunderstanding of the possession of Milk's legacy as the fortune of the possessor rather than that of LGBTQ communities and worldmaking writ large. Such calculation, competition, callousness—not that it matters to the perpetrators in such circumstances—was antithetical to Milk's own lived activism.

And Milk would also prompt us to scrutinize the more benign but no less consequential violence of synecdoche. Milk insisted that he couldn't possibly symbolize all LGBTQ people, which is to say emphatically that there are so many other LGBTQ archives to plumb and so many other stories to tell. At the Books, Inc. event in 2013, activist Michael Petrelis during Q&A chided the audience that in San Francisco there was a surplus of Milk commemoration, while he could think of only two plaques in the city memorializing lesbian community members—the late bar owner Rikki Streicher at the Eureka Valley Recreation Center and Jane Warner Plaza, named for the police officer who had died of cancer. I'm reminded of Horacio Roque Ramírez's heartening and heartbreaking accounts in his essay, "A Living Archive of Desire," recovering and circulating queer Latino communal memory, in particular that of legendary San Francisco performer Teresita la Campesina. And who knows the story of Compton's Cafeteria? (The obfuscation of which in LGBTQ history spurred trans* scholar and activist Susan Stryker to conceptualize "homonormativity"—before Lisa Duggan's important iteration of that critique). And that's just in the urban center of San Francisco. Earnest and laudable memory work on gay, white, middle-class men should continue, but not in decimation of copious, diverse, intersectional engagements with and circulation of the past.

In closing, I'd like to return to a particular manifestation of Milk memory's queer futurity. We might imagine together that Amelia's 8-year-old gay son, in the not-too-distant future and amid important life changes, might become Max Geschwind, a 16-year-old from Los Angeles (Geschwind). After seeing the film *Milk*, Max interned at West Hollywood City Hall, an experience deepened by being assigned to the planning committee for that year's Harvey Milk Day celebrations. So inspired was Max that, already an aspiring filmmaker, he began work on his own tribute, interviewing the mayor of West Hollywood, Council members, and activists who had known and worked with Milk. The *Milk Effect*, as this moving film is called, captured the heart of his school and caught the eye of Dustin Lance Black, the screenwriter who won an Academy Award for the film *Milk* and who said in his 2009 acceptance speech:

> When I was 13 years old. ... I heard the story of Harvey Milk. And it gave me hope. It gave me the hope to live my life, it gave me the hope

> to one day live my life openly as who I am and that maybe even I could fall in love and one day get married. ... If Harvey had not been taken from us 30 years ago, I think he'd want me to say to all of the gay and lesbian kids out there tonight who have been told that they are less than by their churches or by the government or by their families that you are beautiful, wonderful creatures of value and that no matter what anyone tells you, God does love you and that very soon, I promise you, you will have equal rights, federally, across this great nation of ours.

Black met with Max and encouraged him to raise funding to get the film screened—which premiered on Harvey Milk Day and was thus eligible for the Academy's consideration. Although *The Milk Effect* didn't make the final cut for Best Documentary Short, that's not what mattered most about making the film. Max explains:

> The film concludes with a recitation of Harvey's famous "Hope" speech—I had 16 of my friends at my high school recite the speech as a poignant reminder about the next generation of leaders. This part of the film made me extremely proud of the work I had done. For me, this is the most important part of the film because I hope to show the audience that Harvey's message has not died out and that there is a whole new generation of innovative, miraculous, outstanding leaders that can carry out Harvey's messages of equal rights to their cities, counties, states, or even their countries. My classmates were very excited to participate in a project like this one mainly because they had never seen a fellow high school student take on the challenge of such a big and mature topic. They were also proud of me and the work I accomplished. (Geschwind 112)

Amelia's son and Max remind me of Milk's reflections in an interview he gave after finally winning his historic seat on the Board of Supervisors in November 1977:

> When the mayor asked me a year ago what my motivation was, I told him that I remember what it was like to be 14 and Gay. I know that somewhere today there is a 14 year old child who discovers that he or she is Gay and learns that the family may throw that child out of the house. The police will harass that child. The state will say that the child is a criminal and that the intelligence of the Anita Bryants will be screaming at that child. Maybe that child read in the newspaper, "Homosexual Elected in San Francisco," and that child has two options: move to San Francisco or stay in San Antonio or Des Moines and fight. The child has hope. ("Harvey Speaks Out" 161)

Milk's legacy is manifested in these latter-day cases, but as Max and Amelia and the teacher in her son's second-grade classroom make plain, hope requires humility, reflexivity, commitment, work, voice, collaboration, and coalition. My hope is that queers will allow themselves to be recruited and recruit others, that we will find our candid voices and come out, speak out, mobilize Milk memory or some other, and make something of its vibrant presence. As Muñoz envisioned it, "What we need to know is that queerness is not yet here but it approaches like a crashing wave of potentiality. And we must give in to its propulsion, its status as a destination. Willingly we let ourselves feel queerness's pull, knowing it as something else that we can feel, that we must feel" (185). My hope is that we'll chart collectively the as-yet-unrealized possibilities of queer futurity. Long live Harvey Milk!

Acknowledgments

The author thanks generous audiences at previous lectures, as well as Jason Black, Jacqueline Rhodes, Jonathan Alexander, and Albert Rintrona for their valuable responses and advice. As always, this queer work matters most because of the support of Scott Rose.

Works Cited

Amelia. "When My 8-Year-Old Gay Son Taught His Class about Harvey Milk." *The Huffington Post*, 28 Mar. 2013. Web. 3 Jan. 2015.

Black, Dustin Lance. "Academy Awards Acceptance Speech." glad.org. New York. 22 Feb. 2009. Web. 4 Jan. 2015.

Black, Jason E., and Charles E. Morris III, eds. *An Archive of Hope: Harvey Milk's Speeches and Writings*. Berkeley: U of California P, 2013. Print.

Chávez, Karma R. *Queer Migration Politics: Activist Rhetoric and Coalitional Possibilities*. Urbana-Champaign: U of Illinois P, 2013. Print.

Cohen, Daniel. "Review of an Archive of Hope: Harvey Milk's Speeches and Writings." *Times Literary Supplement* 19 July 2013. 27. Print.

Decena, Carlos Ulises. *Tacit Subjects: Belonging and Same-Sex Desire among Dominican Immigrant Men*. Durham, NC: Duke UP, 2011.

Greschwind, Max. "Why I Created a Film about Harvey Milk." *QED: A Journal in GLBTQ Worldmaking* 1.1 (2013): 111–13. Print.

Gross, Larry. *Contested Closets: The Politics and Ethics of Outing*. Minneapolis: U of Minnesota P, 1993. Print.

Gunn, Joshua, and John Lucaites. "The Contest of Faculties: On Discerning the Social Engagement in the Academy." *Quarterly Journal of Speech* 96.4 (2010): 404–12. Print.

Harris, W.C. *Queer Externalities: Hazardous Encounters in American Culture*. Albany: State U of New York P, 2009. Print.

Herman, Didi. *The Antigay Agenda: Orthodox Vision and the Christian Right*. Chicago: U of Chicago P, 1997. Print.

"Homosexual on Board Cites Role as Pioneer." *New York Times* 10 Nov. 1977. 24. Print.

Jenkins, Philip. *Moral Panic: Changing Concepts of the Child Molester in Modern America*. New Haven, CT: Yale UP, 1998. Print.

Jordan, Mark D. *Recruiting Young Love: How Christians Talk about Homosexuality*. Chicago: U of Chicago P, 2011. Print.

Lancaster, Roger N. *Sex Panic and the Punitive State*. Berkeley: U of California P, 2011. Print.
McCune, Jeffery Q., Jr. *Sexual Discretion: Black Masculinity and the Politics of Passing*. Chicago: U of Chicago P, 2014. Print.
Milk, Harvey. "A City of Neighborhoods: First Major Address I and II." In Black and Morris 166–72.
———. "Harvey Speaks Out." In Black and Morris 159–65.
———. "Keynote Speech at Gay Conference 5." In Black and Morris 197–210.
———. "Milk Forum: Teamsters Seek Gay Help." *Bay Area Reporter* 27 Nov. 1974. 2. Print.
———. "On the Milk Stool." *Coast to Coast*. Clippings. 17 May 1978. Box 26, folder #GLC35. Milk-Smith Collection, Harvey Milk Archives, The James C. Hormel Gay & Lesbian Center of the San Francisco Public Library, San Francisco, CA. Accessed 7–11 August 2007.
———. "Political Will." In Black and Morris 245–49.
———. "Reactionary Beer." In Black and Morris 124–26.
———. "You've Got to Have Hope" speech. 24 June 1977. Box 9, series 2D. Milk-Smith Collection, Harvey Milk Archives, The James C. Hormel Gay & Lesbian Center of the San Francisco Public Library, San Francisco, CA. Accessed 7–11 August 2007.
Mitchell, Colleen. "Things I Don't Mean When I Say #BlackLivesMatter." *blessedarethefeet.com*. Mitchell Colleen. 15 Dec. 2014. Web. 3 Jan. 2015.
Morris, Charles E., III. "My Old Kentucky Homo: Abraham Lincoln, Larry Kramer, and the Politics of Queer Memory." *Queering Public Address: Sexualities in American Historical Discourse*. Ed. Charles E. Morris III: Columbia: U of South Carolina P, 2007. 93–120. Print.
Morris, Charles E., III, and Jason Edward Black. "Preface." Black and Morris xi–xiv.
Muñoz, José Esteban. *Cruising Utopia: The Then and There of Queer Futurity*. New York: New York UP, 2009. Print.
Rivaldo, Jim, "Remembering How Harvey Milk Helped Pave the Way." *Bay Area Reporter* 21 Jun. 2001. 40. Print.
Rivera-Servera, Ramón H. *Performing Queer Latinidad: Dance, Sexuality, Politics*. Ann Arbor: U of Michigan P, 2012.
Roque Ramírez, Horacio N. "A Living Archive of Desire: Teresita La Campesina and the Embodiment of Queer Latino Community Histories." *Archive Stories: Facts, Fictions, and the Writing of History*. Ed. Antoinette Burton. Durham, NC: Duke UP, 2005. 111–35. Print.
Sears, Alan, and Craig Osten. *The Homosexual Agenda: Exposing the Principal Threat to Religious Freedom Today*. Nashville: B&H, 2003. Print.
Seidman, Steven. *Beyond the Closet: The Transformation of Gay and Lesbian Life*. New York: Routledge, 2012. Print.
Shilts, Randy. *The Mayor of Castro Street: The Life and Times of Harvey Milk*. New York: St. Martin's, 2008. Print.
Snorton, C. Riley. "'A New Hope': The Psychic Life of Passing." *Hypatia* 24.3 (2009): 77–92. Print.
Snorton, C. Riley. *Nobody Is Supposed to Know: Black Sexuality on the Down Low*. Minneapolis: U of Minnesota P, 2014. Print.

Part II
Troubling Identity

7 The Trope of the Closet
David L. Wallace

Closeting as an identity concept has begun to get traction beyond the basic notion of lesbians, gay men, bisexuals, and trans people coming out of their heteronormative and gender-restricted closets to claim their previously hidden sexual identities or gender expressions. For example, in popular cable television series, characters come out or consider coming out as vampires, shifters, werewolves, and faeries (*True Blood*), as dead (*American Horror Story*), as a serial killer (*Dexter*), and as a high school chemistry teacher turned crack manufacturer (*Breaking Bad*). One can come out as an atheist in a predominantly Judeo-Christian context, as a witch out of the broom closet, as biracial or multiracial, as someone who has had plastic surgery, or as a participant in BDSM sexual practices. Indeed, the trope of the closet has become so well known that Anne Ruggles Gere has argued that:

> [c]oming out as a Christian or an observant member of any faith can be as dangerous as making public one's sexual orientation because the academy has so completely conflated the disestablishment of religion (which opened the way for Jews, Catholics, and agnostics) with secularizing (banishing religion altogether) higher education. (Symposium Collective 47)

In this chapter, I argue that the trope of the closet is critical to an exploration of sexual rhetorics most obviously because it is the one of the dominant ways that homosexuality has a different rhetorical function from heterosexuality. However, the trope of the closet is also more generally useful as a tool to bring other aspects of identity to awareness—some of which may be sexual and some of which may not be. Because the trope of the closet exists only when liminality is invoked to some degree, it is a natural tool for exploring anything—but particularly anything sexual—that falls outside usual expectations and must be actively articulated to have presence in discourse.

The trope of the closet is an important sexual rhetoric, at least for LGBT people, because of the continued existence of the underlying epistemology that continues to pathologize sexual identities and gender expressions that are deemed non-normative. Understanding the operation of the trope of the closet is useful not only because it allows us to better understand the general process of bringing the invisible or unacknowledged into discourse but also because it can help us to understand that not all closets are the same. The appropriation of this trope in the service of identity issues beyond sexual identity and gender expression carries with it the danger of hollowing the meaning of the epistemology of the closet. Particularly important in this regard is reflecting carefully on the difference between the relatively rare and localized effect that Gere mentions and more systemic identity issues like homosexuality that are problematized broadly in culture and may involve not just social discomfort in a limited setting but legal restrictions of civil rights. Despite this danger, there is real potential for those who have felt pressure not to make some part of our essential nature public to use the concepts of *closeting* and *coming out* to better understand our own and others' experiences.

At its most basic level the trope of the closet works simply to bring into discourse something (e.g., homosexuality) that was invisible or visible but unacknowledged. This function fits the definition of a trope throughout much of Western rhetoric and is crystallized by Hugh Blair as a word being used "to signify something that is different from its original and primitive meaning; so that if you alter the word, you destroy the figure" (963). For Blair, tropes are necessary because "[n]o language is so copious, as to have a separate word for every separate idea," and they too often abound (particularly in what he saw as underdeveloped languages) "plainly owning to the want of proper words (964). What Blair's approach to tropes misses, at least in terms of the trope of the closet, is that simply having a word (e.g., "homosexuality") does not change the underlying epistemology that created the closet and makes the trope necessary. This effect is better captured in Frederick Nietzsche's notion of tropes as tools that rhetors use to manage the layers of metaphor inherent in language and rhetoric. He notes, "all words are tropes in themselves" (Gilman, Blair, and Parents 23), and meaning-making is by nature conventional:

> What is usually called language is actually all figuration. Language is created by the individual speech artist, but it is determined by the fact that the taste of the many makes choices. Only very few individual utter *schemata* [figures] whose *virtus* [virtue, worth] becomes a guide for many.
> (Gilman et al. 25)

Nietzsche's understanding of all language as conventional, as tropic in some sense, makes it clear that in some cases what has not been present in discourse—what has been closeted—is not absent by accident but by prior agreement or convention.

Nietzsche's approach to language and to tropes prefigures the postmodern turn in rhetoric by arguing that language does not represent a fixed reality in the one-to-one way that Blair aspired to, but rather language helps to construct reality. The danger in this postmodern turn is that it can erase the roles that language and discursive conventions play in maintaining systems of marginalization. The logic goes like this: because all meaning is conventional and is both subject to deconstruction and dependent on current use to be continually reconstructed, then any knowledge, discourse, or value (even problematic ones) can be deconstructed and changed. Although this is certainly true, it does not go far enough because it does not explicitly account for the fact that the agency one brings to such acts of deconstruction and reconstruction are constrained by previous constructions that place some in visibly marginalized positions and others in closeted positions that require additional rhetorical work to achieve agency.

Henry Louis Gates captures this additional function is his description of signifyin[g] as a master trope in African American rhetoric. He says, "By an act of will, some historically nameless community of remarkably self-conscious speakers of English defined their ontological status as one of profound difference vis-à-vis the rest of society" (47). Further, Gates argues that those who have been marginalized by such systemic equity need to play a rhetorical game that does not seek to be plain to all as a strategy for managing difference. Of course, a critical difference between signifyin(g) and the trope of the closet is that in the former the potential difference issue is nearly always visible while in the latter it is usually invisible or at least unvoiced. However, both begin with the presumption that the marginalized must routinely negotiate problematic epistemologies and the discourse conventions that support them.

In the pages that follow, I first offer principles that unpack the trope of the closet by returning to Eve Sedgwick's discussion of the epistemology of the closet and further exploring connections between closeting and signifyin[g] as master tropes. Then, I explore the ways in which the trope of the closet has begun to function as a kind of master trope that requires additional tropes such as the trope of visibility and the trope of abnormality to better represent the complexities of negotiating closeted identities.

Unpacking the Trope of the Closet

One reason we need to unpack the trope of the closet is that doing so gets to the heart of one kind of rhetoric's transformational power. That is, by putting the previously invisible, dismissed, or unacknowledged into play, we challenge positions of dominance that too often presume a natural order of things. Thus, the trope of the closet is a critical rhetorical tool for exposing and challenging hegemony. Indeed, Sedgwick sees the epistemology of the closet as serving a discursive function in society:

> An assumption underlying the book is that the relations of the closet— the relations of the known and the unknown, the explicit and the inexplicit around homo/heterosexual definition—have the potential for being peculiarly revealing, in fact, about speech acts generally. (3)

In this section, I propose six principles that further delineate the trope of the closet and what it means to come out of a closet.

Principle #1: Closets Have Effects on All

Sedgwick argues that the epistemology of the closet has broad cultural effects that are critical for not only those who are typically closeted. She argues that "any aspect of modern Western culture must be, not merely incomplete, but damaged in its central substance to the degree that it does not incorporate a critical analysis of modern homo/heterosexual definition" (1). Perhaps the easiest example of Sedgwick's point here is how the kinds of gender policing often used to create closets for lesbians and gay men have deleterious effects on straight people as well: men who are discouraged from expressing emotion and having physical intimacy with their own gender and women who are schooled to be ladylike, not to be too aggressive, and to follow rather than lead. Sedgwick's point here is an important one: we all have a stake in the operation of closets, and it is the rare person who is not negatively affected in some way by the range of sociocultural tools used to create and maintain closets. However, both practically and rhetorically, there is an additional effect for those for whom the closet walls off real discourse about a critical feature of identity.

Principle #2: Not All Axes of Marginalization Are Closets

Sedgwick provides help in understanding what counts as a closet in her discussion of how stigmas based on a visible identity feature are different from stigmas that are typically made invisible or unspeakable by closets. She notes that racism, gender, age, size, and physical handicaps are usually (but not always) based on readily seen features of identity and thus would not constitute closets. In contrast, other identity features bear closer resemblance to the closeting function for those whose sexual identities and gender expressions are deemed non-normative:

> Ethnic/cultural/religious oppressions such as anti-Semitism are more analogous in that the stigmatized individual has a least notionally some discretion—although, importantly, it is never to be taken for granted how much—over other people's knowledge of her or his membership in the group: one could "come out as" a Jew or Gypsy, in a heterogeneous urbanized society, much more intelligibly than one could typically "come out as," say, female, Black, old, a wheelchair user or fat. (75)

By Sedgwick's logic, any identity feature that is usually readily visible will not be subject to the particular problems of the epistemology of the closet, although, of course, hosts of other forms of discrimination and prejudice may be associated with that identity feature. A key feature of the trope of the closet, then, is that something must be made visible or moved from the category of the unthinkable or unsayable into discourse. In this sense, closets complicate what it means to take agency for the closeted.

Principle #3: Closeting May Have a Variety of Rhetorical Effects

Undoubtedly, the general effect of closets should largely be seen as negative since they contribute to societal norms that strip those closeted of a critical aspect of identity and, in some cases, of basic civil rights. Thus, the main effect of coming out of the closet is to claim some aspect of identity and to challenge the underlying problematic epistemology—to make the marginalized visible and relevant in discourse. However, in any given situation, closeting may serve other functions. For example, closeting can, at times provide a problematic kind of protection by allowing the closeted person the choice of whether or not to make an aspect of his or her identity part of some interactions. Again, these bits of protection and occasions for rhetorical choice should not be seen as adequate compensation for the many deleterious effects of the epistemology of the closet, but they are central to the trope of the closet. A critical difference in the kinds of discourse used by the closeted to seek social justice and the kinds of discourse used by those whose problematized identity features are readily visible in most situations.

Principle #4: Coming Out of the Closet Is Not a Once for All Act

The usual understanding of coming out of the closet (at least for gay and lesbian people) is that one reveals one's hidden status for the first time often in a dramatic event. However, as important as initial comings out can be, they do not eliminate the closet once and for all. Rather, closets should be seen as porous, as recurring across contexts. Indeed, Sedgwick sees that the act of coming out is never absolute, never final or complete. She says:

> Even at an individual level, there are remarkably few of even the most openly gay people who are not deliberately in the closet with someone personally or economically or institutionally important to them. (67–68)

For Sedgwick, this point is tied to the ubiquity of the closet. She argues that for gay people, sexual identity is not the only important identifying feature, but that for many "it is still the fundamental feature of social life; and there can be few gay people, however courageous and forthright by habit, however fortunate in the support of their immediate communities, in whose lives the closet is not still a shaping presence" (68).

Later theorists have rightly criticized Sedgwick's notion of the closet as being too binary and too tied to an understanding of the hetero/homo divide that does not focus enough on the malleability of sexual identity and its complicated intersections with other identity features such as gender expression. For example, Karen Kopelson has argued for a performative notion of identity that explicitly recognizes that identity is always multiple and continually constructed in discursive acts. From such a perspective, one might argue that we should reject the notion of coming out of the closet, refusing to recreate the problematic binary that requires homosexual people to come out as something different from the presumed heterosexual norm. The difference here is often cast as a distinction between Sedgwick, who is seen as taking an identity-based position, and performative positions *pace* Judith Butler, that take as their mission dismantling problematic binaries. For example, Steven Angelides explains how the mission of queer theory presses beyond the hetero-/homosexual divide that is central to the epistemology of the closet: "Instead of reifying sexual identity categories, queer theory takes as its project the task of exposing the operations of *heteronormativity* in order to work the hetero-homosexual opposition to the point of critical collapse" (168).

Here a distinction between the goals of rhetorical theory and queer theory may be useful. Rhetorical theory, even when it is working in the interests of social justice, would not presume that one can always work at the point of critical collapse. From the standpoint of Angelides and other queer theorists, it might be tempting to argue that the trope of the closet must be fundamentally flawed because it stems from the identity-based distinction made in the epistemology of the closet. However, the discourse practices by which heteronormativity may be challenged and deconstructed rarely occur within the rarefied air of critical theory.

Principle #5: Not All Closets Are the Same

The trope may be used productively in a limited sense for bringing to the fore issues that are not normally closeted but may be invisible or difficult to discuss in specific contexts. However, in doing so, two things are important: (1) recognizing the fluidity and malleability of closets and (2) not trivializing closeting that is both more systemic and that usually involves negotiating potentially detrimental identity issues on a regular, often daily, basis. For example, Gere's claim that coming out as a practicing member of a faith may be more difficult than coming out as a lesbian in some academic contexts illustrates that the values that are generally attached to the homo/hetero binary and the practicing Christian/nonreligious binaries are not absolute; indeed, they are reversed in the situation she describes. However, in using this example, Gere fails to discuss two important differences: the scope of the underlying problematic epistemology and the severity of the effects of that epistemology. Clearly, coming out as a practicing Christian in the United States is not generally necessary; thus, Gere uses the trope of the closet in a narrowly defined setting and, likely, as an occasional strategy rather than as a defining rhetorical feature of her typical discourse with others. Further, Gere also fails to address the likely difference in possible deleterious effects between coming out as a practicing Christian and a lesbian. Freedom of religion is guaranteed in the Bill of Rights; to date, lesbians have no such universal guarantee of civil rights. Indeed, in many states and many universities, LGTB people enjoy no protection of their civil rights and may be legally discriminated against. This example suggests that although the trope of the closet may be a useful tool for understanding how various things that are erased and unacknowledged may be meaningfully brought into discourse, it will be important to tease out differences in the underlying epistemologies of those closets and to do so in ways that respect differences by choosing not to oversimplify them.

Principle #6: Strategies for Negotiating Closets May Not Result in Clarity for All Involved

Discursive strategies for dealing with the implications of the epistemology of closets may function in ways similar to Gates's description of the African American signifyin[g] tropes that "luxuriate in the chaos of ambiguity that repetition and difference (be that apparent difference centered in the signifier or in the signified, in the 'sound-image' or in the concept) yield in either an aural or a visual pun" (45). Gates distinguishes between *signification* in standard English, which "denotes the meaning that a term conveys, or is intended to convey" (46) and signifyin(g) as "the black trope of tropes, the figure for black rhetorical figures" (51) in which double-voicedness is used to negotiate identity relations that are not made explicit to all parties. For example, he explains, "Teaching one's children the fine art of Signifyin(g) is to teach them about this mode of linguistic circumnavigation, to teach them a second language that they can share with other black people" (76).

There is similar play in signifyin(g)—particularly between those in the know and those not—and in closeting: something is unspoken in each, and in each something may be unknown to at least one party. As I discuss in more detail in the next section, the stance that both signifyin(g) and the trope of the closet take against problematic epistemologies is the basis for each to serve as master tropes that underlie and, in some sense, sponsor other related tropes. One critical difference between the two is that the one doing the signifying is presumed to be always in the know about the play, whereas the fellow participant may or may not be in the know. The trope of the closet also may manage a power and a knowledge difference, but having someone explicitly in the know is not a requirement—both parties may ignore homosexuality or alternative gender expression. The queer person may hide queerness, or, in the case of the transparent closet, the queer person may be the last to be in the know.

The Closet as a Queer Master Trope

In the popular and socially progressive network television show *Glee*, Kurt, a flamboyant male character, has a scene in which he stumbles to come out to his father:

KURT: Dad ... I have something I want to say. I'm glad that you are proud of me ... but I don't want to lie any more. Being part of the Glee club and football has really shown me that I can be anything. And ... what I am ... is ... I'm gay.

BURT: [flatly] I know.
KURT: Really?!
BURT: I've known since you were three. All you wanted for your birthday was a pair of sensible heels. ("Transparent")

As someone who first said that I was gay to someone who mattered to me at age 36, this description of the trope of the transparent or invisible closet rings true to my own experience, as there were many people in my life simply waiting for me to be ready to talk with them about my sexual identity. Of course there were others who were surprised, and still others who were not pleased to have their suspicions confirmed. For me, an important moment in the process of my initial coming out centered around talking about my sexual identity with my three siblings and choosing not to talk about it with my father (my mother and I had a moment of understanding several years earlier just before she died). Two of my siblings responded much as Kurt's fictional father did, having been prepared for the moment by spouses to accept me; the third cried for 45 minutes and worked her way through every gay lifestyle and choice stereotype before settling into a don't-ask-or-tell-me-any-more *détente* with me. All three of my siblings soundly criticized me for my decision not to tell my father, who, predictably, felt hurt and excluded when he found out through other means.

I begin this section with the trope of the transparent closet and with one of my own coming-out stories because I feel compelled to account for my own identity as I take positions about the trope of the closet because my lived experiences matter both in what motivates me to take these stances and in what I see as the relevant issues. As a smart, tall, thin, highly educated, white, middle-class man, I enjoy a great deal of privilege in US culture. However, I also spent two decades deconstructing my version of the closet—largely constructed in the culture of evangelical Christianity and in a rural western Pennsylvania community in which LGBT people were visible only as aberrations or dismissible freaks. Not surprisingly, many people I met, including two my siblings' spouses, were able to read me as gay sooner, without judgment, and with much more ease than anyone in my immediate family. Thus, in this example, I illustrate how the epistemology of the closet affected all of us in my family—delaying for many years an explicit understanding of an essential part of who I am, and, in my dad's case, that effect continues. It is important to note here that I could tell many, many stories here—that even though I have had a long, successful career as an academic and even though I am now the dean of a large college, the closet continues to be a presence for me—something that I must negotiate on a daily basis. In a very real sense, the trope of the closet remains the master trope of my life, even though it no longer causes me to deny a central part of who I am and even though I am practiced at dealing with most of its effects.

What I tried to help my siblings understand was that I saw my dad—who said from his literal pulpit that AIDS was God's punishment on gay people—as perhaps the single most important contributor to the construction of my closet. They argued that he had changed or that he had a right to know. I argued that while two of them had given me hints that it was safe for me to tell them, dad had not done so. Of course, as a recently out person who had read no queer theory, I could not clearly articulate these points, so I felt lost in a frustrating sense of personal relationships I had no real tools to understand. Thus, one reason we need a clearer articulation of the trope of the closet and its many complexities is that this set of rhetorical practices has real transformational power in the lives of LBGT and other people who have had a critical part of their identities packed away in closets. To that end, I turn to two descriptions of the continued operation of the trope of closet: Junxi Qian's exploration of the trope of abnormality in gay public cruising and Gail Mason's exploration of the trope of visibility.

Qian's study of gay public cruising in the People's Park in Guangzhou, China, further illustrates both the continued relevance of Sedgwick's epistemology of the closet and the need to move beyond this single binary in understanding how the trope of the closet works. More specifically, Qian proposes that the *trope of abnormality* operates in complicated ways for gay men who cruise or engage in other activities in the "gay belt" of the People's Park. A central claim in Qian's analysis is that the closet is best understood not in purely binary terms but "in terms of a series of *closeted experiences* produced and reproduced through lived and shifting relations, interactions, and practices" (165).

It is important to remember that the particular set of closeting and coming-out experiences that Qian describes for those who frequent the gay belt of the People's Park occur within a larger historical, sociocultural context in which homosexuality remains largely closeted at a national level. For example, Cao Li reported as recently as 2010 that "it is forbidden by law to refer to homosexuality in films, television shows, or literature" and homosexuality was removed from the country's lists of mental illnesses only in 2001 (2010).

Qian, who worked as a sex educator, conducted interviews with 35 people who frequented the gay section of the park and argues that the act of identifying oneself with the gay section of the park had both positive and negative consequences. Among the positive consequences were a sense of communal identity that included real friendships, a "vibrant social" scene, and, for some, a sense of having a "spiritual home" (158–59). Qian goes so far as to argue that cruising in the park can be read as a kind of empowering subversive activity. However, Qian is equally clear that such activities also entail performing a trope of abnormality: "gay cruisers still need to negotiate the association of homosexuality with shame and deviancy, undergirded by a powerful hetero-/homosexual binary" (157). The aspects of shame are complicated by the fact that the gay belt is also the scene of robbery and prostitution leading many of Qian's subjects to the conclusion "that gay men are destined to be victims of their own desire" (165).

Qian's description of the operation of the trope of abnormality in gay cruising in the People's Park serves as an important reminder that the overt epistemology of the closet is very much alive and well in many contexts despite a general trend in many cultures and countries toward greater acceptance for LBGT people. As I write these words at my local coffee shop, I look up from my laptop and see five large rainbow flags on the walls—leftovers from my community's gay pride celebration, and I am reminded of my social and economic privilege—that closeting is less often an issue for me because I can afford to live in this queer-friendly neighborhood. I am also reminded of Steven Seidman's call for narratives about the lives of LGBT people (134) and of Toni McNaron's call for work on sexual identity that does not "distance itself from the material lives of actual lesbians and gay men" (132). This concern has led me to make myself present in this text, and it often makes me dissatisfied with valuable queer theory that I read because I do not see the authors themselves in their texts and also too seldom see any accounts of the lived experiences of LGBT people in those texts. In this regard, I want to be a voice reminding all of us of the continued relevance of the epistemology of the closet.

In addition to reminding us that the effects of the epistemology of the closet are, for many LGBT people, both persistent and overwhelmingly negative, Qian's trope of abnormality also illustrates that coming out acts that have important positive effects may simultaneously involve the negotiation, if not the re-creation, of the epistemology of the closet. For example, Qian explains that for most of the cruisers interviewed, "a deeply entrenched sense of abnormality, imbricated in the new and context-specific experiences of being deviant and non-mainstream, keeps being reproduced through cruising in public" (159). Further, Qian notes that the trope of abnormality disproportionately affects "low income gays who cannot afford other options (saunas, gay only clubs)" (161).

Two things strike me as particularly important about the trope of abnormality for understanding the larger trope of the closet. First, the experiences of the gay cruisers in the People's Park speaks back to queer theory critiques of the epistemology of the closet, providing an important reminder that, although for some LGBT people negative constructions of homosexuality, bisexuality, and transgender or transsexual status may not be tempered by other aspects of identity that mute those negative effects, for other LGBT people the very acts that allow them access to sexual fulfillment and a positive associations with other queer people cannot be separated from those negative constructions. Second, queer theorists are right to ask for more. For example, Qian's analysis and my use of it here focus largely on the experiences of gay men with only limited attention to other identity issues, and, most notably, women's experiences are not the focus of either. The trope of the closet needs to function both to negotiate the ongoing effects of the epistemology of the closet that can be gathered under the heading of the trope of abnormality and to move beyond sexual identity as the single focus of such identity negotiation.

Mason's discussion of the *trope of visibility* further illustrates how closeting continues to be necessary because of problematic epistemologies but may mean many different things in the lives of those who must negotiate closets. For example, she says "lesbians and gay men are involved in the complex daily management of a plethora of choices around the relation between homosexuality and visibility" (39). Mason grounds her argument for managing visibility as a central trope of the closet in a set of interviews that she conducted with 75 women who identified as gay, lesbian, or queer, and focuses particularly on their experiences managing their sexual identity in response to various kinds of potential violence that visibility entails. She explains that the women she interviewed used a variety of self-management strategies to protect themselves from potential physical and emotional violence due to their sexual identities and/or gender expressions. Mason reasons that because such acts of violence are often both ubiquitous and beyond the control of the queer person, queer people often engage in "self-policing their own behavior" in the interest of safety from "the hostility of homophobia" and that such negotiations nearly always involve issues of visibility (33). Mason further argues that such choices are not the same for all who must negotiate closets due to homophobia and heterosexism. Indeed, she notes that gender and ethnicity may play a critical role in how much visibility a person is willing to engage in: "For example, certain acts, such as walking arm in arm, may be a greater signifier of homosexuality for men than for women, or even more acceptable in some ethnic communities than in others" (27). She also sees an important effect for socioeconomic status: "Quite simply, the more money you have, the more options you have for choosing where you live, how you travel in your daily life and where, and with whom, you spend your leisure time" (33).

Mason's exploration of how the trope of visibility operated in the lives of the women she interviewed illustrates that, although the closet remains a central fixture of their lives—one that often had to be negotiated multiple times each day—the closet did not operate in a simple in/out way. Rather, Mason, argues:

> The meanings attached to being in or out of the closet are neither singular nor universal. To be closeted about one's sexuality can be both a form of acquiescence and a form of control. Similarly, the decision to come out may be an act of resistance at the same time that it feeds into the "trap" of visible sexualities. (39–40)

Mason's discussion of the trope of the closet as a set of self-management techniques reminds me of a conversation I had at an LGBTQ ally training session that I attended at my university. During the activities, I made my homosexuality explicit to the group on several occasions, and although I was certainly not closeted with my dean colleagues, my decision to discuss my homosexuality directly opened the door for a discussion with them about the ways in which my homosexuality played out in my role as a dean. I explained that I had had interactions with faculty members who seemed uncomfortable with the fact that I was gay, but given that I was their boss and that the university's antidiscrimination policy included sexual orientation and gender expression, these faculty members had to find other means to challenge me. Thus, my status and the university's policy against discrimination likely forced their homophobia into a closet. I also explained that with some of the donors I worked with, I "edited" myself, particularly with one couple who are conservative Christians. Because I enjoy an odd kind of celebrity with my college's donors, many of whom seek connection and a kind of intimacy with me, how much about myself I choose to share with them, particularly about my sexual identity, feels like privilege that I give to some and not to others. I suspect that the kind of privilege that I enjoy in doling out information about my sexual identity as a reward is fairly unusual for LGBT people, but it illustrates Mason's point that managing the visibility of homosexuality does not always involve a return to an unwelcome closet.

The trope of the closet is alive and well in modern discourse, but, as I have illustrated in this chapter, we need to understand it as much more than a simple in/out binary, and we need to understand coming out as more than a once-for-all event. The effect of the act of coming out and the many similar acts that likely follow it must be understood as having a number of rhetorical effects. The underlying effect is always to bring something previously unseen, something dismissed, or something typically pathologized into discourse. As I have illustrated, those coming out may be claiming a status that others have already attributed to them; may reveal identity as a direct challenge to those who would erase or pathologize them; may reveal identity as a sign of increased intimacy and trust in a relationship; or may flout their status by engaging in overt behaviors that they expect will appear scandalous or attractive to others. In rhetorical terms, what matters in all such uses of the trope of the closet is that the revelation or explicit acknowledgment of some identity feature changes the relationship between the interlocutors in some way. In this sense, the trope of the closet is not only a master trope for the variety of ways that LBGT people manage aspects of their identities that have been erased or marginalized, but it is also a broader rhetorical tool for bringing what has been ignored, misunderstood, marginalized, or otherwise made invisible into discourse. This function makes the trope of the closet and all of its variants some of the most important rhetorical tools we possess to work for an inclusive and just society.

Works Cited

Angelides, Steven. *A History of Bisexuality*. Chicago: U of Chicago P, 2001. Print.
Blair, Hugh. "Lecture XIV: Origin and Nature of Figurative Language." *The Rhetorical Tradition: Readings from Classical Times to the Present*. Eds. Patricia Bizzell and Bruce Herzberg. Boston: Bedford, 2001. 962–974. Print.

Gates, Henry Louis, Jr. *The Signifying Monkey: A Theory of Afro-American Literary Criticism*. New York: Oxford UP, 1988. Print.

Gilman, Sander L., Carole Blair, and David J. Parents, trans. and editors. *Friedrich Nietzsche on Rhetoric and Language*. New York: Oxford UP, 1989. Print.

Kopelson, Karen. "Dis/Integrating the Gay/Queer Binary: 'Reconstructing Identity Politics' for a Performative Pedagogy." *College English* 65.1 (Sept. 2002): 17–35. Print.

Li, Cao. "Gay Rights in China: Road to Respect. *China Daily* 24 Feb. 2010. Web. 19 Aug. 2014.

Mason, Gail. "Body Maps: Envisioning Homophobia, Violence and Safety." *Social and Legal Studies* 10.1 (2001): 23–44. Print.

McNaron, Toni A.H. *Poisoned Ivy: Lesbian and Gay Academics Confronting Homophobia*. Philadelphia: Temple UP, 1997. Print.

Qian, Junxi. "Narrating the Trope of Abnormality: The Making of Closeted Experiences in Gay Public Cruising." *Geoforum* 52 (2014): 157–66. Print.

Sedgwick, Eve Kosofsky. *Epistemology of the Closet*. Berkeley: U of California P, 1990. Print.

Seidman, Steven. "Identity and Politics in a 'Postmodern' Gay Culture: Some Historical and Conceptual Notes." *Fear of a Queer Planet: Queer Politics and Social Theory*. Ed. Michael Warner. Minneapolis: U of Minnesotis P, 1991. 105–42. Print.

Symposium Collective (Deborah Brandt, Ellen Cushman, Anne Ruggles Gere, Anne Herrington, Richard E. Miller, Victor Villanueva, Min-Zhan Lu, and Gesa Kirsch). "The Politics of the Personal: Storying Our Lives against the Grain." *College English* 64.1 (Sept. 2001): 41–62. Print.

"Transparent Closet." *Tvtropes*. Web. 1 Aug. 2014.

8 Sex and the Crip Latina
Ellen M. Gil-Gómez

There have been exhaustive studies and narratives about the experiences and lives of women of color generally—and women *faculty* of color specifically—that analyze the important receptive creative factors that frame women of color identities in academic contexts. Numerous testimonials and personal and analytical narratives have outlined and illuminated these circumstances, though obviously with different specific details and personal stories. In my own early career, the testimonios most important to me and my understanding of these identity elements were *This Bridge Called My Back; Borderlands/La Frontera; Loving in the War Years; Making Face/Making Soul; All the Women are White, all the Blacks are Men, But Some of Us are Brave; Chicana Lesbians: The Girls Our Mothers Warned Us About; Sister Outsider;* and *Compañeras: Latina Lesbians*. There is little need for me to review them in detail here.[1]

As a young graduate student in charge of my own classrooms, I learned from these texts how to understand all of the white supremacism, classism, sexism, homophobia, and postcolonial subjects/objects that I was experiencing in my daily life. My belief was that the main problem was not that I was different from the majority of my students, or their individual acts of reading, but that I was hampered by the forced "multi culti" curriculum and texts that my university prescribed for introductory classes. It was only after conversations with the one other graduate student of color in my program that I realized that we both experienced the same types of criticism and negative responses from our students, and that I was willing to consider that the source of the problem for us both was what our physical bodies represented to our students. This realization deflated my heretofore-unexamined liberal belief that through education everyone might be equal. However, it was still some time before I fully understood and acknowledged the power that my body as "text" carried with or without my own subjecthood.

My focus at the beginning of my career was to try to change myself and my appearance in order to escape the effects of my physical body that I experienced as a graduate student. It was very similar to my impossible high school quest to compose myself into subjecthood—impossible because of the receptive audience rather than the subject. I also foolishly assumed that there were different, more complex factors at work in this world than in the average U.S. high school. I remember reading Emily Toth's columns in the *Chronicle of Higher Education* and her book *Ms. Mentor's Impeccable Advice for Women in Academia*, as I had no actual mentors to turn to. She summed up the options for academic embodiment: "If it's a choice between being chic or frumpy, I think it benefits academics more to be frumpy," said Toth, a professor of English and women's studies at Louisiana State University. "If you look like you spend too much time on your clothes, there are people who will assume that you haven't put enough energy into your mind" (qtd. in Schneider). Toth's rhetoric of costume was particularly helpful to me because it allowed me to imagine a framework where I could make choices for my physical presence in the foreign professional world. What remained problematic in Toth's version of subject-driven choices was the importance of the body below the clothing. I soon found it was not as simple as choosing from the "frumpy" or "chic" racks because my body and its presence in different cultural contexts could be read differently despite specific clothes.

Going back in time to the very formation of my subject identity, I knew from initially seeing myself as a sexual being that understanding my own sexual identity as a woman meant navigating strong pressure from others with the power to objectify and define who I was supposed to be. As I grew into a sexual being, these external forces changed as did my relationship to and understanding of them. Still, what remained consistent was that others seemed to read my sexual role and inclinations from a set of expectations inspired by their interpretation of my identity—perceived or expressed. This became clear to me through experiencing a continual disconnect between how others "read" my desires and my actual desires.

I became aware of my own wish, or even *need*, to compose myself, to create a public identity within these sexual contexts. When I was an adolescent, these acts of composition were merely related to external appearance—a button, the size, color, or style of clothing, specific makeup choices—in order to create an impression or rather to try to reroute a faulty one. As a young, ostensibly straight woman, it appeared that the only potential effect of this composition was to shape my entry into the world of objectification. There seemed no other option, as this was the depth of imagination of average high-school-aged straight cisgendered males. I felt there was never a chance to define myself as a sexual subject within this audience. While my understanding of these options was obviously immature, I did understand, both from my own experiences and through reading the white supremacist heteronormative world I inhabited, that there was a composition process present. However, I still hoped that eventually there would be a way to compose a more coherent identity that might speak who I actually was, and what I wanted, to others.

After high school, I was asked to enter the profession of sex work, and I weighed this choice against beginning college. Ultimately, I chose college because I believed that it might give me more opportunities for a longer duration than the alternative (which it ultimately did). While many people to whom I have told that story laugh over my apparently ridiculous choice, it seemed to me that a profession in sex work seemed a very logical path given my "training" in objectification by a white supremacist, heteronormative, and sexist society. A sex worker was exactly what it wanted me to be, and that was the message: *what you see is what you get.*

When I was a young academic, my greatest concern was that as a woman of color professor I was routinely read as openly sexual—either sexually available or desirous of sex—mainly by students but also certain colleagues. I felt my effectiveness as a professional was continually undermined. I knew that as an attractive woman I was routinely read this way in my private life, but I naively imagined that once I'd succeeded in entering academe, my sex appeal would be diminished, and this factor would no longer be important. I supposed that if I put myself in this intellectually based context, then I would be read intellectually and not from and for my body. I had unknowingly embraced the liberal fantasy that higher education created and led to equality, a fantasy that Bernal and Villapando effectively critique. They argue that the inescapable gender and race "stratification" in the American university system clearly belies the ideal that it is "objective, meritocratic, color-blind, race-neutral, and [bestows] equal opportunities for all" (170). But embodiment continued to contextualize me. For those who actively read my presence this way there were some predictable outcomes. Straight male students would generally choose two paths to read and potentially manipulate me—charm and seduction or intimidation. Straight women tended to react antagonistically, seeing me as a rival or "queen bee" and thus operating within their sphere rather than above it. Lesbian or bisexual women read me as a potential sexual mentor, as a strong woman who could nurture them both intellectually and sexually. Of course, although these where frequent reactions, they did not describe every student or every response I encountered.

These sexual expectations were also profoundly and inextricably connected to equally strong concepts of race and ethnicity. At the universities where I worked that had predominantly white student populations, these sexual readings were the most commonplace. Every term, every class, I would find myself having a difficult conversation with at least one student who wanted to break through the line between professor and student and have a sexual relationship of some sort. Interestingly, the responses of individuals were also influenced by the content of the courses themselves. In courses related to Chicana/o or Latino/a literature or culture or woman of color studies, my main areas of expertise, these sexual readings could actually encourage students to more fully participate in the course and its materials. It seemed that, in general, students could easily read my sexual intent alongside knowledge of these ethnic groups and their literatures. Their opinions of my sexual behaviors and focus actually strengthened their belief that I was competent at my job, at least in these content areas. This did not hold true for courses without these cultural connections, such as American literature, literary theory, or various genre or period topics courses. In those cases, student responses tended to resemble those of colleagues—that I was simply not professional and thus not competent to hold the role of professor. There was a straight line drawn from external appearance to an opinion of my intellectual capacity: my sexuality as an external sign of "Latina-ness" was beneficial for students but not otherwise. While in the context of reading one's external form through clothing specifically, the following example is equally relevant to one's body entire as unique to faculty of color: "The deconstruction of dress weighs particularly heavily upon minority professors. 'There is a special turn of the knife for racial and ethnic women,' says Nell Painter, a black historian at Princeton. 'There are prejudices against people who look too Jewish, too working-class, too Italian, too black, or too much of anything different.' She adds, however, that 'if you look too WASPish, that's probably all right'" (qtd. in Schneider). Thus, there are consequences when faculty of color, or "different" faculty, look *too* different (which is of course relevant); in my experience they can be read as potentially competent about their own cultural communities whereas white academics can inherently transcend these identity and embodied boundaries.

I certainly tried to compose myself in these ways as a professional academic, again focused on my dress as suggested by Toth's "do's and don'ts: For starters, younger women should play down their sexuality. Skirts should be knee-length or below. Pants are never appropriate for interviews. Steer clear of high-heeled shoes. Choose dark colors over light ones. Ms. Mentor recommends dark purple: 'It looks good on everyone'"(qtd. in Schneider). But no matter what I did with my clothes, hair, makeup, and so on, the problem remained remarkably consistent. Ultimately, I concluded that instead of trying to change my outward appearance, I would try to harness the attention I gained through these sexual readings, stereotypes, and desires to impact my classrooms in more positive ways. I found, at last, that once I was confident and comfortable, these readings were constantly created by students I became more able to channel them into productive learning situations and fewer and fewer awkward sexual confessions.

I finally found a way to use my sexual subjectivity in my own professional life so that it served my purposes. Once I had become aware of the overlap and interplay of contexts of gender, race and ethnicity, class and culture, and most important *sex*, I composed a useful and valuable professional self that was attuned to my student audience. I had less success with my colleagues within professional contexts, though, because since there were no sexual confessions and few awkward moments with colleagues, it was not necessary for me to navigate them as with students. Instead I found that my main obstacles there were from older men in positions of power—of course, an important audience in the academic world but one that could be managed. I only cared about trying to manage those men who could directly and negatively impact my career, and for the most part the only important issue within this audience was the issue of my own invisibility. To be read sexually by this group meant to either not exist at all or to exist as a troublemaker as someone not interested in being sexually objectified—even intellectually. For me it became a twofold dance: don't insult the colleague in question by an outright refusal to play the game, but instead, taking a lesson from my own students, directly connect any sex appeal they read as reflective of my ethnic origin and thus knowledge. For example, in my second year in one department, my then-department-chair patted me on the head during a department meeting, when he was speaking of my work coordinating the department's curriculum focused on race and ethnicity. It was an incredibly paternalistic move, and at the time, I felt completely embodied and humiliated. After more than a few moments of stunned silence, and rather than strike out at him in rebuke or with criticism, I instead repeated his words of praise for me and my work, and went further to celebrate the work of my students as well, matter-of-factly and as if he had done nothing wrong. Because of this "good girl" move, I was able to make a case that the department's offerings in minority literatures should be expanded. In other words, I channeled that attention into my "Latina-ness" which went to emphasize my professionalism and competence.

For the most part, this worked to my benefit, as these colleagues read me positively as a "team player" doing my job, or negatively as a "troublemaker" trying to push the boundaries of race and ethnic oppression. Even though these were potentially detrimental responses, they still directed the colleague to reading me within a professional context, into the context of my work life, and not a private sexual one. I had very few issues of this nature with any female colleagues; unlike female students, we more or less shared equal status in terms of power or potential power in the academy, and thus there was no reason to use or read sexual identity as did straight male colleagues.

My tools for composing my identity then became much more developed as my understanding of my own identity broadened, as did my role as subject and my relationship to multiple audiences. Dress was and always is an important element of appearance, of course, but within these professional contexts my physical body and appearance were less critical. Because of the intellectual nature of the academy, the body is routinely invisible; thus colleagues and administrators go out of their way to ignore it and anyone they see as embodied. It's always a risk to be read as embodied, but it's also a risk to be invisible. As Karla F.C. Holloway describes the risk for faculty of color making *statements* about identity with dress that "it makes the other parts of you invisible—your scholarship, your intellect, your seriousness" (qtd. in Schneider) or otherwise stated, all the elements that equate to one's professionalism and competence. I would argue that these choices go beyond clothing and that any and all kinds of embodiment have this same effect. But as I have already said, I learned fairly early on that changing my external appearance was less valuable than developing my own understanding of my audiences and their reading and interpretive processes. Although students were generally quite direct in their readings using stereotypes of all kinds—gender, sexuality, race and ethnicity, and so on—colleagues generally engaged in a constant double speak most focused on my identity as a professor of color more than anything else. They would say one thing while really wanting and meaning something else—in general, creating a far more intellectual dance.[2]

Regardless of these challenges, I was able to teach and work productively for 20-odd years within these contexts. I had to make compromises, of course, through balancing my own desires and professional goals with those of the field, the institution, and my superiors, but I did find a balance that made me content. This all changed, like the rest of my world, when after more than a year of illness, doctor visits, and diagnostic tests, I was finally diagnosed with lupus, fibromyalgia, and a variety of secondary syndromes. Quite abruptly, I was embodied in a way that defied my earlier experiences of my composed self, and that more importantly defied the very nature and possibility of composing embodiment at all. To my surprise, the cornerstone turned out to be sexual identity and desire.

The full scope of my medical journey, return to work, and subsequent struggle with the new professional embodiment as "disabled" is beyond the scope here,[3] but it does serve me to discuss some of the professional contexts and readings of my body that were its result. My first major step in personally coming to terms with this new embodiment was the realization that Susan Wendell aptly describes: "When you are forced to realize that other people have more social authority than you do to describe your experience of your own body, your ... relationship to reality is radically undermined" (254). For me this began in the murky world of doctors' offices and diagnostic tests: trying to differentiate between and articulate different types of pain, hearing again and again that something was wrong, but I couldn't find help in any particular medical department, diagnostics were inconclusive, starting medications stopping medications, and so on. I had to wait months to become more and more ill in order to "present" in a way that made my label clear to my doctors. This long-term limbo, I learned, was nothing new in the world of autoimmune illness, for many patients can suffer undiagnosed for years at a time. It was clear to me that I was ill, but "disabled" was a whole different ball of wax for me. I still believed early on that illness was something one recovers from, and not potentially a continual state of being. It gave me some small sense of control over my own identity to believe that I would improve, and I remember reassuring my family that "I don't plan on being disabled." At this juncture, though I was always clear in my mind that any power was on very thin ice indeed, I believed that there remained an element of will, of choice in the matter as with all compositions of self.

The first major disjuncture came when I improved enough after some treatment and returned to work. As when I was a new professor of color, when I thought that my status as a professional would trump any personal embodiments I brought to the role, I again believed this to be true for my new embodiment. I believed that my thoughts and feelings about my own body, my illness, and my status would only be important for me privately (and maybe some close friends.) What I found was that my body and the meaning of my embodiment were suddenly thrust into public conversation, created suspicion and both individual and institutional valuation. While pity was the first and easiest response to my return, what soon followed, to my surprise, was doubt and judgment.

Basically, like many with disabling chronic illness, my new "difference" was largely invisible. I occasionally had rashes, changes in my skin tone, and evident levels of fatigue; but to the outside world I was not visibly "disabled," and thus once I requested accommodation, colleagues, administrators, and my superiors at various institutional levels directly and indirectly challenged my requests by arguing the legitimacy of my body on brand-new terrain. Once again my embodiment worked against my professionalism, though this time not through sexual identity. Illness is read by the able-ist as a personal failing rather than as a "normal" state, and one cannot be impaired *and* competent because the terms are understood as mutually exclusive. The "public world is the world of strength, the positive (valued) body, performance and production, the able-bodied, and youth. Weakness, illness, rest and recovery, pain, death, and the negative (de-valued) body" (Wendell 248) and are not welcomed in the domain of work.

Thus, my newly embodied identity changed the entire landscape of my professional existence. Much more than my status as a woman of color faculty member, who could be read negatively as a "troublemaker" or a "sexpot" by certain colleagues or even parts of the institution, I was in no way prepared for the torrent of hostile institutional rhetoric and power which was to befall me as "disabled." My own experience is in agreement with Jung's assertion that "[s]uspicion is not a characteristic of a misguided or uninformed individual but is a built-in feature of the disability policy, and suspicion and skepticism are structured into the procedures used to guide the interpretation of human rights codes" (192). I do not know if I had returned to work in a wheelchair, or with a cane or crutches, for example, if these same mechanisms would have been brought to bear with such vehemence, but these examples were routinely given to me in contrast to my own situation as reflective of "legitimate" disability. For example, the Dean of my college said to me in a meeting that she wanted to make clear that assistance would be temporary because "it's not like you're in a wheelchair." It was a horrifying illustration, supporting drama scholar Petra Kruppers's argument that the wheelchair is the most important marker of disabled identity in performance. He writes: "wheelchairs become rhetorical devices carrying narratives and marking identities" (88). I have repeatedly found that this applies to social constructs of disabled identity as well.

The institution has routinely responded to my identity with suspicion and hostility. My conclusion was that the only possible result of my embodied disability was a drain on resources, energy, morale, and a resulting lowering of standards. Indeed, throughout the process the institution has continually responded with rhetoric requiring my abasement and humiliation. As Jung effectively points out: "bodily limitations and impairments are not interpreted as consequences of unequal relations of power or oppressive ideologies, but as personal inadequacies" (196). To be embodied as disabled is to be a symbol of, and agent for, the decomposition of identity—a continual and unwelcomed paradox to be publicly shamed, or better yet, simply erased. "It has been made clear that there is absolutely no benefit to being disabled in the academy; there is no desired student community to whom to appeal or give benefits, no program to develop, no reputable body of knowledge to represent or even symbolize. Unlike my role as a professional woman of color, ultimately there is no status for me as a professional disabled woman" at my institution. (Gil-Gomez, "(In)Visibilities"). If, however, disability theory or "crip theory" eventually gains the status that feminism or queer theory has in academe, there may indeed be a subjective and positional benefit to claiming and/or celebrating "crip" identity. As Carrie Sandahl states: "The term *crip* has expanded to include not only those with physical impairments but also those with sensory or mental impairments as well. Though I have never heard a nondisabled person seriously claim to *be* crip (as heterosexuals have claimed to *be* queer), I would not be surprised by this practice. The fluidity of both terms makes it likely that their boundaries will dissolve" (27). However, I very much doubt even if this is so that parallel changes in ableism will necessarily result.

To return to sex: it was after about a year or so of these experiences and their individual and institutional battles that I realized that sex again was, and had been, an important force in the external composing processes occurring all around me. The battles for and over my personal and public crip identity, as well as my complete inexperience and inability to negotiate them, made me feel that any notion of composing a self was simply a fiction. I came face to face with my own ableist privilege when I imagined one's body is normal as relatively healthy, able, and essentially immutable in its operation and meaning.

I was brought back to understand myself as sexed in two major ways. The first was again in the work context, when I began suffering from a particularly difficult time of organ failure, which led to almost constant nausea, vomiting, and eventually weight loss. As with many symptoms of lupus, as the signs come and go it takes some time to recognize those that are important—those that are consistent and/or worsening—at any given time. In this specific instance, it took me about three months to recognize these changes as important ones.

To go back to the question of dress, I suppose I would categorize myself as always more "chic" than "frumpy" and thus was used to colleagues, and sometimes students, complimenting my clothing, shoes, or hairstyle. After I got sick, however, these compliments, from those who knew about my illness (mainly colleagues), took on a new emphasis, as if to indicate or stand in for "health." No one really wanted my answer to "how are you?" so the new refrain became "you look good," though with the emphasis placed on *look* rather than *good*. I suppose the emphasis indicated some surprise and suspicion but also reflected its fleeting nature. During this specific physical struggle, I was continually barraged with comments about my weight. I soon noticed that the mix of elation and confusion was quite marked in these instances. On one hand, praising a woman for losing weight was an undeniable compliment and spoken with that intention; once spoken though, the speaker clearly struggled with its ensuing significance. I suppose to these speakers I looked better weighing less than I did previously; the conclusion seemed to be that the weight loss was intended to create sexual allure and thus physical attractiveness or health. I could see the paradox on their faces—if you are sexier, how can you be ill? If you are healthier, how can you be disabled? Regardless of the answers, there seemed absolutely no concept that it could actually be negative or a result of my further loss of health. For someone who appears attractive, weight loss is read as the further intent to emphasize attractiveness. It was these moments that helped me see my embodiment as a function of the ableism and gender biases of others. Unlike my previous epiphanies involving my sexual identity in the classroom, these combinations were hidden even from me. Thus, they were a complete surprise, as I had not fully worked through my own ableist concepts, nor was I schooled through a lifetime to expect them from others.

The second context in which I came to understand myself as a sexed being was even more befuddling and unexpected. At times my state of health requires me to use a wheelchair. It occurs primarily in my "private" life (that is, not at work) and at special events that require too much sustained physical effort for me to manage on my own. I would again characterize my general dress on these occasions as "chic," though not in every situation. I soon became aware that every time I needed to use a wheelchair I suddenly became a magnet for young male attention. Men, usually younger men, would fall over each other to hold open doors, bring me drinks, inquire if I needed assistance, double take and blatantly stare, strike up flirtatious conversations, and give me gifts: VIP or backstage passes, special event materials, or personal introductions to honored guests, and on and on. It was if I had become highly visible and with a sex appeal cranked up to an 11. I thought perhaps it was a result of pity, but I had experienced pity routinely at work and it in no way resembled this. The pity response tends to make one *less* visible, not more so; or I should say that one *is* excessively visible when pitied, but people work hard pretending not to see you.

It's that covert effort to make the hypervisible invisible that was missing in these public instances. I thought perhaps it was the paradox of an attractive woman made unattractive or "broken" through the visual rhetoric of the wheelchair; but I think this would have had to some degree inspire pity. Perhaps it would be a more attentive pity than the invisible version operating in my professional world, but pity nonetheless. I've come to believe that what I embody in these cases is most often a form of fantasy—an excess of female passivity and vulnerability in complete need of straight male assistance and thus control. In these contexts, the control is entirely appreciated and useful rather than being a form of oppression or annoyance. Perhaps I embody the always-receptive female cypher to be steered, directed, *taken*. To some degree, it is similar to when I was pregnant and my body became "owned" and consumed by the public world—discussed, touched, and given extra attention. But in those instances, while my embodiment was certainly read as "in need of assistance" there was never any sexual allure involved, no flirtations, and no special favors beyond being offered a place to sit.

In order to work through these dynamics more fully, I turn to Rosemarie Garland-Thomson's work, specifically "Seeing the Disabled: Visual Rhetorics of Disability in Popular Photography," wherein she argues that there is benefit to understanding the relationship between the viewer and the viewed through a "taxonomy of four visual rhetorics of—disability: the wondrous, the sentimental, the exotic, and the realistic" (339). The wondrous creates the "stereotype of the 'supercrip,'" which "estranges the viewer from the viewed, attenuating the correspondence that equality requires" (341). The sentimental "places the disabled figure below the viewer, in the posture of the sympathetic victim" (341). The exotic does not create a specific hierarchy, but instead it "presents the disabled figures as alien, often sensationalized, eroticized, or entertaining in their difference" (343). The realistic "trades in verisimilitude, regularizing the disabled figure in order to encourage a nonhierarchical identification" (344). Ultimately, however, this identification is used to "warn viewers against becoming disabled" (344). Thomson reminds her reader that these modes are neither easily compartmentalized nor discrete but are routinely intertwined and complex (346).

Though clearly not equivalent to social forms of embodiment, these categories still hold useful possibilities for me. It is hard to find an exact equivalent to what I think is the visual rhetoric involved, but I find the first three categories potentially relevant to understanding how and why these embodiments arise. The only one that I feel is irrelevant is the "realistic" because these instances of excessive sex appeal do not reflect the reality of my usual physical presence. I can only conclude that some intensification of sex appeal results from the combination of my body as both *attractive* and *in a wheelchair*. I'm not sure that this is "wondrous," though perhaps there is some notion that attractiveness and sex appeal of any amount are totally incompatible with one's body in a wheelchair and thus it represents the extraordinary. I would say that the "sentimental" is also a possibility here, though as I've stated I don't think that pity is the main response. There is, however, a strong sense of being made "lowly" by the attention as Garland-Thomson puts it, and as I've said, being marked as in need of chivalrous assistance. This lowliness locates me as constant object, thus increasing the potential for male subjecthood. Finally, I am tempted to choose the "exotic," as this is a constant component of my attraction as a Latina, and perhaps there is some "distance" involved in my representation—distance from "normal" women, that is. However, the male response, as I've described it, does not involve any distance; in fact, it arguably produces more coherence and importance in a male counterpart. This form of the exotic does not function as "freak" but again as object that necessitates excessive male chivalry. All of these elements operate in various ways and to differing degrees. What is constant is that I am embodied as a fully receptive object, dependent on others' subjecthood and attention. And in fleeting moments of attention and effort, the emphasis is on the other's ability to provide and resolve.

I feel powerfully all of these processes operating outside myself and my own desires and sense of self, as I always have. They are even more foreign to me than those of gender, sexuality, race, and ethnicity. The difference in my embodiment of disability is the huge differences that are produced, with rules and qualities that I am just beginning to understand. They do feel a part of me now and my understanding of myself, as the others much earlier, but they are so varied and continually surprising to me that I am routinely caught off guard and left confused by their operation. It is because of this constant state of discomposure that I believe decomposition is the more accurate reflection of human identity. In fact, all of our attempts to shape the rhetorics by which we are defined and understood privately and publicly are shaped in such narrow concepts as to be ultimately illusory. It has only been through my embodiment and disembodiment as "disabled" that I have come to understand the paradigms theorized by McRuer:

> Everyone is virtually disabled, both in the sense that able-bodied norms are "intrinsically impossible to embody" fully and in the sense that able-bodied is always temporary, disability being the one category that all people will embody if they live long enough. What we might call a critically disabled position, would differ from such a virtually disabled position; it would call attention to the ways in which the disability rights movement and disability studies have resisted the demands of compulsory able-bodiedness. (30)

Likewise, Garland-Thomson characterizes the potential, mainly theoretical, benefits from embracing disabled decomposition, which she coins as "misfitting." The main benefits of this proficiency, as she puts it, are realizing that the "generic disabled body ... can dematerialize if social and architectural barriers no longer disable it. ... [and] a shifting spatial and perpetually temporal relationship [which] confers agency and value on disabled subjects at risk of social devaluation by highlighting adaptability, resourcefulness, and subjugated knowledge as potential effects of misfitting" (592). For me, these realizations have routinely come through sex: through an understanding and reevaluation of myself as a sexual object and subject; through trying to understand the importance of my sex appeal in different contexts; and through thinking through how sex and embodiment function together, making any process of composition or decomposition possible.

Notes

1. For a full discussion of both statistics and general academic trends shaping the lives of women faculty of color, as well as my own personal journey in this context, see my "Full Circles from *Mestiza* to *Mojada* and Back: A Testimonio View of Some Academic Borders and Crossers."
2. In "Full Circles" I discuss the kinds of doublespeak at play for faculty of color and the choices required to negotiate it.
3. See my "(In)Visibilities—A Woman Faculty of Color's Search for a Disabled Identity That Works" for a full account of these details.

Works Cited

Bernal, Dolores Delgado, and Octavio Villapando. "An Apartheid of Knowledge in Academia: The Struggle ver the 'Legitimate' Knowledge of Faculty of Color." *Equity and Excellence in Education* 35.2 (2002): 169–80. Print.

Garland-Thomson, Rosemarie. "Misfits: A Feminist Materialist Disability Concept." *Hypatia* 26.3 (2011): 591–609. Print.

Garland-Thomson, Rosemarie. "Seeing the Disabled: Visual Rhetorics of Disability in Popular Photography." *The New Disability History: American Perspectives*. Ed. Paul K. Longmore and Lauri Umansky. New York: New York UP, 2001. 335–74. Print.

Gil-Gómez, Ellen M. "(In)Visibilities—A Woman Faculty of Color's Search for a Disabled Identity That Works." *Staging Women's Lives: Gendered Life Stages in Language and Literature*. Ed. Michelle Masse and Nan Bauer-Maglin. Albany, NY: SUNY UP, 2015. Print.

Jung, Karen Elizabeth. "Chronic Illness and Educational Equity: The Politics of Visibility." *NWSA Journal* 14.3 (2002): 178–200. Print.

Kruppers, Petra. "The Wheelchair's Rhetoric: The Performance of Disability." *TDR: The Drama Review* 51.4 (2007): 80–89. Print.

McRuer, Robert. *Crip Theory: Cultural Signs of Queerness and Disability*. New York: New York UP, 2006. Print.

Sandahl, Carrie. "Queering the Crip or Cripping the Queer? Intersections of Queer and Crip Identities in Solo Autobiographical Performances." *GLQ: A Journal of Lesbian and Gay Studies* 9.1–2 (2003): 25–56. Print.

Schneider, Alison. "Frumpy or Chic? Tweed or Kente? Sometimes Clothes Make the Professor" *The Chronicle of Higher Education*. 23 Jan. 1998. Web. 1 Nov. 2014.

Toth, Emily. *Ms. Mentor's Impeccable Advice for Women in Academia*. Philadelphia: U of Pennsylvania P, 1997. Print.

Wendell, Susan. "Toward a Feminist Theory of Disability." *The Disability Studies Reader*. 2nd ed. Ed. Lennard J. Davis. New York: Routledge, 2006. 243–56. Print.

Further Reading

Anzaldúa, Gloria. *Borderlands/La Frontera: The New Mestiza*. San Francisco: Spinsters/Aunt Lute, 1987. Print.

Anzaldúa, Gloria, ed. *Making Face, Making Soul/Haciendo Caras: Creative and Critical Perspectives by Feminists of Color*. San Francisco: Aunt Lute, 1990. Print.

Hull, Gloria T., Patricia Bell Scott, and Barbara Smith, eds. *All the Women Are White, All the Blacks Are Men, But Some of Us Are Brave: Black Women's Studies*. New York: Feminist Press, 1982. Print.

Lorde, Audre. *Sister Outsider: Essays and Speeches*. The Crossing Press Feminist Series. Freedom, CA: Crossing P, 1984. Print.

Moraga, Cherríe. "La Güera." *This Bridge Called My Back: Writings by Radical Women of Color*. Eds. Cherríe Moraga and Gloria Anzaldúa. New York: Kitchen Table/Women of Color, 1981. Print.

Moraga, Cherríe. *Loving in the War Years: lo que nunca pasó por sus labios*. Boston: South End, 1983. Print.

Ramos, Juanita, ed. *Compañeras: Latina Lesbians: An Anthology*. New York: Routledge, 1994. Print.

Trujillo, Carla, ed. *Chicana Lesbians: The Girls Our Mothers Warned Us About*. Berkeley, CA: Third Woman, 1991. Print.

9 Affect, Female Masculinity, and the Embodied Space Between
Two-Spirit Traces in Thirza Cuthand's Experimental Film

Lisa Tatonetti

There's something queer in Indian Country. At the heart of that queerness is a disobedience to dominant Western gender norms that manifests in the unruly bodies of Big Moms and butch dykes as they're depicted in Native American and Aboriginal texts. I discuss this queerness as a radically resistant form of female masculinity and suggest that an examination of such masculinities has potentially significant implications for analyses of gender, sexuality, and Indigeneity together with the rhetorics that construct them.[1] This assertion hinges on three imbricated contentions.

First, rhetorical constructions of female masculinity in Native literature challenge dominant stereotypes about Indigenous masculinities. Such deconstructive analyses are radically important given that, as Brian Klopotek (Choctaw) explains, "For at least the last century, hypermasculinity has been one of the foremost attributes of the Indian world that whites have imagined. … These imagined Indian nations comprise an impossibly masculine race. Because of such perpetually outlandish representations of Indian gender, masculinity has become a crucial arena for contesting unrealistic images of Indians" (251). Klopotek's observation about the weight of rigid expectations on Indigenous masculinity suggests the need to identify the fault lines in these damaging rhetorics. The very existence of *female* masculinity represents one such fault line by fracturing monolithic, externally constructed discourses about Indigenous gender traditions—*recognizing Native masculinities as not only multiple but also mobile requires a paradigm shift.*

Second, affect theory and, particularly, embodied rhetoric, which I read as presenting a useful definition of the embodied nature of affect, offers a productive language to discuss the integrated considerations of body, emotion, and reciprocal relationship that inform female masculinity in Indigenous literatures. Using the affective lens of embodied rhetoric to read contemporary articulations of female masculinity in Indigenous contexts therefore enables us to acknowledge the weight and value of embodied experiences. This rhetorical intersection thus presents a lexicon for what Tanana Athabascan scholar Dian Million terms "colonialism as it is *felt* by those who experience it" (58).

Third, the affective, transformative power of female masculinity holds the trace of Two-Spirit histories, of gender traditions that exist before and beyond the halls of academe. Here, I stake a claim for Indigeneity as the point of departure in any rhetorical reading of gender and sexuality, rather than as the afterthought it so often represents in the (still-prevalent) additive models of multiculturalism.[2] These interlocking claims about masculinity, embodied rhetoric, and Two-Spirit traces show that the study of female masculinity in Indigenous texts makes legible the affective, relational ties between present-day Indigenous literatures and ongoing traditions of gender variance. Ultimately, this intervention expands current analyses of gender and sexuality in Indigenous studies as well as extending the range and value of rhetorical studies of embodiment.

To make this three-pronged argument in the space of a chapter, I focus on one piece, Thirza Cuthand's 2012 *Boi Oh Boi*, a powerful nine-and-a-half minute experimental film in which Cuthand presents multiple articulations of her own masculinity. A Plains Cree/Scots filmmaker, blogger, and performance artist from the Little Pine First Nation in Saskatchewan, Cuthand (b. 1978) began making films at sixteen.[3] Among her many shorts, she has earned accolades for films such as *Lessons in Baby Dyke Theory: The Diasporic Impact of Cross-Generational Barriers* (1995), *Through the Looking Glass* (1999), *Helpless Maiden Makes an 'I" Statement* (2000), and *Anhedonia* (2001). Although she began her successful career as a filmmaker well before formal training, Cuthand completed her degree at the Emily Carr Institute of Art and Design. Throughout her oeuvre, from her earliest films to her most recent, Cuthand challenges static identity constructions by interrogating the intersections of Indigeneity, gender, sexuality, and disability.[4] Cuthand furthers her analyses of these inherently rhetorical junctures through her articulation of female masculinity in *Boi Oh Boi*.

Thinking particularly about the discourses surrounding Indigenous men and masculinity, Aboriginal Studies scholar Sam McKegney defines masculinity "as a tool for describing the qualities, actions, characteristics, and behaviors that accrue meaning within a given historical context and social milieu through their association with maleness, as maleness is normalized, idealized, and even demonized within a web of power-laden interpenetrating discourses" (2). Meanwhile, Kanaka Maoli scholar Ty P. Kāwika Tengan, in *Native Men Remade*, currently the only monograph on Indigenous masculinity, likewise considers "the way cultural and gendered formations emerge through discursive practices" (16). Cuthand examines discursive understandings of masculinity in relation to the *female* body in *Boi Oh Boi*. Although the film looks across several periods of Cuthand's life from adolescence to adulthood, it centers on the six months in which she lived as a trans man and considered physically transitioning. Throughout the film, Cuthand layers a spoken rumination on female masculinity—a running monologue about her gender identity as a Two-Spirited butch lesbian[5]—atop regularly changing shots of the body as she literally and figuratively practices differing forms of masculinity. In addition to embodying a classic butch visual aesthetic—husky body, short hair, jeans—Cuthand also includes numerous thigh-to-stomach close-ups of herself as she packs—at times inserting a banana into her pants, at times a packing penis. The embodied juxtaposition of Cuthand's frank monologue with her array of sometimes funny, sometimes provocative, and often contradictory rhetorical claims for a female-bodied masculinity underscores Jack Halberstam's landmark contention that "masculinity must not and cannot and should not reduce down to the male body and its effects" (1). Yet, even while calling for the necessity of more nuanced analyses of queer practices in *Female Masculinity*, Halberstam recognizes a "general disbelief in female masculinity"; this disbelief represents a "failure in [our] collective imagination ... [given that] female-born people have been making convincing and powerful assaults on the coherence of male masculinity for well over a hundred years" (15). In *Boi Oh Boi*, Cuthand's embodied rhetorical constructions of female masculinity not only complicate the imaginative "failure" Halberstam references, but also highlight the fact that discourses of (what we would now term) female masculinity have existed for a long time in Indigenous contexts.

Female Masculinity and the Affective Turn

From the opening scene of her short film to its final moments, Cuthand represents female masculinity as a rhetorically produced affective circuit—it is an expressive act that comes into visibility through a rhetorical relationship with others. In other words, the body is felt/the body is read/the body is affectively understood and this interactive cycle occurs within the social space of rhetorical exchange. Female masculinity, in this paradigm, is a rhetorical performance that gains discernibility through affiliation and association with others.[6] In fact, *Boi Oh Boi* comments on this active interplay through its depiction of a kind of affectively engendered female masculinity in the opening sequence: "When I was in high school, I asked my soon-to-be one-time lover: Do you think I am butch or femme? I was clearly butch but I hadn't yet identified myself. I really wanted to know. I think she was being polite, because she just said, 'I don't know.'" The audience hears these words while seeing Cuthand in jeans and a black muscle tee looking at herself in a mirror while applying hair product to her short hair and leaning, arms crossed, against a brick wall—visuals undoubtedly intended to function for comic effect, implicitly asking viewers how anyone could look at Cuthand and *not* see her as performing butch identity. Viewers are thus encouraged to practice rhetorical reading—to interpolate Cuthand into the affectively embodied space of the butch body, a space that, as Halberstam has famously shown, is indicative of certain forms of female masculinity.[7]

In this brief introductory segment, *Boi Oh Boi* casts female masculinity, at least for this particular Indigenous filmmaker, as an embodied, relational experience. In rhetorical studies, this sort of felt experience has been described as a form of embodied knowledge.[8] The film argues that Cuthand's masculinity, though unspoken, is read, and, moreover, manifested through the act of rhetorical discourse—Cuthand's interactions with her friend/later-lover speak particular gender possibilities into being through the discursive act of questioning, even if the answer itself remains unspoken at that moment. In this rhetorical exchange, knowledge circulates outside the body, and gender performances can exist without one's conscious awareness ("I was clearly butch but I hadn't yet identified myself."). Yet, the female masculinity that Cuthand had "not yet" recognized, and that her friend refused to verbalize, was an open secret between them, which, to invoke José Esteban Muñoz, hangs in the air like rumor.[9] The embodied knowledge of Cuthand's butch identity is therefore affectively created in the relay between their bodies, in the implied exchange of gazes, and even in that which remains unsaid. The politics of recognition here and, in fact, throughout the film, thus hinge on the embodied routes of intimate knowledge. Cuthand's masculinity exists in just such an affective circuit—that burgeoning, ever-morphing space of possibility within which gender becomes intelligible. As a result, in Cuthand's film, gender identities, even if written on the body, become legible through an affective act of rhetorical exchange.

In *Boi Oh Boi*, Cuthand describes the gender expression her younger self had "not yet" recognized (and that her friend/soon-to-be lover refused to verbalize) as a secret waiting to be acknowledged and articulated through rhetorical interaction. This facet of the film's representations of female masculinity evokes a concept of affect that ties directly to rhetorical understandings of the body. In her theory of embodied rhetoric, which disentangles and delineates the difference between embodied language, embodied knowledge, and embodied rhetoric, A. Abby Knoblauch refers to a "gut reaction," or the "sense of knowing something *through* the body," as embodied knowledge (52). *Boi Oh Boi* represents gender identity as just such embodied knowledge: Cuthand "knows" her butch identity and presents it in recognizable form to others even before she names it as such. Her "gut reaction" operates within a circuit of knowledge production, an affective economy, in which Cuthand presents as butch, is perceived as butch, *and then* comes to self-define as a butch lesbian. In this scene, embodied knowledge is mobilized through the proximity of bodies. Such performance of female masculinity creates an embodied relational circuit—an affective turn—in which, to use Knoblauch's distinctions, *a way of knowing* becomes *a form of knowledge* (51).

Affect integrates these intersecting spaces of mind, body, and knowledge (and self/other/world) in which ways of knowing become forms of knowledge, which is why it is key to rhetorical analyses of female masculinity. In his foreword to *The Affective Turn: Theorizing the Social*, Michael Hardt looks to the foundational theory of Baruch Spinoza to situate affect in the act of synthesis, which we can understand as the syncretic spaces of embodied knowledge. Hardt contends that

> the mind's power to think and its developments are ... parallel to the body's power to act. This does not mean that the mind can determine

the body to act, or that the body can determine the mind to think. On the contrary, ... mind and body are autonomous [though] they nonetheless proceed and develop in parallel. ... [Additionally] the mind's power to think corresponds to its receptivity to external ideas; and the body's power to act corresponds to its sensitivity to other bodies. (ix–xiii)

This relational, reciprocal sense of feeling, knowing, acting, and interacting is evident in *Boi Oh Boi*'s depictions of female masculinity, which nod to the way the body, embodied knowledge, and gender performances coalesce, thereby interrogating *how* such ways of knowing gender become forms of knowledge about gender. Sara Ahmed extends this interaction of bodies and affect by emphasizing that bodies necessarily form in response to others. In *The Cultural Politics of Emotion*, she explains, "Bodies take the shape of norms that are repeated over time and with force. ... How bodies work and are worked upon shapes the surfaces of bodies" (145). Both Hardt and Ahmed, then, suggest the sort of embodied knowledge that Knoblauch describes as necessarily affective; embodied knowledge, even that which we script as "gut reaction," arises from a "sensitivity" to other bodies and to the discursive forces that surround us.

Although the short film is replete with examples of the affective rhetorical circuit I sketch here, I turn to the pivotal scene during which Cuthand narrates a six-month experience of living as a trans man. Cuthand's exploration of the space of transition—that shifting bridge between and among differing articulations of masculinity—relies, at both its beginning and its end, on physical and psychic connections, on affective understandings of the self in relation to others. While the first section of the film narrates a butch identity that was always already present—as my reading of the opening scene demonstrates—Cuthand represents her experience of transition as a tentative, experimental foray into manhood. The physical aspects of masculinity—such as testosterone's potential effect on the libido—are integral to the experience; however they're overtly tied to the *female* body. She explains, "I felt this tingling in my crotch. And also my body temperature rose. And I swear my clit felt just a tiny bit bigger. I wanted a bigger clit, being a show-off butch with big breasts and all." This sense of herself as a "show-off butch," with its implied understanding of a necessary audience, speaks to the relay Cuthand represents between the articulation of masculinity as a butch lesbian and as a trans man. Halberstam reminds us that "not all transsexualities ... present a challenge (or want to) to hegemonic masculinity, and not all butch masculinities produce subversion. However, transsexuality and transgenderism do afford unique opportunities to track explicit performances of nondominant masculinity" (40). For Cuthand, the experience of female (nondominant) masculinity becomes intelligible through a specifically rhetorical web of relationships. In fact, Cuthand narrates the beginning and end of her six months as a trans man through the lens of conversations with those close to her. The embodied rhetorical circuit I previously identified is further privileged through these acts of affective exchange. Correspondingly, *Boi Oh Boi*'s representations of female masculinity enable us to build on Knoblauch's contention that "it is through my body, our bodies, that we know the world" (56). We do understand the world through our bodies; however, Cuthand shows that we only develop such embodied rhetorical knowledge through our "sensitivity to *other* bodies" (Hardt xiii, emphasis added). Embodied rhetoric—that visceral experience of knowledge bound to our particular bodies—can only exist in intimate relationships.

A specific example of my claim for the interplay of embodied rhetorical knowledge and female masculinity lies in Cuthand's description of her first experience with testosterone, which takes place prior to her period of transition. Her exploration with testosterone is marked by attention to interaction and the affective relationship; though the forms of rhetorical embodiment in her two differing articulations of female masculinity—trans and butch identities—function differently. In a scene in which Cuthand describes taking a hormone shot and subsequently informing her friends she has done so, the body is a performative text: Cuthand interprets her gender explorations vis-à-vis the gaze of others. The rhetorical nature of this affective exchange is accentuated by what Cuthand depicts as a marked *need* for audience response. She explains, "I'd had a shot of testosterone a few years before the whole trans thing came up in my life. I was curious. ... I remember going to an opening and sitting on my friend's Rebecca's lap and suddenly announcing, 'I had a shot of testosterone!' I remember everyone's head swiveled around to look at me." While the physical body is discussed—it's after this shot when Cuthand notes that her "clit felt just a little bit bigger"—the emphasis in the scene is not on her physical reaction, but instead on the desire for social interaction and audience response (an affective rhetorical circuit). From sitting on her friend's lap to the public announcement of her testosterone shot, Cuthand employs the body as a communicative space that incites engagement. In other words, my argument here is that even in the corporeality, the physicality of this moment in which Cuthand's body interacts with a chemical compound, she constructs female masculinity not in the body, but *in the affective spaces between bodies.*

This affectively produced rhetoric of female masculinity is likewise privileged through the visuals that play when Cuthand describes her exploration of FTM transition. The sepia-tinged shot begins when Cuthand, wearing a plaid button-down, stands against a white wall as the voiceover describes her brief foray into manhood. She states, "In 2007, when I turned 29, I was considering transitioning to male. I changed my name informally to 'Sarain,' which is what I would have been called had I been born a boy." At this point in the film, Cuthand raises her hand and reveals the black object she'd been holding is a decidedly fake mustache, which she then dons crookedly. The narration continues as Cuthand begins to drape a tie around her neck: "I made a packer out of hair gel, condoms, and a sock, and wore baggy shirts to hide my tits, which didn't really work because I have large breasts.

I tried taking up space differently, but I wasn't interested in aping the irritating aspects of men." Finally, while Cuthand clumsily ties the tie, she notes, "I talked with my doctor about transitioning and she was looking into where the gender clinic was for me." Throughout this scene, both the visuals and the narration craft Cuthand's temporary FTM transition as a form of play, a narrative distinctively at odds with classic transgender plotlines. In such stories, which are often told through memoir, the gender assigned at birth parallels the biologically defined body; however, in most trans memoirs cisgendered pairing is at odds with the trans persons' embodied knowledge of their gender identity. As a result, many trans narratives describe an experience of gender dysphoria that is present from childhood to transition. By contrast, Cuthand experiences only "one really clear moment of gender dysphoria once when I was 20 and looking at myself naked in a full-length mirror. My body didn't make sense to me. Didn't feel like it was mine. It shook me a bit, but then faded away." This representation of trans masculinity crafts a radically different rhetoric of embodiment than the gut reaction that, for Cuthand, marks her butch identity. Instead of arising from (or being indicative of) embodied knowledge, trans masculinity circulates within a performative narrative that relies upon overt, affective exchanges with an audience.[10]

While the forms of knowledge function differently in each case, the film posits each example of female masculinity as an affective part of the rhetorical circuit. It is, then, the interstitial space of relationship, the affective turn, that engenders these rhetorics of masculinity. These intersubjective rhetorics situate female masculinity as both relational and contingent. However, in the first sections of *Boi Oh Boi*, these contingencies, though moored by the body, do not mesh entirely with an understanding of embodied rhetoric. Knoblauch contends that while "embodied rhetoric born from embodied knowledge ... can rattle loose ... privileged white masculinist discourse," such disruptive work requires a recognition that "knowledge comes from somewhere, from a particular body," with a particular history (62). Therefore, such rhetorical practices *must* purposefully address a politics of location: "Embodied rhetoric, when functioning *as* rhetoric, connects the personal to the larger social realm, and makes more visible the sources of all our knowledge" (62). Thus, however interactive Cuthand's affective articulations of female masculinity might be, it is not until the final segment of her film that such embodied rhetorical potential is fully engaged.

Two-Spirit Traces

Until the last third of the film, *Boi Oh Boi*'s commentary on the affective nature of female masculinity rests upon seemingly deracinated evocations of butch and trans identities that, while clearly classed, don't suggest a specifically Aboriginal context. This potentially mainstream queerness fragments when the film engages Two-Spirit ideology. The final section of *Boi Oh Boi* therefore queers the previously identified rhetorical circuit when Cuthand reads gender through a decolonial lens.

The monologue introduces Two-Spirit identity with an almost academic distance. Cuthand says: "I remember reading about Two-Spirited people when I first came out. About women who lived as men and went hunting and to war and took wives, and rode horses bare chested like men. I didn't know if they were trans or butch. They were from a different time when those labels didn't even exist yet." Interestingly, as first articulated, this knowledge of alternate gender roles in Aboriginal communities, rather than being described through the sort of embodied rhetorical language Cuthand employs in her previously discussed depictions of herself as butch, comes not from gut reaction or embodied knowledge, but from texts. Moreover, the existence of Two-Spirit gender performances, or what Lakota anthropologist Beatrice Medicine has called "facets of action," is kept at a temporal distance through the comment that such discourses about gender existed at "a different time."[11]

As Cuthand, who has been working within the intersections of queerness and Indigeneity in her films for nearly 20 years, undoubtedly knows, the term "Two-Spirit" did not gain currency until the 1990s. At the third annual Native American/First Nations gay and lesbian conference in Winnipeg, a group of Indigenous activists and scholars intentionally forwarded the term, which had theretofore been used informally among queer Native people as a replacement for the troubling and commonly used "berdache." While Native nations have tribally specific language for those who take up non-heteronormative gender positions, such as "winkte" among the Lakota and "nàdleehí" among the Navajo, the anthropological term "berdache" holds problematic connotations of sexual deviance. Though Navajo anthropologist Wesley Thomas suggests that "Two-Spirit" was presented as a "working term" that was not meant to be permanent, it has continued to gain currency in both academic and nonacademic settings since the publication of Sue-Ellen Jacobs, Thomas, and Sabine Lang's landmark edited collection, *Two-Spirit People* (1997).[12] "Two-Spirit" intentionally recalls the histories of Indigenous nations that have more complex gender logics while also purposefully distancing queer Indigenous peoples from the monolith of white queer identity that haunts mainstream appellations like "gay" and "lesbian."[13] In this way, the term unsettles the anthropological gaze by insisting on a specific politics of location in which queer Indigenous people name and claim their own discursive reality. As performance studies scholar Jean O'Hara explains in *Two-Spirit Acts*, Two-Spirit "is the only [English-language] word that incorporates Indigenous cultural understandings" (xx). Such an intentional rhetorical act, which deploys language to demand the acknowledgment of a particular history and particular bodies, moves Cuthand's short film firmly into the realm of embodied rhetoric. Thus when Cuthand recovers female masculinity from the unmarked space of whiteness through the invocation of Two-Spirit history, a decolonial reclamation occurs; her embodied rhetoric—a discourse of female masculinity articulated through the affective relay between Cuthand's body and that of others around her—"rattle[s] loose ... privileged white masculinist discourse" (Knoblauch 62) for viewers who might whitewash (whether intentionally or unconsciously) the rhetorical circuit *Boi Oh Boi* constructs.

Over the course of her monologue, Cuthand questions the academic distance that initially severs her gender performances from the space of queer Indigeneity and allows herself to imagine a more expansive sexual rhetoric. She subsequently remarks: "I sometimes think about what my role in my tribe would have been if colonization hadn't happened. If I was dealing with being queer from a position completely uninfluenced by white Western thought." By reflecting on the rhetorical possibilities of Indigenous knowledge, Cuthand revises the troublesome demand that she stand on one side or another of a discrete binary between femininity and masculinity, between a male bodied person and a female bodied person, between a butch lesbian and a trans man. Indeed, when Cuthand refuses to allow her Aboriginal identity to be subsumed by a butchness that presupposes a racially unmarked body, she employs Two-Spirit histories to rewrite female masculinity through a particularly Indigenous lens. In the process, *Boi Oh Boi* reminds audiences of the colonial history of the land they inhabit, thereby enacting what Scott Lyons (Ojibwe/Mdewakanton Dakota) has famously termed "rhetorical sovereignty."

Importantly, too, *Boi Oh Boi* shows Indigenous gender traditions to be not only *still extant* but also *distinctly different from* trans identities. Cuthand explains at one point in the film that, when she was living as a trans man, her mother "refused to call [her] by my boy name, or my chosen pronouns. She basically ignored the whole thing." However, while Cuthand's mother might refuse to accept Cuthand as a *trans* man, by contrast, her mother *invokes* the cultural memory of alternate gender roles in Native communities: "My mom told me I would have been a third gender ... I think that's how I own my butch identity now. I like the overlap between man and woman. The blurring of the lines. Becoming something totally different from man or woman. Owning my curves, my hardness and softness and gentleness. And yes, even for me, that fierceness." The exchange between mother and daughter speaks volumes to the continued circulation of multiple gender roles in Indigenous cultural memory. While Cuthand's mother refuses to acknowledge her in a trans-identified gender performance, she by no means refutes Cuthand's performance of nonheteronormative gender; instead, she makes that embodied rhetorical act legible within a particular Indigenous context. Their affective rhetorical exchange exemplifies the survivance of certain types of cultural knowledge as well as the strength of Indigenous people's rhetorical refusal of settler narratives.[14] Moreover, to return to Knoblauch, we see Cuthand employ a specifically Indigenous form not just of embodied *knowledge* but also of an embodied sexual *rhetoric* here when she makes "a purposeful decision to include embodied knowledge and social positionality as forms of meaning making" (52). Indeed, Knoblauch's contention that embodied rhetoric requires one to speak from a politics of location has particular weight when that bodily location challenges damaging settler ideologies and emphasizes the continued existence of Aboriginal cosmologies. In this case, when *Boi Oh Boi* presents a scenario in which a mother's words negate a Western reading of her daughter's gender and desire, Cuthand's uses an embodied Two-Spirit rhetoric to subvert a settler narrative of queerness.

In the introduction to his recent edited collection *Masculindians,* Sam McKegney interrogates the hypermasculine stereotypes of Indigenous men and calls for a more productive understanding of Indigenous masculinities. McKegney contends that scholars like Kimberly Anderson (Cree-Metis), Robert Innes, and Jonathan Swift "provide a model of [a] type of balance" in conversations about masculinity (4). Indeed, their work further explains that "[s]uch investigation and theorization is not strictly reclamatory but indeed creative. … [The focus of such analyses] therefore, is not on the recovery of a mythic 'traditional' or 'authentic' Indigenous masculinity;. … Rather, the emphasis must be on exploring sources of wisdom, strength, and possibility within Indigenous cultures, stories, and lived experiences and creatively mobilizing … that knowledge in processes of empowerment and decolonization." (4–5). My brief reading of Cuthand's film demonstrates how the discourse of female masculinity in *Boi Oh Boi* exemplifies this type of creative decolonial practice through the purposeful, affective deployment of embodied rhetoric. To do so, Cuthand's smart, funny, experimental short places the range and complexity of masculinities at the center of theoretical inquiry. Through her reveries on butch and trans masculinities and the relay between them, Cuthand shows how the affective spaces between bodies generate embodied knowledge about female masculinities. But significantly, that rhetorical knowledge resides in a particular Indigenous body, on Indigenous land with a specific history. In the end, like the tripartite argument that began this chapter, Cuthand's film packs a threefold punch: in *Boi Oh Boi,* Cuthand's representations of female masculinity construct an affectively produced sexual rhetoric that challenges static concepts of Indigenous masculinity in the dominant culture and expands analyses of gender and sexuality in Indigenous studies while also demonstrating how, through the use of embodied rhetoric, an Indigenous filmmaker can unsettle the settler logics of queerness.

Notes

1. This argument is part of my current book project, *Big Moms and Butch Dykes: Queerness and Female Masculinity in Indigenous Literatures.* I initially engaged female masculinity in *The Queerness of Native American Literature.* This exploration is extended in "'Tales of Burning Love': Female Masculinity in Contemporary Native Literature" (forthcoming 2015), an essay that articulates the three framing claims I extend here.
2. I'm building especially from the groundbreaking work of scholars like Scott Lauria Morgensen, Andrea Smith, and Craig Womack, who have argued for the primacy of Indigenous critical lenses.

Affect, Female Masculinity, and the Embodied Space Between 131

3. Cuthand's artistic talent runs in the family, as her mother, Ruth Cuthand, is a prominent artist who likewise critiques settler politics and draws attention to the activism and histories of Aboriginal people in Canada. See Borsa, *Ruth Cuthand*.
4. Film critic Michelle La Flamme situates Cuthand, who is a member of Canada's Indigenous Media Arts Group (IMAG), as part of "a new First Nations cinema in British Columbia, with Native women at the forefront, [that] has begun to unsettle the West" (404). La Flamme contends that IMAG "challenges the temporality of Western cinema's geographical and historical constructs by placing the margins at the centre. [These Indigenous artists] reconfigure[] the notion of a frontier by supporting the creation of films and videos that have the ability ... to express [the] unconquered territories of First Nation peoples' imaginative spaces" (404–405).
5. I use this identification as per Cuthand's website and most recent films. See "Welcome! Tawaw!" *Thirza Cuthand: Filmmaker, Performance Artist, General Troublemaker*. http://www.thirzacuthand.com, 11 May 2014.
6. My reading of the affective circuit relies on a Deleuzian sense of becoming, which recognizes, and in fact requires, a sense of multiplicity. According to Deleuze and Guattari, such evolving multiplicities have "neither subject nor object, only determinations, magnitudes, and dimensions that cannot increase in number without the multiplicity changing in nature. ... [Thus] the dimensions of a multiplicity ... necessarily change[] in nature as it expands its connections" (*A Thousand Plateaus* 8). Feeling, seeing, and/or knowing are ongoing, interrelated processes rather than discrete, singular events.
7. I discuss Halberstam's work further in "'Tales of Burning Love': Female Masculinity in Contemporary American Indian Literatures."
8. See, for example, William Banks, Jane E. Hindman, and A. Abby Knoblauch.
9. I'm thinking here of Muñoz's theory of queer ephemera. See *Cruising Utopia*.
10. Cuthand represents trans identity as primarily performative *for the filmmaker*; she is not making claims that all trans identity is performative.
11. In a classic essay that circulated for years as a conference paper before being printed in *Two Spirit People*, Medicine explains, "Among the Lakota (Teton Sioux) there is evidence that other facets of action were bounded within the winkte gloss—ritualist, artist, specialist in women's craft production, herbalist, seer, namer of children, rejector of the rigorous warrior role, 'mama's boy' ... and the designation [of male homosexual] commonly stated in anthropology books" ("Changing" 150).
12. Personal conversation with Wesley Thomas at Washington University in St. Louis on 7 February 2014.
13. See Gilley, *Becoming Two-Spirit*; Jacobs, Thomas, and Lang, eds., *Two-Spirit People*; Lang, *Men as Women, Women as Men*; Roscoe, *Changing Ones*; Williams, *The Spirit and the Flesh*. See Driskill on the use of "Two-Spirit" rather than "gay" or "lesbian," "Stolen from Our Bodies," 62n3. For a discussion of the efficacy of the term "queer" in Indigenous studies, see Womack, *Red on Red*, 300–301. For a critique of the pantribal and panhistorical nature of the term "Two-Spirit," see Epple, "Coming to Terms with Navajo Nádleehí."
14. In this interaction, *Boi Oh Boi* mirrors what Tengan discusses as 're-membering' masculinities, a type of gendered memory work that facilitates the formation of group subjectivities through the coordination of personal memories, historical narratives, and bodily experiences and representations" ("Re-membering Panal'au" 27–28).

Works Cited

Ahmed, Sara. *The Cultural Politics of Emotion.* New York: Routledge, 2004. Print.

Banks, William. "Written through the Body: Disruptions and 'Personal' Writing." *College English* 66.1 (2003): 21–40. Print.

Borsa, Joan (author), Lee-Ann Martin (contributor), Gerald McMaster (contributor), and Jen Budney (editor). *Ruth Cuthand: Back Talk, Works 1983–2009/Kihkahtowi-Naskwewasimowin: Astoskewina 1983–2009.* Saskatoon: Saskatchewan: Mendel Art Gallery, 2012. Print.

Cuthand, Thirza. *Boi Oh Boi.* (9:32) Dir. Thirza Cuthand. Saskatchewan: A Fit of Pique Production, 2012.

Cuthand, Thirza. *Helpless Maiden Makes an 'I" Statement.* Dir. Thirza Cuthand. 2000.

Cuthand, Thirza. *Thirza Cuthand's Through the Looking Glass.* Dir. Thirza Cuthand. 1999.

Cuthand, Thirza. "Welcome! Tawaw!" *Thirza Cuthand: Filmmaker, Performance Artist, General Troublemaker.* www.thirzacuthand.com, 11 May 2013.

Deleuze, Gilles, and Felix Guattari. *A Thousand Plateaus: Capitalism and Schizophrenia.* Trans. and Foreword Brian Massumi. Minneapolis: U of Minnesota P, 1988. Print.

Epple, Carolyn. "Coming to Terms with Navajo Nádleehí: A Critique of Berdache, 'Gay,' 'Alternate Gender,' and 'Two-Spirit.'" *American Ethnologist* 25 (1998): 267–90. Print.

Gilley, Brian Joseph. *Becoming Two-Spirit: Gay Identity and Social Acceptance in Indian Country.* Lincoln: U of Nebraska P, 2006. Print.

Halberstam, Judith (Jack). *Female Masculinity.* Durham, NC: Duke UP, 1998. Print.

Hardt, Michael. "Foreword: What Affects Are Good For." *The Affective Turn: Theorizing the Social.* Eds. Patricia Ticineto Clough with Jean Halley. Durham, NC: Duke UP, 2007. ix–xiii. Print.

Hindman, Jane E. "Making Writing Matter: Using 'the Personal' to Recover[y] and Essential[ist] Tension in Academic Discourse." *College English* 64.1 (2001): 88–108. Print.

Hindman, Jane E. "Writing an Important Body of Scholarship: A Proposal for an Embodied Rhetoric of Professional Practice." *JAC* 22.1 (2002): 93–118. Print.

Jacobs, Sue-Ellen, Wesley Thomas, and Sabine Lang, eds. *Two-Spirit People: Native American Gender Identity, Sexuality, and Spirituality.* Urbana: U of Illinois P, 1997. Print.

Klopotek, Brian. "'I Guess Your Warrior Look Doesn't Work Every Time': Challenging Indian Masculinity in the Cinema." *Across the Great Divide: Cultures of Manhood in the American West.* Eds. Matthew Basso, Laura McCall, and Dee Garceau. New York: Routledge, 2001. 251–73. Print.

Knoblauch, A. Abby. "Bodies of Knowledge: Definitions, Delineations, and Implications of Embodied Writing in the Academy." *Composition Studies* 40.2 (2012): 50–65. Print.

La Flamme, Michelle M. "Unsettling the West: First Nations Films in British Columbia." *Women Filmmakers: Refocusing.* Ed. Jacqueline Levitin, Judith Plessis, and Valerie Raoul. New York: Routledge, 2003: 403–18. Print.

Lang, Sabine. *Men as Women, Women as Men: Changing Gender in Native American Cultures,* trans. John L. Vantine. Austin: U of Texas P, 1998. Print.

Lyons, Scott Richard. "Rhetorical Sovereignty: What Do American Indians Want from Writing." *CCC* 51.3 (2000): 447–68. Print.

McKegney, Sam. *Masculindians: Conversations about Indigenous Manhood.* East Lansing: Michigan State UP, 2014. Print.

Medicine, Beatrice. "Changing Native American Roles in an Urban Context and Changing Native American Sex Roles in an Urban Context." *Two-Spirit People: Native American Gender Identity, Sexuality, and Spirituality.* Ed. Sue-Ellen Jacobs, Wesley Thomas, and Sabine Lang. Urbana: U of Illinois P, 1997. 145–55. Print.

Million, Dian. "Felt Theory: An Indigenous Feminist Approach to Affect and History," *Wicazo Sa Review* 24.2 (2009): 53–76. Print.

Morgensen, Scott Lauria. *Spaces Between Us: Queer Settler Colonialism and Indigenous Decolonization.* Minneapolis: U of Minnesota P, 2011. Print.

Muñoz, José Esteban. *Cruising Utopia: The Then and There of Queer Futurity.* New York: New York UP, 2009. Print.

O'Hara, Jean. "Introduction." *Two-Spirit Acts: Queer Indigenous Performances.* Ed. Jean O'Hara. Toronto: Playwrights Canada P, 2013. xix–xxii. Print.

Roscoe, Will. *Changing Ones: Third and Fourth Genders in Native North America.* New York: St. Martin's, 1998. Print.

Smith, Andrea. "Queer Theory and Native Studies: The Heteronormativity of Settler Colonialism." *GLQ: A Journal of Gay and Lesbian Studies* 16. 1–2 (2010): 42–68. Print.

Tatonetti, Lisa. *The Queerness of Native American Literature.* Minneapolis: U of Minnesota P, 2014. Print.

Tatonetti, Lisa. "'Tales of Burning Love': Female Masculinity in Contemporary Native Literature." *Indigenous Men and Masculinities: Legacies, Identities, and Regeneration.* Eds. Kimberly Anderson and Robert Innes. Winnipeg: U of Manitoba P, forthcoming 2015. Print.

Tengan, Ty P. Kawika. *Native Men Remade: Gender and Nation in Contemporary Hawai'i.* Durham, NC: Duke UP, 2008. Print.

Tengan, Ty P. Kawika. "Re-membering Panal'au: Masculinities, Nation, and Empire in Hawai'i and the Pacific." *The Contemporary Pacific* 20.1 (2008): 27–53. Print.

Williams, Walter L. *The Spirit and the Flesh: Sexual Diversity in American Indian Culture.* Boston: Beacon, 1986. Print.

Womack, Craig. *Red on Red: Native American Literary Separatism.* Minneapolis: U of Minnesota P, 1999. Print.

10 The Unbearable Weight of Pedagogical Neutrality
Religion and LGBTQ Issues in the English Studies Classroom

G Patterson

Across a variety of personal-political orientations toward LGBTQ issues, teacher–scholars in English Studies tend to espouse neutrality as pedagogical best practice. Not only do I question this practice, I strongly caution against it. Specifically, I argue that pedagogical neutrality limits the intellectual and political reach of English Studies, encourages uncritical thinking on LGBTQ topics, and unquestioningly centralizes the needs of students from privileged social groups while putting queer and trans students and teachers at risk. To substantiate these claims, I draw from the results of my person-based research project that asks English Studies teachers, across the United States, to reflect on their experiences addressing LGBTQ issues in the classroom.

Before I move on to discuss my study, it behooves me to demonstrate how pervasive neutrality is among pedagogical discussions of lesbian, gay, bisexual, queer, and transgender topics. As I mentioned earlier, a teacher's propensity to address topics in neutral ways says little of their personal-political orientation when it comes to non-normative sexualities, gender identities, and gender expressions. While a handful of studies resist neutrality narratives,[1] by and large, English Studies teachers espouse neutrality toward LGBTQ issues as pedagogical best practice.

On the whole, there are three genres of the neutrality narrative. The first of these narratives portrays conservative Christian students as a new minority, whose right to explore their home literacies is under siege (Perkins 586). Frequently, these scholars appropriate discourses of the oppressed, likening conservative Christian students to brave civil rights agitators or to those who must closet their religious perspectives in the classroom (Rand 361; Stenberg 279). A second strain comes from scholars who advocate for discussing minoritized sexualities[2] in the classroom. While these scholars cite the transformative value of discussing such topics for *all* students, they caution readers against adopting pedagogical stances in the classroom that might "colonize" (religiously) conservative students (Byington and Waxman 158; Miller 251; De la Tierra 169–70). This worry about oppressing (religiously) conservative students extends into the third strain of scholarship. Here, scholars reference non-normative sexualities[3] as just one of many controversial topics about which students might write, and it becomes the teacher's job to set aside his or her personal convictions and help students practice argumentation—regardless of how damaging said argument may be (Downs 40; Hansen 24).

Across these narratives, scholars articulate both LGBTQ people and conservative Christians as subordinate social groups, competing in a zero-sum game that all but requires neutrality to maintain a "fair and balanced" classroom environment. At a basic level, this pedagogical stance flies in the face of decades of critical theory—which point to Christian, heterosexual, and cisgender identities as dominant social groups that get to define reality and have that reality stick for others (Johnson 33). As such, I maintain that those who advocate pedagogical neutrality at the LGBTQ–religious junction practice a false objectivity that maintains an oppressive status quo.

Understanding that there is sometimes a significant difference between what we espouse in pedagogical scholarship and what we actually experience in the classroom, I designed a two-phase, person-based study that asked English Studies teachers to reflect on their experiences addressing LGBTQ issues in the classroom. In the first phase of the study, I designed an online survey and, using a convenience sample, recruited colleagues through the Queer Studies listserv, the Writing Program Administrator (WPA) listserv, and my professional social media accounts. Sixty-four English Studies teachers responded to the survey. Using the survey itself as a recruitment tool for the second, interview phase of my research, 12 of the original participants elected to participate in follow-up interviews. I conducted these interviews via Skype, telephone, and in person; the means of communication depended on convenience for both participants and interviewer. All interviews were recorded and transcribed. For the purpose of brevity, I focus in this chapter on a thematic analysis of nine participants' follow-up interviews.

As a practitioner of sexual rhetorics, I employ participants' narratives as a way to read against the grain of our discipline's dominant pedagogical narratives. This form of reading queerly from the margins allows me to see past those narrative tropes—here tropes of neutrality—that can limit our pedagogical praxis. Building from the work of Deborah Britzman and Jen Gilbert, I articulate sexual rhetorics as a methodology—as a willingness to "be audacious enough to consider the disjunctions, ambivalence ... conflicts [and] 'loose ends'" of our pedagogical narratives (92). Indeed, my motive for interviewing participants was to bypass the disciplinary narratives that often control discourse in more public academic venues. From my own informal conversations with colleagues, I know well that teachers engage in "unsanctioned" disciplinary and pedagogical talk. While person-based research doesn't necessarily mimic the coffee shops, barrooms, hallways, and other comfortable venues in teachers' lives, I hoped to provide a space for participants to "attend to that which lingers in the margins of any story: *what will have been said*" (83).

In what follows, I relay the findings of my interviews with nine participants. To avoid (name) confusion, however, I center my thematic analysis on the stories of five participants: *Will*, a white, gay, cisgender man; *Trixie*, a white, bisexual, cisgender woman; *Michelle*, a white, cisgender, femme-identified lesbian; *Lynn*, a white, cisgender lesbian; and *Aiden*, a mixed-race, pansexual, nonbinary trans person.[4] To varying degrees, Will, Trixie, and Lynn noted their identification with (or participation in) Christian discourse communities. Neither Michelle nor Aiden mentioned religious identifications. With the exception of Aiden, who was still a graduate student at the time of our interview, all other participants were tenured faculty members.

In striking contrast to the pedagogical literature I reference above, my interview participants challenged the pervasive expectation that teachers adopt neutral stances toward LGBTQ issues. Indeed, participants' experiences of conservative, anti-LGBTQ pushback—from students, parents, colleagues, and administrators—demonstrates how much our discipline's pedagogical *practice* is at odds with our discipline's decades-long affair with critical theory. Working from participants' stories, I locate three themes (below) that highlight this tension. All told, I argue that this theoretical/pedagogical disconnect offers us an opportunity to reflect on our discipline's political and ethical commitments:

- First, participants challenged the claim that (conservative) Christian students are an overlooked minority in the English Studies classroom.
- Second, participants questioned the assumption that LGBTQ issues should be presented along neutral, pro/con lines.
- Third, participants challenged the apolitical narrative that the compositionist's job is to "just teach writing" and instead rearticulate the compositionist's job as teaching *socially just* writing.

Questioning (Conservative) Christian Victim Narratives

All participants questioned the claim that (conservative) Christian students are a besieged minority in the classroom. Several participants depicted (conservative) Christian students *and* their parents as a rather empowered constituency—drawing attention to their attempts to police the curriculum. For example, Michelle described an encounter with a (conservative) Christian student who found her pedagogical response to abortion unsatisfactory and, as a corrective, brought in a copy of the Bible and "trained it on [her] like a weapon." As Michelle moved through the classroom, the student adjusted the book so that the words "Holy Bible" were always facing her. When she confronted the student after class, he explained that it was his duty to remind her of God's views on women's sexuality. In a similarly troubling story, Aiden recounted having once received an email from the parents of an 18-year-old student enrolled in their literature course. The parents expressed concern that some course material addressed issues of sexuality and drug use, and in an appeal to the literary canon, the student's parents asked, "Shouldn't you be teaching Shakespeare?" As the email correspondence continued, the parents became more incensed; they decried Aiden's course as both immoral and biased.

Both Michelle and Aiden's encounters clearly describe attempts by conservative Christians to affect curricular change through direct confrontation with marginalized teachers. In each case, conservative Christians operated under the privileged assumption that course material was biased inasmuch as it didn't reaffirm their socially dominant world view—and at public universities, no less.

In a similar vein to these teachers' stories, several participants made a direct link between (conservative) Christian students' sense of entitlement in the college classroom and the availability of right-leaning political action committees that were to assist students with lawsuits against liberal professors. In another of their courses, for instance, a white, het-cis, male student threatened legal action against Aiden, believing he was "being oppressed both as a straight man and as a Christian." While they noted that the student's complaint didn't materialize into an actual lawsuit, Aiden did tell me that their colleague was currently facing a lawsuit based on similar grounds. Commenting on this phenomenon, wherein students from dominant social groups confuse cognitive dissonance with oppression and seek legal retribution, Aiden noted that they were not alone, citing the vulnerability of many professors who "teach programs with the word 'studies' after them." Universities have become so afraid of lawsuits, Aiden observed, that the easiest solution seemed to be radically defunding or altogether gutting programs that study the experiences of minoritized groups.

Lynn's story bears a striking resemblance to Aiden's. Noting the conservative religiosity of her Arkansas students, she emphasized that she was careful about addressing anything during class time that wasn't germane to her Technical Writing course. During a moment before class, however, one of her students inquired about her new wedding band. When she explained to the student that her partner (a woman) had recently proposed to her, an older, white male student became very upset and exclaimed, "This doesn't belong in any classroom!" She was almost certain the student had left the room to report her for misconduct. Legal concerns were ever-present with conservative groups on campus, Lynn explained, and after a colleague was sued by conservative students on campus, "It made people think about what they were saying in their classes."

Of course, the precarity of addressing LGBTQ topics didn't end at inappropriate classroom outbursts. Lynn also recalled a discussion she had with her department chair about the university catalogue's misspelling of her Queer Theory course. When she suggested that the "Clear Theory" typo be fixed, her chair suggested that—given her upcoming tenure review—perhaps the misspelling was for the best. Here too, it seems, departments are so afraid of conservative pushback that the easiest solution is to downplay the academic contributions of queer and trans scholars—or avoid hiring them (for tenure track jobs) altogether.

Clearly, Lynn and Aiden's experiences trouble the alleged marginalized status of (conservative) Christian students. When a group of students has conservative thinktanks and legal organizations at their disposal—waiting for a liberal infraction to occur—this throws doubt on claims that conservative Christians are a minority group. Indeed, the only way to feasibly support such a claim would be to either purposefully misunderstand what constitutes a minoritized positionality or to focus solely on student/teacher dynamics while disavowing the connections between the classroom and the larger political climate.

Interrogating the Neutral Framing of LGBTQ Issues

Eight participants took exception to the popular notion that teachers ought to frame LGBTQ issues neutrally. Across the board, participants observed students, colleagues, and administrators' attempts to justify neutral frameworks as a matter of fairness for "all students." Of course, participants saw through this "fair and balanced" façade, observing this faux "marketplace of ideas" as a reinscription of cultural dominance.

This professionalized expectation of neutrality became a very real issue for Will, particularly as he reflected on a notoriously active email thread posted to the Writing Program Administrator listserv (WPA-L). On July 31, 2010, a WPA-L listserv member posted a vaguely heterosexist screed to the WPA-L, meant as a show of solidarity with Georgia graduate student Jennifer Keeton. For readers who are unfamiliar with this story, Keeton was dismissed from her counseling program after she refused to counsel queer and trans clients, claiming that "homosexuality was a personal choice" (Netter) and that "binary male-female gender ... [was] not a social construct or individual choice[5] subject to alteration" (Rhett Miller). In retaliation, Keeton sued the university, arguing that her counseling program ought to have respected her religious beliefs and remained neutral.

Taking in this conversation on the WPA-L, Will recalled his surprise at how many listserv members echoed messages of support for Keeton, claiming the Bible to be "real and true" and using the opportunity to indict rhetoric and composition for similarly trivializing the beliefs of conservative Christian students. One can easily imagine Will's dismay, given how many participants in the thread were themselves writing program administrators, holding significant sway over composition curricula. Sidestepping disciplinary ethics—including Keeton's dehumanizing regard for LGBTQ people—many listserv participants framed the debacle as a programmatic failure to help conservative Christians acclimate to academic discourse communities. Still others regarded the news story as an interesting, controversial issue to discuss in composition classrooms while, of course, taking care to attend to "both sides" of the story.

Reflecting on these narratives and his colleagues' repeated calls to "respect" the beliefs of (conservative) Christian students, Will said, "I don't believe for a second that ... not being able to say what you feel like saying at a given moment in the classroom is oppression." Honing in on the unspoken cultural dominance of conservative Christianity, particularly their views on LGBTQ issues, Will openly wondered if WPA-L participants would have been equally as passionate about the religious beliefs of non-Christian students. Reflecting on his own classroom experiences, Will noted that when it came to addressing LGBTQ issues, "No one in here asked me about Koran verses. There's nothing in here about the Torah I've been asked to deal with, no Native American spirituality I've been asked to address." Will's points are worth restating. Are teachers truly being fair to "all students" by expressing a culturally dominant *and oppressive* view of LGBTQ people as just one of many viable arguments in the marketplace of ideas? Moreover, what exactly do compositionists mean when they claim that we should "respect" conservative Christian students' beliefs? And should all beliefs, even dehumanizing ones, be respected—particularly in a classroom environment that (presumably) encourages students to reflect on how they're reading and writing the world?

Of course, beyond the ethical issues participants raised, others added that neutral frameworks risk stifling students' intellectual development. In this regard, participants took particular issue with teachers' tendency to frame LGBTQ issues as pro/con debates. Illustrating this point within the context of a string of news reports about anti-gay pastors embroiled in "homosexual scandals," Michelle argued that pro/con debates encourage students to become distracted by "a kind of popular discourse [where] ... all religious leaders who are anti-gay are bad—or we should out them or whatever—or they're all gay." This approach, she added, didn't seem very "productive in terms of understanding the function" of discursive events like "homosexual scandals" in the first place. Similarly, Will noted that pro/con debates encourage students to think that the point of all discussions—and of all research—is to have *The* answer. What gets lost in the process, he claims, is students' ability to ask larger questions about "why people are disagreeing." At the end of the day, Will said, he wants his students to "have the questions." Pro/con arguments, he claimed, prevent students from asking larger questions about how and why LGBTQ issues become "controversial issues" in the first place.

At the same time, some participants noted that debates do have the limited value of getting students' ideas about LGBTQ issues on the table; the problem boils down to the expectation of neutrality. For instance, while Trixie felt that teachers "can't just allow students to say things on one side of the argument," she didn't believe that this somehow obviated a social justice stance. The point of allowing students' perspectives to flourish, she argued, was so that anti-LGBTQ views didn't go underground—where they can't be critically examined. Trixie explained, "You have to have room for students to say all those things if they're ever going to get to some middle place." While Trixie acknowledged that this approach might not encourage students to alter oppressive views about LGBTQ issues, she added that when teachers employ a social justice approach to classroom debates, students are at least encouraged "to change the way they act and react, [the way they] treat other people, the way they look at texts, and the way they look at the media."

In a similar light, Aiden argued that once students begin talking about LGBTQ issues, teachers must complicate binaristic, pro/con arguments. Using the popular classroom topic of gay marriage as an example, Aiden explained that when the only positions that teachers present to students are "for" and "against" gay marriage, a whole host of queer perspectives remain at the margins of public discourse. This is a particularly apt point, given how many queer and trans scholars and activists have identified "gay marriage" as upholding white hetero-patriarchy, noting that issues like prison abolition and universal healthcare are far more pressing for the most marginalized LGBTQ people. Unfortunately, as Aiden observes, binaristic arguments—in their attempt to present "fair and balanced" information—strip students' field of vision with regard to whose lives are worthy of discussing in the first place.

Across a range of personal-political orientations toward non-normative sexualities, gender identities, and gender expressions, composition teachers frequently advocate presenting LGBTQ issues with neutral frameworks. Many take up pedagogical neutrality as a way to create a "safe space" for all students in their classroom. In contrast, participants' accounts illustrate that such an approach has the effect of making the classroom a place "safe" from critical perspectives on LGBTQ issues. Moreover, the assertion that all perspectives on LGBTQ issues are equally valid sidesteps important questions about privilege and power. However generous teachers' motives may be, practicing pedagogical neutrality can only benefit those with heterosexist and cissexist viewpoints (religious or not).

Re-Visioning "Just Writing" as Socially Just Writing

Observing the insidiousness of neutrality, beyond how LGBTQ issues are discussed (or ignored) in the classroom, seven participants took issue with popular pedagogical narratives that strip the compositionist's job to "just" teaching writing. Participants observe that "just writing" narratives are often deployed to thwart social justice pedagogies. Indeed, as the reader may recall from the literature I reviewed earlier, teachers seem to have a special fondness for employing "just writing" narratives, when faced with conservative Christian students who articulate oppressive stances on LGBTQ issues. In these cases, "just writing" narratives encourage teachers to set aside their "personal" views on LGBTQ issues and instead work with the student to strengthen the persuasiveness of their writing—however oppressive that writing may be. Observing a disconnect between critical theory and its practice, participants identify "just writing" narratives as a stealthy way of evading the critical and ethical commitments so widely espoused in the discipline of rhetoric and writing.

Michelle tempered her critique of "just writing" narratives by first acknowledging the uphill battle that queer and trans teachers often face when responding to hetero- and cissexist arguments in students' writing. Referring to her own run-ins with conservative Christian students in the classroom, Michelle reflects:

> Let's say we're talking about a comp class and a student says in a paper, [...] "Well, homosexuality is wrong because god says it's wrong in the Bible." [...] You can make it a purely writing question, and you can say [to the student], "You need to develop your ideas." I'm just not sure. I mean, that's what we've done; as comp people we've done it a lot. I've fallen back on it. Like sometimes you're just sick and tired of talking about this shit—sick and tired of dealing with the student who refuses to complete the task, and so you say: "This is the task. Do it." And I think that's what you need to do sometimes.

Given her earlier account of being policed by a white, het-cis, male student for not taking an appropriate stance on abortion—an "appropriateness" he conflates with Christo-normative mores—the exhaustion Michelle describes here makes sense. Perhaps especially for queer and trans teachers who occupy multiple minoritized positionalities, momentarily adopting a "just writing" approach to oppressive student writing may be a matter of personal-political survival. Indeed, given similar conflicts participants described with colleagues, parents, and teachers, we must also consider how minoritized teachers might articulate their job as "just" teaching writing as a matter of *professional* survival.

All that said, Michelle points out that "just writing" narratives shouldn't be our "first approach" when students articulate hetero- and cissexist arguments based on religious grounds. Citing our discipline's decades-long commitment to critical theory, Michelle argues that there are far more appropriate responses than simply focusing on the writing and helping students strengthen oppressive arguments. While she doesn't advocate engaging students in biblical arguments, which might intellectually ensnare both teacher and student, Michelle does recommend acknowledging students' perspectives while "continuing to highlight the intellectual endeavor" at hand. Modeling an ideal pedagogical response to anti-LGBTQ arguments, she encourages students to consider: "If we're talking about discourse, if we're talking about the way something functions in society, [...] then where does this point take us—*not* 'How can we argue it out, how can we come to a conclusion?'" Highlighting a disciplinary understanding of writing as a means of discovery, Michelle argues that the point of writing is to encourage students to keep asking critical questions.

Picking up where Michelle left off, participants observed that they encountered religiously motivated, anti-LGBTQ arguments in students' writing *most frequently* when responding to argumentative research papers. Overwhelmingly, participants questioned the usefulness of argumentative research papers, claiming they encourage students to select "controversial" topics, arm themselves with cherry-picked research, and take uncritical positions on topics about which they are largely uninformed. Questioning the way these assignments encourage students to think "the point of an essay is to end with an answer," Will articulated a different approach. He explained:

> I say to students, "I'm sorry to disempower you here, but [...] it's the first time you've spent really looking at this question and so it feels wrong to really expect you to have an answer. I've been thinking bout this for ten years and I don't have an answer [...] We're going to walk away from [the argumentative essay]. I want you to have the questions. If you can think about why this issue is a problem, [...] why they are disagreeing, write that up. That is a good thing to figure out."

Will and Michelle aren't alone in distancing themselves from the argumentative research paper. Many participants described themselves as "going rogue" by developing unsanctioned assignments that ask students to think about arguments circulating in the public sphere a bit more critically. Participants' alternative assignments marry critical and rhetorical theories by asking students to perform discourse analyses on topics of interest and encouraging them to pay attention to how arguments about their topic vary by discourse community. Drawing attention to privilege and power, participants' assignments also ask students to consider those arguments that linger on the margins of public debates. For instance, according to Aiden, if a student were to analyze the United States' ban on transgender people serving in the military, attending to the margins might mean drawing attention to trans activists of color who articulate *real* "trans justice" from an anti-imperialist lens. Regardless of the particularities of their alternative assignments, all participants encouraged their students to consider the larger sociopolitical consequences of their arguments—something "just writing" approaches prevent teachers from addressing.

Beyond the above-mentioned concerns of the participants, they also argued that when teachers adopt "just writing" approaches to problematic student writing, they're framing rhetoric and composition as a discipline without ethical standards. Divorcing writing instruction from the sociopolitical impact of discourse flies in the face of years of critical theory—including critical pedagogy—which encourages students to consider the larger consequences of how they read and write the world.

Indeed, Will argues that such "just writing" narratives are a cop-out—one that intentionally prevents teachers from considering disciplinary ethics. He explained: "I think ethics remains a huge problem we do not address. The logic people don't address it; they 'just deal with the logic'—which to me is irrelevant sometimes. [Others will say], 'Well I'm just teaching academic discourse.' I'm like, 'Hmm, you're teaching ethics.'" Will's point here is apt. In spite of the fact that, in our own work as scholars, we operate under foundational assumptions about how rhetoric ought (and ought not) to be employed, we shy away from sharing these disciplinary standards with our students. According to Will, this reticence to address disciplinary ethics in the classroom is *especially* prevalent when teachers encounter students making anti-LGBTQ arguments based on religious grounds. Will observed:

> I think what hasn't happened yet is a reflective move ... is looking at the profession and asking why we keep entertaining that conversation. What is the value [of addressing the intersection of religion and LGBTQ issues]? My guess is that there would be some hope that, like the racist or sexist student, we want to move them beyond that conversation somehow. I think we're more apt to say about racist and sexist students that we want to move them out of that conversation than we are with religious students—that we want to move them outside of their religion—or to a different vision of their religion. And we're very uncomfortable saying that. ... I don't think we talk about it enough because we don't want to be heavy handed and say, 'Well you have to believe what I believe.' But ethics and belief are not the same thing.

The reader may find Will's candor shocking or refreshing, but what ought not to be lost here is his excellent distinction between ethics and belief. Like other participants in my study, Will highlights the way writing teachers tend to "respect" students' anti-LGBTQ arguments precisely because they ground them in religious belief. Too often, writing teachers regard religious-moral frameworks as a super-discourse that is beyond interrogation in the classroom. But what Will and other participants point out is that belief happens to an idea. In other words, religious beliefs are rooted just as much in rhetorical appeals as any other idea, and just like secular beliefs, they should be judged by the conduct they inspire. Too often, those of us who occupy privileged social groups forget that beliefs can translate into action—and those actions can be deadly. Regardless of whether or not students frame oppressive arguments along religious or secular grounds, it is our ethical obligation as compositionists to highlight for students how one's arguments shape who will (and will not) be seen as human.

Across the board, participants made a case for designing curricula and creating assignments that encourage students to see the relationship between rhetorics and ethics from the very beginning of the course. Participants also drew attention to the consequences of not doing this in the classroom, arguing that "just writing" arguments encourage students to ignore the dire consequences their arguments can have.

For example, Trixie urged teachers to consider the larger social consequences of anti-LGBTQ arguments—something that gets eclipsed when teachers "set aside their personal beliefs" and help students strengthen their oppressive arguments. For instance, Trixie noted how neutrality narratives ultimately led to Tennessee's "Don't Say Gay" bill (HB229/SB049). Starting from the assumption that Christians are a minoritized social group, this bill mandated that teachers not speak about LGBTQ issues. Highlighting the effect Tennessee's "Don't Say Gay" bill will have on students, Trixie added, "Schools were already hiding [LGBTQ] books ... in the library. A student had ... to ask for them, which of course defeated the purpose [...] [And for a] number of Gay-Straight alliances, at this point, their *names* are not even allowed—it doesn't make any sense." In the name of respecting (conservative) Christians' beliefs about sexuality, the lives of an already vulnerable student population become even more precarious.

Trixie's point is worth restating. When teachers employ a "just writing" approach, they can only examine whether the writing avoids grammatical errors, makes persuasive appeals, and presents technical information professionally. Professional documents like HB229/SB049 certainly meet these criteria. What gets lost, however, is that HB229/SB049 effectively rendered LGBTQ-identified students and teachers as worthy of discrimination.

Similarly identifying the worldmaking potential of our pedagogies, Aiden critiqued "just writing" approaches as an attempt to create an apolitical, "subject-less discourse," noting that such attempts always fail. Aiden explained:

> Even being apolitical and trying to not have a stance is an ... and that's sort of the liberal move to make things very sanitized. Like this issue of like colorblindness—'I don't see race. Everyone's equal to me.' That's bullshit. We need to be talking about power relations and the intersections of those and hegemony and how that works. I want [students] to critically think about themselves, their own position, the world around them, how it impacts them. So the affect, the aesthetic, and the political, and how all are intertwined. ... We are not just removed from what we learn. When we write, although it is a solitary act, it can be a very interpersonal activity, ... one that reaches out beyond just you and the computer.

Here, Aiden draws our attention to how a "just writing" approach overlooks the way popular discourse—even liberal discourse—can render invisible the violence minoritized communities experience. Throughout their interview, Aiden attended to how morality discourses demonize poor queer and trans people—many of whom, thanks to the workings of kyriarchy, are gender-nonconforming people of color. Aiden claimed that when teachers adopt a false objectivity, in which they don't see difference and in which everyone is equal, they obscure for themselves *and for their students* how belief discourses render minoritized communities as less than human and thus worthy of violence. When teachers refuse to see difference, for example, they lose the ability to demonstrate how racist, heterosexist, cissexist, and Christo-normative discourses intersect in violent ways that cost the lives of queer and trans people of color—like Jessi Hernandez, Goddess Edwards, Lamia Beard, Ty Underwood, Jazmin Vash Payne, Taja Gabrielle de Jesus, and Penny Proud.

As practitioners of rhetoric and composition, we have long understood that arguments must be persuasive *and* ethical. We must share these disciplinary standards with our students. Teaching students to strengthen anti-LGBTQ arguments under the banner of practicing the rhetorical arts not only diminishes the credibility of our field but also contributes to a violent world. To reiterate, participants aren't challenging the value of teaching students to write. They are fundamentally asking us to redefine the "just" in "just writing" narratives—to ground our pedagogies in social justice.

Conclusion

Throughout this chapter, I have articulated sexual rhetorics as a method of reading our oft-cherished pedagogical narratives from the margins. This queer rhetorical practice isn't an empty exercise. As Britzman and Gilbert contend, the repetition of even valuable pedagogical narratives can "foreclose the work of thinking about our thinking" (82). In this study, participants illustrate the divide between theory and practice in allegedly neutral approaches to LGBTQ issues. They interrogate seemingly benign phraseology, like "respecting students' beliefs," "celebrating the marketplace of ideas," and "just focusing on the writing."

While multiply minoritized teachers have sometimes adopted pedagogical neutrality as a matter of survival, this does not give the rest of us an alibi. Too many of us have moved through educational spaces with unchecked epistemic privilege and have adopted neutrality as an extension of genuine goodwill toward our students without questioning how appeals to the student-as-everyman consolidate racial, sexual, gender, cisgender, and religious oppression in the classroom. However good our intentions may be, we can no longer overlook the dire consequences of pedagogical neutrality.

There are ways to address difficult questions our discipline faces without turning to neutrality as an easy way out. Indeed, participants invite us to reconsider "just writing" as *writing with justice*. No simple turn of phrase, this concept requires us to rebuild our curriculums from the ground up. That said, participants haven't left us in a lurch. They model a way of considering the worldmaking power of discourse and its ability to render us (un)human. Rather than framing the rhetorical arts as a zero-sum game, participants' rogue pedagogies encourage questions and highlight our accountability to others for the stories we tell, the stories we repeat, and the stories we refuse. In short, they offer us a story of rhetorics and ethics that is rooted in social justice. The question remains: Are we willing to hear it?

Notes

1. See, for example, Martha Marinara, Jonathan Alexander, William Banks, and Samantha Blackmon's "Cruising Composition Texts: Negotiating Sexual Difference in First-Year Readers" which critiques composition textbooks' pro/con framing of LGBTQ issues.

2. Please note that, on the whole, we've yet to fully explore transgender issues in rhetoric and composition scholarship.
3. Here again, transgender issues rarely come up as a "controversial" issue to be explored in the composition classroom.
4. Please note that Aiden uses singular they/them as pronouns.
5. I'd like to call the reader's attention to the contradictory rhetorical appeals employed by Keeton—wherein the validity of minoritized sexualities are invalidated as a "personal choice," while trans identities are invalidated as something that can never be a "personal choice."

Works Cited

Britzman, Deborah, and Jen Gilbert. "What Will Have Been Said about Gayness in Teacher Education?" *Teaching Education* 15.1 (2004): 81–96. Print.

Byington, Eleanor, and Barbara Frey Waxman. "Teaching Paul Monette's Memoir/Manifesto to Resistant Readers." *College Literature* 24.1 (1997): 156–81. Print.

De la Tierra, Tatiana. "Coming Out and Creating Queer Awareness in the Classroom: An Approach from the U.S.-Mexican Border." *Lesbian and Gay Studies and the Teaching of English: Positions, Pedagogies, Politics*. Eds. William Spurlin. Urbana, IL: NCTE, 2000. 168–90. Print.

Downs, Douglas. "True Believers, Real Scholars, and Real True Believing Scholars: Discourses of Inquiry and Affirmation in the Composition Classroom." *Negotiating Religious Faith in the Composition Classroom*. Eds. Elizabeth Vander Lei and Bonnie Lenore Kyburz. Portsmouth: Boynton/Cook, 2005. 39–55. Print.

Hansen, Kristine. "Religious Freedom in the Public Square and in the Composition Classroom." *Negotiating Religious Faith in the Composition Classroom*. Eds. Elizabeth Vander Lei and Bonnie Lenore Kyburz. Portsmouth, NH: Boynton/Cook, 2005. Print.

Johnson, Allan. *Privilege, Power, and Difference*. 2nd ed. Boston: McGraw-Hill, 2006. Print.

Marinara, Martha, Jonathan Alexander, William Banks, and Samantha Blackmon. "Cruising Composition Texts: Negotiating Sexual Difference in First-Year Readers." *College Composition and Communication* 61.2 (2009): 269–96. Print.

Miller, Richard. "Fault Lines in the Contact Zone: Assessing Homophobia in Student Writing." *Lesbian and Gay Studies and the Teaching of English*. Ed. William Spurlin. Urbana, IL: NCTE, 2000. 234–52. Print.

Netter, Sarah. "Georgia Student Sues University Over LGBT Sensitivity Training." *ABC News*. 27 July 2010. Web. 16 Feb. 2013.

Perkins, Priscilla. "'A Radical Conversion of the Mind': Fundamentalism, Hermeneutics, and the Metanoic Classroom." *College English* 63.5 (2001): 585–611. Print.

Rand, Lizabeth. "Enacting Faith: Evangelical Discourse and the Discipline of Composition Studies." *College Composition and Communication*. 52.3 (2001): 349–367. Print.

Rhett Miller, Joshua. "Lawsuit Claims College Ordered Student to Alter Religious Views on Homosexuality, Or Be Dismissed." *FOX News*. 27 July 2010. Web. 9 Feb. 2015.

Stenberg, Shari. "Liberation Theology and Liboratory Pedagogies." *College English* 68.3 (2006): 271–90. Print.

"WPA-L Listserv, The." *Council of Writing Program Administrators*. Charlie Lowe and Quinn Warnick. Web. 16 Feb. 2013.

11 The Story of Fox Girl
Writing Queer about/in Imaginary Spaces

Martha Marinara

> *Humanness is never simple.*
> —Audre Lorde

Constructing a writing identity is an unpredictable, relational activity of emergence that exists in the decision to cross into the imagined space of the classroom, to write the "self" in ways that may be risky or dangerous for some students, even though current writing pedagogy promises the safety net of tolerance to any difference. The risk and danger come from the possibilities of erasure and invisibility. Note Jonathan Alexander and Jacqueline Rhodes in "Flattening Effects": "multicultural pedagogies frequently rely on narratives of inclusion, which often seek to contain difference in order to make it legible, identifiable, and thus acceptable to a normative readership" (431). Whether physical, virtual or imaginary, the classroom—like writing—is rhetorically situated and exists in its own institutional context, a context that hasn't shed its history of meritocracy or of reproducing the *status quo* despite our continuing, critical questioning of the academy. But what if we look at the classroom as a *queer space*, not a space for students to pass through on their journeys to their professional lives, but as a space to critique identity, history, and notion of social justice? A space for students to "queerly" write the frames with which to perceive identity, culture, and the material conditions of people's lived experience, so that the classroom is part of a transitioning world and its own space simultaneously, a space where students can make meaning(s) that include(s) differences in identity and worldmaking? Is it possible to genuinely engage queer theory in the classroom, or will queerness just become another line item on the list of learning outcomes?

Children love to talk about imaginary spaces and imaginary, fantastical selves. My five-year-old granddaughter claims to have something I have always wanted: an alter ego, a secret self who appears when she wants to do something transgressive, annoying, or bad, something she thinks is fun but her parents do not, a self who, unlike students in the classroom can safely transgress the *status quo* of five-year olds and then reenter it without fear of reprisals or social stigma.

Last spring, I took her to the Peabody Museum at Yale University. She was especially intrigued by the display of gemstones. "I am going to come here at night, break the glass and steal all the jewels," she whispered in my ear, her hair tickling my cheek, its softness framing her outrageous declaration of evil. Of course (even though I am her Nana), I told her that she couldn't do something so wrong, that stealing would hurt many other people. She pouted and said in a lowered voice, "fox girls don't care."

Apparently, not just anyone can be a "fox girl." One has to find a magic ring in the woods or "someplace like a forest." There were several other qualifications and tests that I either didn't understand or couldn't do, so I had to give up the idea of being initiated into the fox pack. Unlike children, and despite evidence to the contrary, I don't slip so easily into make-believe spaces, into accepting the seeming illogic that imaginary spaces require. This is unfortunate because imaginary spaces can give one enormous power and something equally important when one is trying to make political and social changes—hope for social justice in the possible lives on the other side of the threshold.

In fairy tales and other narratives of fantasy, threshold spaces are magical, glowing with risk and promise. Alice falls down the rabbit hole, a space full of bits and pieces of her prelapsarian life—crockery, book shelves and old maps, school books and cupboards, an empty jar that had been presumably filled with orange marmalade—into a world populated by peculiar, anthromorphic creatures that play with our sense of logic, which is precisely the point of Lewis Carroll's novel. But what happens the moment Alice decides to leap down the hole after the bow-tied White Rabbit? Before she crosses over the threshold from a hot and boring Sunday afternoon into the fantastical nightmare that is Wonderland, she is, for a brief moment, a refugee, someone without a country or an identity.

That liminal space, the space where identity—who we are and where we come from—is difficult to maintain; it leaves Alice in exile from both the *status quo* and imaginary places, a space that is decidedly queer. Writes Judith Halberstam,

> Queer uses of time and space develop, at least in part, in opposition to the institutions of family, heterosexuality, and reproduction. They also develop according to other logics of location, movement, and identification. (1)

A place without the stability of landscape or continuity of history and culture is a queer space. What happens when Alice leaps down the hole, before she crosses into the imaginary space is important, for in that liminal, in-between space she must agree to reimagine reality, to look at structures and institutions—and living creatures—in different ways.

I write, and in writing, I enter metaphor and metaphor enters me. I take up space, inhabit an imaginary trope: the lesbian writer/the lesbian reader/

the lesbian subject. Within queer theorizing is the rhetorical practice of disidentification, or the ways in which one situates oneself both within and against the various discourses through which we identify. Sometimes I write in codes and patterns that are endlessly repeated.

Feminist literary scholar Paula Bennett notes the reoccurrences and repetitions of round, organic objects in Emily Dickinson's poetry:

> Dews, crumbs, pearls, and berries occur 111 times, and with peas, pebbles, pellets, beads, and nuts, the total number of such images comes to 261. (113–14)

She notes that these objects act as metaphors, representing Dickinson's clitoris and giving her poetry a kind of feminine, lesbian power. And, although I have done this same task in naming or writing my own self, the endless oversight that includes counting to ensure inclusion, I have noticed that queer presence even in overwhelming numbers does not necessarily denote respect or social equality. And, I want something for my writing identity besides metaphoric smallness, tiny powers, and recursive circles. Paul Ricoeur explains that metaphor as a "categorical transgression" can be understood as a deviation in relation to a structured, logical order:

> This transgression is interesting only because it creates meaning. [...] should we not say that metaphor destroys an order *only to invent a new one*; and that the category mistake is nothing but the complement of a logic of discovery? (22; emphasis mine)

The metaphoric language of peculiarity serves to reveal what culture has historically regarded as deviation, using narrative space to disrupt sameness. So here I am writing metaphors in a tension-filled liminal space, included in and standing against the discourse that explains and produces metaphors.

Note: Writing as disordering, as transgressing, but no repetition, no counting peas. Fox girl does not like counting peas.

We have found that we can queer anything. Queer scholarship bought queer theory and queer studies an academic legitimacy, made it an object of study, a discipline, complete with its own canon that includes Judith Butler, Eve Sedgwick, Michel Foucault, Theresa de Lauretis, Diana Fuss, Biddy Martin, and Michael Warner, to name a few. Graduate students take seminars in queer theory and write dissertations that apply queer theory to pedagogy and writing. But as Warner points out, the trouble with normal is that the "power lies exclusively on the normal side" (44). And the normal side, unlike imaginary spaces, devours difference in the name of tolerance. Or, as my older daughter once said to me when I told her that I liked the music she was listening to, "That's the problem with alternative music. The minute lots of people start liking something, it becomes mainstream and then it stops being alternative."

Alexander and Rhodes, in "Queer: An Impossible Subject for Composition," argue that scholarship on the potent intersections of queer theory and rhetoric and writing "remains relatively sparse and under-read" (178). They continue:

> Queer compositionists have contributed important essays that prod us to think critically about the importance of LGBT content in our writing curricula, to be attentive to the particular literacy and instructional concerns of LGBT students, and even to consider the potential implications of queer theory for the teaching of writing. However, while comparable work in feminist thinking, critical pedagogies, and postmodernity in general have created significant movements within the field of rhetoric and composition studies, queerness and queer theory have not, despite their significant contributions "across the hall," that is, to literary study. (178)

And I would add in other disciplines and departments across campuses, such as student life, where social activism is often encouraged and rewarded.

Why can't queer theory function rhetorically in the classroom, not just in the life of an individual seeking a voice, the student constructing a writing identity, but also when teaching students to write civic discourse and impact public spheres? Can queer rhetorical practice make room for alternative voices, alternative ways of being, and contrary approaches to public policies and social issues? An individual, a subject, can be disciplined and silenced. But rhetorical acts, developed through interventions such as disidentification, emerge collectively over time to queer how the public sphere argues and considers public policies.

The trouble lies in academic legitimacy, a certain kind of assimilation, because legitimacy comes with the cost of stabilization. The problem with becoming mainstream or legitimizing "queer" as a discipline is that it domesticates desire and tames what is imaginary and dangerous about our scholarship, pedagogy, writing, and teaching. In stepping over the threshold of the potential, in placing the impossible and the unrepresentable into the current framework of composition studies, and into what is passable, possible knowledge in English and Rhetoric departments, work in queer composition studies has become domesticated (albeit uncomfortably), part of the house that we desire to contest, submissive to the rhetoric we want to transform. As David Halperin notes in "The Normalization of Queer Theory," faculty who first introduced queer theory to universities and academic scholarship "were motivated first and foremost by an impulse to transform what could count as knowledge, as well as by a determination to transform the practices by which knowledge functioned within the institution" (343). According to Robert Faunce, "the work of our pioneering queer theorists on queer pedagogy establishes a holding environment (not unlike the ones we create for our students) for us to ruminate in on the further uses of queer pedagogy, and its evolution into other forms of pedagogy" (30). In other words, to play within the imaginary worlds afforded by liminal or queer spaces, to ruffle or disturb the boundaries and borders of knowledge and teaching practice already in place in the academy. And at the same time, to remain legitimate, acceptable, respected—all while teetering on the threshold of the doorway to Wonderland.

Many pedagogies use borders or thresholds as their metaphorical and theoretical underpinnings. The goal of border pedagogy is to remove cultural and political barriers to attain a greater conceptualization of the human experience. "Borders," writes Henry Giroux, "call into question the language of history, power, and difference" (51). Within the borders or thresholds, it is possible to critique what lies on either side.

The word "threshold" is derived from the Latin *limen* and is used by some anthropologists when describing a rite of passage, a crossing over, a separate state before reassimilation. Arnold Van Gennep, a French ethnographer and folklorist first introduced the concept of "transition" as a stage an individual passes through during a "life crisis" (vii). His 1909 *Rites de Passage*, a work essential to the development of the concept of liminality, discusses the transition or passage in the context of rituals in small-scale societies. In his observations, he found a tripartite sequence in ritual observance: separation, transition, and incorporation. Van Gennep offered interpretations of the significance of these rites as forms of social regeneration, based on such natural symbols as death and rebirth (xx).

For example, an adolescent can be considered as existing in a liminal state, since the adolescent is no longer fully a child and not yet an adult. The intersection between face-to-face interaction and cellphone conversations is a liminal social space, in which a caller is neither fully engaged with those who are physically co-present, nor fully mentally co-present (except for the technically mediated auditory connection) with the person on the other end of the line. Sadie Plant calls it a "bi-psyche" and points out that "in a way the mobile [phone] has created a new mode in which the human mind can operate, or that the cell phone user is operating as though in two worlds in the psychological sense" (50). No one remains in a liminal state, but merely uses it as a transition, by law, custom, culture, or ceremony, to another state of being such as adulthood.

However, when Victor Turner first borrowed from Van Gennep the concepts of "liminal" and "liminality" in 1967, he focused almost entirely on the transitional or liminal stage of the rite of passage. He noted: "the subject of passage ritual is, in the liminal period, structurally, if not physically, 'invisible'" (95). According to Turner, the state of liminal individuals is socially ambiguous. Turner defined liminality as a state between states, a "betwixt and between," a beginning state and a final state. He further defines the concept: "Liminality may perhaps be regarded as the Nay to all positive structural assertions, but as in some sense the source of them all, and, more than that, as a realm of pure possibility whence novel configurations of ideas and relations may arise" (97). The words "novel" and "pure possibility" tend to support and legitimize the imaginary, "queer space" of rabbit holes and writing classrooms.

This in-between space seems to me to be much like a writing classroom where we ask students to reimagine writing and texts when they enter, but often fail to recognize the complicated contradiction between their identities as writers and their identities as students. Susan Miller points out in *Rescuing the Subject*,

> As a *student*, this writer appropriately points out, but does not personally assert, positions within already well established discourse communities. But as a *writer*, this student must by writing also assert and be accountable for at least a learner's perspective on these communities. (163; emphasis in original).

We want them to think critically, to develop new frames for their windows on the world, to become skeptical, but I worry that we have stopped reimaging the classroom, reimagining the academic hierarchy of knowledge from emerging to mastery. No matter how much we argue about what to add to our list of writing standards because we want to include identity, diversity, difference, queer rhetorics, feminist rhetorics, the contents of the lists of "what students should know" (NCTE, WPA) remain largely the same. When we do include something about diversity or difference, it is an element on the list, added on, rather than presented as a way of thinking, of seeing writing identities, or as a method of teaching and learning. And while I agree that the skills and concepts constructed by NCTE and WPA are necessary for students to successfully navigate the academy, their professions, and their communities, I worry that we are not putting enough emphasis on helping students use language to imagine future communities, to construct—at least on paper—the worlds they'd want to live in and who they want to be. We only allow the traditional and the transgressive to run on parallel tracks, when like fox girl, I want the tracks to run in different directions, to reveal their differences, different selves and different worlds.

In her own Wonderland, the lesbian writer produces joy, play and passion with/in her words, "the body, memory, the language of the writer compels us in a synergistic field of circulating energies, but without the closure such a systemic metaphor suggests" (Meese 85). Instead, we have incompletion, writing that is never finished, teaching that tries to reveal the struggle with identity, but only shows us glimpses.

As a field, rhetoric and composition prides itself on serving as a means to students' public and professional identity, by providing them with opportunities to gain rhetorical awareness and critical frameworks for interpreting discourse, by getting them ready for a "real world," a world we often imagine as an impersonal, disinterested meritocracy, a space where they won't succeed if we don't teach them the discourses that garner political and social power. Too often, however, these efforts to help students succeed underestimate the personal identity negotiations necessary for many students to take up public roles. None of the lists of learning objectives for language arts and college composition explicitly prompts students and teachers to address the multiple aspects of personal identity that are always already part of such negotiations, particularly features of identity that are socially and cultural stigmatized in the dominant culture. Instead, seeing these identity negotiations in a reimagined space better conceptualizes the need to move among a variety of subject positions, often in a cyclical or recursive rather than linear manner.

Queer pedagogies, much like critical pedagogies, can disrupt normal notions of learning and perceive classrooms as situated in larger spheres of politics and power. Lauren Berlant and Michael Warner remind us that "pedagogy should not be about the reproduction of identities or their representation, but about world building, culture making" (548). But even when teaching queer, we rely heavily on our own stereotypes—reproducing notions and representations of drag and camp, butch and femme as the transgressive space when juxtaposed with the dominant straight culture.

Last week, in an effort to get my students thinking, "really" thinking about their writing, I stopped them in the middle of their freewriting exercise (the normal) and asked them to make origami cranes (the transgressive). I was driven by a story I had heard about Ludwig Wittgenstein, the philosopher of logic and mathematics, who wrote and published the Tractatus *in 1921. In just 75 pages, he thought he had said all there was to say about language. Nothing else of his was published in his lifetime. The story I heard as an undergraduate—which is more than likely not true or misremembered—is that later in Wittgenstein's life, after he put a new roof on his sister's house, he revised his ideas about language. A true story or not, there is something about working with one's hands that pushes the brain, manipulates synapses, puts one on edge, and changes how one perceives the world.*

The students were totally out of their comfort zone. Many asked me over and over if I would fix their cranes or show them again how to fold the colored paper. The anxiety in the room was palpable. They went back to their writing and in enormous relief finished far more pages than I thought they would. They did, however, leave with their cranes. Next week, I'll ask them to unfold the cranes and write on the paper.

Queer theory and pedagogy has drawn heavily from Judith Butler's gender theory, developed first in *Gender Trouble* and later in *Bodies that Matter*, built around the idea of gender as performative and sexuality as part of a repetitive system of practice that becomes internalized as a personal ontology of identity based on the imposition of hegemonic power systems. Based on this model of gender and sexuality, performative acts can be classified as either normative, things that are cisgender or heterosexual, or transgressive, including transgender and homosexual behaviors. While foundational to our current queer theory principles, this performative system leaves little room for theorizing identities that are both normative and transgressive simultaneously, a focus that limits Sedgwick's "open mesh of possibilities," challenging what is imaginable regarding authorship, representation, and culture making (8).

The classroom is already a complicated and compelling theater, but understanding "queer pedagogy" in multifaceted ways allows for Foucault's third cultural space, where the illusion of writing conventions can be explored. Foucault's essay "Of Other Spaces: Utopias and Heterotopias," based on a lecture he gave in 1967, contests the traditional notion of linear time and space. For Foucault, contemporary spatial patterns differ from both medieval hierarchical space and the capitalist space of exchange. The essay begins with a concise description of how the discrete and hierarchical spaces of the Medieval era—the celestial, the earthly, the subterranean, the great chain of being—were eventually thrown into question by the fissures opened up by Galilean physics and cosmology (23). According to Foucault, Galileo's epistemological break substituted "extension" for "localization," meaning that a "thing's place was no longer anything but a point in its movement." This set the stage for our present epoch, which Foucault argues is "one in which space takes for us the form of relations among sites" (24).

According to Foucault such spaces—which he refers to as *heterotopias*—are universal and necessary components of human civilization, but their function shifts over time in response to changes in culture. Their overarching functionality, however, remains constant: Heterotopias are always places where incompatible or contradictory kinds of spaces converge; they represent an "absolute break" with the traditional time of their enclosing cultures. They enable us to both confront our illusions and to create new illusions of the utopias we cannot have: "Either their role is to create a space of illusion that exposes every real space. ... Or else their role is to create a space that is other" (30).

However, Foucault's notion of heterotopias describes for me the experience of teaching in university classrooms that are "simultaneously mythic and real contestation[s] of the space in which we live" (29). The real world of Standard English and university writing exists simultaneously with the transgressive aspects of queer culture, but are taught and learned separately. Like really, is there anything campy about punctuation?

According to Gilles Deleuze, contemporary technologies have caused society to move away from the disciplinary societies that organized "vast spaces of enclosure." "The individual," he notes, "never ceases passing from one enclosed environment to another, each having its own laws," the family, the school, the barracks, the factories, the hospitals, and prisons (3). Like other enclosed, soon to be controlled spaces, academic institutions reflect the learned values and beliefs, notions of justice, and reactions to diversity that abound in society as a whole. Although Deleuze predicts an "ultra rapid form of free floating control" that will mark who has access to information, his claim that "rather than erecting factories, we build corporations" as we transition to a networked society reinforces tradition and squeezes out the transgressive (7). In antithesis of Deleuze, Halberstam notes that "queer temporality disrupts the normative narratives of time that form the base of nearly every definition of the human ... to our understanding of the affective and the aesthetic" (152).

Unlike opening a door and walking through, stopping in the imagined or disrupted time and space in the classroom can create a space where the parallel tracks are no longer parallel. The act of forming a rhetorical identity exists in the decision to cross into the imagined space, the heterotopia, the third space of the classroom, that is part of the real world and its own space simultaneously, that does and doesn't exist. So how to avoid the train crash, the clash of the traditional and the transgressive without being asked to make death-defying—or not—leaps over, under, between, or in front of trains? When you can't be a magical fox girl what other choices do you have? Gloria Anzaldúa questions stories about identity that exist in individual, restrictive, and categorized terms. She replaces those definitions of identity but repositions them within a larger framework—one that is relational and mobile:

> Your resistance to identity boxes leads you to a different tribe, a different story (of mestizaje) enabling you to rethink yourself in more global-spiritual terms instead of conventional categories of color, class, career. It calls you to retribalize your identity to a more inclusive one ... reflecting an emerging, planetary culture. (561)

Because it doesn't fit into a system of rules or prescribed patterns of academic thought, queer theory is not a traditional theory that can be described and explicated. Even in application, queer theory takes different, sometimes contradictory forms. Performers of queer theory are boundary strippers, deconstructing the homo/heterosexual binary. In application, in the first-year writing classroom, however, queer theory often simultaneously becomes a boundary defender, constructing gay and lesbian identities as a single community in order to promote tolerance. But, as Joshua Gamson notes, constructing gays and lesbians as a single community "united by fixed erotic fates," simplifies complex differences and complex sexual identities ("Identity Politics" 391). And, I would add, simplifies and stabilizes what is queer about writing and teaching writing in any writing class: "The central difficulty of identity based organizing: the instability of identities, both individual and collective, their *made-up*, yet necessary character" (Gamson "Queer Dilemma" 390; emphasis added).

Note: Fox girl likes the idea of "making up" an identity. But she recognizes that in the classroom, there are limits—learning objectives, textbooks, department expectations, assignments—to taking on identities of instructor and student that already exist.

And the queer community is very complex, multifaceted, and certainly not unified despite HRC stickers and Equality "add your state name" movements. If we are teaching with/about queer, can we expose the differences and divides in the queer community? Is it important to reveal that in the economic hierarchy women make less than men, so lesbians make 82 cents to gay men's dollar? If we are playing show and tell, can we talk about the inability of many in the community to accept trans persons or any gender performance or sexuality not their own, such as bisexuality? Can we discuss the statistics that reveal gay teen suicides are not predominately male, as the media would have us believe, or that gay men are not the only queers that get beat up or beaten to death outside of bars? Drag shows highlight the straight community's notions of queer culture, but what of queer writers, artists, scientists, musicians, and other actors and shapers of queer culture?

I will admit that sometimes working with collective identities is a vital necessity, especially when working for political and social change. Diana Fuss notes that the truth of heteronormativity can only reaffirm itself, "achieve the status of 'compulsory'," if it is seen as an "internal necessity" (2). Collective identities are advantageous to celebrating difference; theorizing sexual identities as culturally readable acts places them in the realm of the ordinary. More significantly, the truth of heteronormativity "renders all other forms of human sexual expression pathological, deviant, unintelligible, or written out of existence" (Yep 167). Queering the composition classroom then becomes significant if it means, as Foucault states in *Power/Knowledge*, to be invested in "detaching the power of truth from the forms of hegemony, social, economic and cultural within which it operates" (133), in revealing that the truth of heterosexuality is violent and harmful to people who exist across a spectrum of genders and sexualities.

Note: What is transgressive about queer theory and queer teaching when we are teaching students to write, to use language effectively? And how do we keep queer theory an alternative pedagogical style so that it doesn't become mainstream and lose its power?

In the classroom, teachers develop pedagogical narratives based on imagined spatial relationships, but these spaces are informed by the historical, social, and cultural—both internal and external differences. A pedagogical threshold is an imagined space—the space between—the moment of difference that holds the potential for learning. Many scholars support a similar metaphor as Foucault, a metaphor of a third space when thinking about learning as relational and mutable. And yet, some student writers must often work to cover over multiple and sometimes conflicting identities in order to succeed in academia and win the promises of professionalism. But the reality for minority identities that are still socially stigmatized, the step into the threshold to learn the language of power doesn't live up to the promise of stepping over it. When they leave the classroom, their identities are still marginalized. Rather than seeing the threshold as something to step over, why not frame this space as a site of meaning and opportunity for teachers and students to rethink the tensions between language and social behaviors. Could we learn a method of valuing the ways in which meaning and institutions can be at loose ends with one another?

Works Cited

Alexander, Jonathan, and Jacqueline Rhodes. "Queer: An Impossible Subject for Composition." *JAC: A Journal of Composition Theory* 31.1 (2010). 177–206. Print.

———. "Flattening Effects: Compositions Multicultural Imperative and the Problem of Narrative Coherence." *College Composition and Communication* 65.3 (Feb. 2014): 430–54. Print.

Anzaldúa, Gloria, and Analouise Keating, eds. *This Bridge We Call Home: Radical Visions for Transformations*. New York: Routledge, 2002. Print.

Bennett, Paula. "The Pea That Duty Locks: Lesbian Readings of Emily Dickinson's Poetry." *Lesbian Texts and Contexts: Radical Revisions*. Ed. Karla Jay and Joanne Glasgow. New York: New York UP, 1990. 104–25. Print.

Berlant, Lauren, and Michael Warner. "Sex in Public." *Critical Inquiry* 24.2 (1998): 547–66. Web. 3 Oct. 2014.

Butler, Judith. *Gender Trouble: Feminism and the Subversion of Identity*. New York: Routledge, 2006. Print.

———. *Bodies that Matter*. New York: Routledge, 1993. Print.

Deleuze, Gilles. "Postscript on the Society of Control." *October* v59 (Winter 1992): 3–7. Cambridge, MA: MIT Press. Web. 22 Sept. 2014.

Faunce, Robert. "Queer and Nondemagogic Pedagogy in the Classroom." *The CEA Forum* Summer/Fall 2013. 30–44. Web. 22 Sept. 2014.

Foucault, Michel. "Of Other Spaces: Utopias and Heterotopias." Trans. Jay Miskowiec. *Diacritics* 16.1 Spring 1986: 22–30. Web. 22 Sept. 2014.

———. *Power/Knowledge: Selected Interviews and Other Writings 1972–1977*. Ed. C. Gordon. New York: Pantheon, 1980. Print.

Fuss, Diana. "Inside/Out." *Inside/out: Lesbian Theories, Gay Theories*. Diana Fuss, Ed. New York: Routledge, 1991: 1–10. Print.

Gamson, Joshua. "The Dilemma of Identity Politics." *The Social Movements Reader: Cases and Concepts 2nd edition*. Jeff Goodwin and James Jasper, Eds. West Sussex, UK: Blackwell, 2009: 383–92. Print.

———. "Must Identity Movements Self Destruct? A Queer Dilemma." *Social Problems* 42.3 (August 1995): 390–407. Web. 22 Sept. 2014.

Giroux, Henry A. "Border Pedagogy and the Politics of Postmodernism." *Social Text* 28 (1991): 51–67. Print.

Halberstam, Judith. *In a Queer Time and Place: Transgender Bodies, Subcultural Lives*. New York: New York UP, 2005. Print.

Halperin, David M. "The Normalization of Queer Theory." *Queer Theory and Communication: From Disciplining Queers to Queering the Discipline(s)*. G. A. Yep, Karen Lovaas, and John Elia, Eds. New York: Harrington Park, 2003. 339–60. Print.

Johnson, Norris Brock. "Sex, Color, and the Rites of Passage in Ethnographic Research." Antonious Robben and Jeffrey Sluka, Eds. *Ethnographic Fieldwork: An Anthropological Reader*. Malden, MA: Blackwell, 2007: 76–91. Print.

Meese, Elizabeth. "Theorizing Lesbianism: Writing—A Love Letter." *Lesbian Texts and Contexts: Radical Revisions*. Karla Jay and Joanne Glasgow, eds. New York: New York UP, 1990. 70–87. Print.

Miller, Susan. *Rescuing the Subject: A Critical Introduction to Rhetoric and the Writer*. Carbondale, IL: Southern Illinois UP, 2004. Print.

Plant, Sadie. "On the Mobile: The Effects of Mobile Telephones on Social and Individual Life." *International Telecommunications Union*, 2003. Web. 22 Sept. 2014. Pdf.

Ricoeur, Paul. *The Rule of Metaphor: Multi-disciplinary Studies of the Creation of Meaning in Language*. Trans. Robert Czerny. Toronto: U of Toronto P, 1977. Print.

Sedgwick, Eve Kosofsky. *Tendencies*. Chapel Hill, NC: Duke UP, 1993. Print.

Turner, Victor. "Betwixt and Between: The Liminal Period in Rites de Passage." *The Forest of Symbols: Aspects of Ndembu Ritual*. Ithaca, NY: Cornell UP, 1970: 93–111. Print.

Van Gennep, Arnold. *The Rites of Passage*. Trans. Monika B. Vizedom. Chicago: U of Chicago P, 1960. Print.

Warner, Michael. *The Trouble with Normal: Sex, Politics, and the Ethics of Queer Life*. New York: The Free Press, 1999. Print.

Yep, Gus A. "From Homophobia and Heterosexism to Heteronormativity." *Journal of Lesbian Studies* 6.3–4 (2002): 163–76. Web. 22 Sept. 2014.

12 "As Proud of Our Gayness, as We Are of Our Blackness"

Race-ing Sexual Rhetorics in the National Coalition of Black Lesbians and Gays

Eric Darnell Pritchard

> *Through examining the combination of our triumphs and errors, we can examine the dangers of an incomplete vision. Not to condemn that vision but to alter it, construct templates for possible futures, and focus our rage for change upon our enemies rather than upon each other.*
> —Audre Lorde, "Learning from the 60s" 135

Audre Lorde spoke these words in a February 1982 speech titled "Learning from the 60s," delivered at Harvard University's "Malcolm X Weekend." In the epigraph, and the longer speech from which it is drawn, Lorde challenges us to look upon the activism and social transformation of the 1960s with clear eyes, open hearts, gratitude, healthy skepticism, and feeling accountable to what the work of freedom and justice calls one to do in their own times so that they too may do the necessary work of creating possible futures. Lorde, who lived in and contributed to the social transformation of the 1960s, was compelled to engage the problematic ways in which the diversity and complexity of Black life and culture is ignored in the fantasy of sameness over the reality of difference. Taking this point then, we are left with the challenge of looking upon histories of the 1960s, and in particular the Black civil rights and burgeoning gay and lesbian rights movement, with a "persistence in examining the tensions within diversity" on our efforts to reach the fullest expression of freedom and justice for the many (Lorde 135). For Lorde, that "many" was more a question of who *could* be in a collective rather than solely a consideration of who already presumed to be in it. That is, Lorde's vision of transformative justice envisioned a collective that included many who may have been hesitant to join the struggle, but whose lives (whether they realized it or not) depended on their being a part of a coalition with individuals whose concerns were also urgent, cross cutting, and complex, such as heterosexual Black women and men, White feminists, and White LGBT people. Through this work, we also simultaneously make legible the presence and contributions of people like Lorde to the civil and gay and lesbian rights movements. Such change is necessary since Lorde and other Black LGBT rhetors slip in and out of historical recognition in narratives about the civil rights, Black power, and LGBT and feminist movements.

At the same time Lorde delivered the speech, a group of activists known as the National Coalition of Black Lesbians and Gays (or NCBLG) were also engaged in questions about the place of Black LGBT people in the history of the civil rights movement. They would also raise similar questions about the history of the then nascent LGBT rights movement. Lorde and the NCBLG's paths converged around this very same issue at key moments in the 1970s and 1980s due to her role as a member of the organization's Board of Directors and an elder to many who regarded her as a role model for whom they held great respect.

This chapter focuses on four actions of the NCBLG's historic interventions to draw connections between the Black civil and LGBT rights movements: the NCBLG's role in organizing the first Third World Lesbian and Gay Conference in 1979; a speech delivered by Audre Lorde at a 1983 March commemorating the twentieth anniversary of the iconic 1963 March on Washington; the organization's AIDS activism on the local and national level; and a published interview with civil rights movement icon Bayard Rustin in the NCBLG magazine *Black/OUT*. Through this work, the NCBLG and other 1970s and 1980s LGBT of color activists and allies helped redefine the texture of US histories of race, sexuality, and politics.

Drawing on an analysis of oral histories I conducted with three NCBLG founders, archival documents, and news reports, I examine key actions in the history of the NCBLG to ascertain the promises and perils of a usable rhetorical past—those historical moments that can be repurposed for rhetorical intervention now—for the contemporary and futurity of scholarly, pedagogical, and activist inquiry and action. I argue that the NCBLG forged new paradigms for social action through a rhetoric of radical "intersectionality" (Crenshaw 93–118). This use of intersectionality queers conceptions of sexual rhetoric as solely concerned with sexuality, into a recognition of sex, sexuality, and sexual rhetorics as always a raced discourse and vice versa. Put simply, we might view sexual rhetorics as the formation of discourses about sexuality that shape the ways sexuality is understood/misunderstood. By examining the ways the NCBLG navigated the sexual rhetorics of their time, we see how this rhetoric is always one that is awake to the collision of race and sexuality in the subject and in the world. To that end, the NCBLG mobilized a series of rhetorical interventions that (1) helped establish a national coalition of LGBT of Color social and activist organizations; (2) made interventions into historical erasure of Black LGBT people; (3) assisted in coalition building among the Black and LGBT political establishment; and (4) envisioned and articulated some paths forward built on the specific ways that race, sexual, and gender experiences of Blackness and queerness would congeal and be expressed in Black queer life, culture, and activism today.

Examining the radical intersectionality of sexual rhetorics as a historical matter with contemporary and future implications is rhetorically necessary because it demonstrates where social movements built around sexual, but also gender and racial justice, get perennially derailed in language, including the ways it frustrates coalition politics; it offers a theory of sexual rhetorics that is accountable to the materiality of the historical subject(s) under examination; and it shows us what were the discursive practices at a specific time in history in which people acted rhetorically and with consequence to reshape dominant, and exclusionary, ideas around sexuality through attention to its own complexity and its intersections with other identities.

The National Coalition of Black Lesbians and Gays: A Brief Historical Sketch

The 1970s and 1980s were watershed years for the emergence of gay and lesbian organizations working at the intersections of race and sexuality. Among the organizations leading the way was the National Coalition of Black Gays or NCBG (later renamed National Coalition of Black Lesbians and Gays [NCBLG]). Founded in the era of massive white backlash against the civil rights movement and heteropatriarchal attempts to dismantle the women's rights gains of the 1960s, the NCBG drew from the politics and strategies of the civil rights, feminist, and burgeoning gay and lesbian movements, while simultaneously challenging the marginalizing effect each of these movements had on black lesbian, gay, bisexual, and transgender people.

Operating as two separate community organizations that began in 1974 and 1975, the Washington D.C. Coalition of Black Gays and the Baltimore Coalition of Black Gays merged in 1978 to form the National Coalition of Black Gays, the first national organization of LGBT people of African descent in the United States (Brinkley). The organization took the official motto: "as proud of our gayness, as we are of our blackness." The organization changed its name to include "lesbians" in 1980, though women were founders and leaders in the organization from its inception. The organization's constitution and bylaws, adopted on November 29, 1980, also noted the commitment to struggles affecting "transpersons" and bisexual people (1).

The NCBG's founding members were A. Billy S. Jones, Dolores Berry, Darlene Garner, Louis Hughes, Gil Gerald, Rev. Renee McCoy, and John Gee. I have located records that confirm there were approximately 17 NCBLG chapters across the United States. The NCBLG Board of Directors included some of the leading writer-activists of what is seen as a Black queer literary renaissance in the 1970s and 1980s, including Lorde, Joseph Beam, and Barbara Smith, founding member of the trailblazing Black feminist organization, the Combahee River Collective.

Throughout its life, the organization was at the forefront of campaigns to call attention to issues specific to the Black LGBT community on political, health, cultural, economic, and social fronts. The NCBLG was also crucial to the social and artistic lives of its members and communities where chapters thrived. They regularly held parties, banquets, and awards galas that created social spaces for Black LGBT people and their allies where none existed and to celebrate the legacy and achievements of Black LGBT people that were not celebrated or noted elsewhere. They also held fundraisers and organized poetry readings, film screenings, art shows, and theater performances that introduced to some, and presented to others, the work of notable writers and artists, including Black gay poet Essex Hemphill and filmmaker Marlon Riggs. No formal announcement of the organization's end occurred, but the NCBLG's formal operations ended in 1990.

1979: The Third World Lesbian and Gay Conference and the First Gay and Lesbian March on Washington

In 1979, the NCBLG led the organizational efforts to convene the first Third World Conference of Lesbians and Gays, which was held in Washington, DC, on October 12–15, 1979, under the theme "When will the ignorance end?" The conference site was the Harambee House, a frequent gathering place for Black people in Washington, DC, and located very near the campus of Howard University, a historically Black college and university (HBCU), which was also the site of some of the conference workshops and caucus meetings. According to the Third World Conference Program booklet, the NCBLG served as the official sponsor of the conference and as "conference planners" (2). The conference program also notes that the conference was specially geared toward "American Indians, Latin Americans, Asian Americans, and Afro Americans," gathering under three goals: "[t]o edstablish [sic] a national network for Third World Lesbians and Gays; [t]o establish an education and communications network for and among Third World Lesbian and Gay organizations; [t]o confront the issues of racism, sexism, homophobia and heterophobia among, by and against Third World Lesbians and Gays" (2). In addition to workshops for gay and lesbian people of color, the program states that additional "workshops and caucuses are open and provided for non-Third World and non-gay persons" (2). Among the caucuses that took place were a "Women's Caucus," "Transperson's Caucus," and various racial/ethnic caucuses and regional caucuses (12).

Certainly, the conference is significant because it is the first national conference to bring together LGBT of color organizations and collectives. This fact alone warrants attention to what LGBT people of color as individuals and collectives felt about the state of race and sexual politics in their times, and also the role of rhetoric in how they went about the tasks that would create, advertise, manage, and then document this occasion. However, I argue that the most significant and available information regarding this rhetoric, and specifically how they were negotiating the terrain of racial and sexual politics in ways that had not been on the national stage prior to their arrival, were the choices that the conferences planners made about the timing and location of the conference, as well as the ways in which the conference would converge and diverge from events surrounding the Gay and Lesbian March on Washington.

One of the first details I wish to foreground in my analysis is the timing of the event. As noted, the conference was deliberately held the same weekend as the first Gay and Lesbian March on Washington to coincide with the tenth anniversary of the Stonewall Rebellion. Conference organizers saw holding the conference the same weekend in DC as the historic first Gay and Lesbian March on Washington as a way to enable coalition-building among LGBT activists of color, and also build alliances with White gay and lesbian activists while holding them accountable to issues of racism, xenophobia, and economic justice (Louis Hughes interview, 2007).

Another way the conference can be seen as a rhetorical intervention is that it was held at Harambee House near Howard University, which are both, again, associated with Washington, DC's Black community, and in the case of Howard, the educational legacy of Black America. By selecting this place as the site of the March the conference planners were, I contend, deliberately centering the lives, concerns, stories, and politics of LGBT people of color in the Black diaspora from D.C. to the Dominican Republic, from Brooklyn to Brazil. This choice is consistent with more than one of the conference's stated goals. The statement of this act is that what effects Black and other people of color is not mutually exclusive of what affects Black and people of color who identity as LGBT as well. Essentially, the claim is that any national initiatives surrounding issues affecting people of color must also be attentive to the specific effects on LGBT people, with emphasis on LGBT people of color. For example, NCBLG co-founder A. Billy Jones, in an article about the NCBLG, stated that the conference put the NCBLG and LGBT people of color on the map as visible on the national stage as far as any attention to any social and political issues concerning LGBT and people of color (Brinkley).

Another way that the conferences' location operated as intervention in sexual rhetoric, framing race and sexuality as separate matters, was that the Third World Gay and Lesbian Conference site was Harambee House, which was located on Georgia Avenue. Georgia Avenue's streets went through the Black community, and according to NCBLG co-founder Hughes, the conference planners thought it was important to not follow the most convenient route to the Gay and Lesbian March on Washington site or even the route that the Gay and Lesbian March on Washington organizers had planned. Instead, Hughes said, they wanted to take the route most direct from Harambee as it would take them directly down Georgia Avenue, the thoroughfare going through DC's Black communities, and into the main mall where they would join the rest of the Gay and Lesbian March on Washington. Doing so, the conference planners were ensuring that the more than 500 attendees of the Third World Lesbian and Gay Conference would arrive together as LGBT people of color to join an almost completely

White group of March attendees. My assessment of this choice is that the NCBLG as conference planners were symbolically linking the Black communities that ran alongside Georgia Avenue, and the various issues affecting those communities and themselves as well as Black LGBT people, to the set of issues noted in the platform for the Gay and Lesbian March on Washington. Thus, in this moment of heightened attention to the gay and lesbian community, and thus a heightened moment of sexual rhetoric, the NCBLG forwarded a counter rhetorical messaging through their language, timing, use of space and location, and embodiment.

1983: March Commemorating the 20th Anniversary of the March on Washington for Jobs and Freedom

The 1983 "We Still Have a Dream" March was billed as a hope for the kinds of legislative change realized by the 1960s Black civil rights movement. In new reports in the *Washington Post*, March organizers stated that the March was linked to its 1963 predecessor in its desire for new civil rights legislation, and that the timing of the March would draw national attention and support for their legislative initiatives on the table when Congress returned in September, including a proposal to make the observation of the birthday of Martin Luther King Jr. a national holiday (Barker C1; Barker A1; Barker and Perl A1).

As recalled by NCBLG cofounder Gil Gerald in his movement memoir essay, "The Trouble I've Seen," in May 1983, he learned of a meeting held a few months prior where an initial list of speakers for the March was presented by March organizers (23). The list was a who's who of civil rights movement legends, politicians, activists, and artists, but no one was included to represent the gay and lesbian community or organizations, nor listed as a speaker or as a representative on the steering committee. Gerald writes that this oversight led activist Michelle Guimarin of Mobilization for Survival to request that a member of the National Gay Task Force (NGTF, now NGLTF) be added to the March steering committee (23). Gerald recalled that Frank C. Branchini of the Gay Rights National Lobby told him that, in response to the request for gay and lesbian representation, DC Congressional Delegate Walter Fauntroy said the rights of gay and lesbian people had as much to do with the March as did the rights of a penguin, and therefore gay and lesbian people should not be included (Gerald 23). After Fauntroy's comments were attributed to him in news articles, he denied ever making such observations, but all the same doubled down on his opinion that gay and lesbian people should not have a speaking role at the March, as reported by the *Washington Post* (Barker C1). This information prompted numerous individuals and organizations to refuse to endorse the March (Gerald 23). The fallout from Fauntroy's alleged comments and the March organizers resistance to the activists request to include gay and lesbian people kicked off a more than six-month set of organized actions led by the NCBLG, including numerous public protests and a sit-in at the congressman's office, resulting in the arrest of NCBLG activists and allies. As the date of the March grew closer, the controversy surrounding gay and lesbians threat of nonsupport for the March began to get more media attention than the March itself. According to Gerald, Coretta Scott King was especially concerned that gay and lesbian organizations would pull out support for the March and wanted a resolution that would most satisfy all parties. They reached terms of such a resolution during a conference call in the late hour of 12:30 A.M. on August 25 between March organizers and gay and lesbian activists and allies (25). Participating in the conference call were Gerald, 1983 March organizer Donna Brazile, Coretta Scott King, leader of the Southern Christian Leadership Conference's Joseph Lowery, the NAACP's Benjamin Hooks, the Congressional Black Caucus's Barbara Williams-Skinner, and the Task Force's Virginia Apuzzo (Gerald 25). Their campaign proved successful. Mrs. King, Lowery, and Hooks individually endorsed what was a pending federal gay rights bill at a press conference the day before the March, though the March organizers resisted having the March itself endorse the bill (Gerald 25–26). In addition, March organizers finally agreed to include a gay or lesbian speaker on the March program (Gerald 26).

On the date of the March, standing on the steps of the Lincoln Memorial, the site where March speakers stood 20 years prior, Audre Lorde, the self-professed "Black lesbian feminist mother poet warrior," delivered a speech as part of the "Litany of Commitment" section of the March program. Her speech gave voice to a vision of liberation that linked the struggle of gays and lesbians to the Black civil rights and other liberation movements throughout the world. She began as follows:

> I am Audre Lorde, speaking for the National Coalition of Black Lesbians and Gay Men. Today's march openly joins the Black civil rights movement and the gay civil rights movement in the struggles we have always shared, the struggles for jobs, for health, for peace, and for freedom. We marched in 1963 with Dr. Martin Luther King, and dared to dream that freedom would include us, because not one of us is free to choose the terms of our living until all of us are free to choose the terms of our living.
>
> Today the Black civil rights movement has pledged its support for gay civil rights legislation. Today we march, lesbians and gay men and our children, standing in our own names together with all our struggling sisters and brothers here and around the world, in the Middle East, in Central America, in the Caribbean and South Africa, sharing our commitment to work for a joint livable future. We know we do not have to become copies of each other in order to be able to work together. We know that when we join hands across the table of our difference, our diversity gives us great power. When we can arm ourselves with the strength and vision from all of our diverse communities then we will in truth be free at last.
>
> (Lorde, "Address" 212)

Lorde's speech serves as a touchstone for the kinds of interventions by the NCBLG I have discussed thus far. In Lorde's archive are multiple early drafts of the speech, from her initial handwritten musings of what she might say through to the typed drafts she finished before settling on the version she read at the March. Thus, some analysis of the finished product alongside the drafts provides important information about the choices Lorde made that cemented the kind of intervention she and the NCBLG sought to make.

Lorde's speech establishes the major vision of broadening perspectives about Black identity and the connections between race and sexual identities for social movements. In early drafts of the "Litany of Commitment" address, there are no explicit references to joining the Black civil and gay rights movements (1). Also, Lorde's early draft speaks of the March as an occasion "recognizing the diversity of the Black community." However, in a later draft and in the final speech, she says that the march "is openly joining the black civil rights movement and gay civil rights movement in those struggles we have always shared. ..." This revision by Lorde is significant in that it shows that the occasion of the March demonstrates the diversity of the Black community in terms of sexuality and gender, and that the Black civil and gay and lesbian rights movements are not as disparate as one might believe.

Lorde's joining of the Black civil and gay rights movements, as well as stating the diversity of Blackness, is further achieved in her riff off of Dr. King's own words. In an early draft of the speech, Lorde writes: "With Dr. Martin Luther King we have each dared to dream that freedom would include us because, not one of us is free until all of us are free." The arrangement of the sentence, and also its meaning, calls up King's powerful and oft-cited words in his "Letter from Birmingham Jail": "Injustice anywhere is a threat to justice everywhere. We are caught in an inescapable network of mutuality, tied in a single garment of destiny. Whatever affects one directly, affects all indirectly" (77). Interestingly, it is this same line that Coretta Scott King often quoted in speeches of support for LGBT people, including her 1996 speech at the Atlanta LGBT Pride Festival.

Lorde's take on Dr. King's words and her own articulation of the ways our freedoms and futures are wrapped up in one another also reflect the use of empathy as a rhetorical strategy that exposes people's direct and indirect role in other people's oppressions and invites the possibility of coalition building. This is also reflected in her saying that "we do not need to become copies of each other in order to work together" or that "when we join hands across the table of our difference, our diversity gives us great power." Both of these statements imply empathy as a tool and process through which we seek to recognize, affirm, and feel what others are going through, and choose to connect *because* of difference not *in spite of* difference. I view Lorde's comments here as a direct challenge to the media coverage prior to the March, which largely attempted to portray the March and its diverse interests and people as disunified.

Overall, Lorde's speech synthesizes myriad concerns, while centering Black and LGBT issues and concerns; it builds a framework through which the contributions of Black LGBT people to the Black civil rights movement destabilizes the stranglehold of narratives that erase Black LGBT people from that history. For her, people of color have a visible face in the LGBT rights movement, another act of intervention which in that moment disrupts discourses of that movement as solely White. Finally, Lorde's speech reflects on the past and the moment in which the speech was delivered as a usable moment for the future of coalition-building across racial and sexual politics.

1985–1987: AIDS Activism, Habari-Habari, and Black/OUT

Although Lorde's 1983 speech articulated the NCBLG's interventions, many of those same issues emerged multiple times in the organization's AIDS activism and writings that appeared in the NCBLG newsmagazine *Black/OUT*. Attention to this part of the NCBLG's work provides another space to explore the sexual rhetorics of those times, how the NCBLG viewed those rhetorics, and the stance the NCBLG adopted which centered race in sexual politics. Two issues of concern were a continued focus on the presence of Black LGBT people in the histories of the Black civil rights and LGBT movements, and also AIDS activism which centered the particular ways that the Black community was being effected in the earliest days of what became a global epidemic.

The NCBLG led campaigns concerning the AIDS crisis. AIDS prevention, treatment, and education remained a key part of the organization's work until the organization's end, and was also a featured discussion in its annual national membership conventions. In examining the early AIDS prevention and education efforts of the NCBLG, we see how they steered the conversation around AIDS to give attention to its impact on Black and other communities of color. By centering race in their AIDS activism, the NCBLG was able to highlight how what was largely being thought of as a gay (read: White) disease was also affecting Black gay men and therefore Black communities. They were also able to expose the limitations on interventions and care that were not attentive to how racial and ethnic as well as class identity played into the discourses around AIDS that were most pervasive for particular communities. Lastly, they created a space for early AIDS prevention and education work that sought out the ways to use culturally, racially, and ethnically situated language to reach people where they stood. For instance, in July 1986 the NCBLG organized "AIDS in the Black Community," known to be the first national conference on AIDS geared toward Black people. A conference pre-registration forms notes that the event was cosponsored by the National Conference of Black Mayors and the National Minority AIDS Council (1). Also, a number of articles in the organization's newsmagazines *Habari-Habari* (also published as *Habari-Daftari*), and *Black/OUT* featured news updates about AIDS nationally and internationally, including initiatives in local communities where NCBLG chapters were located to raise people's awareness about prevention and treatment. They also published poetry, short stories, and nonfiction essays, which were also important in disseminating this information in another pedagogically relevant and specific way familiar to the members of the organization and the readers of its newsmagazines.

The NCBLG's magazine *Black/OUT*, and its precursor the newsletter *Habari-Habari*, provide another layer of insight into the ways the organization's race and sexual politics forged a sexual rhetoric that would intervene into dominant discourses about race and sexual identity, and particularly the Black civil rights and lesbian and gay rights movements. In 1980 *Habari-Habari*, Swahili for "What's the news? What's the news?" was a bimonthly newsletter. The newsletter was later renamed *Black/OUT* Newsmagazine and published quarterly. The organization sold subscriptions to both members and nonmembers and sold the magazine at local bookstores and newsstands, primarily on the east coast.

Joseph Beam was the editor of *Black/OUT* and, again, served on the NCBLG's Board of Directors. Beam is best known as editor of *In the Life* (1986), the first anthology of Black gay men's literature. The Black gay and lesbian presence in, or more commonly, their absence from, history was a theme resounding across many of Beam's writings, as it was clearly also a chief concern of the NCBLG. Beam's writing on this issue continued the clarion call for intervention about overlooking Black LGBT people in Black history, as is apparent in the first lines of a 1985 essay, "Black History Month: Act Like You Know," first published in *Au Courant* newsmagazine, in which he writes about the tactics of thriving despite historical erasure, saying: "to endure with any safety, I must be a historian, librarian and archaeologist, digging up and dusting off the fragments of black history and black gay history" (n. p.). Beam would perform this intervention multiple times in his career, most notably through a 1987 issue of *Black/OUT*. The issue cover foreshadows its claims about history. In large white lettering on a completely black cover appears one sentence: "Because silence is costly" (1). The cover represents the focus of this edition: erasing Black LGBTQ people from Black and LGBT history. Edited by Beam, the magazine particularly emphasizes breaking the silences around Black LGBT life and culture in historiographies of the Black freedom movement. Beam's "The Elder of the Village: An Interview with Bayard Rustin" is the clearest example. It was Rustin, a black gay man, who served as principal organizer of the 1963 March on Washington for Jobs and Freedom. This fact is often overlooked in the historiography of the movement; it also made him a target for exclusion by many of his contemporaries due to their anti-gay bias and bigotry, occurrences that are well-documented in historical accounts, most notably by John D'Emilio.

In the interview with Rustin, Beam disrupts the very language and categories by which history is shaped and disseminated. He writes:

> At another time, on another continent, I might have gone to his [Rustin's] hut to bask in the warmth of his fire and to listen to his words of wisdom

as the elder of the village. But it is another day, and this is certainly another continent, but Bayard Rustin is no less than the wise man of the village of many centuries ago. (17)

Here Beam makes several rhetorical interventions. First, he positions Rustin in the role of griot, traditional within many African cultural and communal practices. In some cultures, among other responsibilities, the griot is keeper of history and extoller of wisdom for a community. Thus, Beam places Rustin in an authoritative relationship to Black history, saying essentially that Rustin would easily have occupied the position of the wise elder if not for the circumstances of time and space or for how homophobia displaces him from being normative enough to inhabit the role. Situating Rustin firmly in discourses of traditional African culture and history, Beam queers notions of the griot by elevating a black gay man to a position generally seen through the prism of heteronormative assumptions. We might read Beam here as challenging not only history, but also the culturally specific frameworks for documenting and theorizing history itself.

Beam extends this critique in another moment from the interview, when he writes:

> Rustin was a Black Gay civil rights activist long before it was lucrative and legitimate, long before the rebellion at the Stonewall Inn in 1969; long before the tumultuous Black liberation struggles of the 60s, long before the Brown vs. Board [sic] Supreme Court decision in 1954. (17)

Beam's comments move in defense of Rustin's legacy, placing the activist at the center of social change in the 1950s and 1960s. In this way, Beam uses Rustin to exemplify larger criticisms about the historical erasure of Black LGBT people, which simultaneously forces one to question whether the frameworks for understanding identity in those histories are problematic, and argues for a connection between movements for race, sexual, and gender justice.

Conclusion

In their own examination of historical intervention into various forms of omission and oversight, rhetorical studies scholars Jacqueline Jones Royster and Jean C. Williams begin with the statement that "history is important, not just in terms of who writes it and what gets included or excluded, but also because history, by the very nature of its inscription as history, has social, political, and cultural *consequences*" (563; emphasis in original). The NCBLG's struggle and contributions to what we might call sexual rhetorical studies is evidenced in an important series of critical events and related texts that reflect the necessity of interventions into historiographies and cultural memory because of its impact on the present. In this case, for instance, the grassroots tactics, public address, and writings by NCBLG members work to excavate the invisible presence of Black LGBTQ people who have always been a part of and central to the modern Black freedom and LGBT rights struggle. What is at stake by not continuing, complicating, and building upon the interventions of the NCBLG and allied activists is the loss of language that has the potential to produce radically intersectional politics that allows for the simultaneity of racial and sexual subjectivities to drive the creation of sustainable coalitions. In addition, by not complicating and building on this rhetorical tradition, we obstruct the possibility of a progressive future for queer politics that brings everybody along, and does not continue the fractious divides and siloed practices of historical and contemporary justice movements. By doing this, we can avoid the hurt resulting from the silence of numerous (white) LGBT activists and organizations regarding the extrajudicial police killings of Black people and the daily harassment, abuse, and murder of transgender people of color, as powerfully discussed in recent open letters by writer-activists Darnell Moore and Charles Stephens, as well as filmmaker Dee Rees. Thus, we see the uses of Black LGBT history in unresolved complexities and unexplored points of connection that will be generative and beneficial in this so-called new era of possibility for coalition-building in American politics.

I have argued here for the significance of the NCBLG and Black LGBT activism of the 1970s and 1980s, as well as a writing and rhetorical theory of those histories, as a useful way to imagining and reimagining the intersections of race and sexual politics. Such a perspective is crucial to a variety of issues in contemporary quests for social justice and the sexual rhetorics therein, from bullying and marriage equality to violence against Black and queer people by the state. I end this chapter as it began, returning to Lorde's Black queer ancestral guidance in "Learning from the 60s" in which she says: "we do not have to romanticize our past in order to be aware of how it seeds our present. We do not have to suffer the waste of an amnesia that robs us of the lessons of the past rather than permit us to read them with pride as well as deep understanding" (139).

Works Cited

Barker, Karlyn. "March Bars Abortion, Gay Issues." *Washington Post,* 19 Aug. 1983: C1. Web.
Barker, Karlyn. "March to Seek New National Agenda: March to Seek national Agenda for 'Jobs, Peace, Freedom.'" *Washington Post,* 25 Aug. 1983: A1. Web.
Barker, Karlyn, and Peter Perl. "Special Spirit Vowed for March." *Washington Post,* 27 Aug. 1983. Web.
Brinkley, Sidney. "The National Coalition of Black Lesbians and Gays: Making History." *Blacklight Online. Blacklight Magazine,* 24 Oct. 2006. Web.
Crenshaw, Kimberle Williams. "Mapping the Margins: Intersectionality, Identity Politics and Violence Against Women of Color." *The Public Nature of Private Violence.* Ed. Martha Albertson Fineman and Rixanne Mykitiuk. New York: Routledge, 1994. 93–118. Print.

D'Emilio, John. *Lost Prophet: The Life and Times of Bayard Rustin*. Chicago: U of Chicago P, 2004. Print.

Hughes, Louis. Personal interviews. 8 Mar. 2007 and 14 Mar 2007.

Jones, A. Billy S. Personal interview. 9 Feb. 2007.

King, Coretta Scott. "1996 Atlanta Gay Pride Festival Speech by Coretta Scott King." Online video clip. *YouTube*. YouTube. 7 Oct. 2009. Web. 17 Nov. 2012.

King, Martin Luther, Jr. *Why We Can't Wait*. New York: Harper & Row, 1964. Print.

Lorde, Audre. "Learning from the 60s." *Sister Outsider: Essays and Speeches*. Freedom, CA: Crossing, 1984. 134–44. Print.

Lorde, Audre. "An Address Delivered as Part of the 'Litany of Commitment' at the March on Washington, August 27, 1983." *I Am Your Sister: Collected and Unpublished Writings of Audre Lorde*. Eds. Rudolph P. Byrd, Johnetta Betsch Cole, and Beverly Guy-Sheftall. New York: Oxford UP, 2009. 212. Print.

Moore, Darnell L. and Charles Stephens. "An Open Letter to Mainstream LGBT Organizations That Have Remained Silent on Black Lives Mattering." *Huffington Post*. The Huffington Post. 16 Dec. 2014; updated 15 Feb. 2015. Web. 20 Feb. 2015.

Rees, Dee. "An Open Letter to HRC." *Huffington Post*. The Huffington Post. 5 Dec. 2014; updated 5 Feb. 2015. Web. 20 Feb. 2015.

Royster, Jacqueline Jones, and Jean C. Williams. "History in the Space Left: African American Presence and Narratives of Composition Studies." *College Composition and Communication* 50.4 (June 1999): 563–84. Print.

Archival Sources

"Because Silence Is Costly" *Black/OUT* (1987), Folder 1, NCBLG, Black Gay and Lesbian Archive, Manuscripts, Archives and Rare Books Division, Schomburg Center for Research in Black Culture, The New York Public Library.

"Black History Month—Act Like You Know" *Au Courant* (Feb. 25, 1985), Joseph Beam Papers, NCBLG Papers, Black Gay and Lesbian Archive, Manuscripts, Archives and Rare Books Division, Schomburg Center for Research in Black Culture, The New York Public Library.

"Early Drafts of 'Litany of Commitment' Speech" (1983), Box 23, folder 66, Audre Lorde Papers, Spelman College Archive.

Gerald, Gil. "The Trouble I've Seen." *Black/OUT* (1987), Folder1, NCBLG Papers, Black Gay and Lesbian Archive, Manuscripts, Archives and Rare Books Division, Schomburg Center for Research in Black Culture, The New York Public Library.

"The Elder of the Village: An Interview with Bayard Rustin." *Black/OUT* (1987), Folder 1, NCBLG Papers, Black Gay and Lesbian Archive, Manuscripts, Archives and Rare Books Division, Schomburg Center for Research in Black Culture, The New York Public Library.

"National Coalition of Black Gays Bylaws" (Nov. 29, 1980), Folder 1, NCBLG Papers, Black Gay and Lesbian Archive, Manuscripts, Archives and Rare Books Division, Schomburg Center for Research in Black Culture, The New York Public Library.

"Pre-Registration Form: 'AIDS in the Black Community' National Conference" (1986), Box 16, Folders 9–10, Joseph Beam Papers, Black Gay and Lesbian Archive, Manuscripts, Archives and Rare Books Division, Schomburg Center for Research in Black Culture, The New York Public Library.

"3rd World Conference of Lesbians and Gays Conference Program" (1979), in author's possession.

Part III
(Counter)Publics

13 "Gay Boys Kill Themselves"
The Queer Figuration of the Suicidal Gay Teen

Erin J. Rand

They were often listed as a group of five—Billy Lucas, 15 years old; Seth Walsh, 13 years old; Tyler Clementi, 18 years old; Asher Brown, 13 years old; Raymond Chase, 19 years old. These are the boys who committed suicide during the month of September 2010; their deaths, cast as a poignant synecdoche for the consequences of homophobia, were the impetus for a new public concern about adolescent bullying in the United States. Of course, as a means of acquiring a limited form of power within an existing hierarchy, bullying itself is not the origin of violent or cruel behavior, but might be better understood as a symptom of a more general cultural orientation toward violence (Collins). As Max S. Gordon suggests, the combination of aggressive politics that glorify war, discriminatory policies such as the Defense of Marriage Act and Don't Ask Don't Tell, and the mean-spirited humor of popular media all model a pathological attraction to violence. This violence, he fears, is internalized and ultimately unleashed in somewhat predictable ways that are culturally overdetermined. That is, when pushed beyond the limit of personal tolerance, "Straight boys kill others, gay boys kill themselves" (Gordon).

Though intended to be hyperbolic, the inevitability implied by this statement is provocative. If we take seriously for a moment the possibility of this sort of overdetermination, that perhaps contemporary US culture does, in fact, produce straight boys who do violence to others and gay boys who do violence to themselves, then the recent public concentration on strategies to prevent bullying and suicide somewhat misses the point. Instead, we need to consider the ways in which we imagine the gay teen who is at risk for bullying and suicide, for whose benefit these prevention efforts are developed. In the background of the public attention to the gay youth suicides, I want to suggest, hover the "gay boys [who] kill themselves," or what I will call the rhetorical and affective figure of the "suicidal gay teen." This figure, produced through public discourse, tells us more about the collective affective investments of US culture than it does about queer youth, and demonstrates the underlying cultural violence wrought by heteronormativity.

The "suicidal gay teen" is not an actual phrase existing in the public lexicon; rather, it is my label for an enthymematic figure that operates affectively and nonrepresentationally to shore up public discourse without ever actually making an appearance. It becomes visible only through its effects, an unstated premise for claims made on its behalf. This figure, unnoticed when public discourse is approached straight on, emerges only by reading queerly, describing that which cannot appear explicitly, vocalizing disavowals and silences. This is, in other words, a queer method of tracing the production of a figure that cannot speak and cannot be spoken.[1]

The suicidal gay teen is a lonely, tragic figure, necessarily male but not explicitly gendered, unable to withstand the abuses of the adolescent social scene, and prone to self-harm. This figure draws on the tradition of what Richard Dyer calls the "sad young man," a young, white, beautiful, sensitive, melancholic stereotype of homosexuality that appeared repeatedly in many forms of high and low culture from the 1940s to the 1960s (40–42). But unlike the sad young man, who could also be an object of secretive desire, the suicidal gay teen is defined primarily in terms of its victimization and dysfunction and therefore resists eroticization or sexual objectification.

While the stories of actual teen suicides contribute to the production of the suicidal gay teen, the figure does not attempt to accurately represent any particular individual, nor is it a subject position that is actually occupied. Instead, it is a collectively imagined symbol, or what Robert Asen calls a "verbal image" that can be deployed toward particular ends. In his work on welfare policy debates, Asen describes the particular images of poor single mothers that emerge, noting that "image" refers to both visual and verbal representations that are the result of collective imagining (286). "Verbal images," he suggests, "offer insights into processes of collective imagining, which proceed through social dialogue as participants in public discussions form shared perceptions of people, objects, and ideas through their discursive interactions" (287). These images can be explicit or implicit and work both descriptively and prescriptively, especially as they affect the implementation of policies and programs related to the groups being imagined.

Similarly, Bonnie Honig describes how the "figure of the foreigner" is a recurring "device" that appears in the classic texts that describe the founding of Western democracy. This figure, imbued with certain qualities associated with foreignness, does important symbolic work in Western political culture as the stories of these texts are retold. Thus, she explains, what is significant about the figure of the foreigner is not its ability to represent or evaluate actual foreignness, but rather the uses to which it is put on behalf of democracy (8). By turning to the figure of the foreigner as a rhetorical construction, she is able to ask, "What problems does foreignness solve for us?" (12)

Borrowing from Asen, I suggest that rhetorical figures, like images, function to influence or justify policy decisions, to explain complex social phenomena in simple terms, and to stand as proxies for larger social issues. They also, as Honig contends, can be deployed strategically to solve cultural problems. However, because the figure of the suicidal gay teen operates affectively, it does not appear explicitly in public discourse, although it certainly functions rhetorically. As Brian Ott suggests about affect's relation to rhetoric, affect might be understood "as incipient attitudes, as energies, intensities, and sensations" which, in combination with reason, may incline us toward particular positions and opinions (50). Therefore, the work of the suicidal gay teen takes place behind the scenes, shaping our perceptions of and responses to the actual lives and deaths of queer youths. It serves as a repository for cultural anxieties about homosexuality, heteronormativity, and masculinity, and absorbs the responsibility for the tragic deaths of young people.

In the remainder of this chapter, I trace the development of the figure of the suicidal gay teen in public discourse, focusing primarily on the five teen suicides in the fall of 2010, but also on the ways this figure has become entrenched in ongoing discussions about bullying and queer youth. I will proceed by describing three crucial characteristics that inhere in this figure: (1) it is uniquely positioned as both the subject and the object of violence; (2) it is apparently alienated from neoliberal discourses of happiness and progress; and (3) it disavows the gendered nature of bullying and the role of masculinity in heteronormativity. Overall, I am seeking to reconsider the violence of queer youth suicide: by refusing to be captivated by the slash of the wrist or the cinch of the noose, the taunt of the bigot or the blow of the bully, we can instead investigate the production of the affective, rhetorical figure of the suicidal gay teen as an enactment of insidious and injurious rhetorical violence. This figure forces us, as Saidiya Hartman puts it, to "reckon with the precarious lives which are visible only in the moment of their disappearance" and to consider the ways in which certain lives remain always illegible and impossible to save (12).

The "Suicidal Gay Teen": Object and Agent of Violence

While the disproportionately high rates of suicide among teenagers who are queer or gender nonconforming (or perceived as such by their peers) received public attention only recently, they have, in fact, long been a dismal reality. Many of the accounts of the fall 2010 suicides cited similar sets of statistics: 21–35 percent of lesbian, gay, and bisexual youth report attempting suicide in the past year, compared to 4–14 percent of heterosexual youth. Forty-one percent of transgender people report having attempted suicide at some point in their lives (Moskowitz). LGBT youth make up 20 to 40 percent of the homeless youth in the United States (often as a result of being unwelcome or feeling unsafe at home because of their sexualities or gender identities), although they represent only 5 to 8 percent of the general population. One in five LGBT students nationwide reports being physically assaulted at school—kicked, punched, or injured with a weapon—and 86 percent have been verbally harassed because of their sexual orientation (Winters).

To be sure, the increased awareness of this problem is a positive step, but much of the mainstream attention focuses almost exclusively on easily definable moments of homophobia, forgoing a more complex analysis of the heteronormative social structures that enable and even encourage violence against queer youth. Two specific features of the media attention to homophobia stand out as particularly important in the production of the figure of the suicidal gay teen.

First, not only is homophobia figured primarily through its contemporary metonym, bullying, but also suicide is understood as bullying's direct effect. For instance, Secretary of Education Arne Duncan released a statement at the end of September 2010, calling the five suicides "unnecessary tragedies" that occurred "because the trauma of being bullied and harassed for their actual or perceived sexual orientation was too much to bear" (Geidner). Or, as Ellen DeGeneres put it on her show, "teenage bullying and teasing is an epidemic in this country and the death rate is climbing" (Erbentraut "LGBT"). Understanding bullying as the direct cause of death of queer teens both overstates the effectiveness of bullying (positing suicide as an inexorable consequence of bullying) and understates the relationship of bullying to the heteronormative values that pervade our culture (depicting bullying as an isolated issue and the single cause for despair in a young queer's life). As Richard Kim asserts, when we "create scapegoats out of child bullies," we "pare down homophobia into a social menace called anti-gay bullying and then confine it to the borders of the schoolyard." In the aftermath of Seth Walsh's death, the superintendent of his school district explained the policies that were in place to inhibit bullying and to teach tolerance, but ultimately conceded the apparent futility of these measures: "But these things didn't prevent Seth's tragedy. ... Maybe they couldn't have" (McKinley). The superintendent is, of course, quite right: to assume that the suicides of queer teens could be prevented simply by setting up more stringent anti-bullying policies is at best naïve and at worst a deliberate refusal to consider the extent of heteronormative pressures.

Second, serious mainstream attention to a culture of homophobia has arisen only with the visibility of suicidal queer subjects turning violence against themselves. That is, though a plethora of broader symbolic and material violence against queers is routinely ignored, the collective attention of the nation is captured by the imagined solitary scene of self-harm. Of course, there are rare moments when incidents of shocking violence against queers—the murders of Brandon Teena and Matthew Shepard, for example—are met with large-scale public grief and outrage. Like gay youth suicides and like schoolyard homophobic bullying, these are examples of what Slavoj Žižek names "subjective violence": the easily visible kind of violence performed by clearly identifiable perpetrators (1). They all have in common a certain compelling, fascinating, horrifying quality that makes us consume the events with rapt attention, all while turning away from any sort of identification: they draw us in precisely insofar as we cannot imagine committing such atrocities ourselves. They also, as Žižek explains, tend to distract our attention from what he calls "objective violence," or the underlying forms of violence that generate both violent acts and our efforts to maintain peace. Objective violence is embodied in our language and in the functioning of our political and economic systems. Unlike subjective violence, which "is seen as a perturbation of the 'normal,' peaceful state of things," objective violence "is precisely the violence inherent to this 'normal' state of things. Objective violence is invisible since it sustains the very zero-level standard against which we perceive something as subjectively violent" (4). In this case, by focusing on specific moments of appalling homophobia, we concentrate on individual pathologies and the development of policies to control such disordered behavior. Therefore, we do not see the objective violence of pervasive and insidious forms of heteronormativity that produce these subjective forms of violence as a logical possibility. To put this simply, our focus on the horrifying spectacle of young people killing themselves actually maintains the violence of heteronormativity that reproduces the conditions that lead to their deaths.

Furthermore, the violence of suicide is unique in that the queer is not just the object but also the agent of violence. The spectacle of the suicide implies that the ultimate cause of death is in the subject's own hands, a result of his or her own weakness or psychological instability, even as most coverage of the suicides has been careful not to make this claim overtly. In fact, many accounts of the victims go out of their way to make it clear that they were normal, healthy kids. For instance, Justin Aaberg and Jamey Rodemeyer, who committed suicide in July 2010 and September 2011, respectively, were both described in overwhelmingly positive terms: Justin's parents are quoted as saying, "Justin was a smiley, happy boy who loved to play his cello," and Jamey's mother insisted that Jamey was "happy" and "strong" and was seeing a therapist as he questioned his sexuality (James).

But even without insinuating that there is something frail, something delicate, something *queer* about these kids that makes them particularly prone to self-harm, the rhetorical figure of the suicidal gay teen nonetheless allows us to believe that their unhappiness is private, arising from within, not from without. By embodying and literally enacting the violence of homophobia, this figure permits us to espouse equality and grieve the suicides as instances of subjective violence, without requiring us to think too long about the ways in which the everyday objective violence of heteronormativity may make the lives of queer youth unlivable. In other words, homophobic violence can become publicly legible and grievable through the figure of the suicidal gay teen precisely because it offers queers themselves—and not the culture of heteronormativity—as the perpetrators of violence.

Neoliberal Happiness and Affective Alienation

Heteronormativity is highly flexible, incorporating queers even as it marginalizes them. Lisa Duggan, and many other scholars who follow her lead, refer to this incorporation as "homonormativity:" "a politics that does not contest dominant heteronormative assumptions and institutions, but upholds and sustains them, while promising the possibility of a demobilized gay constituency and a privatized, depoliticized gay culture anchored in domesticity and consumption" (Duggan 50). Homonormativity situates the queer subject firmly within a neoliberal logic of citizenship, where one's belonging to the nation is both secured and demonstrated by one's economic participation. As Heather Love points out, though, it is not just that queers are expected to fulfill the obligations of mainstream America, but also like all Americans, they are expected to be happy while doing it. She cites the "general American premium on cheerfulness," suggesting that "being a 'gay American,' like being any kind of American, means being a cheerful American" (53). Clearly, this pressure to have a particular affective orientation toward the banalities of everyday life is unrealistic for anyone, but Love suggests that this pressure is even greater for queers: "Because homosexuality is traditionally so closely associated with disappointment and depression," she explains, "being happy signifies participation in the coming era of gay possibility" (54). Being an unhappy queer, then, represents a refusal of progress and neoliberal citizenship.

This happiness obviously functions normatively, since one is not meant to be happy about just anything, but about very particular things that are culturally valued. As Sara Ahmed explains, "happiness is attributed to certain objects that circulate as social goods" ("Happy Objects" 37). Aligning oneself in relation to those objects—such as marriage and the family—means not just orienting oneself to be happy, but also performing one's membership within a particular group. Social groups cohere "around a shared orientation toward some things as being good, treating some things and not others as the cause of delight" ("Happy Objects" 35). She offers the family as an example: "The family would be happy not because it causes happiness, and not even because it affects us in a good way, but because we share an orientation toward the family as being good, as being what promises happiness in return for loyalty" ("Happy Objects" 38). Importantly, this orientation leads us to act accordingly, making certain choices about how we maintain our families, how we use our resources, and how we expend our energy.

The narrative of the happy family requires heterosexuality because heterosexual love is understood as "what life is aimed toward" and "what gives life direction or purpose," and deviation from the heterosexual happiness script threatens unhappiness (Ahmed, *The Promise* 90–91). One becomes a sort of stranger to one's community, what Ahmed calls an "affect alien," if one does not experience the appropriate affective response to the objects valued by one's community (Ahmed, "Happy Objects" 37). Indeed, an affect alien can produce discomfort in the *entire* community, creating awkwardness by disrupting the shared orientation toward the happy object. Thus, the "unhappy queer," by violating the heterosexual happiness script, functions as an affect alien who disrupts our shared orientation toward such happy objects as marriage and the family, and is "attributed as the cause of unhappiness"

(Ahmed, *The Promise* 95). The affect alien, in other words, is perceived to be "the one who converts good feelings into bad, who as it were 'kills' the joy of the family" (Ahmed, *The Promise* 49). Pointing out the trouble with happy objects leads to being labeled as the trouble oneself; or, as Ahmed puts it, "the exposure of violence becomes the origin of violence" ("Happy Objects" 39).

Understanding the circulation of affect around particular objects and within cultural groups in this way goes far to help explain why we are so ready to recognize the violence of homophobia when it is manifested in a violent act that takes the queer as both its object and its agent. The violence of heteronormativity can be at least partly covered over insofar as queers are incorporated, homonormatively, into the neoliberal American dream, and insofar as they demonstrate the appropriate happiness at such an inclusion. But the suicides of queer youth illustrate quite starkly the lie of neoliberal equality. The rhetorical figure of the suicidal gay teen, because it reveals a disruption of the shared cultural orientation toward happy objects, is catachrestically labeled, like Ahmed's affect alien, as the origin of the violence. This is not to suggest that the figure of the suicidal gay teen is being blamed for homophobia, but rather that the violence produced and disavowed by heteronormative discourses of happiness is transferred onto this figure.

That the moment of the suicide attempt is often portrayed as one of profound loneliness and isolation—rather than as a moment in which the unbearably crowded cacophony of the social becomes too much to bear—helps to disguise the intensely social nature of the tragedy. The production of the figure of the suicidal gay teen thus enables a discourse of empathy and concern for equality, allowing us to imagine ourselves as would-be saviors rather than as accomplices. The figure of the suicidal gay teen enacts the violence of a heteronormative culture, and in the deaths of queer youth, provides an opportunity to perform the grief, compassion, and outrage befitting liberal democratic citizens who are confronted with subjective violence. In other words, the foregrounding of this figure does a great deal of rhetorical work for us and serves a profoundly social function: it allows us to condemn homophobia (most directly, through the metonym of the bully) and to reaffirm our shared orientation toward marriage and family as happy objects, but does not require us to notice or take responsibility for the alienating heteronormative effects of our affective connections.

Gendering the Suicidal Gay Teen

One of the most notable commonalities among the suicides of September 2010 is that all of the five teens were boys. But this commonality is, in fact, rarely noted. If anything, the gendering of the suicides is masked by the language deployed in most of the mainstream news stories about them. Many articles, for example, talk about the heartbreaking stories of "queer kids," or the "increase in suicides among gay students," and the need to improve anti-bullying policies to protect "gay and lesbian" students or to reach out to "gay, lesbian, bisexual, and transgender youth." This language is intended to be gender-neutral and inclusive, but it belies the fact that the ensuing stories often refer exclusively and explicitly only to boys (Bramlett; "Campus Forum"; McCarty; Erbentraut, "Dan Savage"). Failing to attend to the importance of gender by allowing masculinity to remain unmarked "has the effect of blinding us as we desperately search for clues about how to respond" (Katz and Jhally). The production of the rhetorical figure of the suicidal gay teen depends on this gender-blindness, even as the policing of gender norms is one of bullying's primary features.

Discussions of bullying repeatedly instantiate masculinity as a key feature of the problem without seeming to notice that they do so. For instance, Richard Kim begins by talking about "queer kids" (a nongendered category), but his specific example quickly reminds us that bullying is a problem of masculinity: "There's nothing—nothing—that raises my hackles more than seeing an effeminate boy being teased." Later, he describes the "rash of suicides by gay teenagers, most of them boys," but then proceeds to provide a list of suicide victims that includes *all* boys, and he does not offer an explanation for the gender imbalance of the phenomenon. Likewise, Charles P. Pierce, in an otherwise apt criticism of Michigan's newly passed but severely flawed anti-bullying legislation, offers illustrations of bullying that assume both parties—the target of the bullying and the bully—are boys. Furthermore, the type of bullying he imagines is explicitly homophobic, where, in his words, one child "thinks another kid is a great big 'faggoty-fag-fag.'"

These comments do not just point up the lack of attention to female bullies and female victims; they also reveal the ways in which the act of bullying—and by implication, the figure of the suicidal gay teen—is always already gendered. Boys who taunt other boys by calling them "faggots" are commenting not so much on their actual or perceived homosexuality, but on their association with femininity. In a study of adolescent boys in high school, C. J. Pascoe argues that "achieving a masculine identity entails a repeated repudiation of the specter of failed masculinity." This performance of masculinity often takes the form of what Pascoe calls the "fag discourse:" labeling other young men as "fags" while attempting to avoid having that label applied to themselves (5). In other words, tormenting "faggots"—gay or not—is a means of establishing manhood and represents a defense against being perceived as insufficiently masculine. Thus, understanding teen suicides only in terms of homophobia and bullying misses the crucial role of masculinity in upholding heteronormative categories of gender and sexuality.

Pascoe also notes that for teenage boys, masculinity is often understood as "a form of dominance usually expressed through sexualized discourses," and as such, it is built upon the bodies of their female classmates (5). Demonstrating their access to female bodies—through sexual teasing, "playful" physical harassment, and uninvited and sometimes aggressive touching—is a means for adolescent boys to prove their heterosexual masculinity to their male peers. Thus, when boys attempt to gain power in a masculine hierarchy by deploying the "fag discourse," they do so at the expense not only of the boys who are labeled as "faggots," but also of the girls whose femininity and female bodies are understood to be so despised. As Gordon writes, he had been bullied as a child because of his race, but nonetheless participated in the victimization of a female schoolmate by teasing her about her developing body. He remembers, "at the age of 10, it was already clear to us, as boys, that we had a right to objectify her body, to insult her ... the message was already established; her body was there for our amusement and violation." Hugo Schwyzer puts it quite clearly: "what we often see as homophobia is really thinly disguised misogyny," and the taunting of "faggots" serves to denigrate homosexuality, but even more so, communicates contempt for femininity.

I am suggesting, therefore, that the "queerness" of the figure of the suicidal gay teen is premised on an assumed and undesirable association with femininity. Female bodies are the index by which male masculinity is gauged, and the menace of feminization defines the bullying through which masculinity is hierarchized. Even when the bullying of boys is overtly homophobic (when they are called "faggots"), it may be more properly understood as a policing of heteronormative gender expectations. It is no surprise, then, that the bullying of girls also targets gendered norms of heterosexuality and femininity, most often through the invocation of promiscuity. For instance, Ashlynn Conner, who committed suicide at 10 years of age in November 2011, was teased about looking like a boy when she cut her hair short; she was called ugly and fat (in other words, told that she was unsuccessfully performing femininity) and was even labeled a slut (Grimm and Schlikerman). Phoebe Prince, who committed suicide at 15 years of age in January 2010, was ridiculed and physically assaulted by classmates for dating a popular senior boy; she was called "an Irish whore" and was told to "close her legs" and "stop being a ho" ("Irish Teenager"). Just as a boy need not actually be gay to be labeled a fag, a girl need not actually be promiscuous—or even sexually active—to be labeled a slut. Both terms serve policing functions, but there is a crucial difference: while girls are taught that they must avoid being seen as "bad girls," boys are taught that they must not be girls, period. Indeed, this is articulated quite literally in an article by Jimmy Bramlett, which calls for empathy for the queer teen boys who killed themselves and urges other teens to make a different choice: "And I keep thinking that these kids should know this message, that suicide is wrong, that they were such pussies for taking their own lives and leaving a mess for their families to deal with." His use of the word "pussies" as opposed to, for instance, "cowards," is not incidental: even in the aftermath of the tragedy of suicide, the ultimate denigration is to be associated with the female body.

This is not simply to suggest that what is perceived as homophobia is actually misogyny, or that at the root of the oppression of queers is a more fundamental oppression of women. It is not, in other words, to posit a hierarchy of cultural restrictions on sexuality and gender, respectively. Rather, it is to note that when a discourse of homophobia drives our understanding of adolescent boys' suicides, we fail to recognize that teenagers of all genders are subject to overwhelming heteronormative pressures that sometimes manifest themselves in seemingly homophobic bullying. It is also to caution that when the rhetorical figure of the suicidal gay teen is implicitly gendered male and becomes visible primarily as a target of homophobic bullying, the lives and deaths of queer girls, straight girls, and trans* and gender nonconforming kids inevitably recede even further from view, illegible through homophobia's insufficiently fine optic.

Conclusion: The Violence of the Promise

The figure of the suicidal gay teen, as I have shown, operates implicitly and affectively behind the scenes of public discourse, shaping the ways in which we frame the problem of queer youth and therefore how we imagine we might make it better. This figure emerges as a site of self-imposed violence, affectively alienated from a tolerant culture, in which masculinity's role in upholding heteronormativity can be disguised. As I suggested at the outset, the production of this figure tells us little about actual queer adolescents, but much about our cultural anxieties concerning queer lives and deaths. As such, it carries out the social functions suggested by Honig and Asen: it can be deployed to solve cultural problems, it simplifies complex social phenomena, it stands in as a proxy for larger social issues, and it influences or justifies policy decisions.

I would like to address this last function—the ways in which the suicidal gay teen drives policy decisions—by focusing for a moment on the It Gets Better Project—perhaps the most visible and popularly known suicide prevention effort targeting queer youth, and one that arose directly in response to the September 2010 suicides. Launched by author and editorialist Dan Savage and his partner, Terry Miller, the It Gets Better Project houses a collection of user-created videos that are intended "to show young LGBT people the levels of happiness, potential, and positivity their lives will reach—if they can just get through their teen years" ("What Is"). The project has been incredibly popular, now boasting well over 50,000 videos, and has the potential, as West, Frischherz, Panther, and Brophy argue, for a kind of queer worldmaking that emphasizes "the creative capacities of individuals, together and alone, to forge relations that evade the complete capture of compulsory heteronormativities" (57). But It Gets Better has also been roundly criticized for, among other things, being a form of "slacktivism" that does not involve making any real changes; for suggesting that queer lives will get better merely with the passage of time rather than with political action; for presenting a kind of life that is available only to particularly privileged segments of the population; and for valuing a positive and upbeat message over true diversity and dissent (Meyer; Gray; Halberstam; Puar). In short, many of the critiques of It Gets Better are leveled at precisely the neoliberal logic I described earlier, which asserts happiness as a measure of progress and participation in heteronormative and homonormative institutions as proof of success. Affect, here, is deployed rhetorically: it is the mechanism through which the neoliberal demand is carried out, and it is through the inducement to happiness that the hetero- and homonormative thrust is reframed as a desirable form of progress. The It Gets Better Project reaches out to the queer adolescent who is cast as affectively alienated and alone, who needs to be reminded that "the good life" is within reach. It asks that teenager to not engage in the act of violence that a heteronormative culture seems to suggest, promising in exchange for complicity a life of normality.

But the flimsy promise of It Gets Better is exposed by kids like Jamey Rodemeyer and Eric James Borges, who created their own hopeful It Gets Better videos meant to encourage others and then later killed themselves anyway. The figure of the suicidal gay teen, the justification for projects such as It Gets Better, is the disavowed exclusion of the hetero- and homonormative neoliberal ideal, but the only solution offered by this project is a repackaged version of the same damaging ideal. If this solution fails to help, as it failed for all the kids who are remembered in this chapter, then the figure of the suicidal gay teen—isolated, radically alienated, and the agent of its own demise—is only rendered more poignant, more rhetorically and affectively forceful.

Approaching the suicidal gay teen queerly, as I have attempted to do here, is therefore an effort to break away from the captivating brightness of neoliberal discourses of tolerance, to risk a few surreptitious glances into the shadows in the hopes of a glimmer of recognition in return. It is, in other words, to read queerly for the rhetorical violence that figures the suicidal gay teen as the repository and agent of the violence of a heteronormative culture, and to understand the lives and deaths of queer youths in relation to this figuration. As Lee Edelman explains, politics does not depend on essential identities but "on the figurality that is always essential *to* identity, and thus on the figural relations in which social identities are always inscribed" (24). Consequently, the value of a queer reading strategy "resides in its capacity to *expose as figural* the symbolic reality that invests us as subjects insofar as it simultaneously constrains us in turn to invest ourselves in *it*, to cling to its fictions as reality, since we are only able to live within, and thus may be willing to die to maintain, the figures of meaning that pass as the very material of literal truth" (24; first emphasis added). To recognize the figural as figural, as a rhetorical and affective effect, can lead us to reconsider the interventions we presume to make on behalf of queer youth; it can also goad us to acknowledge that the figure of the suicidal gay teen serves as a sort of queer salve for the wounds of heteronormativity, and that the production of this figure is a covert and repeated performance of rhetorical violence. Such queer recognition admits that the inevitability signaled by "gay boys kill themselves" is best understood not as a lament but as a devastating cultural imperative.

Note

1. My thanks to Dan Brouwer, who, during the queerly suspended temporality of a flight delay in Houston's George Bush Intercontinental Airport, helped me articulate the queerness of this method.

Works Cited

Ahmed, Sara. "Happy Objects." *The Affect Theory Reader*. Eds. Melissa Gregg and Gregory J. Seigworth. Durham, NC: Duke UP, 2010. 29–51. Print.
Ahmed, Sara. *The Promise of Happiness*. Durham, NC: Duke UP, 2010. Print.
Asen, Robert. "Women, Work, Welfare: A Rhetorical History of Images of Poor Women in Welfare Policy Debates." *Rhetoric and Public Affairs* 6.2 (2003): 285–312. Print.
Bramlett, Jimmy. "A Plea for Empathy." *LAist*. 1 Oct. 2010. Web. 28 Apr. 2015.
"Campus Forum to Discuss Suicides among Gay Teens, Students." Pennsylvania College of Technology press release. 7 Oct. 2010. Print.
Collins, Randall. "The Inflation of Bullying: From Fagging to Cyber-Effervescent Scapegoating." *The Sociological Eye*. 7 July 2011. Web. 28 Apr. 2015.
Duggan, Lisa. *The Twilight of Equality*. Boston: Beacon, 2003. Print.
Dyer, Richard. *The Matter of Images: Essays on Representations*. 1993. New York: Routledge, 2013. Print.
Edelman, Lee. "The Future Is Kid Stuff: Queer Theory, Disidentification, and the Death Drive." *Narrative* 6.1 (1998): 18–30. Print.
Erbentraut, Joseph. "Dan Savage Tells LGBT Youth 'It Gets Better.'" *Chicagoist*. 22 Sept. 2010. Web. 28 Apr. 2015.
Erbentraut, Joseph. "LGBT Community Mourns String of Suicides." *Chicagoist*. 1 Oct. 2010. Web. 28 Apr. 2015.
Geidner, Chris. "Education Sec'y on Teen Suicides: 'Every one of us ... needs to stand up and speak out.'" *Poliglot: A Queer Spin on Politics*. 1 Oct. 2010. Web. 28 Apr. 2015.
Gordon, Max S. "Troy Davis and Jamey Rodemeyer: By a Jury of Our Peers." *The New Civil Rights Movement*. 2 Oct. 2011. Web. 28 Apr. 2015.
Gray, Mary. "It Doesn't Get Better for Anyone If We Don't Make it Better for Everyone." *Queer Country*. 4 Mar. 2011. Web. 28 Apr. 2015.
Grimm, Andy, and Becky Schlikerman. "10-year-old Girl's Death Stuns Small Town." *Chicagotribune.com*. 17 Nov. 2011. Web. 28 Apr. 2015.
Halberstam, J. Jack. "It Gets Worse ..." *Social Text: Periscope*. 20 Nov. 2010. Web. 28 Apr. 2015.
Hartman, Saidiya. "Venus in Two Acts." *Small Axe* 26 (2008): 1–14. Print.
Honig, Bonnie. *Democracy and the Foreigner*. Princeton, NJ: Princeton UP, 2001. Print.
"Irish Teenager Phoebe Prince's Suicide Outrage Sparks Mass US Backlash." *Belfast Telegraph*. 19 Apr. 2010. Web. 28 Apr. 2015.
James, Susan Donaldson. "Jamey Rodemeyer Suicide: Police Consider Criminal Bullying Charges." *ABCNews.go.com*. 22 Sept. 2011. Web. 28 Apr. 2015.
Katz, Jackson, and Sut Jhally. "The National Conversation in the Wake of Littleton Is Missing the Mark." *The Boston Globe*. 2 May 1999. Web. 28 Apr. 2015.
Kim, Richard. "Against 'Bullying' or On Loving Queer Kids." *The Nation*. 6 Oct. 2010. Web. 28 Apr. 2015.

Love, Heather. "Compulsory Happiness and Queer Existence." *New Formations* 63 (Winter 2007/2008): 52–64. Print.
McCarty, Mary. "Suicides Make Anti-Bullying Policies Essential." *Dayton Daily News*. 10 October 2010. Web. 28 Apr. 2015.
McKinley, Jesse. "Suicides Put Light on Pressures of Gay Teenagers." *New York Times*. 3 Oct. 2010. Web. 28 Apr. 2015.
Meyer, Elizabeth. "It Gets Better: Helping or Hurting?" *PsychologyToday.com*. 10 Dec. 2010. Web. 28 Apr. 2015.
Moskowitz, Clara. "High Suicide Risk, Prejudice Plague Transgender People." *Live Science*. 19 Nov. 2010. Web. 28 Apr. 2015.
Ott, Brian L. "The Visceral Politics of V for Vendetta: On Political Affect in Cinema." *Critical Studies in Media Communication* 27.1 (2010): 39–54. Print.
Pascoe, C.J. *Dude, You're a Fag: Masculinity and Sexuality in High School*. Berkeley: U of California P, 2007. Print.
Pierce, Charles P. "A Dangerous Law and the New Formula of Conservatism." *Esquire*. 4 Nov. 2011. Web. 28 Apr. 2015.
Puar, Jasbir. "In the Wake of It Gets Better." *The Guardian*. 16 Nov. 2010. Web. 28 Apr. 2015.
Schwyzer, Hugo. "Boys, Girls, the Fag Discourse and Compulsive Heterosexuality: A Review of CJ Pascoe's Book." Web. 28 Apr. 2015.
West, Isaac, Michaela Frischherz, Allison Panther, and Richard Brophy. "Queer Worldmaking in the 'It Gets Better' Campaign." *QED: A Journal in GLBTQ Worldmaking*. Inaugural Issue (Fall 2013): 49–86. Print.
"What Is the It Gets Better Project?" *ItGetsBetter.org*. Web. 28 Apr. 2015.
Winters, Rosemary. "LGBT Kids Coming Out Earlier." *The Salt Lake Tribune*. 17 May 2010. Web. 28 Apr. 2015.
Žižek, Slavoj. *Violence*. New York: Picador, 2008. Print.

14 Consorting with the Enemy?
Women's Liberation Rhetoric about Sexuality[1]

Clark A. Pomerleau

Since the women's liberation movements' (WLMs) upsurge in organizing in the 1960s, American feminists have debated what stances to take regarding gendered sexuality. Coverture's legacy continued through the twentieth century; heterosexual marriage and motherhood remained rationales to limit women's legal rights, economic opportunities, social standing, and sexual autonomy (Kerber). Feminist rhetors had to debunk received wisdom to root out sexist assumptions that pervaded individual relationships and institutions, so they often rejected mainstream authorities. Instead, they created knowledge from experience, including their process or feelings in arguments, generalizing from the individual to the group to forge commonality and invite coparticipation. Oppositional rhetoric meant to create collective feminist identity often used binaries that symbolically reversed normative values, but women disagreed on whether these dichotomies had essential or social constructionist origins. Women transgressed feminine passive acceptance of norms by willingly hearing or reading feminist critiques. Feminist consumers of rhetoric, however, might resist one interpretation by privileging their own experience and values over another's. Women's actions also signaled the effectiveness of rhetoric meant to change behavior. For all the effort to reevaluate dominant views, feminist views on sexuality sometimes blended with societal biases, and radical propositions created in the late 1960s through mid-1970s have remained at odds with neoliberal values.

Intercourse, Vaginal Orgasm, and Heterosexual Marriage as War Tactics

Between 1965 and 1968, most denunciations of the ways sexism permeated men's behavior and society argued that men and women needed to retrain themselves and create institutional equality (Baxandall and Gordon 21–22, 25, 28–29). Valerie Solanas, in contrast, called on women "to overthrow the government ... and destroy the male sex." Her extended criticism reversed Aristotelian bias by calling maleness biologically inferior, an "incomplete female," "a deficiency disease" (1). Her mimeographed tract, *SCUM Manifesto*, became a bestseller after she shot pop art leader Andy Warhol. In addition to introducing essentialist reversal that devalued males, Solanas declared all sexual relationships unimportant and love/friendship with men impossible (23, 26–28, 36). Some denounced Solanas's ideas as insane based on psychiatric diagnosis at her trial, but *SCUM Manifesto* influenced key early self-styled "radical feminists" and entered anthologies (Morgan, *Sisterhood* 514–19).

Ti-Grace Atkinson's positions added divisiveness to questions of sexual behavior, and after she spoke widely and gained popular press acclaim, the speeches and essays she published in 1974 reached more readers. Life experiences such as unwanted marriage at 17 and divorce after five years in 1961 influenced her position. Attending a New York-National Organization for Women (NY-NOW) founding meeting connected her to women's rights work. By the end of 1967, members elected her president. She also began doctoral study in philosophy at Columbia University, which focused her on argumentation and put her in the epicenter of New York's WLM. NY-NOW members feared negative publicity when Atkinson supported Solanas. When two-thirds of the members also rejected Atkinson's 1968 call for a nonhierarchical structure, she left to form a group soon called The Feminists (Atkinson 98). Atkinson's collection, *Amazon Odyssey*, documented her frequent analogy to war. She portrayed herself as having "always been in the midst of battle." Atkinson took credit for "drawing up the lines of battle very early" (xxiii). One of her first essays while she was in The Feminists argued that Freud "concocted" a theory of vaginal orgasm to support intercourse in marriage, an institution that exploited women (13).[2] Atkinson picked up on Solanas's rejection of sex while opposing biological essentialism historically used against women. By April 1969, she denounced marriage on the premise that male sexism created romantic love and the institution of marriage to perpetuate oppression. "Radical Feminism and Love" asked rhetorically, "Why do women, even feminists, consort with the enemy? For sex? Very few women ever say that; that's the male-role reason. What nearly all women mutter in response to this is: 'for love'" (44).

Atkinson accepted the notion that society tried to deprive women as a class of power and posited that romantic love was a main way women linked themselves to men to gain men's power vicariously. She concluded that the woman "*in love with* the man ... is going from the political, the power*less* identification, to the individual, one-to-one unit. She is disarming herself to go into the enemy camp" (45). Atkinson attempted to convince female readers to dis-identify with the "She" that represented all women in love with the "enemy." In April 1969, her "Radical Feminism: Declaration of War" presented "a detailed understanding of what *his* battle strategy has been that has kept us so successfully pinned down" (47). Here, synecdoche implied that all men warred against women, whereas "us" invited female solidarity. Atkinson criticized movement participants for not exploring "the significance of the fact that women form a class" (48):

> The "battle of the sexes" is a commonplace, both over time and distance. But it is an inaccurate description of what has been happening.

> A "battle" implies some balance of powers, whereas when one side suffers all the losses, such as in some kinds of raids (often referred to as the "rape" of the area), that is called a *massacre*. Women have been massacred as human beings over history, and this destiny is entailed by their definition. As women begin massing together they take the first step from *being* massacred to *engaging in* battle (resistance). Hopefully, this will eventually lead to negotiations—in the *very* far future—and peace. (49)

This passage heightened the sense of personal threat with the word "rape," while accurately associating rape with military massacre months before revelations that soldiers attempted to rape women and girls at My Lai before murdering them.[3] The WLM had not yet problematized drawing parallels between privileged US women and Vietnamese villagers or enslaved people, but both analogies were common in the writings of white feminists. Atkinson continued with advice to create feminist analysis: "When any person or group of persons is being mistreated or, to continue our metaphor, is being attacked," "the victim determines how much damage was done," whence the attack came, "how can you win the immediate battle," "why did he attack you?", and "how can you win (end) the war?–offensive measures. –moving within his boundaries." (50). Atkinson addressed head-on her use of military terminology, arguing that women must deprogram nonresistance and fight back. She advocated developing feminist analysis to gauge the best places to strike and opposed incorporating enemy programming like hierarchy into the WLM. After hypothesizing about how sexism developed, she raised and dismissed biological arguments, concluding that "the sex roles—both male and female—must be destroyed, not the individuals who happen to possess either a penis or a vagina, or both, or neither" (55).

The December 12, 1969, issue of *Life* magazine publicized The Feminists' protest that the New York City Marriage License Bureau committed "fraud with malicious intent." The Feminists' leaflet asked provocative questions that accurately reflected ways coverture continued to diminish married women's rights:

> Do you know that rape is legal in marriage?. ...
> Do you know that love and affection are not required in marriage?. ...
> Do you know that you are your husband's prisoner?. ...
> Do you know that, according to the United Nations, marriage is a "slavery-like" practice?
>
> (Morgan, *Sisterhood* 536–37)

Life did not cite the leaflet; the reporter just quoted Atkinson explaining that The Feminists' quota against more than one-third of members marrying or living with a man showed that "[w]e reject marriage both in theory and in practice" (Davidson 69). Atkinson advocated celibacy and hoped test-tube babies would better society (Davidson 69; Atkinson 99).[4] She told the reporter, "The more I understand what's going on with men, the less I miss male companionship and sex. Men *brag* about domination, conquest, trickery, exploitation" (69). In a separate speech, Atkinson criticized societal pressure to marry, clarifying that although "[m]y husband was very good to me," marriage created "this feeling of despair, of closing the door on my life." When society mandates marriage, a "woman by definition has no life, no destiny, no identity" (Atkinson 26). By the end of 1970, Atkinson had shifted from solely attacking the system and calling heterosexual love a "mass hysteria" to branding women who remained married "collaborators" (Atkinson 5–8, 13–45, 131–32).

The war analogy could energize women whose consciousness-raising highlighted that their personal struggles with men fit into prevalent political injustice. After Betty Friedan's withering critique of the sexist legacies of psychoanalysis in *The Feminine Mystique*, however, Atkinson's claims that women in heterosexual love were hysterics risked alienating audiences, as did oppositionally placing women "collaborators" with male enemies. Women who differentiated between male loved ones and systemic sexism were likely to reject the war analogy, along with derogatory designations. Furthermore, Atkinson as the messenger was contentious. Her 1970 resignation from The Feminists reflected continuous movement concerns over women who gained "leader" status based on their public presence. Unlike leaderless consciousness-raising groups, Atkinson's frequent speeches and media interviews invested her with authority, but other feminists who also came to the fore, like Robin Morgan and Susan Brownmiller, derided her "inflammatory rhetoric" that vilified other feminists as part of her frequent exits from groups (Brownmiller 1999 230; Morgan, *Saturday's Child* 305).

Alliances for Equal Duties

The WLM generation had the highest rate of marriage seen in a century; obviously, most did not heed Atkinson's call. Alix Kates Shulman and Robin Morgan used marital experiences to prove that couples could consciously divide labor equally. After her divorce, Shulman did not renounce marriage and motherhood, as Atkinson had. She remarried. Shulman started writing after having two children and struggled to gain solitary time to write while also participating in New York Radical Women (NYRW) and Women's International Terrorist Conspiracy from Hell (WITCH). Her "A Marriage Agreement" is a first-person narrative about how having two children changed her marriage from easily divided household tasks to the burden of domestic life falling to her:

> We automatically accepted the traditional sex roles that society assigns. My husband worked all day in an office; I left my job and stayed at home, taking on almost all the burdens of housekeeping and child raising.

> ... now I was restricted to the company of two demanding preschoolers and to the four walls of an apartment. It seemed unfair that while my husband's life had changed little when the children were born, domestic life had become the only life I had.
>
> (Baxandall and Gordon 219)

The personable account echoed scenes from *The Feminine Mystique*. Shulman related that she tried to cope until consciousness-raising sessions showed "other women too felt drained and frustrated as housewives and mothers." "Eventually, after an arduous examination of our situation, my husband and I decided that we no longer had to accept the sex roles." Shulman later wrote of her 1969 call for married men and women to split domestic duties equally, "At the time the idea was so outrageous that my piece was reprinted widely, in *New York* magazine, *Ms.*, *Redbook* (where it received more reader letters than any other article *Redbook* had ever published), and, in 1972, *Life* magazine, where it was the subject of a six-page spread" (Ohioana Authors; Love 422). Women read that they were not alone. They could list their household's specific jobs and adopt the same premise: "As parents we believe we must share all responsibility for taking care of our children and home—not only the work, but the responsibility. At least during the first years of this agreement, *sharing responsibility* shall mean dividing the *jobs* and dividing the *time*. ... And deviation from 50–50 must be for the convenience of both parties" (Baxandall and Gordon 219).

Robin Morgan, like Atkinson, has been an early and high-volume voice, both instrumental and criticized. She simultaneously joined New Left and feminist groups. Her jointly founded NYRW gained publicity by staging a peace protest that eschewed reliance on motherhood and then by protesting 1968 Miss America pageant objectification. As NYRW dissolved, Morgan formed WITCH (1969) (Morgan, *Saturday's Child* 257). The same *Life* article in which The Feminists protested marriage pictured Morgan holding her baby. The reporter counted her among many who were

> restructuring their nuclear families. Robin Morgan, a member of WITCH, who is a poet, editor and former child actress ..., has been married seven years and has a 5-month-old son. Robin and her husband, Poet Kenneth Pitchford, have consciously worked to share all roles. Both have part-time jobs, he in the mornings, she afternoons; while one works, the other takes care of the baby. "We're both mothers," Robin says. "He bottle feeds, and I breast feed." ... Robin hopes they will be living in a commune before Blake grows up. "Our arrangement is one attempt at an interim solution. But no personal solution will work until we have a complete social and economic revolution which stresses the liberation of 51% of the people."
>
> (Davidson 71, 78)

Morgan's comparison of infant care rejected biological determinism. She portrayed her husband as an equal partner with a shared vision. A year later she was more wary. Morgan famously quit co-gender New Left participation in 1970, asserting, "We have met the enemy and he's our friend. And dangerous" before she catalogued New Left men's betraying sexist behavior (Baxandall and Gordon 53). She wove personal experience into her introduction to *Sisterhood Is Powerful*, arguably one of the era's most famous books to spread "radical feminism," asserting that male partners' "reprisals" were part of the oppression authors faced in creating the anthology: "I twice survived the almost dissolution of my marriage" (xiii–xiv). Like Shulman and Atkinson, Morgan deemed the nuclear family unit oppressive to all involved because the woman became legally dependent, "paying for her keep with an enormous amount of emotional and physical labor." By 1970, Morgan rejected men's alternatives such as "divorce or 'just living together' or communal living" as creating more difficulties for women. For another 12 years, her introduction and own life prioritized marriage over divorce, which implied that she would retain marriage within women-created alternatives: "we must create the alternatives that *we* want, those we imagine to be in our self-interest. I, for one, think that some form of extended family structure (… [with] living companions of choice) might be the answer" (xxxii–xxxiii).[5]

Gender war rhetoric would have imperiled Shulman and Morgan's identities as mothers of boys in heterosexual marriages. They sought collective identity formations that recognized how heterosexuality and roles for mothers disadvantaged women, but they did not generalize "us/them" as broadly as Atkinson.

The Lavender Herring/Menace

Debates over heterosexual relationships overlapped with shifting views about the relationship between lesbian identity and feminism as some lesbian women divided their time between feminist and gay liberation movement (GLM) activism. In a 1973 interview, Atkinson claimed to have invented "the whole concept of political lesbianism which is now popular" (Reynolds 5, 8). Initially, Atkinson wondered why opponents hurled the term "lesbian" at feminists. She concluded in a February 1970 speech to college women that men perceived lesbians as resistant because they did not need men. At this stage, however, Atkinson stereotyped lesbians as apolitical reactionaries because "lesbianism involves role-playing and, more important, because it is based on the primary assumption of male oppression, that is, sex, lesbianism reinforces the sex class system" (83, 86). Like her antithesis between friendship and love, this reductive definition of lesbianism as role-played sexual interest did not recognize that lesbian relationships could fulfill multiple emotional needs with relational equality. Her "experiential" knowledge consisted of believing she saw roles that imitated heterosexuals.

Gay Liberation Front (GLF) member, Martha Shelley, debunked the sexology model that women with same-sex attraction imitated husband–wife roles. Her 1969 "Notes of a Radical Lesbian" summarized confining options for heterosexual women, while "The Lesbian" was "freed of dependence on men for love, sex, and money." Shelley stated from experience, "I have never met a Lesbian who was not a feminist. ... I have met straight women who would die to preserve their chains. I have never met a Lesbian who believed that she was innately less rational or capable than a man; who swallowed one word of the 'woman's role' horseshit.'" She asked, "Isn't love between equals healthier than sucking up to an oppressor?" In a move that implied universal bisexual (a.k.a. "bi") potential, Shelley posited reasons for homophobia before concluding with a call to revolution:

> Men fear Lesbians because they are less dependent, and because their hostility is less controlled.
>
> Straight women fear Lesbians because of the Lesbian inside them, because we represent an alternative. They fear us for the same reason that uptight middle-class people fear hip people. They are angry at us because we have a way out that they are afraid to take.
>
> (Morgan, *Sisterhood* 307–10)

Shelley and other GLF women joined lesbian former members of NY-NOW as the Lavender Menace (a.k.a. Radicalesbians) when NOW cofounder, Betty Friedan, denounced lesbians who pressed NOW to support lesbian rights as raising a "lavender herring" that distracted from important issues and as menaces to NOW's reputation. Lavender Menace refuted nonlesbian feminists' homophobic stereotypes in their May 1970 takeover of a NOW conference. Their position paper, "The Woman-Identified Woman," defined lesbians as choosing the highest political solidarity with women. This definition reversed norms that considered heterosexuality positive and lesbianism negative. The paper built on concerns that heterosexual women exhibited male-identification, false consciousness through identifying with the oppressor's power, ego, status, protection, and acceptance, an internalized enslaved role, self-hatred, and alienation from themselves and other women. Lesbians, in contrast, exemplified personhood outside male role distinctions (Jay and Young 172–75).[6] Lavender Menace speakers challenged women to embrace the derogatory associations within lesbian-baiting:

> As long as the label "dyke" can be used to frighten women into a less militant stand, keep her separate from her sisters, keep her from giving primacy to anything other than men and family—then to that extent she is controlled by the male culture.
>
> (Jay and Young 174)

The Lavender Menace implied that any woman who was woman-identified could achieve autonomy. "The Woman-Identified Woman" dramatically changed the definition and scope of lesbianism in ways that had lasting impacts for gender expression and sexuality by defining lesbians as women focused holistically on other women without male-imposed behavioral norms. Initial WLM responses included hostility, hesitation, and growing support for recognizing that women's autonomy to choose a female partner was a feminist issue. The mostly white NOW members passed a resolution denouncing homophobia with another problematic race analogy: "Asking women to disguise their [lesbian] identities so they will not 'embarrass' the group is an intolerable form of oppression, like asking black women to join us in white face." Nonetheless, sexual orientation continued to divide feminists through the 1980s. Dominant society stigma against lesbians remained a threat. Conflicting assertions of vanguard feminist status based on sexual orientation and behavior, including promulgations on how women should look, act, and be sexual, continued to raise ire (Pomerleau, "Empowering Members" 847).

Atkinson was among women without erotic attraction to women who, in the wake of "The Woman-Identified Woman," carved out a vanguard feminist place for women who rejected sexual relationships with anyone. By the end of 1970, she revised her view of lesbians, claiming that their political significance was "this commitment, by choice, full-time, of one woman to others of her class." Contesting women's self-identification, she derided women who married men but had sexual relations with other women: "These women are not lesbians in the political sense. These women claim the right to 'private' lives. They are collaborators." And she praised "other women who have never had sexual relations with other women, but who have made, and live, a total commitment to this movement. These women are 'lesbians' in the political sense" (132). Atkinson had a short-lived membership in the New York homophile group, Daughters of Bilitis, during which she denounced women who became lesbian after joining the WLM as former reactionaries, while simultaneously advocating "I am a lesbian" buttons to confuse oppressors and to further WLM goals (145). Denouncing formerly heterosexually identified women highlighted Atkinson's dichotomy between those solely concentrating on feminism (good) and any sexual focus (bad). Her tactical alliance with lesbians for feminist gains included no GLM goals.

Flanking Bisexuality

When the Lavender Menace asked for support at their NOW takeover, NY-NOW and NYRW member, Kate Millett, came out as lesbian. Privately, she had a relationship with a woman and publicly with a man she married to prevent U.S. deportation (Millett 5, 24). Within the WLM, Millett had circulated a manifesto that asserted feminism would advance "bisex, or the end of enforced perverse heterosexuality" (Echols 74, 167, 211). In the ensuing seven months, Millett's life and intramovement talk became national news when mainstream media featured her as indicative of feminism. Many reviews heralded her book, *Sexual Politics*. *Life* compared it to Marx's

Capital. Life also pictured her kissing husband Fumio Yoshimura and noted that "she belongs to a number of women's liberation groups, including ('though I'm not into that') a radical lesbian organization" (Wrenn 22). The picture and "I'm not into that" quotation infuriated Radicalesbian members, one of whom interrupted a talk Millett gave at Columbia. Millett later described the scene:

> Teresa Juarez yelling at me from the audience, "Are you a Lesbian? Say it. Are you?" ... saying it like it was a joke, my credentials: founding member of Columbia Women's Liberation and bisexual. ...
> ... "Say it! Say you are a Lesbian." Yes I said. Yes. Because I know what she means. The line goes, inflexible as a fascist edict, that bisexuality is a cop-out. Yes I said yes I am a Lesbian.
> (Millett 14–15)

A *Time* reporter covered that lecture, and the December 14, 1970, issue claimed that Millett was "the high priestess of the Women's Liberation movement," only to round on the book and author to discredit the WLM. *Time* named five academic or journalist critics who

> raised some provocative questions. Can the feminists think clearly? Do they know anything about biology? What about their maturity, their morality, their sexuality? Ironically, Kate Millett herself contributed to the growing skepticism about the movement by acknowledging at a recent meeting that she is bisexual. The disclosure is bound to discredit her as a spokeswoman for her cause, cast further doubt on her theories, and reinforce the views of those skeptics who routinely dismiss all liberationists as lesbians.
> (Women's Lib 68)

In the space of six sentences, *Time* committed the fallacies of arguing from authority, hasty generalizations with false dichotomies, and a series of ad hominem attacks that equivocated by exchanging "bisexual" for "lesbian" to prejudice readers against feminists. Shifting definitions of Millett's sexuality crystallized both feminists' media concerns and hostility against bisexuality from heterosexual and lesbian feminists.

Time's slide from bisexual to lesbian, Millett's characterization of bi identification as a "cop-out," and her heralding of "bisex" captured three conflicting views that vied for predominance in the 1970s. By questioning Millett's/feminists' morality, *Time* upheld a long tradition that nonreproductive sexuality was sinful. *Time*'s ad hominems about maturity and sexuality dovetailed with Freud's notion that bisexuality did not exist in adults, so identifying as bi represented failure to mature properly (Blumstein and Schwartz 279). American sexology and culture tended to label any amount of same-sex attraction homosexual despite Alfred Kinsey's caution against moralizing and determination that sexual attraction fell into a continuum, not a dichotomy (Storr 20, 32). The GLM fought homophobic stereotypes but split on whether to glorify bisexuality as an ideal potential within all people or to prioritize gay and lesbian identity based on concern that "swinging" behavior had become chic, and people whose attraction were not limited to one gender could always retreat from political conflict and stigma by expressing as heterosexual. Even GLM leaders who considered bisexuality developmentally superior urged those with bi attraction to identify as gay or lesbian for gay liberation's sake. The globally distributed 1970 manifesto by Carl Wittman epitomized this political advice:

> Bisexuality: Bisexuality is good; it is the capacity to love people of either sex. The reason so few of us are bisexual is because society made such a big stink about homosexuality that we got forced into seeing ourselves as either straight or non-straight. ... Gays will begin to turn on to women when 1) it's something that we do because we want to, and not because we should, and 2) when women's liberation changes the nature of heterosexual relationships.
>
> We continue to call ourselves homosexual, not bisexual, even if we do make it with the opposite sex also, because saying "Oh, I'm Bi" is a cop out for a gay. We get told it's OK to sleep with guys as long as we sleep with women, too, and that's still putting homosexuality down. We'll be gay until everyone has forgotten that it's an issue. Then we'll begin to be complete.
>
> (Jay and Young 331)

In addition to the wariness that bi people would not remain politically engaged, lesbians used choice against bisexuality. From the 1970s through the 1980s, the competing terms "sexual orientation" and "sexual preference" reflected the disagreement of gay spokespeople over whether sexual attraction was something outside one's control and not one's "fault," or whether one had a right to choose consensual sexual expression. Lesbian separatists were most likely to develop "Woman-Identified Woman" to claim lesbianism was a superior choice available to all women (Pomerleau, *Califia* 72–74). That position rendered bisexuality a failure to focus energy exclusively on other women.

Despite media claims that the mid-1970s heralded "bisexual chic," biphobic attitudes predominated among psychologists and most people with heterosexual or homosexual identity (*Newsweek* 27 May 1974 in Rust, *Bisexuality* 554–55). Philip Blumstein and Pepper Schwartz's 1974 study found that only "libertarian" groups of swingers and threesome participants deemed bisexuality positive (Blumstein and Schwartz 292). Lesbians perpetuated negative discrediting. Participants with bi identity ranged from considering a partner's gender irrelevant to having had a few same-sex experiences to believing all people were inherently bi. Although lesbian participants overwhelmingly had heterosexual experience (including after lesbian identification), those who embraced lesbian identity often discounted bisexuality as a precursory phase before fully coming out. These women mistrusted bisexuality and pressured those in their community not to express openness to a future relationship with a man (283–85, 289, 291). Blumstein and Schwartz relayed the idea that a

> significant part of the community, especially those women active in radical feminist organizations, feels that bisexuality is dangerous and that the bisexual is consorting with the enemy. The existence of women claiming to be bisexual creates the specter that homosexual relations among women are not sufficient, that dependence upon men remains, and that separatism (or at least autonomy) is therefore not a viable all one paragraph—put citation after political form. (291)

We return to the war imagery of "consorting with the enemy" along with arguments that retaining attraction for men continued dependence and somehow delegitimized lesbianism as inadequate.

Stalemate

Because US society identified women and girls as sexualized objects men should possess, feminist arguments for equality and liberation had to contend with the concept of sexuality. Sexuality represented central ideological pressures on women to exist for men's approval and prioritize marriage, reproduction, and childcare over other goals. Nearly compulsory imperatives to marry and mother prescribed how women should comport their bodies, express their emotions, and primarily identify themselves. In the ensuing two generations, feminists have advanced women's legal rights, economic opportunities, social standing, and sexual autonomy, but neoliberal backlash has chipped away at progress. Separatism and sex-negative propositions that prioritized movement gains have lost what traction they had in a sex-saturated society that touts individualism.

The majority of US women have not extracted themselves from heterosexual relationships, even though marriage rates declined from 84 percent of US-born 30- to 44-year olds in 1970 to 60 percent in 2007 (Fry/Cohn). The majority of households (60 percent) that have minor children have continued Shulman and Morgan's family structure—two working parents with children. Statistically, individual solutions have inched such couples closer to parity in unpaid labor and equalized total work hours. Since 1965, such fathers have more than doubled their hours of housework and nearly tripled their childcare time. In these families, mothers still average *two-thirds* of the unpaid labor, while fathers' more hours of paid work equalize couples' total work hours. Conservative economic pressures have encouraged two-income households (Parker and Wang). Neoliberal goals of privatization and capitalist control prevented Americans from supporting heterosexual families through nationalized childcare and medical care and well-funded education. The 2007–2009 Great Recession increased the small minority of stay-at-home fathers to 2.2 million and created more multigenerational households, but social pressure and national mortgage policies have continued to keep fathers in paid labor and push nuclear family homeownership over communal or other alternatives (Livingston).

Americans have become more tolerant of nonheterosexual attraction in a context of reformist marriage equality rather than radical attempts to dismantle heterosexist institutions. From 1996 to 2014, American support for extending secular state legal marriage to gay and lesbian couples rose from 32 to 55 percent (McCarthy). The marriage debates capitalized on liberal ideals of individual rights, freedom, and equality, terms that are easily assimilated into neoliberal discourse. Neoliberal rearticulation of British-American classical liberalism and American myths of self-made "men" and rugged individualists are hegemonic rhetorical touchstones through which reformist Americans can explain their quest for the thousand legal rights and social approval marriage grants. In contrast, the feminist movement's prioritization of collective struggle and delayed satisfaction over individual sexual pleasure has been a hard sell.

Older feminist views have maintained some sway through distinct stakes in lesbian feminist biphobia. Paula Rust's survey of over 400 nonheterosexual women found the same incongruities between identity and behavior that Blumstein and Schwartz did (Rust, "'Coming Out'" 50–54). The demographics of her 1990s sample looked similar to those of the1960s–1970s feminist authors: primarily young but spanning ages 16 to 78, predominantly white with six percent racial diversity, well educated, and employed (56). Rust found that 90 or 100 percent of women had sexual relations with men before identifying as lesbian or bi, respectively, and 43 percent of lesbian-identified women had had a relationship with a man since identifying as lesbian (Rust, "The Politics" 375–76). Rust attributed "lesbian cultural belief that bisexuality is a phase" to findings that 24 percent of lesbian-identified women first came out as bi and that bi women were more willing to shift back and forth between labels (Rust, "'Coming Out'" 59). Lesbian and bi women disputed the importance of feelings in sexual identity and "the range of experience in which homosexual feelings and behaviors are predominant but not exclusive" with bi women labeling feelings for men and women bisexual, while "[a]mong lesbians, heterosexual feelings can coexist with lesbian identity as long as these feelings are not translated into behavior" (380–81). These lesbians still considered their position a challenge to heterosexist patriarchy. They incorporated women into their circles based on shared current identification as lesbian and rejection of their heterosexual pasts. Therefore, they saw bi women's lack of separatism as "the threat of heterosexism" because the bi women did not structure their identity as an oppressed gender against an oppressor gender (382). For women interested in building bi identity, "previously radical claims of lesbian legitimacy have come to represent a new conservative ideology that denies legitimacy to bisexuality" (382).

Is there one persuasive argument about sexuality? Feminists of the 1960s–1980s exposed compulsory heterosexuality to promote role-less relations; encouraged contexts where women could experiment with (competing) forms of lesbian identity; and contended with a parallel rise in bi identity. Rhetoric to create collective feminist identity against a clear opponent (us/them) did not keep up with the complexities of identities. Attempts to patrol behavior seemed crucial as women considered how women supported patriarchy, but vanguardism created conflict. Contemporary leading feminists and organizations tend to be wary of vanguardism, "sex wars," and transphobia, turning from those conflicts by deeming those issues private, individual responsibilities or rights. Privatization, responsibility, and rights, however, are problematically shared between liberalism and neoliberalism.[7] Researchers from Kinsey through Rust advanced data that people's behavior and identity do not completely correspond. People have articulated their identities to fit what can be changing social contexts, so changes in sexual identity and behavior may be "expected of mature individuals as they maintain an accurate description of their position vis-à-vis other individuals, groups, and institutions" (Rust, "'Coming Out'" 50). The realization that sexuality changes and gains its meaning from our social situations collides with the seemingly comforting commonplace that sexuality is stable. Individuals often experience their sexual identities as essential (Rust, "'Coming Out'" 70). It will take a lot more talk to persuade people to discard their often unexamined senses of self.

Notes

1. I am grateful for Agatha Beins and Jennifer Jensen Wallach's feedback. To be succinct, I confined sources to earliest articulations by women that mainstream media exalted whose work anthologies reprised. They set terms others reiterated or denied. Alice Echols gives much more context.
2. More famously see The Feminists member, Anne Koedt's, 1970 "The Myth of Vaginal Orgasm," anthologized in Baxandall and Gordon 158–62.
3. Hal Wingo, "The Massacre at MyLai," *Life* Magazine 67.23 (December 5, 1969): 36–45; Army correspondent Jay Robert's recollection of sexual assault on page 43. Susan Brownmiller, *Against Our Will*, 103–105.
4. Shulamith Firestone's 1970 bestseller, *The Dialectic of Sex*, popularized the ideal of technology freeing women from reproductive labor and has been widely anthologized (e.g., Nicholson 19–26). Atkinson knew Firestone and shared what Robin Morgan later called a "naive assumption that technology would be an unmixed blessing that would automatically free women" (*Saturday's Child*, 257n6).
5. Shulman and Morgan expressed significantly more objections to their ex-husbands and division of labor in later memoirs, but they did not argue universally against marriage and they mirrored the dissatisfaction of many women in their generation (Shulman, *Drinking the Rain*; Morgan, *Saturday's Child*).
6. Also anthologized elsewhere, for example, Nicholson 153–57.
7. Space constraints did not permit me to delve into the mid-1970s–1980s feminist "sex wars" over appropriate sexual behavior or essentialist assertions that if

doctors labeled someone male at birth, that person could not be a woman. These fights were rife with attacks that opponents were male-identified or, in the case of trans women, Morgan's assertion that they were "the Man," "an infiltrator, and a destroyer—with the mentality of a rapist" (Pomerleau, *Califia Women*, 28–29, 78–90).

Works Cited

"Alix Kates Shulman: Highlights of a Life." Ohioana Authors. N.d. Web. 16 Jan. 2015.
Atkinson, Ti-Grace. *Amazon Odyssey*. New York: Links Books, 1974. Print.
Baxandall, Rosalyn, and Linda Gordon, eds. *Dear Sisters: Dispatches from the Women's Liberation Movement* and *Radical Feminism: A Documentary Reader*. New York: Basic Books, 2000. Print.
Blumstein, Philip W. and Pepper Schwartz. "Lesbianism and Bisexuality." *Sexual Deviance and Sexual Deviants*. Ed. Eric Goode. New York: William Morrow & Co., 1974. Print.
Brownmiller, Susan. *Against Our Will: Men, Women and Rape*. New York: Simon & Schuster, 1975. Print.
Davidson, Sara. "An 'Oppressed Majority' Demands Its Rights." *Life*. 12 Dec. 1969: 67–78. Print.
Echols, Alice. *Daring to Be Bad: Radical Feminism in America 1967–1975*. Minneapolis: U of Minnesota P, 1989. Print.
Fry, Richard, and D'vera Cohn. "Women, Men and the New Economics of Marriage." *PewResearch*. 14 Jan. 2010. Web. 20 Jan. 2015.
Jay, Karla, and Allen Young, eds. *Out of the Closets: Voices of Gay Liberation*. New York: Jove/HBJ, 1977. Print.
Kerber, Linda K. *No Constitutional Right to Be Ladies: Women and the Obligations of Citizenship*. New York: Hill and Wang, 1998. Print.
Kessler-Harris, Alice. *In Pursuit of Equity: Women, Men, and the Quest for Economic Citizenship in 20th-century America*. New York: Oxford UP, 2001. Print.
Livingston, Gretchen. "Growing Number of Dads Home with the Kids." *PewResearch*. 5 June 2014. Web. 19 Jan. 2015.
Love, Barbara J., ed. *Feminists Who Changed America: 1963–1975*. Urbana: U of Illinois P, 2006. Print.
McCarthy, Justin. "Same-Sex Marriage Support Reaches New High at 55%." *Gallup*. 21 May 2014. Web. 20 Jan. 2015.
Millett, Kate. *Flying*. New York: Knopf, 1974. Print.
Morgan, Robin. *Saturday's Child: A Memoir*. New York: Norton, 2001. Print.
Morgan, Robin, ed. *Sisterhood Is Powerful: An Anthology of Writings from the Women's Liberation Movement*. New York: Vintage, 1970. Print.
Nicholson, Linda, ed. *The Second Wave: A Reader in Feminist Theory*. New York: Routledge, 1997. Print.
Parker, Kim, and Wendy Wang. "Modern Parenthood." *PewResearch*. 14 Mar, 2013. Web. 19 Jan. 2015.
Pomerleau, Clark A. *Califia Women: Feminist Education against Sexism, Classism, and Racism*. Austin: U of Texas P, 2013. Print.
———. "Empowering Members, Not Overpowering Them: The National Organization for Women, Calls for Lesbian Inclusion, and California Influence, 1960s–1980s." *Journal of Homosexuality*. 57.7 (2010): 842–861. Print.

Reynolds, Beatrice K. "An Interview with Ti-Grace Atkinson: Her Speeches and Speechmaking." *Today's Speech*. (Fall 1973): 3–10.
Rust, Paula C. Rodríguez, ed. *Bisexuality in the United States: A Social Science Reader*. New York: Columbia UP, 2000. Print.
———. "'Coming Out' in the Age of Social Constructionism: Sexual Identity Formation among Lesbian and Bisexual Women." *Gender and Society* 7.1. (Mar. 1993): 50–77. Print.
———. "The Politics of Sexual Identity: Sexual Attraction and Behavior among Lesbian and Bisexual Women." *Social Problems*. 39. (1992): 366–386. Print.
Shelley, Martha. "Notes of a Radical Lesbian." *Sisterhood Is Powerful: An Anthology of Writings from the Women's Liberation Movement*. Ed. Robin Morgan. New York: Vintage, 1970, 306–10. Print.
Shulman, Alix Kates. *Drinking the Rain*. New York: North Point, 1995. Print.
Solanas, Valerie. *SCUM Manifesto*. New York: Olympia, 1968. Print.
Storr, Merl, ed. *Bisexuality: A Critical Reader*. New York: Routledge, 1999. Print.
"Women's Lib: A Second Look." *Time* 96.24 (14 Dec. 1970): 68. Print.
Wrenn, Marie-Claude. "Women Arise." *Life*. 69.10 (4 Sept. 1970): 16–23. Print.

15 Sex Trafficking Rhetorics/Queer Refusal

Ian Barnard

> We believe that one can't be a feminist, or a human rights advocate, or a conscious human being and not see sex trafficking as one of the central issues of the twenty-first century.
> —Giddings, in "Trafficking Sex" 174

I

As I write this chapter, students at my university campus are mounting an awareness campaign against sex trafficking; a chamber opera about sex trafficking is being performed in downtown Los Angeles; and anti-sex trafficking discourses are proliferating in scholarly and activist conferences and books, national and international legislation, political campaigns, newspapers and television shows, and on Facebook, subway trains, and billboards. Sex trafficking, it seems, is everywhere. And so are rhetorics about (against) sex trafficking.[1] However, in the past two decades, feminist scholars and activists have offered a wide-ranging critique of the panoply of feminist and other anti-sex trafficking rhetorics currently suffusing global and US national legal, political, and cultural stages. These critiques identify the abolitionist (anti-sex work) agenda that drives much anti-sex trafficking discourse, especially in and from the United States (e.g., Hesford; Parreñas); the failure to distinguish sex trafficking from sex work in much anti-sex trafficking discourse (e.g., Doezema; Parreñas); the failure to distinguish sex trafficking from other kinds of trafficking or the ignoring of other kinds of trafficking (e.g., Murray 54–55; Vance); the ways in which campaigns against sex trafficking can be covers for or at least facilitate increased policing of (national) borders and clampdowns on migration (e.g., Hesford; Hua); the problematic transnationalism and Western universalism that characterize much of the discourse about sex trafficking (e.g., Hesford; Hesford and Kozol; Hua[2]); problematic representations of women as passive and only as victims in anti-sex trafficking rhetorics (e.g., Hesford; Hua); the focus on (individual) human rights at the expense of attention to the role of transnational capitalism, neocolonialism, and other systemic structures and relations in producing various kinds of trafficking and abuse of women (e.g., Hesford; Hua); representations of trafficked subjects as deserving victims in need of (white) rescue (e.g., Baker; Hesford; Hua); constructions and reproductions of racist and classist stereotypes of Third World women in assumptions of who is trafficked and who is not (e.g., Doezema; Hua); the privileging of certain types of narratives in creating and representing sex trafficking stories (e.g., Hesford; Hua); problematic constructions of children (e.g., Hesford); and efforts to contain women's sexuality and to reinscribe heteropatriarchal ideas of family.

Although many of these tropes and their effects are interconnected (for instance, sexual disciplining is race-specific, and the construction of certain subjects as trafficked and others as not overlays dispositions and policies distinguishing desirable from undesirable migrants), in this chapter I am particularly interested in bringing together, building on, and teasing out the implications of one strand of these critiques that implicitly or explicitly points to the ways campaigns against sex trafficking are invested in recuperating and promoting—sometimes forcefully—patriarchal and heteronormative sexualities and family structures, and in repressing and displacing queerness more generally.

Unsurprisingly, *pace* Eve Sedgwick's celebrated opening lines to *Epistemology of the Closet* and the evocative list of oppositions that she argues intrinsically structure and are formatively shaped by the homosexual/heterosexual divide even though they at first glance seem to have nothing to do with homosexuality, these displacements themselves often take the form of displacement, and the patterns of displacement that trace anti-sex trafficking rhetorics may themselves be seen as the traces of their anxieties around queerness. If queerness in all its shape-shifting enigmaticness is really an epistemological bottom line, then all the more reason for the displacements around its anxiety to be so far-fetched and far removed. Anti-sex trafficking rhetorics, like child molester panic, are imbricated in heteronormative attachment and defensiveness, though in the case of sex trafficking panic the routes of attachment are more elliptical and dispersed than the more obviously queerphobic displacements in child molester panics.[3] Queerphobic panic and queer reactive impetuses inform and even impel much anti-sex trafficking rhetoric and activism, not necessarily instead of other fears and anxieties and ethical imperatives, but alongside and inflected by them (and vice versa), and given an understanding of "queer" as elliptical, complex, multidimensional, and expanding, and as never only coterminous with glbt (though more often than not including glbt concerns and people). I use "queer" here in solidarity with Gayle Rubin's 1984 formulation of the "outer limits of sexuality" ("Thinking Sex" 13). Rubin's sex hierarchy included "Heterosexual," "Non-commercial," and "In private" in the "charmed circle" and "Homosexual," "Commercial," "Casual," and "Cross-generational" in "the outer limits," in some ways anticipating contemporary uses and understandings of "queer" as both tied to but not conterminous with homosexuality. In her 2011 reflection on the 1984 piece, Rubin notes with satisfaction its "protoqueerness" in accounting for the "cross-identifications and multiple subject positions that most of us occupy" ("Blood" 40), and, indeed, Rubin's 1984 lists can help us to think suggestively (in multiple senses of the word) about queer's limits and confluences. I want to allow for queer's compass to include sex work and other proscribed and dissident sexual practices, institutions, and relations (including the gender dissidences evoked in the category "transgender"), while also keeping queer's homoerotic resonances (and the concomitant homophobia that characterizes resistance, phobia, and backlash) in play, and without determining in advance how far queer might become de-anchored from the homosexual (or even from the sexual) and how important it might be to retain queerness as ethical, moral, or desirable.[4]

Beginning with Rubin's own observations about anti-sex trafficking campaigns, one possible (achronological) trajectory for a chain of displacements and interrogations in the sex trafficking wars might start to look like this:

- Rubin has explicitly linked recent sex trafficking panics to the feminist sex wars of the 1980s and 1990s, arguing that the (losing) antiporn faction in the earlier conflict reinvented itself to focus its efforts on behalf of more popular, more winnable, and more socially acceptable initiatives against sex trafficking in the twenty-first century ("Blood" 35). Rubin's point is that some of the same people (with new allies) are fighting some of the same battles but under the cover of contesting sex trafficking (e.g., Janice Raymond). Multiple apparatuses of bait-and-switch, transference, and metamorphosis are at work: antiporn feminism becomes anti-sex trafficking (feminist) activism—the feminism is somewhat silent here in order to disavow the linkage; the 1980s and 1990s are thrust forward into the twenty-first century; sex trafficking rhetorics become covers for the disavowed positions in the sex wars (here, especially, opposition to prostitution); and outrage at sex trafficking covers over seeping anxieties about queerness (more on this later).
- Several scholars have pointed to Victorian anxieties around "white slavery" as the origins and antecedents of contemporary campaigns against sex trafficking and other sex panics (e.g., Doezema; Lancaster; Murray; Vance). The history of anti-sex trafficking discourses shows that they have always been entangled with moral and legal outrage about and campaigns against prostitution in general. Jo Doezema traces current concerns around sex trafficking to early international attempts to address prostitution that were influenced by nineteenth-century feminist activism (35). In Britain in the late 1800s, the "social purity" movement was driven by panics around child prostitution and the white slave trade (Doezema 35) (According to Doezema, most women identified as victims of sex trafficking were actually migrating prostitutes.) The social purity movement then expanded to the United States and the rest of Europe, and by the end of the nineteenth century the "white slave trade" began to be regulated internationally. The League of Nations adopted

two conventions concerning the traffic in women and children, and in 1949 the UN adopted the Convention for the Suppression of the Traffic in Persons and the Exploitation of the Prostitution of Others (Doezema 35). International concern about sex trafficking was revived by feminists in the 1980s (Doezema 35).

- Why do campaigners pay so much attention to sex trafficking when many more people are trafficked for other purposes like nonsexual labor exploitation? Sex trafficking in fact constitutes a relatively modest percentage of human trafficking; according to Siddharth Kara, of the world's 28.4 million slaves at the end of 2006, 1.2 million were sex slaves (x). The lopsided attention to sex trafficking could be said to offer further evidence that this really is a sex panic,[5] that the underlying and even unconscious motives for this attention swirl around phobias, anxieties, and panics about sex rather than opposition to human exploitation. Similar rebuttals were made to the obsession with pornography rather than other forms of exploitation of women during the feminist sex wars.

II

The clearest signals of the sex-policing agenda at the heart of much anti-sex trafficking rhetoric come in the interdictions against prostitution in much (though not all) sex trafficking regulation and representation. One of the most blatant examples, cited by both Wendy Hesford and Julietta Hua, was the insistence by the George W. Bush administration that organizations' abilities to qualify for funding under the Victims of Trafficking and Violence Protection Act of 2000 be tied to a requirement that they "make a public declaration opposing sex work and prostitution" (Hua 38). Women's sexuality and agency is reigned in and spoken for in the name of protectionism. Additional ways in which anti-sex trafficking rhetorics can and are being deployed to shore up reactionary gender relations have been analyzed by Carrie Baker, who shows how filmic representations of sex trafficking, whether fictional or documentary, in addition to presenting racially problematic rescue narratives where white (male) saviors liberate white and Third World women from sexual slavery, often seem intent on "restoring patriarchal authority through males saving females from traffickers" (211). (Baker also compliments some media representations on their more nuanced depictions of sex trafficking. In Section III below, I discuss some encouragingly complicated popular culture representations of sex trafficking and their possible significance.)

In their overt or implied excoriation of Rubin's "outer limits of sexuality," feminists at the forefront of the anti-sex trafficking movement often make common cause with unlikely bedfellows—or perhaps not so unlikely, given the US precedents of the feminist sex wars, the specter of antiporn feminists testifying before the Meese Commission on Pornography in 1986, and so on. Whether intentionally or not, their work against sex trafficking sometimes dovetails with calls for returns to "family values" that underlie some other anti-sex trafficking rhetorics. As Carole Vance puts it, referencing Rubin's 1975 "The Traffic in Women" essay, sex trafficking panic's trajectory deplores one kind of "traffic in women" while implicitly (and sometimes explicitly) privileging another—heterosexual marriage (135). Hua points out that anti-sex trafficking abolitionist activism has served to "construct the idea of sex as mutually exclusive of work" (38; see also 88), thus legally, morally, and socially circumscribing acceptable work within class- and culture-specific parameters and confining sex to the side of procreation. In her analysis of newspaper accounts of sex trafficking, Hua finds further evidence of the ways in which anti-sex trafficking campaigns reproduce distinctions between "good" and "bad" sex in the trope of johns who become boyfriends (56). When trafficked women are working for the johns, the sex is seen as coerced, but when a john has a change of heart and "saves" one of these women by becoming her boyfriend, the sex switches over to the realm of the legal, the wholesome, and the healing. Promiscuous, nonprocreative, paid-for sex is exploitative. Presumptive monogamous and potentially procreative "romantic" heterosexual sex within a coupled relationship is redemptive. Hua also suggests anti-sex trafficking rhetorics' disavowal of the "outer limits of sexuality" in her discussion of the history of Asian mail order brides being seen as possible sites of sex trafficking in the United States (37). This assumption reinscribes legal and moral force to historically and culturally specific constructions of marriage revolving around ideologies of love and romance, and deny and/or repudiate the force of other marriage models, motivations, necessities, and realities. In addition to exposing the cultural biases that underlie the specific permutations of US and supposedly universal anti-sex trafficking rhetorics,[6] projections such as these underline the ideological alliances of anti-sex trafficking rhetorics with bourgeois, heteronormative sexual moralities.

The 1995 UNESCO report on Contemporary Forms of Slavery is quite explicit in articulating the conjunction, calling for "strengthening the family nucleus and respect for moral values" (Murray 54) as an antidote to trafficking, prostitution, and sexual exploitation, a copula that makes uncomfortably clear how morality and value are symbolically and materially embedded in the (nuclear) family and its attendant imperatives toward heteronormativity in so much of the anti-sex trafficking imaginary (more on "family" below). The confluence of these imbricated discourses and narratives around gender, family, and nation-state paternalisms in anti-sex trafficking rhetorics suggests that sex trafficking panic may serve as a cover, or at least an impetus, for backlashes against the global crescendo of movements for gender equity, sexual liberation, and queer rights.

We can see the traces of these backlashes and panics—sometimes convolutedly and unconsciously exposing anti-sex trafficking zeitgeists—worked through in the spectrum of cultural artifacts, from ballot initiatives, legislation, activism, international aid work, newspapers accounts and memoirs about sex trafficking, to fictional and nonfictional television documentaries and dramas. A paradigmatic case in point is Kathryn Bolkovac's 2011 memoir, *The Whistleblower: Sex Trafficking, Military Contractors, and One Woman's Fight for Justice*. The book chronicles the author's work for the private military contractor DynCorp International, contracted by the US State Department to support the UN's peacekeeping mission in Bosnia in the late 1990s and early 2000s, and her discovery of and efforts to put the brakes on an insidious network of sex trafficking in Bosnia. As is common in much anti-sex trafficking discourse, "trafficking" is conflated with sex trafficking throughout Bolkovac's book, illustrating the generation and privileging of sex panic. And even though Bolkovac accuses others of conflating trafficking with prostitution, she herself does this (e.g., 111, 129, 132). Tellingly, before going to Bosnia for DynCorp in 1991, the author worked in a Nebraska police department unit not unlike the special New York City police unit represented in *Law and Order: SVU*, the iconic and hugely successful US television series about the detectives who investigate "sexually based offenses": "I was placed on the Youth Aid unit, now known as the Special Investigations Unit, and, in my three years there, made over sixty felony arrests and had a 95 percent conviction rate of predators of women and children" (21). Bolkovac also unnecessarily mentions that a suspect whom she shot during her pre-Bosnia police work in Nebraska was HIV-positive (23). To complete the book's tracing of Rubin's "outer limits of sexuality," together with the necessity of distinguishing inner from outer positions, Bolkovac's narrative is also, in part, the story of how she met her husband, Jan, in Bosnia. In the contexts of the author's line of work and her stories about her tomboy childhood, it's also possible to see the story of Jan in *The Whistleblower* as a kind of lesbian panic rectification. When Bolkovac discusses Venetta, a woman from Florida whom she met and admired during the week of training in preparation for her mission in Bosnia, Venetta's experience in "vice, drug, and prostitution undercover work" (27) is counterposed with mentions of her boyfriend and her "kids back home" (27), almost as if to check Venetta's contamination by those outer limits with a reminder of her insider status. The book's intersecting (and, I would argue, mutually constituting) plots and subplots mirror conflicting subterranean impulses and formations around sex and sexuality at work in the book and in the discursive fields around sex panic and sex trafficking in which it circulates and participates.

California's Proposition 35, a ballot measure passed overwhelmingly by presumably well-meaning voters in 2012, represents the activist political outcome of the sex trafficking rhetorics I have been chronicling, and also illustrates their possible material consequence. It concatenates for public consumption and in legal jargon many of the features of the anti-sex trafficking discourses of Bolkovac and others, as well as capitalizing on sex panics around children. In popular culture, pedophilia is a hypersaturated signifier, often the "secret" that wraps up a plot or that explains a character's dysfunction and/or shame (e.g., *Broadchurch*, *Mystic River*, and even Lars von Trier's *Nymphomaniac*). And the sanctity and purity of children, their supposed sexual innocence, seems to top the list of taboos that cannot be questioned and that are able to summon up apparently limitless reserves of unreflective fear, panic, anger, and hysteria.[7] In addition to enacting the now familiar slippage between human trafficking as a whole and sex trafficking, Proposition 35 made blatant appeals to emotions and values embodied in clichéd and self-righteous platitudes about protecting children. Right from the start, Sec. 2., following the title, proclaimed that "The people of the State of California find and declare: 1. Protecting every person in our state, *particularly our children*, from all forms of sexual exploitation is of paramount importance" (Secretary 101, my emphasis), and according to Sec. 2.3., "Upwards of 300,000 American children are at risk of commercial sexual exploitation" (ibid.). More disturbingly, Sec 2.3 declared that "Because minors are legally incapable of consenting to sexual activity, these minors are victims of human trafficking whether or not force is used" (ibid.). Here "sex trafficking" becomes a particularly nebulous categorization, since it can include sex workers who are neither trafficked nor coerced but whose situations can invoke substantive law enforcement and other campaigns because of a technicality that constructs them as trafficked by definition.[8]

My point here is not that we should not take seriously the matter of whether minors are capable of consent or that age of consent laws are worthless, but that failure to distinguish between very different types of abuse or possible abuse is indicative of a cynical (and abusive) use of sex trafficking panic that engulfs a variety of people and practices and that ultimately makes "sex trafficking" a meaningless term, doing a calamitous disservice to those who are sex trafficking victims and those who are fighting on their behalf. Others do this via prostitution; Proposition 35 does it via children. In each case, the invoked class (prostitutes, children) reinforces—however indirectly—distinctions between approved and disapproved sex and sexuality, and between privileged and marginalized relationships. Needless to say, (heteronormative) procreative sex is always on the first side of the binary. The (nuclear) family that is connotatively invoked in many of these anti-sex trafficking rhetorics inevitably calls upon a weighted history of discourses of family, and the racial, class, sexual, and gendered affiliations that are variously advocated and sanctified in the name of family,[9] and to what Michael Warner and Harriet Malinowitz have termed, respectively, "reprosexuality" and "pronatalist culture" to designate social, political, and economic institutions, operations, imperatives, and people (often, nowadays, including glbt people) that privilege normative sexualities and family structures. In 1991, Warner wrote in the introduction to the "Fear of a Queer Planet" issue of *Social Text*, "The family may be a site of solidarity and value for racial and ethnic struggle, for example, but current definitions of the family are abysmally oppressive for lesbians and gays. Familial language deployed to describe sociability in race- or gender-based movements (sisterhood, fatherhood, fatherland, mother tongue, etc.) can be a language of exile for queers" (12–13).

In attending to Bolkovac's book and Proposition 35, I have purposefully worked through a sampling of seemingly well-meaning and innocuous texts in order to show the continuities across apparently diverse treatments of sex trafficking; to demonstrate how easily anti-sex trafficking work gets inscribed into the sex panics rhetorics I have been outlining; to suggest how the contours of heteronormativity, queerness, and queer-anxious backlash seep into, through, and from these rhetorics; and to point to the rippling-out consequences of these anxieties and backlashes that are formative and material. (For example, the increased penalties proposed under Proposition 35 compound the horrific problems around California's obscenely large prison population, a particularly ironic outcome given that California voters in 2012 also passed Proposition 36, aimed at ameliorating the state's "three strikes" law that has resulted in the incarceration of huge numbers of Californians—especially men of color—for relatively minor offenses.)

III

The final textual representation of sex trafficking I will offer develops a more critical take on anti-sex trafficking rhetorics and comes, unsurprisingly perhaps, in the form of popular culture and *Law and Order: SVU* itself. True to form, popular culture not only taps into prevailing zeitgeists around sex trafficking discourses, but also bursts beyond the political (and scholarly) platitudes of anti-sex trafficking rhetorics in some ways by revealing their inconsistencies and slippages in (surprisingly) sophisticated embodiments. And, not unexpectedly, *Law and Order: SVU* has become a touchstone fictional representation par excellence of the anxieties and manipulations propelling sex trafficking panic. From connecting sex trafficking to terrorism (Al Qaeda + 9/11 + sex trafficking in the 2012 "Acceptable Loss" episode—talk about heightening the sex panic!) to conflating prostitution with sex trafficking (the 2007 "Debt" episode) to an imbroglio on the intersections between forced labor and sex trafficking (the 2010 "Merchandise" episode), intersections that are missing in most anti-sex trafficking scholarship and political discourse, *SVU* seems to have it all. In 2010 Demi Moore even posted a Facebook status promoting one of SVU's sex trafficking-themed episodes: "Tonights episode of Law and Order: SVU is on Human Sex Trafficking great to see this issue getting more awareness!" [*sic*] (Moore)—as if to exemplify the crossover between fiction and nonfiction in the hyperbolic melodrama of sex trafficking discourse, the fashionableness of taking on sex trafficking as a social/political cause, the seeming no-brainerness of attacking sex trafficking, and the assumption that any treatment of sex trafficking (and *SVU*, in particular) would make a simple didactic appeal against sex trafficking. But *SVU* is smarter.

SVU's most interesting take on sex trafficking was developed in the 2009 "Hothouse" episode, where sex trafficking is actually revealed to be a ruse.

The story begins with the discovery of the murdered body of Elsa, a 14-year-old Ukrainian girl. The detectives on the case assume/deduce that Elsa was a sex trafficking victim, but these assumptions are overturned when it is eventually revealed that Elsa was, in fact, physically and psychologically abused by her father and murdered by her competitive roommate at an exclusive New York City private school for child geniuses. The school is also assigned its share of the blame, since it was prescribing drugs to the students to increase their academic performance and its own status, and encouraging a mindset that valued academic achievement and cut-throat competition above all other social and personal values. The sex trafficking subplot is quickly dropped as we realize that Alik, the accused sex trafficker, is telling the truth about not knowing Elsa, and that the burns and other bruises on Elsa's body were inflicted by her authoritarian father, not Alik. In some ways, this episode can be said to enact sex panic by revealing its ruse. Moreover, Alik, despite his initial presentation as a villainous stereotype (slick suit, foreign accent, piercing eyes, smirk on the lips, misogynistic, physically aggressive), when interviewed by the detectives actually makes some of the same arguments against sex trafficking panic, albeit in a vulgar form, as those forwarded by scholars I have discussed in this chapter (economic issues drive women into the sex industry, the women are better off with him, he gives them nice things). Although sex trafficking does not make a return in this episode after it is revealed to be a ruse in the case of Elsa, this is not to say that the episode dismisses sex trafficking out of hand. We do meet a character who seems to be an actual sex trafficking victim and who does not have very nice things to say about Alik or what he did to her, so the episode is quite nuanced in its treatment of the topic. There does appear to be an unstated and familiar assumption in the episode, though, that the women who work for Alik are forced into prostitution. Prostitution is forced prostitution. Or prostitution = sex trafficking. The unstated assumption is itself telling, reenacting the problematic conflation of prostitution with sex trafficking at the same time that the episode exposes sex trafficking panic by untangling sex trafficking from other practices and dispositions that have been contaminated through denotative, discursive, and activist association with sex trafficking. The conflicted nature of the episode mirrors the contradictions that characterize so much of the scholarly and other rhetorics against sex trafficking.

Another untangling: "Hothouse" also seems to urge us to complicate our representations and constructions of children, who play such pivotal symbolic roles in all kinds of sex panics, as instanced in my discussion of Proposition 35 in Section II above.[10] This episode of *SVU* is assertively about children *not* as victims of sex trafficking, in counterposition to much dominant discourse about sex trafficking. In fact, children are as much villains as victims here, since both the murdered girl and her murderer are children. Even this reversal is challenged, though, as the SVU detectives, recognizing that the 14-year-old murderer was put under enormous pressure from her school, fight to have her not tried as an adult. And the episode ends with yet a further complicating twist when a second juvenile defendant enters the courtroom, accused of raping and murdering his six-year-old stepsister. The prosecutor asks sarcastically if the detectives want leniency for him as well. What looks like compassion and commonsense from one perspective might look like injustice, incompetence, and even abuse from another.

I see *SVU*'s admirable refusal of reductive moralizing and easy binaries as a working through of the sex panics that suffuse current culture, not so much precipitating or critiquing the panics (though, certainly, the series could be read in both these ways) as nurturing an important space that allows us to understand them in complex articulations, since the panics themselves are so lacking in self-reflection. The fact that this enormously resilient and successful television series is so centrally concerned with sex panics attests not only to the cultural obsession with these panics (I use "culture" to indicate both the social animus that is concerned with sex panics and the artistic creations that construct and mirror them) but also to its role in fulfilling a need to engage with and respond to sex panics with/in sustained, complex, and even contradictory multiple faculties, logics, and emotions.

The family as site of abuse in "Hothouse" (the father's physical and psychological torture of Elsa and her sister) underscores the queer critiques and queer abjections that I have been identifying in anti-sex trafficking rhetorics and in *SVU*. Here violence against children is relocated from the expected sex panic (sex trafficking) to the supposed safety of the nuclear family that is constructed as the antidote to sex trafficking in the UNESCO Report on Contemporary Forms of Slavery, a symmetrical undoing of the conservative reversal enacted by another episode of SVU ("Web"), in which a depleted but resilient nuclear family is recuperated as the last/only corrective to the "fake families" supposedly deceptively invoked by child molesters.

But queer (dis)identifications are always difficult to track and pin down. In sex trafficking *SVUs*, queer alignments frequently form along unexpected trajectories. The "terrorist" posing as a trafficked sex slave in the "Acceptable Loss" episode—another instance of sex trafficking revealed as a ruse—turns out to be quite sympathetic when we discover that her father was killed by a US drone strike in Waziristan, and the episode ends with the two women cops (Detective Benson from the SVU and Lieutenant Eames from Homeland Security) having a drink together. When Detective Benson's companion muses on how it had felt like she was married to her long-term (male) police partner, Benson reminds her, "But you weren't." Benson is here also reflecting on her own long-term but recently ended police partnership with Detective Stabler (and viewers' difficulties letting him go), as well as alluding to the difficulties the cops in the show have with their personal relationships at home, the complicated nature of their relationships with their police partners, and her own single status. The husband-to-be, boyfriend, and "kids back home" of *The Whistleblower* are strikingly absent from SVU. The cops' relationship patterns are non-normative, and their relationships defy conventional categories, singularities, and boundaries. It's common for popular culture to represent police officers as loners or outcasts who don't fit within society's social norms because of the demands of their job, but *SVU* pushes this common trope a step further by not only emphasizing the otherness of its lead cops, but also by aligning them against the nuclear family, with terrorists, queers, and child molesters.

This cluster of sex trafficking *SVU* episodes dramatically enacts and corrects the slippery landscape of sex trafficking as it also calls into question easy binaries between victims and villains, cops and queers, families and abusers. Although *SVU* by its nature is doomed to create and reproduce (or at least pander to) sex panics, its consistent undercutting of dominant anti-sex trafficking rhetorics ensures that its relationship to those panics is as convoluted as the queer apotheosis of anti-sex trafficking rhetoric and as queer's own imbrication in a larger sociality.

IV

One could argue that the kinds of heteronormalizing effects and the reactions against them that I have been tracing structure all aspects of heterosexist culture (to return to the opening of Sedgwick's *Epistemology*). I would probably concede this point, but nevertheless maintain the value of identifying and understanding specific local and global permutations of queerphobia as a way of insisting on the multiple forms and effects it manifests even as it effects a global and all-encompassing reach. Sex panics around sex trafficking also help to show how gender and queerness can be entwined in nuanced and covert ways, while simultaneously reminding us quite unflinchingly, via feminist anti-sex trafficking activism, of Sedgwick's Axiom 2: "antihomophobic inquiry is not coextensive with feminist inquiry" (*Epistemology* 26).

But queer remains quite slippery. At the beginning of this chapter, I invoked Rubin's chronicle of the "outer limits of sexuality" in order to make a case for an expansive understanding of "queer." What is the value of this connection between queerness and the outer limits of sexuality? Is it possible to sever homosexuality from the other inhabitants of the outer limits of the sexual order? Is it possible to sever "queer"? Maybe. But the connection can help queer maintain a radical (sexual/gender) politics and assert an intersectionality and interconnectiveness that repudiate the possibility and desirability of single-issue and singular politics, identities, identifications, and power relations. Contrapuntally, it sutures the outer limits of sexuality to an anti-homophobic analysis and politics. If and how homophobia might shape and inform other kinds of panics, whether sexual or not, is in my view less a matter of claiming homophobia's centrality as suggested in the opening lines to *Epistemology of the Closet* than an invitation to see how elliptical and unexpected linkages reveal homophobia in unexplicit places. Is there something foundational about homophobia—perhaps the primal scene of male homosexual anal intercourse? Perhaps the realization, following Wittig, that "lesbians are not women"? Perhaps anti-transgender panic about the instability of gender? Perhaps an anxious insistence on teleology that the dystopian/antisocial thesis in queer theory has disdained?[11]—that makes it the root of a host of other repressions, anxieties, and interdictions? Certainly these questions (or, at least the fascinations, desires, and anxieties that inform them) seem to hold unending social and cultural fascination to the extent that they and their stand-ins get worked over, reasserted, and reconfigured in the gamut of political and cultural terrains.[12]

Notes

1. For brief histories of contemporary anti-sex trafficking campaigns, see Doezema, Hua, Hesford, Murray, and Vance.
2. See also earlier critiques of imperialist feminism offered by Grewal, Grewal and Kaplan, and Mohanty.
3. See Rubin, "Blood," for a recent critique of child molester panic.
4. For further discussion of queer's multiple signifying possibilities, see Rallin; Sedgwick, *Tendencies* 8–9; Chapter 1 of my *Queer Race*; and Chapter 3 of Sullivan.
5. See Lancaster for further discussion and histories of sex panics in general.
6. Rhacel Parreñas points out that the abolitionist faction of global anti-sex trafficking activism is largely based in the United States (9).
7. For further discussion of sex panics around children, see Rubin, "Blood."
8. For additional critiques of Proposition 35, see Diamond; Grant.
9. For further discussion of the coercive teleology of rhetorics of "family," see Sedgwick, *Tendencies* 5–6; Nair 5–6.
10. See Chapter 5 of Hesford's *Spectacular Rhetorics* for discussion of Western constructions of non-Western children and childhood.
11. Lee Edelman's book *No Future: Queer Theory and the Death Drive* is often seen as the founding text of the contemporary "antisocial" turn in Queer Theory. For discussion of queer "ahistoricism," see Boone, Dinshaw et al., Goldberg and Menon, Halberstam, and Rohy.
12. I thank Kent Baxter, Naz Keynejad, and Aneil Rallin for generously pointing me toward helpful sources and resources as I worked on this chapter, and the anonymous outside reviewer for her generous and formative suggestions for revision. I am also grateful to the interlibrary loan staff at Chapman University's Leatherby Libraries for their conscientious assistance in locating sources for this research.

Works Cited

Baker, Carrie N. "An Intersectional Analysis of Sex Trafficking Films." *Meridians: feminism, race, transnationalism* 12.1 (2014): 208–26. Project Muse. Web. 15 Jan. 2015.

Barnard, Ian. *Queer Race: Cultural Interventions in the Racial Politics of Queer Theory*. New York: Peter Lang, 2003. Print.

Bolkovac, Kathryn. With Cari Lynn. *The Whistleblower: Sex Trafficking, Military Contractors, and One Woman's Fight for Justice*. New York: Palgrave Macmillan, 2011. Print.

Boone, Joseph Allen. *The Homoerotics of Orientalism*. New York: Columbia UP, 2014. Print.
Diamond, Greg. "I Despise Human Trafficking, But I Oppose the Badly Drafted Prop 35." *The Orange Juice Blog* 31 July 2012. Web. 29 Dec. 2013.
Dinshaw, Carolyn, et al. "Theorizing Queer Temporalities: A Roundtable Discussion." *GLQ* 13.2–3 (2007): 177–95. Print.
Doezema, Jo. "Forced to Choose: Beyond the Voluntary v. Forced Prostitution Dichotomy." *Global Sex Workers: Rights, Resistance, and Redefinition*. Ed. Kamala Kempadoo and Jo Doezema. New York: Routledge, 1998. 34–50. Print.
Edelman, Lee. *No Future: Queer Theory and the Death Drive*. Durham, NC: Duke UP, 2004. Print.
Goldberg, Jonathan, and Madhavi Menon. "Queering History." *PMLA* 120.5 (2005): 1608–17. Print.
Grant, Melissa Gira. "California's Prop 35: Targeting the Wrong People for the Wrong Reasons." *truthout* 4 Nov. 2012. Web. 29 Dec. 2013.
Grewal, Inderpal. "'Women's Rights as Human Rights': Feminist Practices, Global Feminism, and Human Rights Regimes in Transnationality." *Citizenship Studies* 3.3 (1999): 337–54. Print.
Grewal, Inderpal, and Caren Kaplan. "Introduction: Transnational Feminist Practices and Questions of Postmodernity." *Scattered Hegemonies: Postmodernity and Transnational Feminist Practices*. Ed. Grewal and Kaplan. Minneapolis: U of Minnesota P, 1994. 1–33. Print.
Halberstam, Judith. *In a Queer Time and Place: Transgender Bodies, Subcultural Lives*. New York: NYU P, 2005. Print.
Hesford, Wendy S. *Spectacular Rhetorics: Human Rights Visions, Recognitions, Feminisms*. Durham, NC: Duke UP, 2011. Print.
Hesford, Wendy S., and Wendy Kozol. "Introduction." *Just Advocacy?: Women's Human Rights, Transnational Feminisms, and the Politics of Representation*. Ed. Hesford and Kozol. New Brunswick, NJ: Rutgers UP, 2005. 1–29. Print.
Hua, Julietta. *Trafficking Women's Human Rights*. Minneapolis: U of Minnesota P, 2011. Print.
Kara, Siddharth. *Sex Trafficking: Inside the Business of Modern Slavery*. New York: Columbia UP, 2009. Print.
Lancaster, Roger N. *Sex Panic and the Punitive State*. Berkeley: U of California P, 2011. Kindle.
Law and Order: Special Victims Unit. NBC. Television series.
    "Acceptable Loss" (Season 14), first aired 2012.
    "Debt" (Season 6), first aired 2004.
    "Hothouse" (Season 10), first aired 2009.
    "Merchandise" (Season 12), first aired 2010.
    "Web" (Season 7), first aired 2006.
Malinowitz, Harriet. "Unmotherhood." *jac* 22.1 (2002): 11–36. Print.
Mohanty, Chandra Talpade. "Under Western Eyes: Feminist Scholarship and Colonial Discourses." *boundary 2* 12–13 (Spring–Fall 1984): 333–58. Print.
Moore, Demi. Facebook post. 6 Oct. 2010. Web. 25 Jan. 2014.
Murray, Alison. "Debt-Bondage and Trafficking: Don't Believe the Hype." *Global Sex Workers: Rights, Resistance, and Redefinition*. Ed. Kamala Kempadoo and Jo Doezema. New York: Routledge, 1998. 51–64. Print.

Nair, Yasmin. "Against Equality, Against Marriage: An Introduction." *Against Equality: Queer Critiques of Gay Marriage*. Ed. Ryan Conrad and Yasmin Nair. Lewiston: Against Equality, 2010. 1–9. Print.

Parreñas, Rhacel Salazar. *Illicit Flirtations: Labor, Migration, and Sex Trafficking in Tokyo*. Stanford, CA: Stanford UP, 2011. Print.

Rallin, Aneil. "A Provocation: Queer Is not a Substitute for Gay/Lesbian." *Harlot* 1 (2008). harlotofthearts.org. Web. 3 Aug. 2014.

Rohy, Valerie. "Ahistorical." *GLQ* 12.1 (2006): 61–83. Print.

Rubin, Gayle. "Blood Under the Bridge: Reflections on 'Thinking Sex.'" *GLQ* 17.1 (2011): 15–48. Print.

———. "Thinking Sex: Notes for a Radical Theory of the Politics of Sexuality." 1984. *The Lesbian and Gay Studies Reader*. Ed. Henry Abelove, Michèle Aina Barale, and David M. Halperin. New York: Routledge, 1993. 3–44. Print.

———. "The Traffic in Women: Notes on the 'Political Economy' of Sex." *Toward an Anthropology of Women*. Ed. Rayna R. Reiter. New York: Monthly Review, 1975. 157–210. Print.

Secretary of State, California. *Official Voter Information Guide: California General Election, Tuesday, November 6, 2012*. 2012. Print.

Sedgwick, Eve Kosofsky. *Epistemology of the Closet*. Berkeley: U of California P, 1990. Print.

Sedgwick, Eve Kosofsky. *Tendencies*. Durham, NC: Duke UP, 1993. Print.

Sullivan, Nikki. *A Critical Introduction to Queer Theory*. New York: New York UP, 2003. Print.

"Trafficking Sex: Politics, Policy, Personhood: Keynote Conversation: April 18, 2013." *Meridians: feminism, race, transnationalism* 12.1 (2014): 172–200. Project Muse. Web. 15 Jan. 2015.

Vance, Carole S. "Thinking Trafficking, Thinking Sex." *GLQ* 17.1 (2011): 135–43. Print.

Warner, Michael. "Introduction: Fear of a Queer Planet." *Social Text* 29 (1991): 3–17. Print.

Wittig, Monique. "The Straight Mind." *Feminist Issues* 1.1 (1980): 103–11. Print.

16 Sexual Counterpublics, Disciplinary Rhetorics, and Truvada

J. Blake Scott

When I attended this past year's World AIDS Day event in downtown Orlando, I was struck by the consistencies across several speakers' testimonials. Men my age or older, these speakers had lost friends and lovers—and had nearly lost their own lives—to the epidemic. But they were survivors, and as such implored us to learn from their histories of loss and triumph. Wearing red "Getting to Zero" t-shirts, the speakers went to the stage, one by one, to testify about their hard-won survival, to lament the ongoing exigency of so many new infections, especially among younger men, and to implore the audience to "Get tested, get treated, and use a condom every time." What was missing from the speakers and larger event—which included HIV testing and prevention materials, including condoms—was any mention of other, newer tools, including PrEP or preexposure prophylaxis, also known by the drug brand name *Truvada*, a once-a-day pill that can nearly eliminate the chance of infection if exposed to HIV.

The message to use condoms stood out as familiar but in need of revision, or at least amplification, particularly given the speakers' recognition of an unwaning epidemic. The United States sees over 50,000 new infections (with MSM or "men who have sex with men" comprising over 60 percent of the newly infected) each year, and in recent years has seen a 22 percent increase in the HIV rate among MSM aged 13 to 24 ("Preexposure" guidelines). The number of MSM reporting recent unprotected sex in CDC surveys rose nearly 20 percent from 2005 to 2011 (McNeil). One journalist called this situation the "condom conundrum," arguing that "It's high time for a different approach" (Sandler).

Truvada, a mix of the drugs tenofovir and emtricitabine, has been used as part of a treatment for people living with HIV (PLWH) for some time. In November 2010, the *New England Journal of Medicine* published the results of a major three-year, international study of Truvada as a prevention therapy, which found that the drug dramatically lowered gay and bisexual men's risk of getting HIV—by 92 percent for those who took it consistently ("Pre-Exposure" fact sheet).[1] In May 2012, the FDA approved the use of Truvada as a preexposure prevention drug for HIV, and in May 2014, the CDC recommended the drug for hundreds of thousands of at-risk people in the United States, including gay men who have sex without condoms and patients who regularly have sex with anyone they know is infected.

This policy shift has been off to a slow start. Although PrEP is now mostly accepted by public health officials, few state and local health departments have included it in their prevention efforts (New York being the first), and some have noted a largely indifferent response from physicians (Tuller). Although it is covered by most insurance companies and recommended for up to a half million people in the United States, only a few thousand patients (almost half women) have been prescribed Truvada for PrEP (Tuller). A number of HIV/AIDS-focused NGOs serving gay men (e.g., the San Francisco AIDS Foundation, AIDS Foundation of Chicago, Project Inform) have launched educational campaigns about PrEP, but other HIV/AIDS NGOs and activists have opposed it, some more vehemently and completely than others ("Divide"). The FDA approval of Truvada sparked a heated debate among gay HIV/AIDS activists, largely waged online and involving a zigzagged set of back-and-forth responses. Indeed, the debate has become more than about safer sex prevention practice to raise larger questions about HIV disclosure, gay sexual identity, communal memory and responsibility, and the relationship of gay publics to heteronormative power.

This chapter examines this ongoing debate, teasing out the contested meanings of Truvada and the participants' rhetorical constructions of them. In addition to a lively debate about risk, the little blue pill has generated fault lines across the network of HIV prevention and gay activists, creating what we might call *countering* counterpublics. The confessional and advocacy discourse of gay men taking Truvada or PrEP, who some have called PrEPsters (Duran, "Evolved"), has even generated a new counterpublic. In this chapter I explain how the Truvada debate can extend our thinking about rhetorical and sexualized notions of risk and counterpublics. My discussion of counterpublics is grounded in a rhetorical notion of publics, which Michael Warner and others have defined as networks of subjects but also social spaces organized by and recognizable through interlinked, visible, and ongoing discursive action (413, 421). As material-discursive entities, publics are "formed by people coming together to discuss common concerns, including concerns about who they are and what they should do, and as a result construct social reality together" (Palczewski, Ice, and Fritch 236). Counterpublics, in turn, can be conceived as "parallel discursive arenas where members of subordinated social groups invent and circulate counterdiscourse to formulate oppositional interpretations of their identities, interests, and needs" (Fraser 123). Although publics and counterpublics share some of the same characteristics (e.g., mechanisms for discursive interaction and circulation), counterpublics, Robert Asen explains, develop as "explicitly articulated alternatives to wider publics that exclude the interests of potential participants" (425), alternatives that can be reactive but also proactive. For example, a counterpublic of gay HIV/AIDS activists formed partly out of the need to develop and circulate prevention strategies and norms in the face of a deadly slow public health response to the epidemic and as an alternative to what Cindy Patten calls a heterosexist "national pedagogy" that locates risk in queer bodies and identities. At the same time, Asen explains, the discourse of counterpublics "reconnect[s] with the communicative flows of a multiple public sphere" (425). It took a number of years, but eventually mainstream HIV prevention efforts followed the lead of gay activists in adopting condoms (if not other queer erotic tactics) as a crucial safer sex tool, at least for certain risk groups.

Like other cultural discourses about HIV, the Truvada debate has involved slippages between sexual behavior and identity-based risk through what I have called elsewhere "disciplinary rhetorics." Disciplinary rhetorics are bodies of persuasion that work with other actors (e.g., desires, embodied and habituated practices, the virus itself) to help shape the normalization, identification, and embodied experiences of sexualized subjects (Scott). We can understand both the rhetoric *about* Truvada—such as who should be taking it and why—and the sexual rhetoric around Truvada's *use*—such as confessional disclosure and negotiated sex practices—as disciplinary in this Foucaultian sense of the word. The notion of disciplinary rhetorics, I argue, can help explain the relationship between Truvada's sexual bodies, as normalized constructs, and embodied experiences. It can also serve as one way to understand how counterpublics, as discursive arenas, can include a corporeal dimension involving embodied actors and practices.

The following analysis maps and examines some of Truvada's contested meanings circulating among the counterpublics shaping the PrEP debate, explaining how this discourse can function as a disciplinary rhetoric involving sexualized bodies, values, and practices. Finally, the analysis considers what the debate might suggest about sexual counterpublics and their relationship to disciplinary rhetorics.

Truvada's Meanings and Counterpublics

Truvada's Contested Meanings

Although those arguing about Truvada and PrEP have staked a range of positions that comprise a continuum of (dis)agreement, I have found it useful to compile and categorize some of Truvada's contested meanings in two clusters, one more supportive of its widespread use and one less so. Supporters of Truvada have characterized it in the following ways:

- a new tool for sanctioned public health HIV prevention efforts that also include condom use and HIV testing
- the linchpin of, or even new paradigm for, prevention efforts targeting MSM, particularly younger gay men and gay men of color
- a responsible strategy for the individual management of risk, particularly as a safeguard for or replacement of inconsistent condom use
- a mundane but important option, similar to the reproductive management option of the birth control pill

- a way to heighten sexual intimacy, remove "barriers" in both senses of that word
- a means to liberation from worry and anxiety about sex and its negotiation
- a way to open up communication around sex-related risk and its management
- a leveling mechanism creating a new category of "HIV equal"

For those opposing its widespread use to varying degrees, Truvada is:

- an HIV prevention strategy foolishly conceived as a magic bullet, threatening to supersede other essential prevention-related efforts, such as community-based outreach focusing on stigma
- inappropriate and potentially dangerous as a widespread prevention strategy for gay men, given the likelihood of poor adherence among those who need it the most
- an unproven medication with serious health-related side effects (e.g., kidney problems) and unknown long-term side effects
- a "poison pill" created to boost the profits of the pharmaceutical industry and approved through the collusion of this industry with the government
- a false sense of security, in part because it does not prevent other sexually transmitted diseases
- a betrayal of hard-won safer-sex prevention efforts and norms around condom use, and a threat to the memory of the gay community's struggle, loss, and triumph surrounding HIV/AIDS
- an enabler of new, resistant strains of HIV and the conduit (or petri dish) for a new inevitable epidemic
- a party drug that will be used mainly by financially well-off white gay men as a license to be promiscuous
- a means of limiting HIV status disclosure and conversations about risk in the negotiation of sex
- an assimilationist strategy in line with heteronormative values

Truvada's Countering Counterpublics

A number of these meanings-in-tension have circulated among a longstanding network of gay HIV/AIDS activists who have fought the epidemic for decades and who have been called the "safer sex generation" (Stern, "I Have Learned"). This network and its discourse constituted a counterpublic that worked to promote prevention strategies, lobby for research, and demand access to treatment, as documented by Patten, Steven Epstein and others. In this sense, part of the countering stance of this counterpublic became accepted and absorbed into mainstream discourse and policy, and some activists became public health advisors and officials who have influenced such policy from the inside, while others maintained an oppositional stance to mainstream institutions of authority like public health agencies and the pharmaceutical industry.

The tensions dividing this counterpublic around Truvada are captured by an interview-based article about two former ACT UP allies (Shapiro). One of these allies, Peter Staley, has served as a government advisor to President Clinton's National Task Force on AIDS Drug Development and New York Governor Cuomo's AIDS Task Force, which has embraced Truvada and PrEP as a key part of its prevention effort. "You have to let science guide your activism," argues Staley in the interview, pointing to the impressive data about Truvada's prevention efficacy. On the other, more cautious side of the PrEP debate, Sean Strub, the founder of *POZ* magazine, acknowledges a limited role for PrEP for particular patients who would take it every day but worries that too much emphasis on PrEP will lead to limited conversation and strategies around safer sex and will take attention away from related problems, such as stigma and lack of access to quality healthcare. "There's no pill to treat stigma," he points out.

Perhaps the most vocal opponent to the widespread adoption of PrEP has been the AIDS Healthcare Foundation (AHF) and its president, Michael Weinstein. Weinstein and other representatives of the AHF spoke against the FDA approval of Truvada for PrEP, questioning the medical research supporting PrEP and the objectivity the FDA's approval process. Later, Weinstein and the AHF called the CDC's May 2012 recommendations for PrEP "reckless," predicting that PrEP's widespread implementation "will be a catastrophe for HIV prevention in this country" (Moisse). Arguing that stubborn HIV infection rates should be attributed to an underimplemented strategy of condom promotion rather than a failed one, Weinstein worried, like Strub, that an emphasis on PrEP is a "typical American easy way out," adding that "men don't need more excuses not to use condoms" (Moisse). Although federal recommendations for PrEP include condom use, Weinstein articulated the widely shared fear that PrEP would replace condoms for many, leading to other STDs and less precaution around HIV. Additionally, he and AHF have pointed to Truvada's serious side effects and, more importantly, the possibility of inefficacy and resistance from lack of adherence. On this point, the AHF conducted its own survey of potential drug users, which found that close to 40 percent of respondents did not indicate they would be "very likely" to take the pill every day (Ramos). This likelihood would create a "false sense of security," according to a Texas regional director of AHF (Ramos).

A number of other responses contributed to the counterdiscourse of this backlash against PrEP. One PrEP opponent launched a "scare campaign" on the social media app Secret, claiming that PrEP failed to keep him uninfected (Staley). Echoing Weinstein's characterization of Truvada as a "party drug" (McNeil), Regan Hofmann, former editor-in-chief of *POZ*, called Truvada a "profit-driven sex toy for rich Westerners" (Glazek). Users of social media sites quickly picked up on and began using the derogatory designation of "Truvada whore," coined in a *Huffington Post* piece by David Duran ("Truvada"), who has since changed his position to tout a number of PrEP's empowering benefits.

Reinforcing the argument that PrEP is an easy way out, a *New York Post* article titled "False Prophets: Questioning the Crusade for a New Gay Equality" compares PrEP to "offering insulin to the obese—rather than fresh vegetables and gym membership" (Kaufman). Shortly after the CDC's guidelines were published in 2014, longtime activist Larry Kramer offered this critique in *The New York Times*: "There's something to me cowardly about taking Truvada instead of using a condom. You're taking a drug that is poison to you, and it has lessened your energy to fight, to get involved, to do anything" (Healy). Here Kramer captures several perceived dangers of PrEP but especially the risk of exacerbated apathy—a bitter pill to activists who have tirelessly promoted safer sex norms, discussions, and responsiveness among gay men.

The questioning of PrEP could be viewed as a backlash against not only federal recommendations, but also what critics saw as an overenthusiastic endorsement by other activists and journalists. In January 2014, a *Slate* writer called Truvada a "miracle drug" (Stern, "There Is a Daily Pill"), and, along with other blog entries and news articles, advocated for the ubiquitous use of PrEP similar to women's use of the birth control pill. "Is This the New Condom?" posed an *Out* magazine article, going on to compare the replacement of condoms with Truvada to a replacement of diaphragms with "the pill" (Murphy). Other stories also emphasized the psychosocial and cultural impacts of PrEP, including sexual freedom from anxiety and stigma. A featured *New York* magazine story celebrated Truvada's potential to enable "Sex without Fear" (Murphy), while another piece argued that "PrEP has the potential to liberate us, because it gives gay men who have managed to stay HIV-negative an opportunity to sever the cord between sex and HIV" (Sandler). Some proponents tied the liberating power of PrEP to a new sexualized, destigmatizing identity politics, wherein gay men would all be "HIV-equal"—the name of a nonprofit promoting PrEP (Kaufman).

The range of arguments promoting and questioning PrEP that I've mapped thus far point to a nuanced notion of counterpublic that can account for multiple, shifting, and countering values, positions, and tactics. If counterpublics are defined by a shared oppositional stance, the tension among gay HIV/AIDS activists such as Staley and Strub complicates discerning their collective discursive action as shared. Some have pointed to countering responses to PrEP along generational lines, with younger men more likely to view PrEP as an empowering tool to counter the fear and stigma around sex and to meet contemporary challenges posed by the epidemic. One of PrEP's most prominent advocates, therapist and blogger Damon Jacobs, makes this generational distinction when asserting that "[g]ay men who embraced the condom message and survived the trauma of 30 years ago have PTSD" (McNeil). To some older activists, such responses threaten to erase the exigency for remembering safer sex norms and the people who sacrificed to develop them. One HIV survivor in New York City expresses his misgivings about PrEP's cultural impact this way: "I want people to understand why they're able to take this right now. It's on the backs of people who have died and suffered" (Murphy, "Sex").

An Emergent Counterpublic

In diagnosing the slow adoption of PrEP, one writer observed that "PrEP lacks a built-in constituency to advocate for it" (Glazek). Yet a number of gay men taking Truvada have met this challenge, forming through their discursive and embodied actions a new counterpublic that we might call a backlash to the backlash. These men chronicle their experiences with and perspectives on PrEP in confessional blogs and articles, and a few have formed online educational and advocacy sites and become frequent commenters on online stories critiquing PrEP. The discourse of this counterpublic could be viewed as a set of disciplinary rhetorics shaping a new sexual identity of a responsible gay man as well as revised forms of identification with sexual desire and risk management.

Participants in this emergent discourse include the anonymous blogger with the pseudonym Jake Sobo, who authors the "My Life on PrEP" blog, and PrEPsters posting on the "My PrEP Experience" blog sponsored by the AIDS Foundation of Chicago. Manhattan therapist Damon Jacobs, the most outspoken member of this counterpublic, began telling his story with PrEP and educating others about it through a Facebook page ("PrEP Facts: Rethinking HIV Prevention and Sex") in 2013, and he later cofounded an educational website called "PrEP-o-licious." He has been the subject of a number of interviews, including one in *The Body* titled "This PrEP-ed Life: Damon Jacobs on Sex and Dating in a New Era of HIV Prevention" (Rodriguez). Jacobs is also a frequent commenter on blogs and stories about PrEP, often posting to correct misunderstandings with scientific information from PrEP studies and public health guidelines.

These confessional PrEPsters, as I will call them, see their role as educating and empowering others, countering critiques that PrEP users are irresponsible with their personal testimonies of how they have taken charge; "I Haven't Given Up, I've TAKEN CHARGE" one My PrEP Experience blogger asserts (Literski). They write about why they were good candidates for PrEP (they weren't using a condom every time), why they tried it (they wanted another way to protect themselves and also sometimes to enjoy the intimacy of condom-less sex), how they accessed it, and how they have benefited from it. On this latter note, these PrEPsters report that although they maintain a healthy respect for the risk of HIV, their sex lives are no longer riddled with fear and anxiety. Although some PrEPsters, like Jacobs, emphasize the empowerment afforded by PrEP more in terms of private, individual prevention management, others, such as Sobo, add to this a more explicitly community-focused objective. As part of his quest to promote destigmatizing discussions about PrEP and the intersexual politics around it, Sobo gives his gay audience advice about how to talk to their friends or potential sex partners about PrEP and its benefits.

Some PrEPsters, including Sobo, have responded to charges of reckless promiscuity in a more direct, perhaps queerer way. Led partly by Adam Zebowski (aka "pupbones"), an HIV test counselor and community prevention educator in San Francisco, a number of men have launched a testimonial campaign around the tongue-in-cheek admission that "I am a Truvada Whore." The campaign includes a website, hashtag, and t-shirt, and asks Truvada users or "allies" to help "take the word back, wear it as a scarlet letter, be loud and proud."

As Zebowski explains in his post to the My PrEP Experience blog, the campaign seizes and reappropriates the derogatory "Truvada whore" charge on social media (and sex pick-up) sites, following earlier gay activists' reappropriation of the term "queer," which "subsequently lost its power as a derogatory word." In addition to sparking conversations rather than knee-jerk judgments about the use of Truvada, Zebowski views the campaign as a way to "create a better sense of community and belonging." Longtime activist Staley views this campaign as a "beautiful movement" enacting a powerful new destigmatized sexual identity, but one that also enacts the historical counterdiscursive tactic of "coming out" that has been "the secret ammo for the LGBT movement from Day 1" (Stern, "I Have Learned").

Truvada's "Promiscuous" Counterpublics and Disciplinary Rhetorics

In linking Truvada's potential health and cultural impacts, arguments shaping the debate have proliferated differing takes on desire, risk, safer sex, responsibility, and identity for gay men, both on the individual and communal levels. These arguments also point to some of the ways rhetorics—more specifically disciplinary rhetorics—function as vectors to variously normalize gay sexuality and thereby shape the identification and practices of embodied subjects.

Arguments about the relationship between condoms and Truvada are fraught with tension about gay sexual norms and responsibility. Staley and other PrEP proponents have positioned Truvada as a timely and responsive addition to the gay community's toolbox, a desperately needed intervention into the exigency of new infections among gay men (especially younger men and men of color) (see Shapiro). In addition to assuming that PrEP will replace consistent condom use, a questionable assumption, Weinstein and other critics position Truvada outside the realm of safer sex strategies, including queer ones (see "Divide"; Weinstein). Condom use has been the most widely promoted and accepted of these strategies, which also include non-penetrative sex and other erotic acts (see Crimp). For most prevention activists, what has been historically and decidedly not part of a safer sex repertoire is barebacking, or anal sex without a condom. PrEP threatens this demarcation by making condomless HIV prevention possible and thereby changing the definition of safer sex (see Sandler).

While a number of gay prevention activists view condoms as a queer technology of safer sex (even as they are endorsed by public health officials), others have linked condoms to the anxiety and stigma surrounding gay sexuality and HIV. For these men, PrEP enables the removal of two barriers at once, shedding the shame, fear, and identity-based internalization of risk associated with heterosexist norms. In this sense, PrEP can be viewed as a counterpublic tool that affords gays an expanded repertoire and freedom, and a healthier relationship to sex, similar to those enjoyed by heterosexuals. Conversely, Weinstein and other PrEP critics portray the fear of HIV as a healthy motivator of gay responsibility and an important reminder of the gay counterpublic's historical struggle and survival (Weinstein).

Arguments comparing Truvada to another sex technology—the birth control pill—also point to differing values about and understandings of gay sexuality. According to some advocates, PrEP affords not only new forms of safer sex responsibility, but also a sanctioning of expanded sexual desires. Tim Dean, the author of a book on the subculture of barebacking, references such desires in relation to the risk of bucking longstanding community-based norms, stating that, "to acknowledge that we want raw sex entails a big risk in itself, because that doesn't fit in with the image of the good, responsible gay man who dutifully practices safe sex" (Juzwiak). PrEP proponents tend to affirm such desire as natural and human. The director of the AIDS Foundation of Chicago makes this universalizing move in imploring his gay audience to recognize that, "[y]ou're here because people barebacked. Your grandmother was a barebacker." Pointing out a double standard of desire, he further states, "With a gay man, it's like, 'Oh my God. You're reckless, you're careless, you're insane, you're self-destructive, you want to hurt yourself and others.' And we ignore the fact that gay men have the same needs to feel close and intimate and pleasure" (Juzwiak).

PrEP critics have portrayed the standardization of Truvada in the manner of a birth control pill—and the related act of condomless sex it leads to—as a move toward heterosexist norms and away from queer safer sex knowledge and tactics. An exception to the largely generational divide, a younger gay blogger labels this an assimilationist move that "insults" queer sexual creativity (Lowder). This same blogger connects sex assimilation to a larger shift away from counterpublic prevention efforts, asserting that PrEP "feels like a straight bureaucratic approach to a queer communal problem" (Lowder). Here safer sex strategies are linked to a communal identity and norms.

Discourse around Truvada has produced multiple and sometimes competing sexualized identities and forms of identity disclosure. Some PrEP advocates have pointed to the equalizing power of no longer needing to disclose HIV status—the identity of HIV neutral. One advocate approached PrEP identity another way, adding the new status of "I'm negative on PrEP" to five other variations of HIV status (including "I don't know my status") (Barucco); he goes on to hierarchize the statuses from the safest to the least safe, illustrating how the disciplinary rhetorics around PrEP can add to rather than replace problematic identity-based notions of risk and minoritizing safer sex strategies. While PrEP critics have invoked the normalized risky bodies of irresponsible and reckless gay men, proponents have responded with countering notions of pragmatically empowered PrEP-sters and outspoken "Truvada whores," notions that sanction new identifications with sexual desire and community. PrEP critics and advocates have positioned themselves as guardians and empowerers, respectively, of a gay counterpublic, and have accused each other of being less "counter" and more assimilationist and self-destructive.

Even some proponents and users of Truvada have questioned whether it is a long-term solution or just the next important step in managing risk and the larger epidemic. The research around drug-based HIV prevention continues with follow-up studies about adherence with PrEP, and with studies of other drugs and new forms and doses of Truvada, including the possibility of an injection every three months (see Tuller; Cohen). As these new or extended forms of prevention are approved, adopted, and debated among gay/bisexual men and other stakeholders, we are sure to see an accompanying proliferation of new or extended sexual conceptions, norms, practices, and counterpublics. Yet even the snapshot of the ongoing PrEP debate that I provide here suggests several conceptions of sexual counterpublics that rhetoricians might find useful.

First, as mentioned earlier, counterpublics—like sexuality—are multifaceted and fluid. We might even say counterpublics are promiscuous in the various countering positions, conceptions, tactics, and identities they produce. Even though gay HIV prevention activists have shared common opponents of the virus, apathetic government and cultural responses, and stigmatizing notions of risk, they have also positioned themselves to these entities and to each other in markedly different ways, largely in response to changing exigencies. My analysis of Truvada's counterpublics affirms some of the more general characteristics identified by Robert Asen and Daniel C. Brouwer—including their permeable boundaries and potential imbrications with the state. It also resonates with Brouwer's recognition of different modes of corporeal expressivity across HIV/AIDS activist zines. In critiquing what she views as Warner's too-easy dichotomy of public/counterpublic, Melissa Deem proposes that we worry less about whether a public is "counter" and instead "examine rhetorics that cross these nominally different public formations" (446). Deem uses the notion of "minor rhetorics" (447) to track this movement, but we could also track circulating notions of desire or risk. Instead of asking, "Who are the real counterpublics here?" we might ask, "How do disciplinary rhetorics of HIV risk circulate across, get taken up and adapted by, and, in turn, transform public formations?"

Second, counterpublics are enacted and maintained through both discursive and embodied practices, as well as through affective dimensions of embodiment. Although I read Warner to emphasize the discursive dimension of counterpublics and their maintenance, Brouwer has observed and compellingly illustrated Warner's theorizing of linguistic and corporeal modes of counterpublicity working together. Conceptualizing the counterpublics shaping the Truvada debate as discursive arenas is certainly useful, given the ways they constituted and positioned themselves through online arguments. The confessional PrEPsters and "Truvada whores," in particular, are primarily discernible through their repeated discursive forms, including confessional stories, linguistic reappropriations, and circulating hashtags designed to enroll others in promoting alternative sexual norms. At the same time, we would overlook an important dynamic if we failed to account for the corporeal, embodied experiences, performances, and interactions of these counterpublics, from their lobbying government officials to their negotiations of safer sex to their embodied identifications in t-shirts. In line with Hayles' theorizing of the body–embodiment distinction and relationship—wherein a body is a normalized/normalizing construct and embodiment is a particular contextual, material experience (196–97)—we might further understand the relationship between the discursive and corporeal dimensions of counterpublics in terms of a feedback loop. In the dynamic of this feedback loop, "changes in experiences of embodiment bubble up through language" and "discursive constructions affect how bodies move through space and time" (Hayles 206–7). We can see this in the way the embodied experiences of PrEPsters, both before and after they began taking Truvada, shape the alternative norms and identities proffered in their confessional blog entries and other discourse, which in turn (potentially) shape the embodied identification and risk negotiations of their audiences. We can also see this dynamic at work in the way counterpublic norms around responsible safer sex were enacted through shared condom-centered sexual interactions, and in the way in which the normalized construct of the responsible gay citizen has shaped the enactment of desire and embodied feelings of anxiety and fear around condomless sex.

Finally, this analysis of the Truvada debate illustrates how the disciplinary rhetorics of counterpublics can be both sexualized and sexualizing—a more specific version of the feedback loop just described. The multiple enactments of counterpublicity around PrEP were indebted to and interpellated by sexualized risk-based identities, even when they were attempting to offer alternative identifications. Counterpublics, in turn, can offer new ways of disciplining sexual subjects, through, say, enabling particular orientations toward, identifications with, and negotiations of risk while disabling others. For example, arguments and online interactions invoking the stigmatizing construct of the "Truvada whore" have dissuaded some at-risk men from self-identifying as potential PrEP users, and the intimate experiences of other activist men have informed their reappropriation of this term as one of empowerment and self-determination. Reading the sexual enactments of counterpublics as disciplinary rhetorics can identify ways that bodies of persuasion facilitate the mutual conditioning of sexualized constructs and practices. Reading the disciplinary rhetorics of Truvada's counterpublics as sexual can offer another way to understand rhetoric's fluidity or promiscuity, even as it is enacted across embodied experience and corporeal expressivity.

Note

1. Some have cited a 99 percent efficacy rate for Truvada as PrEP, an estimate based on a retrospective analysis of study data. See Barro for an interesting meta-analysis of this analysis.

Works Cited

Asen, Robert. "Seeking the 'Counter' in Counterpublics." *Communication Theory* 10.4 (Nov. 2000): 424–46. Print.
Asen, Robert, and Daniel C. Brouwer. "Introduction: Reconfigurations of the Public Sphere." *Counterpublics and the State*. Eds. Asen and Brouwer. Albany: State U of New York P, 2004. 1–32. Print.
Barro, Josh. "Is Truvada, the Pill to Prevent H.I.V., 99 Percent Effective? Don't be So Sure." *The New York Times* 16 July 2014. Web. 2 Dec. 2014.
Barucco, Renato. "Beyond 'Poz' and 'Neg': Five HIV Statuses, Plus a New One." *Huffington Post* 27 Mar. 2014. Web. 31 Mar. 2014.
Brouwer, Daniel C. "Counterpublicity and Corporeality in HIV/AIDS Zines." *Critical Studies in Media Communication* 22.5 (Dec. 2005): 351–71. Print.
Cohen, Jon. "A Bid to Thwart HIV with Shot of Long-Lasting Drug." *Science* 343: 7 Mar. 2014. Web. 2 Dec. 2014.
Crimp, Douglas. "How to Have Promiscuity in an Epidemic." *October* 43 (Winter 1987): 237–71. Print.
Deem, Melissa. "Stranger Sociability, Public Hope, and the Limits of Political Transformation." *Quarterly Journal of Speech* 88.4 (Nov. 2002): 444–54. Print.
"Divide Over HIV Prevention Drug Truvada Persists." *USA Today* 6 Apr. 2014. Web. 3 Dec. 2014.
Duran, David. "An Evolved Opinion on Truvada." *Huffington Post* 27 Mar. 2014. Web. 3 Dec. 2014.
Duran, David. "Truvada Whores?" *Huffington Post* 12 Nov. 2012. Web. 3 Dec. 2014.
Fraser, Nancy. "Rethinking the Public Sphere: A Contribution to the Critique of Actually Existing Democracy." *Habermas and the Public Sphere*. Ed. G. Calhoun. Cambridge, MA: MIT Press, 1992. 109–42. Print.
Glazek, Christopher. "Why Is No One on the First Treatment to Prevent HIV?" *The New Yorker* 30 Sept. 2013. Web. 2 Dec. 2014.
Hayles, N. Katherine. *How We Became Posthuman: Virtual Bodies in Cybernetics, Literature, and Informatics*. Chicago: U of Chicago P, 1999. Print.
Healy, Patrick. "A Lion Still Roars, With Gratitude." *The New York Times* 21 May 2014. Web. 3 Dec. 2014.
Juzwiak, Rich. "What Is Safe Sex? The Raw and Uncomfortable Truth about Truvada." *Huffington Post* 5 Mar. 2014. Web. 31 Mar. 2014.

Kaufman, David. "False Prophets: Questioning the Crusade for a New Gay Equality." *New York Post* 30 Nov. 2014. Web. 3 Dec. 2014.
Literski, Nick. "I Haven't given Up, I've TAKEN CHARGE: One Man's Story of Taking HIV Meds for Prevention." *My PrEP Experience*. AIDS Foundation of Chicago 23 May 2012. Web. 3 Dec. 2014.
Lowder, Bryan. "Twenty-One Attempts at Swallowing Truvada." *Slate* 5 Dec. 2014. Web. 12 Dec. 2014.
McNeil, Donald. "Advocating a Pill, U.S. Signals Shift to Prevent AIDS." *The New York Times* 14 May 2014. Web. 3 Dec. 2014.
Marcus, Julia L., et al. "No Evidence of Sexual Risk Compensation in the iPrEx Trial of Daily Oral HIV Preexposure Prophylaxis." *PLOS One* 18 Dec. 2013. Web. 3 Dec. 2014.
Milioni, Dimitra L. "Probing the Online Counterpublic Sphere: the Case of Indymedia Athens." *Media, Culture, and Society* 31.3 (2009): 409–31. Print.
Moisse, Katie. "Truvada for HIV Prevention: Pros, Cons of Popping a Pill." *ABC News* 9 May 2012. Web. 31 Mar. 2014.
Murphy, Timothy. "Is This the New Condom?" *Out* 9 Sept. 2013. Web. 3 Dec. 2014.
Murphy, Timothy. "Sex without Fear." *New York Magazine* 14 July 2014. Web. 3 Dec. 2014.
Palczewski, Catherine H., Richard Ice, and John Fritch. *Rhetoric in Civic Life*. State College, PA: Strata, 2012. Print.
Patten, Cindy. *Fatal Advice: How Safe-Sex Education Went Wrong*. Durham, NC: Duke UP, 1996. Print.
"Pre-Exposure Prophylaxis (PrEP)." Centers for Disease Control. United States Public Health Service 30 Sept. 2014. Web. 2 Dec. 2014.
Preexposure Prophylaxis for the Prevention of HIV Infection in the United States: A Clinical Practice Guideline. Centers for Disease Control. United States Public Health Service 2014. Web. 2 Dec. 2014.
Ramos, Steve. "Truvada: Why the Emotion?" *Dallas Voice* 21 Mar. 2014. Web. 31 Mar. 2014.
Rodriguez, Mathew. "This PrEP-ed Life: Damon Jacobs on Sex and Dating in a New Era of HIV Prevention." *The Body* 13 May 2013. Web. 2 Dec. 2014.
Salahi, Lara. "Daily Use of Antiretroviral Drugs Cuts AIDS Transmission." *ABC News* 23 Nov. 2010. Web. 31 Mar. 2014.
Sandler, Carl. "A Pill to Prevent HIV." *Huffington Post* 6 Nov. 2012. Web. 31 Mar. 2014.
Scott, J. Blake. *Risky Rhetoric: AIDS and the Cultural Practices of HIV Testing*. Carbondale: Southern Illinois UP, 2003. Print.
Shapiro, Lila. "The Most Celebrated, Mistrusted Little Pill in the World." *Huffington Post* 1 Dec. 2014. Web. 3 Dec. 2014.
Sobo, Jake. "My Life on PrEP." *Frontiers Media* 18 Oct. 2012. Web. 31 Mar. 2014.
Staley, Peter. "Anti-PrEP Scare Tactics." *Huffington Post* 17 July 2014. Web. 3 Dec. 2014.
Stern, Mark Joseph. "'I Have Learned Not to Underestimate the Stigma': Peter Staley on Truvada, Condoms, and HIV Prevention." *Slate* 22 May 2014. Web. Accessed 3 Dec. 2014.
———. "There Is a Daily Pill that Prevents HIV. Gay Men Should Take It." *Slate* 6 Jan. 2014. Web. 31 Mar. 2014.
Tuller, David. "A Resisted Pill to Prevent H.I.V." *The New York Times* 30 Dec. 2013. Web. 3 Dec. 2014.

Vilensky, Mike. "Truvada, the Drug in Cuomo's AIDS-Eradication Plan, Spurs Debate." *The Wall Street Journal* 13 July 2014. Web. 2 Dec. 2014.

Warner, Michael. *Publics and Counterpublics*. Cambridge, MA: Zone, 2005. Print.

Weinstein, Michael. "Truvada Can't Make Us Let Our Guard Down." *The New York Times* 18 June 2014. Web. 3 Dec. 2014.

"World AIDS Day." World Health Organization, n.d. Web. 3 Dec. 2014.

Zebowski, Adam. "I am a Truvada Whore." *My PrEP Experience*. AIDS Foundation of Chicago. 28 March 2014. Web. 3 Dec. 2014.

17 Presidential Masculinity
George W. Bush's Rhetorical Conquest

Luke Winslow

By international comparisons, US voters display irrational, apathetic, and ignorant political attitudes. About half do not know that each state has two senators, and three-quarters do not know the length of their terms. About 70 percent cannot say which party controls the Senate. Over half cannot name their congressperson, and 40 percent cannot name either of their senators. Slightly lower percentages know their representatives' party affiliations (Caplan). More recent surveys suggest that about 30 percent of Americans could name the Vice President, about 35 percent could not assign the proper century to the American Revolution, six percent could not circle Independence Day on a calendar, and 18 percent think President Barack Obama is Jewish (only ten percent think he is Muslim) (Bruni).

The causes of this ignorance vary: US voters are said to be overloaded with information, struggle integrating information about their political choices, and lack incentives to seek out the kind of information that will help simplify the political process (Popkin). The result is a significant number of US citizens who possess underdeveloped political philosophies, uncertain motivations to deliberate carefully on policy issues, and a tenuous command of important facts (Entman).

This ignorance has a profound impact on how voters *make sense* of individual political actors, forcing many to rely heavily on heuristic shortcuts to navigate what might otherwise be an unmanageably complex political climate (Caplan). These shortcuts are increasingly reliant on affect. Affect does not require the conscious awareness of having gone through the difficult steps of researching, weighing evidence, or inferring a conclusion. Rather, affect activates the intuitive and automatic thought processes that influence how voters *feel*, not what they cognitively, analytically, and deliberately *know*.

For a helpful analogy, imagine a motorist successfully navigating a busy intersection. To do so, the motorist must gather as much information as possible about the intentions of other drivers and the speed, acceleration, direction, and mass of their cars. At many intersections, however, there is a substitute for all of this information: a traffic signal. For voters, affective heuristics effectively function as that traffic signal. A voter does not need to know if a political candidate can speak Mandarin, chart the treasury yield curve, or has written a doctoral dissertation on the most relevant political issue of the day. If the candidate fails to pronounce the name of the local football field correctly or doesn't look good in hunting camouflage, a voter may have all the material necessary for making a heuristically plausible assessment of the candidate.

How does this description of US political discourse inform a larger exploration of rhetoric, sexuality, and regimes of discursive control? The primary purpose of this book is to trace the emergence and unacknowledged presence of sexual rhetorical practices into the public sphere in order to offer a more comprehensive understanding of the dense and complicated ways sexuality constitutes nexuses of power, constructs identity, and carries the weight of ideological pressure. Several of the chapters in this book explore this process by analyzing the meaning-making and exchange process where historically underrepresented and marginalized sexual identities are constructed, affirmed, and struggled over. Although all the chapters in this book are tied together by a shared purpose, this chapter's focus on the interconnectedness of gender, sexuality, and style in US political discourse hopefully adds breadth to the book's overall inquiry by illuminating the meaning-making and exchange process in traditional, formal corridors of power. More specifically, I want to demonstrate how affective heuristics are operationalized as one of the most important factors US voters use to make political decisions by way of gendered and sexualized representations. To do so, it is important to understand the interconnectedness of gendered and sexualized performances in US political discourse. While most are likely aware that the term "sex" describes biological differences between men and women, and "gender" describes the social, cultural, and political experiences of those differences, consider how affective heuristics in American political discourse works to negate that distinction by containing the contradictions, fissures, and ruptures that inevitably bubble up when political attitudes and judgments are being formed. The construction, affirmation, and regulation of sexualized and gendered performances in American political discourse are often represented as a timeless and transcendent biological inevitability, not the struggled-over, contingent, and up-for-grabs cultural production that it is. Ultimately, the interconnectedness of gender and sexuality simplifies and orders the attitudes of voters related to what a politician can be, organizes the meaning making and exchange process, and performs an important rhetorical function by locating politicians within regimes of power, effectively shaping democratic discourse and influencing public opinion by creating and affirming specific vocabularies.

The process is not unique to politics. We all use gendered and sexualized signifying practices to constitute our identity as social subjects (Butler, *Gender*; Eagleton; Whitehead). Gender and sexuality order our existence and produce the lived relations by which we are connected to other people. When we are subjectified as a "man" or "woman," we are assuming a position in a complex social structure. Gender and sexuality do not do this alone, however; we cannot assume an isolated gendered or sexualized identity, just as we cannot assume an isolated racial or class identity. Gender and sexual identities are always raced and classed, in the same way race and class are always *made meaningful* within a gendered and sexualized lens (C. Crenshaw; K. Crenshaw; Dace; Guillaumin; Winslow, *Promise*). Our identities are cobbled together through a confluence of several markers—through the intersectionality of distinct characteristics such as gender, sex, and race, as well as sexual orientation, class, religion, education, and political and regional affiliations. However, for scholars interested in the relationship between sexual normalization and regimes of discursive control through which bodies are disciplined in public spheres, the significant role gender and sexuality play in the relationship between political actors, news media, and cultural paradigms offers a rich and valuable site of scholarly inquiry. This is especially true for the US presidency.

The US presidency is legally open to all native-born citizens who have had permanent residency in the United States for at least 14 years and are over the age of 35. But we know that is not true. There are clear constraints that limit who can be president. Gender has historically functioned as one of the most effective. The outcome of a presidential election often hinges on who can best assume a particular image of the ideal US male (Malin; Morreale; Traister). US voters expect their president to embody a specific masculine image that signifies the moral and social cues for the country. Brenton Malin argues that US conceptions of presidential masculinity work to organize cultural meanings and resources, outline our national will, and construct representations of an imaginary national unity. Through such representations, candidates enact the culturally constructed desires intimately linked to who we want to be (Wahl-Jorgensen). Shawn Parry-Giles and Trevor Parry-Giles extend this claim, arguing that to be perceived as capable of filling the station of president, a candidate must not only adopt a gendered persona, but the most valued set of gendered expectations. Karlyn Kohrs Campbell adds that the American president is to represent what we pretend is a single, universally accepted ideal for American manhood. Ultimately, presidential masculinity functions as an important form of discursive control through which particular sexualized bodies are empowered and disempowered in an important public sphere.

The presidency of George W. Bush offers a vivid and rich case study. If the 2000 and 2004 presidential elections hinged on who could best assume the image of the ideal American male, Bush dominated Al Gore and John Kerry. Bush was consistently able to bolster his masculine credentials and appeal to southern NASCAR fans and Wal-Mart moms in a way Gore and Kerry could not. Compared to Bush and his affinity for barbecue, nonalcoholic beer, and brush cutting in the Texas heat, Al Gore seemed stiff, inauthentic, and academic. Four years later, John Kerry's Boston Brahmin roots, along with his Botox injections, fake tans, and $75 haircuts hindered his ability to *outman* Bush. The purpose of this chapter is to find out why. I aim to contribute to a larger conversation about the relationship between affective heuristics, sexuality, and the US presidency by exploring the role of *style* in political deliberation. More specifically, I seek to develop a theoretical rationale for the important relationship between style and sexuality in political discourse. I call this *presidential masculinity*.

Presidential masculinity accounts for the process by which governmental and social elites, media, and the public frame political actors through the symbolic activation of the aesthetic dimensions of public presentation. George W. Bush, in relation to Al Gore and John Kerry, illuminates this process. Al Gore and John Kerry ran unsuccessful presidential campaigns. They lost for a wide variety of reasons. I don't intend to explain them all. But as a starting premise, it is important to recognize that Al Gore and John Kerry faced unique stylistic challenges in relation to George W. Bush. Or more humbly, I assert that journalists paid close attention to each candidate's style and often used style to explain the status of each candidate's campaign. Ultimately, these stylistic explanations functioned affectively through a sexualized conduit of identity creation and constitution. The common theme woven across the time period, political party, and the social and economic situation is that Bush, Gore, and Kerry were framed by journalists in a way that shaped their ability to connect with the cultural paradigms and sexualized expectations of a significant number of voters. I hope to identify enough of these stylistic references so that the reader will accept as plausible that each presidential candidate's style impacted the viability of their candidacy.

In so doing, I hope to accomplish four objectives. First, I would like to contribute to a larger conversation related to understanding the way gendered and sexualized rhetorical practices function in the public sphere by activating affective heuristics to simplify political judgments and equip voters with the techniques of public deliberation needed to navigate an increasingly complex political landscape. Second, I hope to illuminate the oscillating relationship among style, sexualized representations, and social formations by exploring how the aesthetics of presidential masculinity issue a demand whose precise effect emerges in an intersubjective encounter between with the rhetor and the social orientations the meaning-making process is operating within. Third, I want to contribute to conversations related to the role of identity markers in political deliberation by advancing our understanding of how the gendered and sexualized framing of an individual political actor, like George W. Bush, leverages the visual for its rhetorical potency. Finally, I hope to contribute to a larger conversation about the role of constitutive rhetoric in the twenty-first century and lend insight into the role of aesthetic rationales in a milieu marked by increasing social fragmentation, hybrid identities, diffused technologies, and extreme heterogeneity.

I begin by exploring masculinity. I then unpack in more detail what I mean by style. I use the stylistic dimensions developed in Barry Brummett's 2008 book *The Rhetoric of Style* to synthesize and integrate the references journalists from mainstream print media coverage in newspaper and magazines from 1999 to 2004 used to make meaning out of George W. Bush, Al Gore, and John Kerry in ways that coalesced into a coherent and useful framework voters used to guide political deliberation. Presidential masculinity and the aesthetic references at its foundation hopefully offer several larger conceptual lessons related to one of the key constructions of a political rhetoric in the twenty-first century: the rhetoric of style. I hope to capture the relevant themes and patterns that emerge out of the way journalists used style to make sense of each candidate in ways the public responded to. I encourage the reader to be mindful of the way these stylistic dimensions branch out across politics to other areas of deliberation and meaning-making across different texts and experiences.

The Rhetoric of Masculinity

Although being sexed is a necessary part of what it means to be human, how we socially make meaning out of our reproductive organs produces multiple and often competing versions of gendered representations (Jaggar). Gender is never fixed or final, objective or detached, but instead is part of a complex system of symbols used to create, transfer, and advocate who one is and can be as a human being. Therefore, an accurate understanding of masculinity in presidential political discourse acknowledges the significant role rhetoric plays in illuminating the relationship between identity and gender. Masculinity is not a transcendental anchor, but is instead part of a varying confluence of networks that begins with the symbolic and ends with the rhetorical. Whenever masculine-gendered expressions come out as social actions—as in a presidential debate or television commercial for Bud Light—they are mediated through environmental conditions and external contingencies (Whitehead). Like women, men need to define themselves—they can't just *be*. This is because all gendered representations operate as a kind of language relying on the symbolic creation and transference of meaning between a sender and a receiver. Masculinity is a discourse that includes "communication" in the narrow and traditional sense as verbal symbols, vocal sounds, and the grammatical rules governing those sounds, but expands to a rhetorical system that comprises a rich ecology of meaning-making and exchange constructing, organizing, and influencing cultural practices (McCann and Kim).

This broader description of the relationship among gender, rhetoric, and identity moves my inquiry onto the terrain of *style*. To understand the rhetorical function of masculinity and the political and social work it supports, one must see it as a style. Style is a term that both stretches beyond rational discourse and is fundamentally connected to political and social struggle. Style is a socially held symbol system that includes not only oral and written discourse, but also a wide range of rhetorical purposes across the cultural spectrum, such as personal appearance, voice and vocabulary, clothing, body shape and physical size, grooming, costume, tone, timing, sensibility, taste, and manners (Brummett, *A Rhetoric*). This description of style also accounts for the way these aesthetic dimensions are used to organize our social world, particularly how style pulls together actions and objects that define sexual identity and gender. Style is not only read and noticed by others but is also used to call individuals into coherent audiences, publics, and communities. Style is the tool that ultimately activates the subject; it is a referential tool that, consciously or not, allows us to make important judgments about ourselves and others based on aesthetic presentation (Hariman, *Political Style*; Lockford).

Style is fundamental to the performance of gender. As Judith Butler has shown, the meaning-making and meaning-transmitting possibilities of sexuality are deeply embedded in the performance of a stylized body constituting the illusion of a coherently gendered self (Butler, *Performative*). The relationship between the stylized performance of sexuality and the affectively constructed political judgment operates below our critical radar, carrying the weight of ideological pressures on bodies and minds—often without voters even knowing it. In turn, the performance of a particular gendered and sexualized style constructs a coherent identity that allows individuals to be made meaningful and ultimately positioned within our social hierarchy.

Defining style in this way aligns it well with the rhetorical function of masculinity. Style helps an audience read off socially useful information about gendered representations. In other words, style operates as the terrain upon which masculine power is struggled over. Masculinity orders, arranges, and aligns individuals through a rhetoric of exclusion in which identity is created by defining oneself against outgroup members. The rhetoric of exclusion offers men a category in which they can define themselves against what they fear: the effeminate, emasculated, and helpless man. This is done by separating what is masculine from what is feminine and dividing the traits that can be connected to each into dichotomous binaries.

This process lends insight to the general function of identity creation. A secure identity without reference to another group is impossible to maintain. Our identities come together by looking at the certain ways our social affiliations are categorized in relation to surrounding groups from which we are distinct. Accordingly, masculinity depends on a variety of Others for its substance, its characteristics, and its sense of identity. Even if no one knows what being a man is, we like to think we know what being a man is not. Masculinity and exclusivity work together to calm men's deepest doubts about not being fully male by offering men a way to construct an orientation *against* what they most fear becoming. Often this means men define themselves against the effeminate, usually women or gay men. But if exclusivity is the foundation, outsiders can also be constructed out of men who are the wrong color, the wrong social class, from the wrong part of the country, the wrong height, weight, or wear the wrong clothing. Masculinity is always and already defined by exclusion and opposition right from the start (Volli). Consequently, much of our gendered discourse seeks to contain, marginalize, and punish those who adopt the "wrong" style. Gender distinctions are predicated and categorized based on the presence of dissimilar others, often with an important political impact. The political forces structuring social groups today are based on a desire for affiliation that is displayed through similar styles (Maffesoli). In US political discourse, this process is most evident in the rhetorical construction and affirmation of the term *presidential*.

Presidential is an important visual and material component of our political culture that organizes the expectations we have for what our head of state should look and sound like. We consume it on a daily basis, and thus, this style is emotionally charged and always with us, carried around on the back of the one who is to symbolize of our national image. Because social hierarchies of power are largely managed through aesthetic dimensions, *presidential* locates a candidate in social space by virtue of his or her relationships and memberships that this style implies. Taken together, presidential masculinity functions ideologically by producing a set of meanings connected to certain groups and distanced from others. Just as we can read a "hippie style" or a "hipster style" as a certain way of talking, dressing, behaving, and living, there is a system of signs that come together as a rhetorical unit of coherence in presidential masculinity. This system of signs is important because we hold it accountable to representations of reality. Just as we want doctors and police officers to assume a style that reflects their social positions, we want our presidents to do the same. The system of signs that comes together to constitute and reflect presidential masculinity connotes a narrow and specific identity fused together by the most dominant gendered markers.

The Stylistic Dimensions of Presidential Masculinity

Aesthetic Rationales: What Is Attractive and What Is Good

In our larger social milieu, we use the aesthetic as a criterion on which to make many important decisions (Ewen; Postrel). In Barry Brummett's words, what counts as *good* is often that which is aesthetically pleasing (*A Rhetoric*). In politics, the aesthetic dimensions of public presentation play an important role in organizing attitudes, judgments, and behaviors. Understanding why candidates get elected and why bills get passed depends on hairlines and waistlines, as much as policy statements and political experience. Political actors are aware of the effect their aesthetic sensibilities have on voter judgment. The sheer amount of stylistic references attributed to political actors themselves or their handlers indicates how important political actors think style is in crafting their public image in particular ways. Al Gore and John Kerry, for example, were aware of their stylistic deficiencies, and they knew how those deficiencies harmed their ability to connect with voters. Thus, the construction of presidential masculinity begins at the top.

The primacy of aesthetic rationales is made clear in Gore and Kerry's attempts to improve their style. Journalists often referenced failed stylistic attempts and efforts by each candidate to improve. Al Gore, for example, struggled throughout his campaign with stylistic deficiencies. Similarly, John Kerry assumed stylistic deficiencies that George W. Bush did not. Journalists also make the relationship between style and larger assessments about connection and likeability explicit. Here is where sexuality bubbles close to the surface. In contrast, George W. Bush seemed to enjoy a definitive stylistic advantage over his two opponents. For example, Jacob Schlesinger and Jackie Calmes in the *Wall Street Journal* cited a poll that showed Bush leading Kerry 45 percent to 28 percent on who was more "easygoing and likeable" (A4). Schlesinger and Calmes then develop likeability in more detail. They quote pollster John Zogby, who wrote, "Likeability is a very important factor. It means approachability, accessibility, compassion and understanding, all of which are leadership virtues." Schlesinger and Calmes articulate the implications of likeability when they cite polls that show undecided voters are generally dissatisfied with George W. Bush and side with John Kerry on many issues, but they cannot bring themselves to vote for Kerry. Schlesinger and Calmes quote Zogby again when he said undecided voters think Kerry is up to the job intellectually, but they're not sure they can bond with him.

By operating affectively, style functions as a powerful heuristic that often lurks beneath a voter's critical awareness. Journalists, media, and political actors work together to appropriate the symbols of social relations and processes through which the aesthetic is represented in ways that become so deeply integrated into public conversation they become taken for granted, simultaneously validated and hidden from view. In effect, the aesthetic dimensions of politics are largely unacknowledged within our own experience. The relationship between aestheticization and rhetorical engagement is based on implicit movement guided by emotional rather than programmatic logic (Hariman, *Prudence*). This does not mean voters are unaware of style's impact. More accurately, for style to operate below voter's critical radar means they are not as aware of the connection between style and more substantive assessments, such as morality, intelligence, and competence (Brummett, *A Rhetoric*). This is why style can function as the grounding category that pulls together our expressions of language, dress, and nonverbal behavior into a coherent gendered identity.

Primacy of Text—George W. Bush and "George W. Bush"

The heuristic offered by presidential masculinity is particularly well suited to an era in which voters never get to know presidential candidates. Instead, voters look to a set of cultural artifacts that serve as material manifestations of a larger, more abstract symbol system called "George W. Bush." These sets of cultural artifacts are known as *texts*. The text is a primary component of presidential masculinity because the affective heuristics voters rely on to make political decisions are increasingly represented in texts rather than direct experience. The political-actor-turned-text becomes the imaged representation that cuts through political clutter. When a political actor is turned into a text, his or her image serves a cohesive, unifying, and moralizing function that connects with voters. The real-life George W. Bush becomes "George W. Bush the text" through the unification of verbal and visual signs, artifacts, and symbols by which individuals can recognize, share, and cohere around. Voters do not need to know Bush, read the 415 pages of his prescription drug plan, or churn through the legal and moral rationale of his extraordinary rendition program. If he is a text, they have a recognizable symbolic representation they already understand.

George W. Bush's stylistic dominance coheres around a loose collection of references to his affiliation with a masculine western aesthetic. Media coverage concedes that even though Bush, Gore, and Kerry come from wealthy, powerful families, Bush successfully shed the appearance of elitist and out-of-touch through this style. His opponents could not. Several articles reference George W. Bush's use of aesthetic to draw a sharp distinction between him and his father. Nicholas Kristof wrote that George H.W. Bush taught George W. Bush what to avoid on the campaign trail (A-20). Kristof wrote that Bush "is campaigning this year as the anti-Dad. His campaign organization has a beyond-the-beltway, down-home Texan feel to it that his father's did not." Kristof continued, "For all his father's efforts to enjoy pork rinds and boycott broccoli, George W. Bush has a far more natural Bubba quality to him. More than his father, he genuinely seems delighted by the chance to work crowds. George W. Bush comes across as by nature remarkably cheerful, relaxed and free of neurosis or inner conflict." Al Gore's style is described in aesthetic terms that cohere around themes related to boring, stiff, dull, and robotic. Similar stylistic deficiencies harmed John Kerry.

Cataloguing the stylistic dimensions that turned Bush, Gore, and Kerry into a "text" helps contribute to a richer understanding of how political actors, media, and voters interact. It seems that textual constructions must fall within a particular frame of intelligibility and permitted meanings that are pieced together, in part, out of the aesthetic dimensions listed above. From these examples, we have a better understanding of how style turns political actors into texts. We also have a better understanding of the sexualized terrain on which certain discourses carry ideological potency into the public sphere.

Imaginary Communities: Turning Individuals into Voting Blocs

In presidential politics, the success of a particular textual construction hinges on turning an imaginary community into a significant voting bloc. Aesthetic dimensions work together to produce a textual version of political actors that explains, in part, political potency. More broadly, presidential masculinity explains how political actors may attempt to create a community of voters hailed by specific aesthetic artifacts. These artifacts are contingent upon a number of variables. However, some clear patterns emerge across these candidates that reveal a consistent set of primary aesthetic dimensions, including hair and grooming, body shape, gesture, and posture, and voice and vocabulary.

For example, George W. Bush successfully leveraged his masculine western aesthetic in a way that resonated with a dominant media frame related to confidence and competence. Jonathan Raban in the *Financial Times* called Bush a man "at home in his own skin" (16). Taft Wireback for the *Greensboro News Record* wrote that George W. Bush "looked natural during the Boston debate" with Al Gore (A6). Julia Keller wrote that Bush demanded a less formal, sit-down debate with Al Gore because "the more conversational ambience would favor the Texas governor's laid-back demeanor" (5.1). Finally, Dave Harmon writing in the *Austin American Statesman* quoted a political scientist who reviewed a Bush/Gore debate by saying, "There was a plastic quality to (Gore), and I thought Bush was much more natural" (A10).

George W. Bush was able to use his unique voice and vocabulary, including his folksy accent, fragmented grammar, and imprecise word choice to connect with voters in a way that seemed to be more appealing than Gore or Kerry. The rhetorical force of creating an imaginary community comes from a shared method of noticing and responding to these stylistic dimensions (Brummett, *A Rhetoric;* Winslow, *The Imaged*). Audiences congeal around a shared reading. It is the cohesive nature of aesthetic references that allows a certain hairstyle or an endearing verbal miscue to act as a unifying center pulling together diffused identities into collective groups. The rhetoric of style ultimately focuses on the product of the interpellation process: the construction and affirmation of ordering mechanisms and the hierarchies of power they prop up. People do in fact make attributions about social relationships and identity markers like sexuality and gender based on aesthetic textual representations (Ewen; Hebdige). Through this process, categories are marked, experiences are organized, values are affirmed, and political functions are performed.

Implications and Conclusions

A set of further questions and future directions are prompted by these findings. First, this chapter hopefully encourages continued inquiry into the way sexual rhetorical practices work in relation to the unique peculiarities of the US voter. Cynically, the features of US political discourse discussed here reveal a polity that can lack humility in what can be confidently known for certain, nuance in understanding the complexity of modern political life, and the mindfulness necessary for a healthy democracy. The concern—if these voting behaviors spread—is that more US voters will adopt the primary characteristic of the worst kind of public citizen: the know-it-all who knows very little. Presidential masculinity functions as one powerful source for creation of this type of voter. Future research should aim to identify other symbolic resources that work together with our affective heuristics to simplify political judgments and allow voters to navigate an increasingly complex political landscape.

Second, this chapter encourages future research on the relationship between style and audience. We know that style works *with* audiences, not *on* them. Future research should continue to explore the relationship among rhetoric, style, and social orientations. In political discourse, these relationships are marked by the declining institutional strength of political parties in ordering and categorizing voter attitudes, the increased personalization of politics fueled by candidate-centered campaign paradigms that emphasize the individual candidate's persona and personal attributes, and the decline of blatant forms of sexual bigotry in mainstream political discourse. Hillary Clinton's widely anticipated presidential candidacy in 2016 will surely bring these issues into public conversation in theoretically valuable and political urgent ways.

Third, this chapter encourages future research on framing. We know that scholars from a variety of disciplines—including political science, journalism, and communication and rhetorical studies—have looked closely at how issues and events are framed (see Entman; D'Angelo and Kuypers; Reese, Gandy, and Grant). This line of research could now benefit from further exploration into the gendered framing of individual political actors. This may involve more scholarship on the relationship between framing and the visual. Although it is clear that the visual is an important site for the construction of meaning, much of our attention focuses on verbal, cognitive, and content-level messages, which in turn leaves us with a limited explanation of one of the most important social touchstones of our day (Entman; Hariman, *Political Style*; Sartwell; Vivian).

Finally, this chapter encourages further exploration into the role of constitutive rhetoric in the twenty-first century. One of Kenneth Burke's many contributions to the state of contemporary rhetorical studies was his ability to document how rhetoric moved from a traditionally *referential* function (the rhetoric of Aristotle and Cicero in which an audience is assumed to be given and a rhetor appeal to an audience in an attempt to create effects) to a *constitutive* function (in which rhetoric carves out an audience as a result of rhetoric) (see also Brummett *A Rhetoric*). Burke's observation is all the more salient in our fragmented and heterogeneous milieu. As I have tried to do here with presidential masculinity, future research illuminating the process by which sexualized aesthetic rationales constitute particular audiences would lend important insights into who we are and what we value.

Works Cited

Brummett, Barry. *A Rhetoric of Style*. Carbondale: Southern Illinois UP, 2008. Print.
———. *Rhetorical Homologies: Form, Culture, and Experience*. Tuscaloosa: U of Alabama P, 2004. Print.

Bruni, Frank. "America the Clueless." *New York Times* 12 May 2013: Print.
Burke, Kenneth. *A Rhetoric of Motives*. Berkeley: U of California P, 1950. Print.
Butler, Judith. *Gender Trouble: Feminism and the Subversion of Identity*. New York: Routledge, 1990. Print.
———. "Performative Acts and Gender Constitution: An Essay in Phenomenology and Feminist Theory." *Feminist Theory Reader: Local and Global Perspectives*. Eds. Carole R. McCann and Seung-Kyung Kim. New York: Routledge, 2003. 416–27. Print.
Campbell, Karlyn Kohrs. "The Sound of Women's Voices." *Quarterly Journal of Speech, 75*, (1989): 212–20. Print.
Caplan, Bryan. *The Myth of the Rational Voter. Why Democracies Choose Bad Policies*. Princeton, NJ: Princeton UP, 2007. Print.
Crenshaw, Carrie. "Women in the Gulf War: Toward an Intersectional Feminist Rhetorical Criticism." *Howard Journal of Communication* 8 (1997): 219–35. Print.
Crenshaw, Kimberle. "Mapping the Margins: Intersectionality, Identity Politics, and Violence Against Women of Color." *Stanford Law Review* 43 (1991): 1241–99. Print.
Dace, Karen L. "Had Judas Been a Black Man … Politics, Race, and Gender in African America." *Judgment Calls: Rhetoric, Politics, and Indeterminacy*. Ed. John M. Sloop and James P. McDaniel. Boulder, CO: Westview, 1998. 163–81. Print.
D'Angelo, Paul, and Jim A. Kuypers. *Doing News Framing Analysis: Empirical and Theoretical Perspectives*. New York: Routledge, 2010. Print.
Eagleton, Terry. *Ideology: An Introduction*. London, Verso, 1991. Print.
Entman, Robert. *Projections of Power: Framing News, Public Opinion, and U.S. Foreign Policy*. Chicago: U of Chicago P, 2004. Print.
Ewen, Stuart. *All Consuming Images: The Politics of Style in Contemporary Culture*. New York: Basic, 1988, Print.
Guillaumin, Collette. *Racism, Sexism, Ideology, and Power*. London: Routledge, 1995. Print.
Hariman, Robert. *Political Style: The Artistry of Power*. Chicago: U of Chicago P, 1995. Print.
Hariman, Robert, ed. *Prudence, Classical Virtue, Postmodern Practice*. University Park: Pennsylvania State UP, 2001. Print.
Harmon, Dave. "Analysts: Call It a Draw, With Both Showing Strengths." *Austin American Statesman* 4 Oct. 2000: A10. Web. 20 Apr. 2015.
Hebdige, Dick. *Subculture*. London: Methuen, 1979. Print.
Jaggar, Alison. *Feminist Politics and Human Nature*. Totowa, NJ: Rowman & Littlefield, 1988, Print.
Keller, Julia. "Sit and Deliver." *Chicago Tribune* 11 Oct. 2000: 5.1. Web. 20 April 2015.
Kristof, Nicholas D. "Living in His Father's Shadow Has Helped Shape George W. Bush." *Pittsburgh Post – Gazette* 29 Oct. 2000: A-20. Web.
Lockford, Lesa. *Performing Femininity: Rewriting Gender Identity*. Lanham, MD: AltaMira, 2004. Print.
Lupia, Arthur, and Matthew McCubbins. *The Democratic Dilemma: Can Citizens Learn What They Need to Know?* New York: Cambridge UP, 1998. Print.
Maffesoli, Michel. *The Contemplation of the World: Figures of Community Style*. Trans. Susan Emanuel. Minneapolis: U of Minnesota P, 1996. Print.

Malin, Brenton. *American Masculinity Under Clinton: Popular Media and the Nineties "Crisis of Masculinity."* New York: Peter Lang, 2005. Print.

McCann, Carole R., and Seung-Kyung Kim, eds. *Feminist Theory Reader: Local and Global Perspectives.* New York: Routledge, 2003. Print.

Morreale, Joanne. *The Presidential Campaign Film.* Westport, CT: Praeger, 1993. Print.

Parry-Giles, Shawn. J., and Trevor Parry-Giles. "Gendered Politics and Presidential Image Construction: A Reassessment of the 'Feminine Style.'" *Communication Monographs,* 63 (1996): 337–53. Print.

Popkin, Samuel. *The Reasoning Voter: Communication and Persuasion in Presidential Campaigns.* Chicago: U of Chicago P, 1996. Print.

Postrel, Virginia. *The Substance of Style: How the Rise of Aesthetic Value Is Remaking Commerce, Culture, and Consciousness.* New York: HarperCollins, 2003. Print.

Raban, Jonathan. "Man of the People: Bill Clinton Brought Huggability to the US Presidency." *Financial Times* [London] 18 Nov. 2000: 16. Web. 20 Apr. 2015.

Reese, Stephen. D., Oscar H. Gandy, and August E. Grant, eds. *Framing Public Life: Perspectives on Media and Understanding Our World.* Mahwah, NJ: Erlbaum, 2001. Print.

Sartwell, Crispin. *Political Aesthetics.* Ithaca, NY: Cornell UP, 2010. Print.

Schlesinger, Jacob M., and Jackie Calmes. "In Bush vs. Kerry, Part II, Style Matters; Town-Hall Debate Offers President, Challenger Chance to Connect Directly to Voters." *Wall Street Journal* 8 Oct. 2004: A4. Web. 20 Apr. 2015.

Traister, Bryce. "Academic Viagra: The Rise of American Masculinity Studies." *American Quarterly,* 52 (2000): 274–304. Print.

Vivian, Bradford. "Style, Rhetoric, and Postmodern Culture." *Philosophy and Rhetoric* 35 (2002): 223–42. Print.

Volli, Ugo. "Odysseus and Male Cunning: Myths and Images of Masculinity in Western Culture." *Material Man: Masculinity, Sexuality, Style.* Ed. Giannino Malossi. New York: Harry N. Abrams, 2000. 114–21. Print.

Wahl-Jorgensen, Karin. "Constructing Masculinities in U.S. Presidential Campaigns: The Case of 1991." *Gender, Politics, and Communication* Eds. Annabelle and Liesbet van Zoonen. Cresskill, NJ: Hampton, 1999. 53–70. Print.

Whitehead, Steven M. *Men and Masculinities: Key Themes and New Directions.* Malden, MA: Polity, 2002. Print.

Winslow, Luke. "The Imaged Other: Style and Substance in the Rhetoric of Joel Osteen." *Southern Communication Journal,* 79.3 (2014): 250–71. Print.

———. "Promise Keepers and the Rhetoric of the Stylized Other." *Journal of Communication and Religion* 35.1 (2012): 69–104. Print.

Wireback, Taft. "Few Changes Expected in Wake Debate." *Greensboro News Record* [Greensboro, NC] 8 Oct. 2000: A6. Web. 20 Apr. 2015.

18 Liberal Humanist "Rights" Discourse and Sexual Citizenship

Harriet Malinowitz

In the United States, the notion of rights and fairness is at the very core of our national identity. By asserting that national goods and entitlements have been denied them, LGBT people have done two crucial things in one move: they have framed discrimination against them as a fundamental flaw in the system (which all rational citizens would agree must be remedied), and they have also *performed* their status as authentic Americans, in that they clearly hold constitutional truths to be both self-evident and just.

The mainstream lesbian and gay rights movement works toward legal and social acceptance of homosexuals on the grounds that queers, like heterosexual people, are—or strive to be—"normal" actors in the symbology and practices of everyday life. Within this desire and attainment of normality lies the very conception of "citizenship." There are different sorts of citizenship. Here I am concerned with the distinction between *legal* citizenship—based in a constitutionally-grounded notion of "rights" and reserved for those either born into that privilege or those who enter it by swearing their loyalty to the nation and its ideology—and *cultural* citizenship, which relies on one's relationship, or claim, to the symbols and meanings that define the nation. Cultural citizenship preserves pluralism and multiculturalism to the extent that such will not disrupt the master narrative of cohesive national identity and the unalloyed American brand. It is an essential characteristic of M&Ms, after all, that they encompass a variety of colors, though they must be identical in all other ways. In the United States, it is in the realm of cultural citizenship that one becomes authorized—or not—as a *real* American within the national imagination. This authorization becomes fundamental to whether or not one can actually lay claim to material legal entitlements. Thus, dissidents or any who do not endorse, identify with, perform, or otherwise incarnate national ideologies consequently find themselves off the grid of "equal opportunity." So may anyone who simply does not *appear* to personify canonical national values, such as Islamists, the homeless, non-English-speakers, prostitutes, and non-seatbelt-wearers. At its most serious level, cultural citizenship distinguishes those citizens who are seen as deserving the protection of police from those who are murdered by them with impunity.

The Constitution, on which our notion of "rights" is based, is certainly an ambiguous symbol in itself, representing at once the fundamental values

Americans profess to revere and the meddlesome government they want to shrink. The LGBT movement, like most other modern movements for social justice and equality, has molded its "rights" discourse, derived from that Constitution, according to the template established by the black civil rights movement of the 1950s and 1960s. In this schema, via a massive act of social persuasion which essentially involves hoisting the status quo on its own petard, those who have been outliers in the matrix of American democracy become those whose *inclusion* in the matrix is considered to be the very embodiment of American democracy.

The rightness of "rights" achieves widespread recognition and sympathy through various (often sentimentalized) vehicles of symbolization. One of these rights I would describe as "the brave act of defiance"—standing up for what one knows (laws notwithstanding) to be a basic, or "natural," entitlement. This move is most famously embodied by the fable of Rosa Parks, who is configured in popular accounts as a heroine of impulse, stripped of her activist acumen and strategic plan. The LGBT movement doesn't have any such individual heroic figure except perhaps for celebrities in highly publicized coming-out events (Ellen DeGeneres, Laverne Cox, Michael Sam); our iconic turning point was the group-generated event of Stonewall.

Another, and contrasting, vehicle through which "rights" are symbolized I would describe as "the spectacle of cruel and unusual victimization of the innocent." In the black civil rights movement, this symbolization was embodied perhaps most flagrantly by the four girls killed in the Birmingham church bombing; in the LGBT movement, it was the tortured and slain body of 21-year-old gay student Matthew Shepard from the University of Wyoming.

In 1998, Richard Goldstein argued in the *Village Voice* that Matthew Shepard's killing resonated with the imagery of a lynching:

> As in a lynching, Shepard's body was strung up as if the killers intended it to be displayed. ... And just as the rationale for lynching is typically some sexual transgression on the victim's part, Shepard's accused killers gave police the classic justification for antigay violence: they said he had come on to them. (67)

In *Vanity Fair,* Melanie Thernstrom called Shepard's killing a "crucifixion" (as did others, such as religious philosopher Gracia Fay Ellwood). These accounts led many to envision Shepard dying in a Christ-like position, although in actuality he was left almost horizontally on a fence just inches off the ground, his hands tied behind him (Wypijewski). But these representations also miss a much more urgent breach of the martyrdom story: a 2013 book by award-winning gay journalist Stephen Jimenez revealed that Shepard was a crystal meth addict and dealer who had had both drug and sexual trafficking associations with at least one of his killers—and that therein lay, at least in part, the key to the motive behind the murder. In a most starkly disillusioning way, the death turned out not to tell the lesson it had been groomed to do. Still, its widely interpreted poignancy gave birth and a name—along with that of James Byrd, Jr., a black man who was killed by white supremacists in another grisly 1998 act—to landmark national hate crimes legislation. As a *Wall Street Journal* review excerpt blurbed on the paperback edition succinctly put it, *The Book of Matt: Hidden Truths about the Murder of Matthew Shepard* "shows how a desire for Manichaean morality tales can lead us to oversimplify the human experience."

Many in the LGBT community did not receive the news well. Neal Broverman, in an Op-ed for *The Advocate* called "Why I'm Not Reading the 'Trutherism' about Matt Shepard," sulked that revealing the true facts about the "fragile and adorable" Shepard felt "lurid and cruel," and he wondered, "[W]eren't there more worthy tales to pick apart?" On the other hand, gay rights activist John Stoltenberg, while acknowledging that burnishing Matt's innocent image had been "the agenda of many gay-movement leaders," pointed out quite aptly: "Ignoring the tragedies of Matthew's life prior to his murder will do nothing to help other young men of our community who are sold for sex, ravaged by drugs, and generally exploited. They will remain invisible and lost" (quoted in Bindel). To wit: there have been no hate crimes bills named for Eddie Northington, the gay, HIV-positive, homeless, frequently obnoxious, 39-year-old alcoholic who was beheaded in Richmond, Virginia, in 1999. Nor has his murder been classified as a hate crime, his name become known in the LGBT community, or his murderer found. Guy Trebay wrote in *The Village Voice* that following his death, "there were no angry protests in Richmond, no handbill campaigns, no demonstrators from the capital city's sizeable gay population taking to the streets in rage." He points out that Northington's severed head was discovered in a city park where the police had been busting cruising gay men in a venture called Operation Park Clean Up, and suggests that it may have been found elsewhere but relocated to the park for effect. "It occurs to me," he writes, "that hierarchies of worthlessness are deployed in order to render the killing of Eddie Northington an anomaly, another unsolvable episode in the ongoing Grand Guignol of the South." Legal scholar Ruthann Robson makes a similar point when she talks about the predicament of lesbian criminal defendants: "The pursuit of equality has a rhetorical inconsistency with criminality," she writes. "By focusing on equality, the lesbian and gay civil rights movement has sought to present images of what I call 'but for' lesbians, who, 'but for' their lesbianism, are 'perfect.' These 'but for' images of lesbians are intended to contradict the pathological depictions of lesbians advanced by conservatives" (181). Lesbian felons, such as serial killer Aileen Wuornos, are not generally draped under the rainbow flag in Pride tableaux to the strains of Sister Sledge's "We Are Family," notwithstanding the discrimination they may face as lesbians.

In any case, Matthew Shepard "hate crime" imagery and metaphors, whether overtly articulated or symbolically suggested, can only be persuasive to mass audiences once those audiences are *already* inclined to believe that the lynched or crucified body represents the victim, not the justly avenged cause, of social rupture. And they are generally inclined to believe this only after a long, slow paradigm shift has taken place. This paradigm shift involves an alteration in metaphorical status for members of a despised group: they must cease to be metaphors of pollution which would threaten the health of the polity and instead become metaphors of the polity itself. They must signify, that is, the very *essence* of the polity so that fellow citizens will view them as collaborators in staving off yet other pollutants that threaten from the outside.

This notion is integral to a phenomenon that feminist/queer/ethnic studies scholar Jasbir K. Puar has called *homonationalism,* or "homonormative nationalism" (38): a process involving "homosexual sexual exceptionalism," in which certain "domesticated homosexual bodies" (4) are featured in the national imaginary to promote an image of Western modernity and enlightenment. In this Orientalist schema, the putatively forward-thinking, democratic, inclusive state sparkles against a backdrop of crude and lewd Muslim savagery; Western "tolerance" is a beacon of hope for otherwise abject "others" who would most likely suffer beheading in the boorish Eastern backwaters of the planet. (Ironically, cases such as Eddie Northington's are simply photoshopped out of the picture; Americans almost by definition don't behead gay people.) Queers of a certain acceptable sort become the West's new fetish objects in the "clash of civilizations." The spectacle of erstwhile outsiders publicly enthusing about their insiderhood affords the ultimate endorsement of mainstream American values. Meanwhile, the spectacle of the conservators of national ideology embracing the enthusiastic erstwhile outsiders affords the ultimate certification of their liberal, democratic humanism.

Gay Rights and Liberal Democracy

The conventional argument for gay rights was summed up by Michael Nava and Robert Dawidoff in their 1994 book *Created Equal: Why Gay Rights Matter to America.* The authors state that the basic, cumulatively logical arguments that support the contention of their title—that gay rights *matter to America,* not just to gays—are these: that the purpose of American constitutional government is the protection of individual rights; gays and lesbians, as American citizens, are entitled to the exercise of those rights, but they are denied it on spurious grounds rooted in ignorance and bias; the organized opponents of gay rights aim to substitute sectarian religious morality in place of constitutional guarantees; and these forces are using the issue of gay rights as a test case in order to promote a broader agenda, the purpose of which is to limit individuality itself (xii). Thus, to be anti-gay is to be anti-American. Or, as gay legal scholar Richard Mohr has put it, "Liberalism makes moral sense of gay issues; gay issues make moral sense of liberalism" (5). By the second decade of the twenty-first century, as caterers and wedding planners around the country cash in on same-sex nuptials and *Heather Has Two Mommies* has morphed into the aphorism "Heather Has Two Genders" (Gurdon), this notion has certainly come of age.

The "liberalism" that gay rights arguments invoke has its roots in natural rights and social contract theory (Hobbes, Locke, Rousseau), Kantian ethics, Mill's "greatest happiness principle," and those ideologies' adaptation, amalgamation, and rearticulation by the U.S. Founding Fathers. But as legal philosopher Morris Kaplan, author of *Sexual Justice: Democratic Citizenship and the Politics of Desire* has detailed, there are three subcategories to the gay "rights" argument that actually create "divergent strands" of the movement.

The first subcategory Kaplan describes is focused on the argument for "decriminalization of homosexual activities between consenting adults" (14). This was the focus of overturning the "sodomy laws," and its constitutional basis lies in what many have called the "right to privacy" (though no such right is explicitly articulated in the Constitution). It found its ultimate expression, and hit its ultimate wall, in the ill-fated *Bowers v. Hardwick* case of 1986.

In fact, the majority ruling's rationale for overturning *Bowers* in the *Lawrence v. Texas* decision of 2003 addressed, instead, Kaplan's second subcategory of "rights" arguments, which are concerned with "the prohibition of discrimination against lesbians and gays in employment, housing, education, and public accommodations" (14). This is a "civil rights" argument that places lesbians and gays squarely within the tradition established by other minorities and the Civil Rights Acts of 1964 and 1968 by appealing to the Equal Protection Clause of the Fourteenth Amendment (15). This was the issue that came to national prominence via the 1992 anti-gay referenda in Oregon and Colorado; and it was Colorado's Amendment 2 that the Supreme Court struck down as unconstitutional in 1996 by a six-to-three majority in *Romer V. Evans,* citing its relegation of homosexuals to "second-class citizenship" (159).

The third subcategory of the "rights" argument, according to Kaplan, concerns "the legal and social recognition of the ethical status of lesbian and gay relationships and community institutions" (14). At specific issue here are, among other things, same-sex marriage and domestic partnership, health insurance benefits, hospital visiting and medical decision-making privileges, child custody and adoption, the legitimization of lesbian and gay organizations in schools and within professions, and the right for queers to gather unharassed in public social spaces.

It is worth mentioning that the *Lawrence v. Texas* ruling, one of the most pivotal events emblematizing the historic "progress" of the LGBT "rights" movement, sits beside the Matthew Shepard ur-"hate crime" in the annals of LGBT apocrypha. Minneapolis law professor Dale Carpenter disclosed what actually happened in his book *Flagrant Conduct: The Story of Lawrence v. Texas,* which received a good deal of praise when it came out in 2012. In a felicitous comedy of errors, John Geddes Lawrence and Tyron Garner were busted in a Houston apartment on September 17, 1998 for the crime of sodomy in Lawrence's bedroom. Yet they apparently had *not* been having sex, were not lovers, knew each other only minimally, and were not even in the same room when the police burst in—though they both were gay and were having a rather rowdy, intoxicated evening. They were persuaded by gay civil rights activists to change their plea from "not guilty" (which would probably have been successful, given the flimsiness of the charge against them) to "no contest" in order to become plaintiffs in a bigger case for the greater good. This required keeping their real identities largely hidden from public view. As Dahlia Lithwick wrote in her review of Carpenter's book in *The New Yorker*:

> The story told in *Lawrence v. Texas* was a story of sexual privacy, personal dignity, intimate relationships, and shifting notions of family in America. ... Lawrence and Garner understood that they were being asked to keep the dirty secret that there was no dirty secret. ... In order to appeal to the conservative Justices on the high court, the story of a booze-soaked quarrel was repackaged as a love story.

Gay "Rights"-Based Arguments of the 1990s

High-profile LGBT advocates during the publicity boom of the Gay Nineties capitalized enormously on the discourses of rights and fairness. Melinda Paras, Executive Director of the National Lesbian and Gay Task Force and Policy Institute from 1995 to 1996, advocated using the notions of "fairness" and "compassion" to gain mainstream sympathy and support for lesbian and gay rights because, she said, these words strike a powerful chord in the American psyche; they invoke American ideals of democracy and freedom that we have held since our inception as a nation. Paras contended that even people who profess religious objections to homosexuality may be disarmed enough to counter an anti-gay ballot initiative if we say things like, "You and your partner are allowed to marry and raise children together; my partner and I aren't, even though we love each other and are in a totally committed, permanent relationship. Is that fair?"

Paras—whose appointment to head the Task Force was heavily contested by gay conservatives because of her affiliation with Marxist organizations in the past—was ironically advocating the very rhetoric that gay conservatives were simultaneously propounding. Also in the mid-1990s, Richard Tafel, executive director of the gay conservative Log Cabin Republican Club, was on the speaking circuit explaining that the goal of the Log Cabin Club was "equality"—that is, to have gays treated the same way as others. He said: "When people understand us and we understand them, we'll have equality. We just need to think of the world as those we've educated versus those we haven't educated." Like Paras, he asserted that the American people are fundamentally *fair*—and that when they are educated about an injustice, they will inevitably sympathize with those who are wronged.

Conservative gay writer Bruce Bawer's 1993 book, *A Place at the Table: The Gay Individual in American Society,* was a much-publicized pitch for gay acceptance which appealed to the "integrity" of traditional Americana, capitalism, assimilation, and nuclear family values, and rejected what Bawer called "the gay subculture" and "the multicultural mindset." Bawer, who pointedly identified himself as "a monogamous, churchgoing Christian" (25) and part of "the 'silent majority' of homosexuals" (26), drew on examples of gay goodness (and purportedly inadvertent lapses in mainstream fairness) such as the case of James Dale, the Boy Scout who didn't lie about his homosexuality because he'd taken an oath to be trustworthy: "[I]nstead of being honored for his courage and rectitude," wrote Bawer, "and recognized on this account as a superb role model for gay and straight boys alike, he was ejected [from his troop]" (67). Meanwhile, Bawer lambasted what he called "the far-left political correctness crowd," composed of those he said were "prejudiced against whites and males," who "increasingly control the humanities and social science departments of America's universities and local politics in places like New York City" (45), and who irritatingly "tie gay rights to other issues to which it has no natural relation" (47)—such as racism, sexism, and classism.

Yet Bawer, like Tafel, located his appeal within the old liberal tenets of "fairness" and "compassion," which are themselves rooted in the belief that a despised group is in fact abject and harmless, eager to comply with the rules of the dominant culture, and above all, *similar* to others in that culture—their difference being only chimerical, after all:

> If the heterosexual majority ever comes to accept homosexuality, it will do so because it has seen homosexuals in suits and ties, not nipple clamps and bike pants; it will do so because it has seen homosexuals showing respect for civilization, not attempting to subvert it. (51)

The central contradiction of Bawer's argument, of course, was that he appealed to the heterosexual majority to be fair to a homosexual minority who was just like them, while simultaneously exhorting the homosexual minority to *become* just like the majority who, apparently, they did not yet adequately resemble.

Urvashi Vaid, a predecessor of Melinda Paras's at the helm of the Task Force, and like Paras, a controversial figure because she is a woman of color with an allegedly "radical" agenda in a movement too often controlled by the wealth of powerful gay white men, published in 1995 her book, *Virtual Equality: The Mainstreaming of Lesbian and Gay Liberation.* Vaid, in a move reminiscent of Bawer (though from a very different angle), fell away from some of the radical positions she started out promulgating—her argument, on one level at least, was for a more grassroots-based, left, feminist, multiracial queer politics—and into the mainstream center, which again was defined by "fairness." She did begin by contending that the civil rights-based "legitimation" (or mainstreaming) model of change that provided the dominant framework for persuasive discourse aimed at straight society wouldn't get gays and lesbians very far. If they were to learn from their predecessor movements—mainly the black civil rights and women's movements—they would see that "rights" alone bring *access* to courts, but not the eradication of the prejudice that led us to take our grievances there to begin with.

Yet Vaid also made repeated overtures to popular American sensibilities. "Morality" remained, in her book, entwined with religious discourse, albeit more benign than the "rights" version; and gays and lesbians in the military during the Gulf War were described as "willing to serve their nation." She envisioned an "intersectional" queer politics deeply informed by race, class, and gender issues, yet she also homogenized and idealized the queer community, engaging on its own terms the very mainstream she claimed to want to transform. She offered statements such as: "Gay and lesbian people embrace the most welcoming and pluralistic notions of American democracy ... we are ourselves a moral people, of a wide variety of religious faiths, anchored by values to which we feel deeply bound: values of freedom, equality, inclusion and justice" (26–27). Vaid, like her Republican colleagues, well knew that the American mainstream wouldn't really believe the more nonconformist members of the queer community to be deserving of their "fairness" and "compassion"—and so, like those colleagues, she "fronted" those members with other members who were mainstream in all ways except for their queerness.

Another public spokesperson for lesbians and gays in the 1990s, former *New Republic* editor and hawker of centrist rationality Andrew Sullivan, articulated in his 1995 book *Virtually Normal* a vision that capitalized on liberalism's public–private dichotomization: homophobes would be left to enjoy and deploy their *personal* bigotry, while the state would have to enforce equality in the public sphere. The most significant gains for lesbians and gays, in his view, would be "equal opportunity and inclusion in the military; and legal homosexual marriage and divorce" (171–72). Marriage, he said, is "the highest public recognition of personal integrity" (179), and gay marriage is "a profoundly humanizing, traditionalizing step" (185). He called the military ban a stark example of the government's "unfairness" in that it withheld recognition for valorous acts and forced people to be dishonest (173). Yet he admitted that the politics of representation, which are not always amenable to reason, do have an enormous impact on public policy:

> Prohibitionists ... won the military issue because of its symbolic power. The acceptance of open homosexuals at the heart of the state, at the core of the notion of patriotism, is anathema to those who wish to consign homosexuals to the margins of society. (174–75)

Of course, this changed. Prompted by a range of stimuli—from the courts to television studios to people "coming out" to family, coworkers, and neighbors—incremental shifts in public opinion propelled institutions and legal bodies to chip away at old homophobic prejudices (displacing them with Islamophobic ones and, no doubt, others). Which brings us back to the notion of *homonationalism*: at this point, to be pro-gay *is* to be patriotic; that is, white, gay American people have been spooned into the putative melting pot where they too now baste in the special sauce distinguishing them from the benighted, the barbarians, and, of course, the beheaders.

The Persuasive Power of Symbols and the Construction of the "Cultural Citizen"

The power of symbolism is, I believe, the Achilles heel of the "fairnesss" argument. Laws, after all, are formulated and adopted according to popular sentiments and perceptions, and these are molded by elements within the technically "private" realm, those that Althusser calls "ideological state apparatuses"—religious groups, workplaces, trade unions, the media, the arts, the family, and so on. It is because of these sentiments and perceptions that we have seen crime bills, welfare reform legislation, anti-immigrant legislation, the Patriot Act, Obamacare, gun laws, green policies, anti-gay marriage acts—and ultimately, pro-gay bills, acts, and rulings, as well as more anti-immigrant legislation—surge quickly to the top of the US domestic agenda.

Liberal humanist rhetoric figures heavily in the creation of those sentiments and perceptions, consistently focusing on ways that we are all really the same, ergo deserving of equal rights as citizens. Blurring differences, they overlook the ambiguity inherent in the notion of "citizenship" itself. Ostensibly a stable (and thus emotionally reassuring) term invested with notions of guaranteed rights and entitlements, the claims of "citizenship" rest precariously on a presumed (yet nonexistent) fixity and homogeneity within and among the individual selves that comprise a society. Though "pluralism" is commonly held to be a democratic value, pluralistic society is limited by its tolerance only for established social groups that it *already* recognizes as coherent, if somewhat odd, configurations. Tolerance does not extend to groups molded outside the master cultural template who don't conform in some recognizable way to dominant social principles. Thus, for instance, the mainstream gay rights movement has worked toward legal and social acceptance of homosexuals on the grounds that, just like heterosexual people, they have desires to live within monogamous nuclear families, worship in the church or synagogue of their choice, aspire to conventional middle-class lives, and/or express their patriotism through military service. But in fact, many homosexuals *and* heterosexuals desire promiscuity, solitude, or childlessness; are atheists, Muslims, Buddhists, or Pagans; cannot imagine working within the exploitative conditions of corporate capitalist structures (sometimes because their communities have received the brunt of that exploitation—by virtue of having provided inadequately compensated labor, or having endured practices such as toxic waste dumping, uranium mining, land and fishing rights violations, union busting, foreign trade agreements, or outsourcing); or are deeply opposed to the chronic policing projects of the US military (sometimes because they have immigrated from, or have family in, countries that we have ravaged). Among the ranks of both homosexuals *and* heterosexuals may be found drug addicts, thieves, child molesters, tax cheaters, perjurers, fake faith healers, drunks, and Mafioso.

Yet all of this seems to have little effect on popular liberal LGBT rights discourse. Neither do mainstream LGBT rights advocates suggest that "homosexuals" and "heterosexuals" are quite often not discrete categories, though we are boxed, census-like, into them.

The notion of "citizenship" elides these unruly realities, implicitly invoking instead a generic person with a legal claim to an equal share of certain material, political, and moral resources. "Citizenship" suggests factuality, not indeterminacy. Yet the facts of legal citizenship do not necessarily correspond to the different narratives of cultural and political citizenship which many citizens of this country have told. Citizens remain distinctly unequal in their claims—and access—to the symbols and meanings that define the United States, as well as to the cultural heritage of the United States. Certain groups automatically receive, while others have to fight for, access to the powers that be. Certainly monetary, linguistic, educational, and affiliative resources are necessary in order to access the legal system. Yet who even imagines that he or she has the "right" to claim legal redress for unfairness or mistreatment? Who imagines that the narrative that he or she tells will hold cultural legitimacy, enter public discourse, wield persuasive power, find a place within the logic wherein the "common good" is determined? Who does (and who doesn't) imagine oneself to be an integral part of the whole? Who is (and who isn't) depicted in official and cultural representations of citizenship? Who is (and who isn't) considered to be a "good American" or a "real American"? Who will a jury believe, and who will it condemn or acquit? Whose videotaped murder can a grand jury watch and yet not believe anything indictable happened?

These questions of membership and entitlement determine how knowledge is constructed in particular spheres via the meanings and symbols that shape public life. For example, at LGBT pride marches, there is always some haggling over the order (and even inclusion) of particular contingents. What sort of message does the spectacle of Dykes on Bikes first, accompanied by Scouts for Equality, the Gay Officers Action League, the American Cancer Society, the New York Civil Liberties Union, Diet Coke, and Delta Airlines— with others lined up for miles behind—send to onlookers and participants in New York City? Will the inclusion of the Butch/Femme Society, the Leather Pride Contingent, and the Chelsea Manning Support Network fuel right-wing fundamentalist scare tactics? Will the presence of P-FLAG, Gotham

Volleyball, Wal-Mart, Netflix, couples exchanging wedding vows on floats, churches, politicians, banks and insurance companies, museums, colleges, union locals, and the fire department deflate the fears that are raised? How do the choices to march, to be a cheering spectator, to stare blankly from far back on the sidewalk, to visually sign gay pride slogans in a Rainbow Alliance of the Deaf contingent, to stand in front of St. Patrick's Cathedral with a sign that says, "Sodomites Will Go to Hell," to wear a t-shirt that says, "I love my lesbian daughter," or to roll oneself down Fifth Avenue in a wheelchair stickered with pink triangles—how do these define citizenship in a shared physical space on an unofficial, yet traffic-stopping, city holiday?

If we are to understand the relationship between citizenship and sexuality as truly a cultural, and not merely "rights"-based or legal, phenomenon, we need to seriously explore the ways that queers as a group are like others in the society who *don't* have power, instead of only whimsically invoking the ways we are like those who *do*. For example, arguments for the acceptance of sexual orientation as a "protected" category will mean little outside of a context in which the dismantling of other "protections" can be examined. How helpful will it be for queers to claim that we are "exactly like" heterosexual Latino youths who are deported, heterosexual black men who are murdered by white police, poor heterosexual women who get fired from minimum-wage jobs for staying home with a sick child, heterosexual cancer patients with inadequate health insurance, or Steven Salaita, the heterosexual Palestinian-American professor who was "de-hired" from the University of Illinois because of his passionate tweets deploring the carnage in Gaza during the summer of 2014?

Attempts to fashion lesbians and gays in the public mind as a "minority," which began with the work of the Mattachine Society in the early 1950s and continues in LGBT mainstream organizing today, will certainly benefit from an understanding of, in Alexis de Tocqueville's (and latterly, the legal scholar Lani Guinier's) words, the ways that "the tyranny of the majority" has promoted disenfranchisement for minorities in a "winner-take-all" democratic system. Research suggesting the biological determination of homosexuality, believed by some to point the way toward full legal rights, needs to be informed by the history of other groups' persecution based on biologically determined characteristics—for example, with the eugenics movement. And human rights advocates need to become cognizant of the ways that gay "rights" are cynically championed in the service of neoliberal and Orientalist agendas. Columbia law professor Katherine Franke, unbeguiled by "conservative U.S. politicians and commentators [who] highlighted sexism and homophobia in Iran as a justification for the denunciation of [Iranian President Mahmoud Ahmadinejad when he spoke at Columbia University in 2007]," notes that their condemnation spectacularly disregarded Christian fundamentalist sexism and homophobia in the United States. She describes their impromptu burst of broadmindedness simply as "reinforcement for the widely held view that Iranian culture was particularly intolerant and primitive compared to Western modernity and cosmopolitanism" (22), and sums up, "Revulsion toward gay men gets articulated as the most visible trope deployed by political leadership seeking to hold on to local control and governance, while tolerance toward homosexuality is demanded of those nations that seek membership in economic and political communities" (23).

Beyond Anti-Normativity Fetishism

Critique of liberal humanist normativity has, since the 1990s, become a hallmark of academic queer theorizing, and the ideas that I have put forth in this essay are, to some extent, synthetic rather than new. "Queer," though sometimes simply an umbrella term for a range of nonheteronormative identities, has often come to signify—especially within vanguard academic scholarship and in the borough of Manhattan—a transgressive stance that rejects the objective of social inclusion for LGBT people under the "We are all the same" rubric. In this chapter I have attempted to buttress that very antinormative queer ideal, while also showing that "radical" critiques sometimes end up employing—at least implicitly—the very same liberal humanist rhetoric and assumptions in relation to which they would claim outlaw status. As UK-based legal scholar Aleardo Zanghellini has put it, sometimes queer theory "is not as counter-normative as it would have us believe" (7). The same can be said for "radical" queer politics. Despite all, says Zanghellini, "a commitment to the idea that personal autonomy and diversity are intrinsically valuable (other things being equal) appears foundational to these queer critiques of mainstream understandings of law." Thus, he asserts persuasively that, certainly at least in the field of law, "queer critique and the normative commitments that animate it cannot be logically separated" (6).

Since June 2013, when the Supreme Court handed down the *United States v. Windsor* and *Hollingsworth v. Perry* "same-sex marriage" landmark legal decisions—in the midst of other vast societal changes for LGBT people—it has been especially difficult for queer theorists to articulate to a celebrating public just why enjoying these claims to the public good is so bad. Indeed, questions have started to be posed—smart and critical ones, not just banal and vanilla-soaked ones—about the normative/antinormative dichotomies that have long animated our discussions. (See, for example, Robyn Wiegman, Aleardo Zanghellini, Eleanor Wilkinson.) Lisa Duggan suggests some of the inevitable demise of the dichotomy in her article "A New Queer Agenda." While underscoring the crucial importance of the brilliant 2006 manifesto "Beyond Same-Sex Marriage: A New Strategic Vision for All Our Families and Relationships" and asserting that she is "shocked at the way lesbian and gay leaders and organizations have prioritized same-sex marriage," she explains why she and her ex-lover nonetheless registered as domestic partners in New York City after September 11, 2001: "[W]e both grasped the significance of that term 'next of kin' as we never had before"—though, she says significantly, "we had to lie and claim we lived together as a conjugal couple." On the line to register, they met many heterosexual couples doing the same thing: "They did not want to be married, or they were not romantic couples, but their experiences since September 11 had convinced them that they wanted the basic legal recognitions that domestic partnership registration would provide." A revelatory take-away from Duggan's story: *most people are not, in fact, "just like everyone else," but know that they still have to masquerade as them if they need help in a crisis.*

Works Cited

Althusser, Louis. "Ideology and Ideological State Apparatuses (Notes towards an Investigation)." *Lenin and Philosophy and Other Essays.* New York: Monthly Review, 1971. Print.

Bawer, Bruce. *A Place at the Table: The Gay Individual in American Society.* New York: Simon & Schuster, 1993; Touchstone Edition, 1994. Print.

"Beyond Same-Sex Marriage: A New Strategic Vision for All Our Families and Relationships." beyondmarriage.org. 26 July, 2006. Web. 10 Dec. 2014.

Bindel, Julie. "The Truth Behind America's Most Famous Gay-Hate Murder." *The Guardian,* 26 October 2014. Web. 2 November 2014.

Broverman, Neal. "Why I'm Not Reading the 'Trutherism' about Matt Shepard." *The Advocate.com.* 24 Sept. 2014. Web. 23 Nov. 2014.

Carpenter, Dale. *Flagrant Conduct: The Story of Lawrence v. Texas.* New York: Norton, 2012. Print.

Cranston, Maurice. "Introduction." *The Social Contract.* By Jean-Jacques Rousseau. Trans. and Intr. Maurice Cranston. Baltimore, MD: Penguin, 1968. Print.

Duggan, Lisa. "A New Queer Agenda." *The Scholar and Feminist Online.* Issue 10.1–10.2/Fall 2011/Spring 2012. Web. 10 Dec. 2014.

Ellwood, Gracia Fay. "The Crucifixion of Matthew Shepard." *University of Southern California Personal Web Pages,* 1998. Web. 24 Nov. 2014.

Franke, Katherine. "Dating the State: The Moral Hazards of Winning Gay Rights." *Columbia Human Rights Law Review* 1 (2012). Web. 20 Sept. 2014. PDF.

Goldstein, Richard. "The Hate that Makes Men Straight." *The Village Voice.* December 22, 1998: 64, 67, 70. Print.

Guinier, Lani. *The Tyranny of the Majority: Fundamental Fairness in Representative Democracy.* New York: The Free Press, 1994. Print.

Gurdon, Meghan Cox. "Heather Has Two Genders." *Wall Street Journal.* 14 Sept. 2014. Web. 8 Dec. 2014.

Jimenez, Stephen. *The Book of Matt: Hidden Truths about the Murder of Matthew Shepard.* Hanover, NH: Steerforth, 2013. Print.

Kaplan, Morris B. *Sexual Justice: Democratic Citizenship and the Politics of Desire.* New York: Routledge, 1997. Print.

Lithwick, Dahlia. "Extreme Makeover." *The New Yorker,* 12 Mar. 2012. Web. 23 Nov. 2014.

Mohr, Richard. *Gays/Justice: A Study of Ethics, Society, and Law.* New York: Columbia UP, 1988. Print.

Nava, Michael, and Robert Dawidoff, *Created Equal: Why Gay Rights Matter to America.* New York: St. Martin's, 1994. Print.

Paras, Melinda. "The Rhetoric of the Radical Right." Talk at Conference on College Composition and Communication, Washington, DC, Mar. 1995.
Puar, Jasbir K. *Terrorist Assemblages: Homonationalism in Queer Times*. Durham, NC: Duke UP, 2007. Print.
Robson, Ruthann. "Convictions: Theorizing Lesbians and Criminal Justice." *Legal Invasions: Lesbians, Gay Men, and the Politics of Law*. Eds. Didi Herman, Carl F. Stychin. Philadelphia: Temple UP, 1995. Print.
Said, Edward. *Orientalism*. New York: Vintage, [1978] 1979. Print.
Sullivan, Andrew. *Virtually Normal: An Argument about Homosexuality*. New York: Knopf, 1995. Print.
Tafel, Richard. Speaker on "Strategies" panel at *Identity/Space/Power: Lesbian, Gay, Bisexual, and Transgender Politics* conference, Feb. 9, 1996, Center for Lesbian and Gay Studies, CUNY Graduate Center, New York City.
Thernstrom, Melanie. "The Crucifixion of Matthew Shepard." *Vanity Fair*. March 1999. Web. 10 Dec. 2014.
Tocqueville, Alexis de. *Democracy in America*. Vol. 1. New York: Vintage, [1835] 1990. Print.
Trebay, Guy. "Overkill." *The Village Voice*. 6 Apr. 1999. Web. 24 Nov. 2014.
Vaid, Urvashi. *Virtual Equality: The Mainstreaming of Lesbian and Gay Liberation*. New York: Anchor /Doubleday, 1995. Print.
Wiegman, Robyn. "Eve's Triangles, Or: Queer Theory Without Anti-Normativity." UCD Humanities Institute, Dublin. Sept. 2012. Web. 10 Dec. 2014. Podcast.
Wilkinson, Eleanor. "Anti-normative Normativities: Queer Theory Beyond Sex." "Queer Geographies and the Politics of Anti-Normativity" Panel. RGS-IBG Annual International Conference 2013. University of Exeter, Devon, UK.
Wypijewski, JoAnn. "A Boy's Life." *Harper's Magazine,* Sept. 1999: 61–74. Print.
Zanghellini, Aleardo. "Queer, Antinormativity, Counter-Normativity, and Abjection." *Griffith Law Review* 18.1, 2009. Web. 10 Dec. 2014. PDF.

List of Contributors

Jonathan Alexander is Professor of English, Education, and Gender & Sexuality Studies at UC Irvine, where he was the founding Director of the Center for Excellence in Writing and Communication. The author, co-author, or editor of nine books, Jonathan writes about sexuality, technology, and literacy—sometimes all at the same time. His most recent books include *Understanding Rhetoric: A Graphic Guide to Writing* (with Elizabeth Losh; Bedford, 2013) and *On Multimodality: New Media in Composition Studies* (with Jacqueline Rhodes; NCTE, 2014). In 2011, he won the Charles Moran Award for distinguished contributions to the field of Computers & Composition Studies. He is the general editor of *College Composition and Communication*.

Jacqueline Rhodes is Professor of English at California State University, San Bernardino. Her scholarly work focuses on intersections of rhetoric, materiality, and technology, and has been published in a variety of venues, including *College Composition and Communication*, *JAC: A Journal of Composition Theory*, *Computers and Composition*, *Enculturation*, and *Rhetoric Review*. She is the author of *Radical Feminism, Writing, and Critical Agency: From Manifesto to Modem* (SUNY, 2005) and co-author, with Jonathan Alexander, of *On Multimodality: New Media in Composition Studies* (NCTE, 2014), winner of the 2015 CCCC Outstanding Book Award and the 2015 Computers and Composition Distinguished Book Award.

***

Ian Barnard is Associate Professor of Rhetoric and Composition at Chapman University and Professor Emeritus of English at California State University, Northridge. Ian's work on feminist and queer theory has appeared in *Genders*, *Women's Studies*, *Feminist Teacher*, and other journals, and in the anthology *Postcolonial and Queer Theories: Intersections and Essays* (ed. John Hawley). Ian is also the author of two books: *Queer Race: Cultural Interventions in the Racial Politics of Queer Theory* (Peter Lang, 2004) and *Upsetting Composition Commonplaces* (Utah State UP, 2014).

List of Contributors

Heather Lee Branstetter earned her Ph.D. from the University of North Carolina and is now an independent scholar and writer. She studies how underground or subversive groups of people respond to systemic forces that proscribe the available means of persuasion. Her work seeks to understand how networked communities create and change culture by negotiating values across various media. Currently, she is completing a book-length project documenting how orally transmitted stories, small talk, and gossip constructed and maintained attitudes toward illegal yet openly operated, locally regulated brothel-based sex work in her rural hometown from 1884 to 1991.

Meta G. Carstarphen, Ph.D., APR, is a Professor at the University of Oklahoma in the Gaylord College of Journalism and Communication. Her research interests include rhetoric and writing, historiography, race/gender/class diversity, and tourism media and diversity. An award-winning magazine author, her books include *Sexual Rhetoric: Media Perspectives on Sexuality, Gender and Identity* (Greenwood, 1999), *Writing PR: A Multimedia Approach* (Allyn & Bacon, 2004), *American Indians and the Mass Media* (U of Oklahoma P, 2012), and *Race, Gender, Class, and the Media* (Kendall Hunt, 2014). She teaches classes in race/gender/class and the media, public relations, and graduate rhetoric.

Ellen M. Gil-Gómez is Professor of English at California State University, San Bernardino, where she teaches Chicano/a Cultural Studies and literature, comic narratives, graphic novels, and feminist and LGBTQ Theories. She has published mainly in Chicano/Latino and Women of Color Studies, including her book *Performing La Mestiza* (Garland, 2001) and numerous articles and chapters. Her most recent publications focus on comics, disability studies, and online pedagogy.

Jordynn Jack is Professor at the University of North Carolina, Chapel Hill, where she directs the Writing Program and teaches courses in rhetorical theory, rhetoric of science, women's rhetorics, writing in the natural sciences, and composition. Her scholarly work focuses on the rhetoric of science, women's rhetorics, and genre. She is the author of *Science on the Home Front: American Women Scientists in World War II* (U of Illinois P, 2009) and *Autism and Gender: From Refrigerator Mothers to Computer Geeks* (U of Illinois P, 2014), *How Writing Works* (Oxford, 2016), and an edited collection, *Neurorhetorics* (Routledge, 2012). Her articles have appeared in *College English, College Composition and Communication, Rhetoric Society Quarterly, Rhetoric Review, Quarterly Journal of Speech*, and *Women's Studies in Communication*.

Harriet Malinowitz is currently Lecturer in the Department of Writing at Ithaca College. She is the author of *Textual Orientations: Lesbian and Gay Students and the Making of Discourse Communities* (Heinemann, 1995), and essays, articles, and reviews in publications including *College English,*

JAC, PRE/TEXT, The Women's Review of Books, Peitho, NWSA Journal, CommonDreams.org, Radical Teacher, The New Lesbian Studies, Feminism and Composition Studies, and *The Right to Literacy*. She is involved in an ongoing research project on Zionism and propaganda and is active in Jewish Voice for Peace, serving on its national Academic Advisory Council.

Martha Marinara is an Associate Professor of Writing and Rhetoric at the University of Central Florida. Marinara earned an MA in Creative Writing (SCSU 1989) and a PhD in Rhetoric (Lehigh University 1993). Her academic publications have appeared in *College Composition and Communication, Pedagogy and Culture,* and *The Journal of Basic Writing*. She writes poetry and fiction, publishing recently in *Clockhouse Review, Pelican Review, Lost Coast Review,* and *Broken Bridge Review*. Marinara won the 2000 Central Florida United Arts Award for Poetry. Her novel, *Street Angel*, nominated for a Lambda Literary Award and a Triangle Award, was published in 2006.

Jacqueline M. Martinez is Associate Professor of Communicology at Arizona State University, where she teaches courses on semiotics, phenomenology, culture, and communication. She is the author of *Communicative Sexualities: A Communicology of Sexual Experience* (Lexington, 2011) and *Phenomenology of Chicana Experience and Identity: Communication and Transformation in Praxis* (Rowman & Littlefield, 2000). She has published articles in *Hypatia, The American Journal of Semiotics,* and *The Journal of Homosexuality*, among others. She is a Fellow with the International Communicology Institute and President of the Interdisciplinary Coalition of North American Phenomenologists.

Charles E. Morris III is Professor of Communication and Rhetorical Studies and LGBT Studies at Syracuse University, and Co-Editor-in-Chief of *QED: A Journal of GLBTQ Worldmaking*. Some of the observations herein earlier appeared in Jason Edward Black and Charles E. Morris III, eds., *An Archive of Hope: Harvey Milk's Speeches and Writings* (U of California P, 2013) and were delivered in lectures hosted by the University of Richmond, the University of St. Thomas, Vanderbilt University, the University of Colorado-Denver, and Syracuse University. His books include *Queering Public Address: Sexualities in American Historical Discourse; Remembering the AIDS Quilt;* and *An Archive of Hope: Harvey Milk's Speeches and Writings*, a 2014 Lambda Literary Awards finalist.

Jason Palmeri is Associate Professor of English and Director of Composition at Miami University in Oxford Ohio. He is the author of *Remixing Composition: A History of Multimodal Writing Pedagogy* (Southern Illinois UP, 2012). Jason's current research and teaching engages multimodal rhetorics of social movements in both digital and offline spaces.

List of Contributors

G Patterson is a visiting Assistant Professor of English and an affiliate in Women's, Gender & Sexuality Studies at Miami University Hamilton, where ze teaches courses in composition and rhetoric, technical communication, creative writing, and women's studies. Hir research interests include curriculum development, rhetorics of social justice, and queer and transgender studies. Hir work was published in two edited collections, on the topics of digital writing curriculums and queer pedagogy. G was awarded the 2014 CCCC Lavender Rhetorics Award for hir dissertation, *Doing Justice: Negotiating the LGBTQ-Religious Junction in English Studies*.

Clark A. Pomerleau is Associate Professor of History at the University of North Texas who specializes in the histories of gender, sexuality, feminism, and countercultural social movements in the United States. Author of *Califia Women: Feminist Education against Sexism, Classism, and Racism* (U of Texas P, 2013), he is now researching the back-to-the-land movement in Maine.

Eric Darnell Pritchard is Assistant Professor of English at the University of Illinois at Urbana-Champaign. His research focuses on the intersections of race, queerness, sexuality, gender, and class with historical and contemporary literacy and rhetorical practices, as well as popular culture. Pritchard's scholarly writings have appeared in various scholarly journals and anthologies including *Harvard Educational Review*, *Literacy in Composition Studies*, *Palimpsest*, and *Home Girls Make Some Noise: Hip Hop Feminist Anthology*. Pritchard's book, *Fashioning Lives: Black Queers and the Politics of Literacy*, is forthcoming from Southern Illinois UP.

Erin J. Rand is Associate Professor of Communication and Rhetorical Studies and affiliated with LGBT Studies at Syracuse University. Her research focuses on resistance and rhetorical agency in activist and social movement discourses, with an eye to understanding the rhetorics of social change and queering the rhetorical tradition. Rand's work has appeared in *Quarterly Journal of Speech*, *Communication and Critical/Cultural Studies*, *Rhetoric and Public Affairs*, *Text and Performance Quarterly*, and *Women's Studies in Communication*, and she is the author of *Reclaiming Queer: Activist and Academic Rhetorics of Resistance* (U of Alabama P, 2014).

Jonathan Rylander is a Doctoral Candidate in the Composition and Rhetoric PhD program at Miami University and Assistant Director of the campuswide writing center. His current research explores intersections among queer and coalitional rhetorics in the context of writing program administration.

J. Blake Scott is Professor in the Department of Writing and Rhetoric at the University of Central Florida, where he directs three undergraduate degree programs (including a new major) and teaches courses in rhetoric, professional communication, and health and medical writing. He has several publications about HIV/AIDS rhetorics, including his book *Risky Rhetoric: AIDS and the Cultural Practices of HIV Testing* (Southern Illinois UP), which was recently reprinted with a new afterword. His civic engagement experience has included serving in leadership positions on the Orlando-area HIV community planning body charged with assessing and prioritizing needs and allocating federal Ryan White Modernization Act funding.

Lisa Tatonetti is Professor of English at Kansas State University where she studies, teaches, and publishes on queer Native literatures. She is co-editor of *Sovereign Erotics* (U of Arizona P, 2011), an award-winning collection of Two-Spirit creative work, and author of *The Queerness of Native American Literature* (U of Minnesota P, 2014). Her current project is tentatively entitled "Big Moms and Butch Dykes: Female Masculinity in Indigenous Literatures." When not writing or teaching, she can be found walking the Konza prairie or renovating her 1920s house under the watchful eye of Samson the wondercat.

David L. Wallace is Dean of the College of Liberal Arts at the California State University, Long Beach. He is author of *Compelled to Write: Alternative Rhetoric in Theory and Practice* (Utah State UP, 2011), coauthor with Helen Rothschild Ewald of *Mutuality in the Rhetoric and Composition Classroom* (Southern Illinois UP, 2000), and author of many articles and chapters on the teaching of writing and the need to address the intersections of multiple identity issues.

Luke Winslow is an Assistant Professor of Communication at San Diego State University. He joined the faculty at SDSU in the Fall of 2014 after teaching for five years in the Department of Management at the University of Texas at Austin. His teaching and research interests include contemporary rhetorical criticism, political communication, and rhetoric and social justice. His work has appeared in *Critical Studies in Media Communication*, *Rhetoric and Public Affairs,* the *Western Journal of Communication,* the *Southern Journal of Communication, Communication Studies,* and the *Journal of Communication and Religion*. He earned his PhD from the University of Texas at Austin and lives in San Diego with his wife, Addie.

Index

Aaberg, Justin 179
ableism 115–16
Aborigines and female masculinity 121, 127–30
activism 11, 33–41, 83, 159–60, 167–9, 193, 204–7
Adorno, Theodor 73
aesthetic dimensions of presidential masculinity 237–8
affective alienation of the suicidal gay teen 179–81, 184–5
affective rhetoric 37, 123–7, 129, 177, 231–4, 236
affect theory and female masculinity 121–30
African American rhetoric 97, 101
agencement theory 32
agency 7, 66, 72, 76, 97–98, 118
Ahmadinejad, Mahmoud 254
Ahmed, Sara 125, 180
AIDS activism 167–9
Alexander, Jonathan 4, 6, 18, 40, 147, 150
Althusser, Louis 252
Ambivalent Sexism Inventory (ASI) 65–66
Amen, Daniel G. 58
American presidency 233–41
Anderson, Kimberly 130
Angelides, Steven 100
antigay rhetorics 6
anti-normativity fetishism 255–6
anti-sex trafficking: campaigns 203–14; and popular culture 210–13; rhetorics 11
Anzaldúa, Gloria 155
Applegarth, Risa 17
approach, defined 19
Apuzzo, Virginia 165
archives of sexuality 2–4, 8
argumentative research papers 141–2

Asen, Robert 176, 184, 218, 219, 226
Atkinson, Ti-Grace 189–91, 193–5

Baird, Allan 87–88
Baker, Carrie 206
barebacking 225
Barnard, Ian 11
Bartky, Sandra Lee 50–51
battle of the sexes 189–91
Baudrillard, Jean 60
Bawarshi, Anis 61
Bawer, Bruce 250
Beam, Joseph 161, 168–9
belief and ethics 142–3
benevolent sexism 66, 69
Bennett, Paula 149
berdache 128
Berlant, Lauren 24, 153
Bernal, Dolores Delgado 110
Bessette, Jean 17, 26
bigotry 10, 84–85, 168, 241, 251
billboards 39–40
bi-psyche 151
birth control pill 219, 222, 225
bisexuality 11, 104; and feminists 195–9
Black, Dustin Lance 89–90
Black, Jason Edward 79
Black civil rights movement 245; connecting with the LGBT rights movement 10, 159–70
Black LGBT 160–70
Black/OUT 167–8
Blair, Hugh 96
Blanchard, Ray 63
Blauwamp, Joan M. 72
Blumstein, Philip 197–8
bodies: assemblage of in art project 34–41; control of as "straight," 1; embodied spaces between 121–30; females despised by boys 182–3; imagination of 2; in pornographic

images 63–64; representing physical 108–18
Boi Oh Boi (film) 122–30
Bolkovac, Kathryn 208
Borg, Charmaine 62, 64
Borges, Eric James 185
Bowers v. Hardwick 248
boys as suicidal gay teens 181–4
brain: heterosexual perspective in studying 9; as a sex organ 58
Bramlett, Jimmy 183
Branchini, Frank C. 164
branding of immigrants and LGBT citizens 33–34
Branstetter, Heather Lee 8
Brazile, Donna 165
Britzman, Deborah 135, 145
Brouwer, Daniel C. 226, 227
Broverman, Neal 246
Brown, Asher 175
Brownmiller, Susan 191
Brummett, Barry 234, 237
bullying, adolescent 11, 175–85
Burke, Kenneth 59, 61, 241
Bush, George H. W. 239
Bush, George W. 12; as ideal American male 233–41
butch identity 122–7
Butler, Judith 9, 59, 75, 100, 153, 236
Byrd, James Jr. 246

Califia, Pat 50
Calmes, Jackie 238
Campbell, Karlyn Kohrs 233
candor 9, 83–86
Carpenter, Dale 248
Carstarphen, Meta G. 5, 9
Chase, Raymond 175
chastity movements 6
Chávez, Karma 17, 35, 82
Chivers, Meredith L. 63
Christians 10, 100, 106, 134–44
Ciclitira, Karen 64
Cikara, Mina 65, 67
citizenship 35, 244, 252–5
civil rights 248–9
Civil Rights Acts of 1964 and 1968, 248
civil rights movement 159–60
classroom as a queer space 147–57
Clementi, Tyler 175
Clinton, Hillary 241
closeting 96–101, 104–5
clothing reflecting sexuality 109, 111–12

coalitional subjectivity 82
coalition politics 87–88
Cobb, Michael 5
Cohen, Daniel 87
collective identities 155–6
collective imagining 176
color feminism 36
Combahee River Collective 161
"coming-out," 9–10, 45, 55, 83–84, 95–106; as never ending 99
composition courses 4–6
condoms to prevent AIDS 217, 221, 224–5
Connor, Ashlynn 183
consciousness related to experience 47–51, 53
conservative Christians 10; and LGBTQ issues in the classroom 134–45; questioning as oppressed minority in the classroom 136–8
constituting consciousness 47
constitutive rhetoric 234, 241
Coors Boycott 87–88
corporeal intending 9, 54
countering counterpublics 218, 220–4
counterpublics 3, 4, 7; and Truvada debate 218–28
Crary, Jonathan 60
crip theory 115
critical imagination 23, 26
critical theory 140–2
cultural citizenship 244, 252–5
cultural dominance of conservative Christianity 138–9
cultural violence 175–85
culture industry 73
Cuthand, Thirza 10, 122–30
Cvetkovich, Ann 3, 4, 24

Dale, James 250
Daughters of Bilitis 195
Davy, Kate 22–23
Dawidoff, Robert 247
Dean, Tim 225
Deem, Melissa 226
DeGeneres, Ellen 178
de Jong, Peter J. 62, 64
Deleuze, Gilles 24–25, 27, 32, 154–5
Dickinson, Emily 149
differential belonging 82
Dingo, Rebecca 41
DiProse, Rosalyn 75
disability and sexuality 10, 115–18
disabled as embodied identity 113–18

disciplinary rhetorics 11, 217–28; sexualized and sexualizing 227–8
disidentification 149
Doezema, Jo 205
domestic duties being shared equally 191–3, 198–9
dominance and submission 50–51
dominant lifeworld 7
"Don't Say Gay" bill 143–4
Duggan, Lisa 33, 179, 255
Duncan, Arne 178
Duran, David 222
Dussauge, Isabelle 58–59
Dyer, Richard 176
DynCorp International 208

Eberhardt, Jennifer L. 65, 67
Edelman, Lee 185
Ellwood, Gracia Fay 245
embodied knowledge 124–30
embodied rhetoric and female masculinity 121–30
English studies and LGBTQ issues 134–45
entitlement 244–5, 252–3
ephemera documents 3–4
equality of gays and lesbians 249–50
Equal Protection Clause of the Fourteenth Amendment 248
eroticization of dominance and submission 50–51
Esperanza Peace and Justice Center 82
ethical rhetoric 46–47
ethical status of lesbian and gay relationships 248
ethics and belief 142–3
ethnicity: influencing visibility of homosexuality 105; and sexual expectations 110
ethos 4, 6
evidence, rhetorical treatments of 50–51
exclusion, rhetoric of 236
"experience of" differing from "ideas about," 47–50
experience related to consciousness 47–50, 53–55

Facebook 72
facets of action 128
fag discourse 182–3
FAIR Education Act 81
fairness argument for gay rights 249–51
family: branding of 33–34; oppressive to lesbians and gays 209–10; orientation and affective alienation 180–81; and sex trafficking 207, 212
Faunce, Robert 150
Fauntroy, Walter 164
feedback loop in disciplinary rhetorics 227
female bullies and victims 182
female impersonators 69, 70
female masculinity 10; in Indigenous literature 121–30; as a rhetorically produced affective circuit 123–7
female passivity 116–17
females as sexualized objects, 182–3, 198
feminine sexual masochism 50–51
femininity contempt by heterosexual boys 182–3
feminism: and activism in anti-sex trafficking 205–7; and intersection of identities 74–75; and lesbian identity 193–5; and women's response to pornography 65–69
feminists: on feminine sexual masochism 50–51; on sexuality 188–200
Feminists, The 189
figure of the foreigner 176
Finnegan, Cara 60
Fiske, Susan T. 65–68
Flaxman, Gregory 25
Foucault, Michel 2, 53, 154, 156
framing 241
Franke, Katherine 254
Friedan, Betty 191, 194
Fuller, Linda K. 5
functional magnetic resonance imagery (fMRI) 65, 66, 69
Fuss, Diana 156

Gamson, Joshua 155
Gaonkar, Dilip P. 19
Gardner, Christine J. 6
Garland-Thomson, Rosemarie, 117, 118
Garner, Tyron 249
Gates, Henry Louis 97, 101
Gauntlett, David 72, 75
gay agenda 86
gay and lesbian archives 2–4
Gay and Lesbian March on Washington 163–4

268 Index

gay and lesbian rights movement: connecting with Black civil rights movement 159–70
Gay Liberation Front (GLF) 193–5
gay liberation movement (LGM) 193–200
gay marriage 7, 251, 255
gay public cruising 103–4
gay rights: arguments of 249–52; and liberal democracy 247–9
gays 33, 81–82, 87–88, 155, 197, 225. *See also* LGBTQ; black 159–70
gender 235–6; dysphoria 127; expressions and coming out 95–106; fluidity of 68; in Indigenous studies 122; influencing visibility of homosexuality 105; multiple roles 129; as performative 153–4; policing 98; and response to pornographic images 62, 66–69; and sexuality and politics 232; theory 153–4
gendered framing 241
gendered rhetoric 9
gender identity: as affective act of rhetorical exchange 123–4; as embodied knowledge 124–7; as a performance 75, 124
genre: and the image 60–70; and visual rhetoric 59
Georgiadis, Janniko R. 62, 64
Gerald, Gil 164
Gere, Anne Ruggles 95, 96, 100
Geschwind, Max 89–90
Gibson, Michelle 4, 40
Gilbert, Jen 135, 145
Gil-Gómerz, Ellen M. 10
Giroux, Henry 151
Glick, Peter 65–66, 68
Goldstein, Richard 245
Goncalves, Zan Meyer 6
Gordon, Max S. 175, 183
Gore, Al 233–4, 237, 240
G-spot 62
Guattari, Félix 32
Guimarin, Michelle 164
gut reaction 124–5

Habari-Habari 167–8
Habermas, Jürgen 6
Halberstam, Judith (Jack) 3, 24, 123, 125, 148, 155
Halperin, David 150
Harambee House 162–3
hard-core rhetoric 58–70

Hardt, Michael 124, 125
Harmon, Dave 240
Harris, W. C. 86
Hartman, Saidiya 177
Harvey Milk Foundation 81
Haskins, Ekaterina 26
Hekman, Susan J. 74
Hemphill, Essex 162
Hernández, Catalina 73
Hesford, Wendy 206
hetero/homosexual divide 99–100, 103
heteronormativity 100, 156, 210; and homophobia 175, 178–9; and sex trafficking rhetorics 204; and suicidal gay teen 179–81; and understanding of sexual response 59–60
heterosexuality 11, 45–46, 58, 62–63, 68–69, 155–6, 180, 183, 188–91, 193–200, 207, 250, 254
heterotopias 154
HIV prevention 217–28
Hofmann, Regan 221
Hogg, Charlotte 22
Hohmann, Marti 62
Hollingsworth v. Perry 255
Holloway, Karla F. C. 112
homonationalism 8, 31–33, 247, 252
homonormative nationalism 247
homonormativity 33, 89; and the suicidal gay teen 179–81, 184–5
homophobia 3, 83–85, 105, 175, 178–9, 194, 213, 254
homophobic bullying 11, 175–85
homosexuality 96, 103–6, 138, 141, 176–7, 182–3, 197, 204, 249–55; as an identity category 3; decriminalization of activities 248; and pedophiliac predation 86–87
homosexual recruitment 86–88
Honig, Bonnie 176, 184
Horkmeimer, Max 73
hostile sexism (HS) 65–66
hostile sexuality 69
Howard, John 26
Hua, Julietta 206, 207
Hughes, Louis 161, 163
human trafficking 206
hypermasculinity 121

"I am Undocuqueer" art project 34–40
"ideas about" differing from "experience of," 47–50
identity: as collaborative and tactical assemblage 35–37; collective 155–6;

construction 72–77; creation of 1, 236–7; decomposition of 115, 118; as disabled 113–18; disclosure of HIV 225–6; issues 5, 9–10, 32; multiple *versus* binary mode of 99–100; negotiations 153; sexual identity as a woman 109–13; visible features *versus* invisible and closeting 98; Žižek, Slavoj 178
image genres 60–70
images evoking sexual response 59–70
imaginary communities 239–40
imaginary spaces 147–57
immigration and LGBTQ rights activism 33–40
Indigenous masculinity 121, 127–30
Innes, Robert 130
intellectualism 47
intersectionality 160, 233; as a lived experience 76–77; and queer assemblage 32–40; of realities 31–42
It Gets Better Project 184–5

Jack, Jordynn 9
Jacobs, Damon 222, 223
Jacobs, Sue-Ellen 128
Jensen, Robin E. 5
Jimenez, Stephen 245
Johnson, Nan 23
Jones, A. Billy 163
Jordan, Mark 86
Jung, Karen Elizabeth 114, 115
"just writing" narratives 136, 140–5

Kaite, Berkeley 63, 64, 67
Kaplan, Morris 248
Kara, Siddharth 206
Kawika Tengan, Ty P. 122
Keeton, Jennifer 138
Keller, Julia 240
Kerry, John 233–4, 237
Kim, Richard 178, 182
King, Coretta Scott 165, 166
Kinsey, Alfred 196
Kirsch, Gesa E. 23, 26
Klopotek, Brian 121
Knoblauch, A. Abby 124–30
Koedt, Anne 62
Kopelson, Karen 99
Kramer, Larry 222
Krassas, Nicole R. 72
Kristof, Nicholas 239
Kruppers, Petra 114

Lancester, Roger 86
Lang, Sabine 128
Lang, Thomas 128
language: being sexualized 6; maintaining systems of marginalization 96–97; and speech 47–48
Latina-ness 111–12
Lavender Menace 194–5
Law and Order: SVU and sex trafficking 208, 210–13
Lawrence, John Geddes 249
Lawrence v. Texas 248–9
legal citizenship 244
Lesbian Herstory Archives 2
lesbianism, defined 193
lesbians 155–6, 246–51; black 160–70; coming out of the closet 95–105; and gays as a minority 250, 254; in historiography 22; identity and feminism 193–5; as mothers 5; and solidarity with other women 194–5
LGBTQ 31; archives 2–4; and humanist rights 244–5; issues in the classroom 134–45; and migrant activism 33–40; preserving and pleasing their memory 80, 88–91; recognition of 33; rights movement 159–60
Li, Cao 103
liberal democracy and gay rights 247–9
liberal humanist rights 244–56
liberation movements and activism 11
liminality 151–2
liminal stage of the rite of passage 151–2
Lithwick, Dahlia 249
Logan, Shirley Wilson 76
Log Cabin Republican Club 249
Lopez, Rogelio Alejandro 38
Lorde, Audre 36, 159–61, 165–7, 170
Love, Heather 24, 180
love rejected by feminists 189
Lowery, Joseph 165
Lucas, Billy 175
Lyons, Scott 129

mainstream values 21–22
male gaze 73–7
males rejection by feminists 188–91
Malin, Brenton 233
Malinowitz, Harriet 6, 12, 209
marginalization, various types 98
Marinara, Martha 10, 40

marriage: equal division of domestic duties 191–3, 198–9; gay 7, 251, 255; rejected by feminists 190–1; and sex trafficking 207
Martinez, Jacqueline M. 8
masculinity: definition 122; presidential 232–41; proving heterosexuality by contempt of femininity 182–3; representations of 11–12; rhetoric of 235–7
Mason, Gail 103, 105–6
materiality of queer assemblage 38–40
McKegney, Sam 122, 130
McNaron, Toni 104
McRuer, Robert 118
meaning-making 2, 6, 232, 234, 235
media. See popular media
Medicine, Beatrice 128
Meem, Deborah 40
memory: politics 81; preserving and pleasing of LGBTQ's 80, 88–91
Merleau-Ponty, Maurice 46–50, 52–54
metaphor as a categorical transgression 149
migrant rights of undocumented queers 34–40
military gay ban 251
Milk, Harvey 9, 79–91; candor of 83–86; legacy of 88–91; and recruitment 86–88; as symbol of hope 80–83
Milk, Stuart 81
Milk Day 79
Milk Effect (film) 89–90
"Milk memory," 79, 80
Miller, Susan 152
Miller, Terry 184
Millett, Kate 195–6
Million, Dian 121
minor rhetorics 226
misfitting of the disabled 118
misogyny 183; oppression 50–52
Mohr, Richard 247
Moore, Darnell 170
Moore, Demi 210
Morgan, Robin 191–3
Morris, Charles 2, 3, 7, 23–24
Morris, Charles E. III 9
Morris, Chuck 17
Morris, Sammie L. 26
Moscone, George 80
Mulvey, Laura 73–74
Muñoz, José Esteban 24, 79, 91, 124

National Coalition of Black Gays (NCBG) 161
National Coalition of Black Lesbians and Gays (NCBLG) 160–70
National Gay Task Force (NGTF) 164
national identity 5
Native American literature and female masculinity 121–30
naturalistic enthymeme 60
naturalization of sexual difference 59
Nava, Michael 247
neoliberal happiness and the gay teen 179–81, 185
neuroscience studies of sexuality 58–70
neutrality towards LGBTQ issues 138–45
New Left 192, 193
New York-National Organization for Women (NY-NOW) 189, 194, 195
New York Radical Women (NYRW) 191–2
Nicoletta, Dan 79
Nietzsche, Frederick 96
nonhuman agency influence 32
normal, what constitutes as 2
normativity as a common enemy 37–38
norms being challenged 21–22
Northington, Eddie 246

Obama, Barack 231
objective violence 178–9
ONE National Gay and Lesbian Archives 2
oppression 3
other sex panic 11
Ott, Brian 176–7
outer limits of sexuality 204, 206–8, 213

Painter, Nell 111
Palmeri, Jason 8
Paras, Melinda 249, 250
Park, David 60
Parks, Rosa 245
Parry-Giles, Shawn 233
Parry-Giles, Trevor 233
Pascoe, C. J. 182
pathos 4
patriarchy and sex trafficking rhetorics 204, 206
Patten, Cindy 218–19
Patterson, G 10
Paynes, Medora 81

pedagogical neutrality 134–45
pedophilia 208–9
perception of others 54
performativity to gender and identity 75
Petrelis, Michael 89
Phelps, Fred 6
phenomenological reduction 47–49, 51–54
physical body as text 108–9, 111–12
Pierce, Charles P. 182
pity response 116
Plant, Sadie 151
pluralism 252–3
politics: of access of queer assemblage 38–40; ignorance of 231; interconnectedness of gender and sexuality 232
popular media and gendering identity 72
pornographic images: as an image genre 61, 64, 66–67; as stimulus 59–70; and women's response 61–65; and women's response from feminist perspective 66–69
Portnoy, Alisse 76
power to interpret 74–76
power to produce 76–77
power to read 72–74
praxis of hope 82
preexposure prophylaxis (PrEP) 217–18
presidential masculinity 232–41; stylistic dimensions of 237–40
Prince, Phoebe 183
Pritchard, Eric Darnell 10
professional embodiment 109–18
promiscuity linked to deviance and pathology 18
promiscuous approaches to rhetorical research 17–28; building more inclusive archives 26–27; challenges of 21–25; legitimating 22–24; publishing in nontraditional venues 24–25; using community-oriented-immersion methodology 26–27
pronatalist culture 209
Proposition 35 (California) 208–9, 211
prostitution 205–7, 211
Puar, Jasbir 8, 31–33, 247
public candor 84–86
public cruising by gays 103–4
public identity with sexual contexts 109–13
public memory 26–27
public-private dichotomization 251
public spheres 6–7, 11–12

Qian, Junxi 103–4
queer: experiences being archived 2–4; and promiscuity 18; and sex trafficking 212–14
queer archivist rhetorics 31; figuration of the suicidal gay teen 175–85; queer panic 11; pedagogy 150–1, 153–4; sexism 68–69; space 148–49; subjects 4–6
queer assemblage as rhetorical methodology 8, 31–42; materiality, circulation and politics of access 38–40; tactical representation 34–40; using collaborative forms of composing 40–42
queerness: displaced with anti-sex trafficking rhetorics 204–14; as futurity 9, 79–91; in Indigenous literature 121–30
queer theory 155, 255; in the classroom 147; and literary study 150–1
Queer Undocumented Immigrant Project 34
Queer Undocumented Youth Collective 34

Raban, Jonathan 240
race: and sexual expectations 110; and sexuality 10; and sexual rhetorics 160–70
racist gentrification policies 39–40
radical feminism 188–9, 193
radical possibility of speech 53
Rand, Erin J. 11
Rawson, K. J. 23–24, 26
religion: and LGBTQ issues in the classroom 134–45; and sexual rhetorics 5–6
religious affiliation and identity 10
religious freedom 10
reprosexuality 209
rescue, recovery, and (re)inscription research methods 23
research methods using sexed and intimate methods 23
Reumann, Miriam G. 5
revisioning of history 2
rhetoric: African American 97, 101; antigay 6; being promiscuous 18; changing and shaping of 41; constitutive 241; disciplinary 11, 217–28; of dress 109, 111–12; embodied 121–30; of exclusion 236; of gender 72, 75; gendered 9; as

a hermeneutic 19; is sexual 80; of masculinity 235–7; minor 226; sex trafficking 203–14; 34–40; visual 59
rhetorical ethics 46–47; of sexual expression 50–51
rhetorical historiography 8, 17, 19, 22–23; revisionist 23–24
rhetorical methodology and queer assemblage 8, 31–42
rhetorical promiscuity 17–28
rhetorical research 17–28
rhetorical sovereignty 129
rhetorical studies and lack of sex/uality in 4–5
rhetorical theory differing from queer theory 100
rhetorical treatments of evidence 50–51
rhetorical violence 177–85
Rhodes, Jacqueline 18, 40, 147, 150
Ricoeur, Paul 149
Riggs, Marlon 162
rights: and fairness 12; and sexual citizenship 244–56
rights-based work 11
rite of passage 151–2
Rivaldo, Jim 87
Rivera-Servera, Ramón 82
Robinson, Frank 79
Robson, Ruthann 246
Rodemeyer, Jamey 179, 185
Romano, Susan 73
Romer v. Evans 248
Roque Ramírez, Horacio 89
Rose, Shirley K. 26
Royster, Jacqueline Jones 23, 26, 76–77, 169
Rubin, Gayle 50, 204–5
Rust, Paula 199
Rustin, Bayard 160, 168–9
Rylander, Jonathan 8

sadomasochism 50
Salaita, Steven 254
Salgado, Julio 31, 34–40
same-sex marriage 7, 251, 255
Samois 50–51, 53, 54
Saraswati, L. Ayu 68
Savage, Dan 184
Schacht, Steven P. 70
Schlesinger, Jacob 238
scholarship methods 21–25
Schwartz, Pepper 197–8
Schwyzer, Hugo 183

Scott, J. Blake 11
Sedgwick, Eve 97, 98, 99, 103, 204
Seidman, Steven 104
Seif, Hinda 35
self-disclosure 9
self-harm 178–9
self-identification 9
Sequoyah 72–73
Seto, Michael C. 63
sex: appeal of the disabled 115–18; dealing with expectations based on physical body 109–18; influenced by cultural norms 62; rejected by feminists 189
sexed methods 17–92
sex education 5
sexism 65–69, 188–9, 254; and heterosexuality 68–69; and homosexuality 68–69
sex panic 205, 206, 208, 210, 211–13
sex trafficking 209. *See also* trafficking; panic 11; popular culture representations of 206; rhetorics 203–14
sexual expression 9, 46, 49, 51, 54
sexual freedom 50–51
sexuality 1; approached as a problem 5–6; archives of 2–4; as assemblage of affective processes 32; being rhetorical 1–2, 18; considered with citizenship status 35; as culturally influenced 59; feminist views on 188–200; and gender and politics 232; hostile 69; identities and coming out 95–106; impacting migration 33–34; in Indigenous studies 122; in mass media 5; neuroscience studies of 58–70; as power 1; as process 31–34; as rhetoric 1, 79; rhetorics in political discourses 11–12; and style in politics 234; as a topic of inquiry 6
sexualization of women impacting men 65–69
sexually deviant 18
sexual normalization 1
sexual orientation and fluidity 68
sexual penetration as core of sexual activity 62–63
sexual preference impacting response to visual sexual stimulation 62–63
sexual rhetorics 129–30; definition 1; emergence of practices 8; by feminists 188–200; historicizing

72–77; as a methodology 135; and national identity 5; phenomenology of 46–47; and race 160–70; research methods 8
sexual subjectivity 111–12
sex work 109–10, 203, 205–6
Sharer, Wendy 23
Shelley, Martha 193–4
Shepard, Matthew 178, 245–6, 248
Shilts, Randy 88
Shulman, Alix Kates 191–2
signification 101
Smith, Barbara 161
Snorton, C. Riley 82
Sobo, Jake 223–4
social devaluation of the disabled 113–18
socially just writing 136, 140–5
social purity movement 205
socioeconomic status influencing visibility of homosexuality 105
sodomy laws 248–9
Solanas, Valerie 188–9
speech as gesture 53–54
speech speaking and speech spoken 46–49, 53, 55
Spinoza, Baruch 124
Staley, Peter 221, 224
"staying-in," 45
Stephens, Charles 170
Stoltenberg, John 246
Stonewall Inn Riots 3
strategic contemplation 26
Streicher, Rikki 89
Strub, Sean 221
Struthers, William M. 58
Stryker, Susan 89
students as writers 152–3
style: dimensions of presidential masculinity 237–41; and sexuality in politics 234–6
subjective violence 178–9
suicidal gay teen 11, 175–85; as affective, rhetorical figure 177–85; boys associated with femininity 182–3; driving policy decisions 184–5; females 183–4; gendering 181–4; as object and agent of violence 177–9; as a verbal image 176
Sullivan, Andrew 251
Swift, Jonathan 130
symbolism, power of 252–5

Tafel, Richard 249
Tatonetti, Lisa 10

Teena, Brandon 178
Teresita la Campesina 89
text and power to influence 73
textual version of politicians 238–9
Thernstrom, Melanie 245
Third World Lesbian and Gay Conference 160, 162–4
Thomas, Wesley 128
Thompson, Julie 5
threshold as a rite of passage 151
Tocqueville, Alexis de 254
Toth, Emily 109
trafficking 208. *See also* sex trafficking
transexuality 125
transgender archives 3
transgenderism 125, 134, 142, 161, 170, 177, 205
Trebay, Guy 246
trope of abnormality 103–4
trope of the closet 95–106; cultural effects of 98; differences and fluidity of 100–1; epistemology of 97–101, 103–4; excludes visible identity features 98; having variety of rhetorical effects 99; as a queer master trope 101–6; as a recurring event 99; as self-management techniques 105–6; signifying and lack of clarification 101
trope of visibility 103, 105–6
troubling identity 95–171
Truvada 11, 217–28; compared to birth control pill 219, 222, 225; meanings and counterpublics 219–24
Tumblr 38–39
Turner, Victor 151
Two-Spirit traces 122, 127–30
tyranny of the majority 254

undocumented queers and migrant rights 34–40
"UndocuQueer" activist movement 31
undocuqueer as a singular term 35–36
United States v. Windsor 255

vaginal orgasm 189
Vaid, Urvashi 250–1
Vance, Carol 207
Van Gennep, Arnold 151
"vicious circle of proselytism," 86
Victims of Trafficking and Violence Protection Act (2000) 206
Villapando, Octavio 110

violence: culturally overdetermined 175; objective 178–9; rhetorical 177–85; subjective 178–9; and visibility of homosexuality 105
visual rhetoric 59; of disability 116–18
visual sexual stimulation and sexual preference 61–65
voice and ability to produce 76–77
voters and gender and sexuality for political decisions 232–41
voting blocs 239–40

Wallace, David 4, 9, 95
Wallace, Howard 87
Walsh, Seth 175, 178
Ward, Jane 68, 69
Warhol, Andy 188
Warner, Jane 89
Warner, Michael 6–7, 149, 153, 209, 218, 227
way of knowing becomes a form of knowledge 124
Weinstein, Michael 221
Wendell, Susan 113
Wesselink, Peggy 72
West, Isaac 17
"We Still Have a Dream" March 164–7
wheelchair as a rhetorical device 114, 116–17
White, Dan 80

white slavery 205–6
Williams, Jean C. 169
Williams-Skinner, Barbara 165
Wingard, Jennifer 33
Winslow, Luke 11
Wireback, Taft 240
Wittgenstein, Ludwig 153
Wittman, Carl 197
Wolf, Naomi 58
women: of color in academia 108–18; exhibiting visibility of homosexuality 105; responding to visual sexual stimulation 61–65; sharing domestic duties with males 191–3, 198–9
Women's International Terrorist Conspiracy from Hell (WITCH) 191–2
women's liberation movements (WLMs) 188–200; war analogy of 189–91
writing: gay and lesbian identities 4–6; identity 147; socially just 136, 140–5
Wuornos, Aileen 246

Yoshimura, Fumio 196

Zanghellini, Aleardo 255
Zavoina, Susan 5
Zebowski, Adam 224
Zogby, John 238
"zoned" pornographic images 64